CONSEQUENCES

CONSEQUENCES

A PERSONAL AND POLITICAL
MEMOIR

JOHN G. TOWER

LITTLE, BROWN AND COMPANY

BOSTON   TORONTO   LONDON

She forgave my transgressions and was always constant,
She raised our children and made my career possible,
And in the hour of my travail, she held my hand and said,
"You know I've always believed in you."
This book is dedicated to Lou Tower.

First Edition

Acknowledgments of permission
to quote selected material appear on p. 389.

Library of Congress Cataloging-in-Publication Data

Tower, John.
    Consequences : a personal and political memoir / John G. Tower. — 1st ed.
        p.   cm.
    Includes index.
    ISBN 0-316-85113-2
    1. Tower, John.   2. Legislators — United States — Biography.
3. United States. Congress. Senate — Biography.   4. United States —
Politics and government — 1945–   I. Title.
E840.8.T68A3   1991
328.73'092 — dc20   90-42687

10   9   8   7   6   5   4   3   2   1

HC

*Published simultaneously in Canada
by Little, Brown & Company (Canada) Limited*

Printed in the United States of America

CONTENTS

CONTENTS

ACKNOWLEDGMENTS

THE WRITING of a political memoir is anything but a solitary endeavor. Over the course of pulling together and refreshing one's recollections of a long public career, it is necessary to tap the memories of many friends and associates whose involvement was central to some part of that career, somewhere along the way.

Once amassed, those recollections must be distilled and knit into a cohesive narrative. That significant effort was undertaken by Roger Gittines in the fall of 1989, before which time he and I had never met. While the story is mine, the form of this book is the product of his considerable talent as a writer, involving working from hundreds of hours of interviews and volumes of research material, as well as frequent and lengthy conversations between the two of us.

We are both grateful to the many people who contributed to this book in myriad ways — most particularly Carolyn Bacon, former senator Howard Baker, Will Ball, Howard Beasley, Richard Billmire, Phil Charles, Senator Bill Cohen, Rhett Dawson, Paul Eggers, Nola Gee, Read Hanmer, Bill Hildenbrand, French Hill, Dan Howard, John Knaggs, Tom Korologos, Ken Krieg, Ron Lehman, Senator John McCain, Fred McClure, Jim McGovern, Mattie McKee, Michele Markoff, Sherrie Marshall, José Martinez, Kathy Maxa, Dr. Bill Narva, Rose Narva, Bill Perrin, Dr. Roy

Shilling, Carl Smith, Curt Smothers, the Reverend David Switzer, Ken Towery, and Ruth Wilson.

My staff — Kim Garven, Martha Kirkendall, and Marian Tower — also shared in the effort, and their support was a major ingredient in getting the job done. And in the best spirit of team play, Roger Gittines's wife, Jane Berger, helped immensely by transcribing many interviews and editing copy.

My literary agent, Margret McBride, and my editor, Fredrica Friedman, were constant sources of encouragement and wise counsel.

Finally, this book would not have been written without the loving support of my three daughters, who, of course, figure prominently in this memoir.

To one and all who gave this book life, named and unnamed, I express my deepest appreciation.

INTRODUCTION

THIS IS NOT THE BOOK I originally intended to write. Something happened between the spring of 1987, when I began to discuss the project with my publisher, and the spring of 1989, when I at last began to record my thoughts for these pages.

That "something," of course, was my nomination by President George Bush to serve as secretary of defense, and its subsequent rejection by the Senate.

As a political scientist by academic training and practical experience, I would have preferred spending twelve months of labor on an in-depth study of the strained and potentially dangerous state of relations between the executive and legislative branches of government. There is much of importance to be said on the subject. Instead, due to circumstances in large measure beyond my control, I have been compelled to construct a narrative framework for this thesis, and other matters of concern, out of the events of recent history.

The confirmation battle amounted to roughly four months of a career in politics and public service that spanned nearly four decades. It could be argued that it merits, perhaps, one chapter out of an entire political memoir. Yet, to so limit my discussion, I would have to ignore a few inescapable facts of life. As I said shortly after the vote, history will remember me as the first cabinet-designee of a newly elected president of the United States to be rejected by the Senate. In addition, far too many of my contemporaries know nothing of me aside from the caricatures and contempt that spewed forth with such a ruinous effect on my career, my professional standing, my place in history, and my family's serenity.

Those of us who enter the political arena must be prepared to make sacrifices and suffer defeat. To dismiss the confirmation battle and its outcome as nothing more than politics as usual, however, would be to overlook an important distinction. We must use our political process to promote the public interest. When it degenerates into a form of theater, blood sport, partisan pursuit of power and prerogative, that process fails its purpose.

In the chapters ahead, I have sought to pull together an agglomeration of what I regard as some of the most important events of my career, personal experience, observations on the Senate, working insights into the U.S. government as a whole, and perspectives on arms control, defense policy, and the prominent people I have known and served with, rounded out with a few recommendations for congressional reform. Then, like limestone, a rock that is composed chiefly of shells, coral, and other organic matter, these fragments of a life have been cut into blocks, from which I have fashioned a story about what happened to John Goodwin Tower, why it happened, and what its future consequences may be.

There was a time when I would have agreed that "sweet are the uses of adversity," and perhaps one day I will again. It has been painful for me to relive the confirmation fight. At times I have questioned the wisdom of doing so. But to the degree that this adversity can be used to stimulate a constructive dialogue about how to keep our political process from ever again taking such an ugly, destructive turn — then I am satisfied with those consequences.

June 1990
Dallas, Texas

CONSEQUENCES

ONE

THE HONOR
OF THE THING

Mr. ADAMS."

"No."

"Mr. Adams, no.

"Mr. Armstrong.

"Mr. Baucus."

"No."

"Mr. Baucus, no.

"Mr. Bentsen."

"Aye."

The assistant legislative clerk of the United States Senate called the roll, recording the yeas and the nays. The tone was flat, unemotional, as it always is, no matter what may hang in the balance. But there is a cadence to every roll call vote. Some march hard and fast, rushing straight into the guns and history; others stumble; a few limp. Those who wait to hear their names, to answer, to give assent or withhold it, supply this foot soldier's rhythm — eager, reluctant, indifferent, resigned. Each, in turn, makes a decision. Out of those one hundred individual decisions, a majority is made, and once made, the majority rules.

"Mr. Bentsen, aye."

No one else in that office suite across the river from the Capitol, where I was watching the vote on television, heard the cadence change, and maybe it was meant for my ears alone. But by coming early in the roll call, Lloyd Bentsen's vote broke the momentum and marred the smooth acceleration toward the inevitable outcome. Thereafter, what transpired was not a mechanical playing out of an abstract process. Each no, each aye, from then on was a personal judgment rendered one at a time that would stand on the historical record unadorned by ideology, partisan considerations, or self-justification.

I sat there, perched on the arm of a battered government-issue leather chair, watching a career being extinguished vote by vote.

"Mr. Biden."

"No."

I wasn't surprised, or angry, or hurt. I had slid into an emotional void. There was nothing there to feel except the overwhelming desire to get it over with.

"Mr. Biden, no."

And another no from Bingaman reminded me that inside of a quarter of an hour the Senate would finally be free to turn to other business and I could return home to Texas. My nomination to be secretary of defense was headed for defeat. If there is one thing that I am, or have a reputation for being, it is a good vote counter. And this one was easy. The Democratic party controlled the Senate, and while a few defections on the grounds of friendship, fairness, or principle would be tolerated, nothing was going to be allowed to stand in the way of Sam Nunn, the chairman of the Senate Armed Services Committee, and his determination to deny the president his choice for secretary of defense.

An aye from Christopher Bond of Missouri, and then David Boren's name was called. Hearing no response, the clerk moved on without recording a vote. Senators who arrive late or remain silent on the first round until they can see which way the tide is running are passed over, to be recognized at the end before the final tally is announced. A handful of my Pentagon transition staff was gathered around me, watching the television set that had been tuned to C-SPAN almost constantly since the Senate floor debate on my nomination had begun nearly a week before. I'd had work to do as secretary of defense designate, important work, and I'd fought the temptation to sit there by the hour and watch the proceedings. Occasionally I'd come out of my private office for a few minutes to turn up the sound and see what was happening. Mercifully, the phone would ring to summon me back to my desk to pick up where I had left off, surrounded by empty bookshelves and bare walls that seemed to symbolize my predicament: I was there in the Pentagon — right where I had wanted to be — but I wasn't really there at all. However, on Thursday, March 9, the phone didn't ring, and there was no longer any point to returning to my desk; so I sat in front of the television thinking about Dave Boren, whose uncle had hired me for my first teaching job, at Midwestern State University, in Wichita Falls, Texas. Boren is a Democrat, but connections like that help change the chemistry between political adversaries. Although you do not expect to agree on everything, when there is room for compromise, room for doubts, those personal ties are important. Boren did not answer the roll call on the first round, but I knew he would and how he would vote. It would be one more no.

Like a salesman who must ask for the sale, politicians must ask for the vote, and I had called Dave Boren, whom I regarded as a friend, to ask. He told me that he was sorry . . . Sam Nunn needed his vote; Sam Nunn was a good friend.

The roll call moved into the C's and there was a satisfying run of ayes, including one from William Cohen of Maine, which changed the cadence again. Bill and I had served together on the Senate Armed Services Committee. During my chairmanship, he played a key role in helping us rebuild U.S. military strength after years of decline and deterioration. During the uglier moments of the confirmation fight, some claimed that I had no friends in the Senate. That was one of many fallacies. I count Bill Cohen as a good friend.

The roll call moved on, and there were no surprises.

"Mr. Dixon."

"No."

"Mr. Dixon, no."

Dixon of Illinois, who had told me not to bother stopping by his office as I was making the traditional nominee's courtesy calls on members of the Armed Services Committee. There would be no need for that, he said, since he remembered favorably our work together on the committee and was pleased with my nomination.

"Mr. Dodd."

"Aye."

"Mr. Dodd, aye."

A second Democratic vote and a precious one. Twenty years before, I had refused to cast my vote to censure his father for breaking Senate rules that had been recently formulated and applied to him retroactively. I based that vote on fairness. It was unfair to Thomas Dodd. I did not hold an IOU on Chris, but I did hold an expectation that he would judge me fairly, and I wasn't disappointed.

"Mr. Exon."

"No."

"Mr. Exon, no."

James Exon of Nebraska, Sam Nunn's stalking-horse on the drinking allegations that were hurled at me. And what an irony! An astonishing and blatantly hypocritical choice for the job. He has a reputation as one of the most excessive regular boozers in the Senate.

"Mr. Heflin."

"Aye."

"Mr. Heflin, aye."

The third Democrat to cross over. A former judge, Howell Heflin knew a lynch mob when he saw one, I think.

The clerk moved into the middle of the roll.

"Mrs. Kassebaum."

"No."

"Bitch!" A woman on my staff flung the word at the screen, and for a moment the spark of her anger seemed to warm up the bleak office.

"Mrs. Kassebaum, no."

A Republican. The only one to turn away from me. A disappointment. And by choosing that bland word I'm not underplaying my reaction. It was a disappointment to lose Nancy Kassebaum's vote. Unlike my staff, I couldn't summon up an epithet. I have a doctor friend who is a bone specialist; a few years ago he was badly injured in a car accident. As the ambulance crew was extracting him from the wreckage, he was telling them exactly what to do, diagnosing his own injuries. The confirmation fight had dragged on for so long that I knew where I was hurting, what bones were broken, what would mend and what wouldn't; I looked on it in a very clinical way.

"Mr. McCain."

"Aye."

"Mr. McCain, aye."

There was steel in that yes, and there is steel in the man, hardened by almost six years in a North Vietnamese prisoner of war camp. He was with me, fighting all the way. John McCain does not bend or break under any circumstances.

"Mr. Nunn."

"No."

"Mr. Nunn, no."

Unlike the response to some of the other no votes, there weren't any derogatory comments from my staff after the chairman of the Senate Armed Services Committee cast his. At that point, there was nothing left for us to say.

"Mr. Shelby."

"No."

"Mr. Shelby, no."

The group in my office laughed when I mimicked Shelby's Alabama drawl and repeated the comment he made when he indicated privately to me that he would vote for my nomination: " 'I'd never trust a man who didn't drink a little and chase a little. . . .' "

"Mr. Stevens."

"Aye."

"Mr. Stevens, aye."

Ted Stevens and I had some ferocious legislative battles over the years. But I had never seen a legislator as enraged as he was when, in the midst of the Democrats' onslaught, he shouted, "He is my friend . . . and I thought he was your friend. And I want some justice for my friend." Ted Stevens is too big a man to permit even spirited differences to sully a friendship.

And Thurmond.

"Aye."

"Mr. Thurmond, aye."

"Mr. Wallop."

"Aye."

"Mr. Wallop, aye."

"Mr. Warner."

"Aye."

"Mr. Warner, aye."

"Mr. Wilson."

"Aye."

"Mr. Wilson, aye."

"Mr. Wirth."

Timothy Wirth of Colorado did not answer, and so the clerk began recognizing those senators who had missed or passed on the first round. On a close vote, a wise tactician holds some of his forces in reserve just in case of surprises. With just a few minutes left to go, Dale Bumpers of Arkansas and Tom Harkin of Iowa were still unrecorded. Should Bumpers have felt pressure to vote with regional interests, and had Harkin, who was facing a difficult reelection contest in 1990, decided he required help from Iowa Republicans and independents, the margin that Sam Nunn needed would have vanished. Nancy Kassebaum had promised to support me if her vote proved to be decisive. Until the clerk reads the totals, a senator is free to change a vote, and I saw it happen many times during my twenty-four years in the Senate. A tie would have been broken in my favor by Vice President Dan Quayle, who was in the presiding officer's chair. However, Bumpers and Harkin hewed to the Democratic line, as I had expected. William Armstrong and Arlen Specter, both ayes, were the final two votes.

It was over. I had already written my final statement. The news media were gathered in the secretary of defense's private dining room one floor below us. I glanced down at the sheet of paper and said, "Let's go." I steeled myself for the delivery of my vale-dictory.

For the most part, I had little direct contact with the press for the first five or six weeks of the Bush transition. Under the circum-stances it seemed the appropriate and prudent thing to do. I di-vided the time between my home base in Dallas and my Washington, D.C., office, catching up on personal business after the long presidential election campaign.

I had been in the trenches fairly steadily since I introduced George Bush at the rally in Houston where he formally announced his candidacy in the fall of 1987. The vice president had surprised me with a telephone call to ask if I would introduce him to the gathering, which would start him down that road to the Repub-lican nomination and to the White House.

It is always nice to be asked to dance, and while I had not as yet committed myself to any of the well-qualified Republican candi-dates, I was not being coy, looking for the best offer. I had been the Texas state chairman for the Reagan-Bush campaign in 1984, but since I had been retired from the U.S. Senate for three years, I did not expect the phone to be ringing off the hook.

The call from George Bush was flattering, and I quickly accepted the invitation, assuring him that he had my full support. I promised to help the campaign in any way that would be useful. Before long

I was traveling around the country making speeches, participating in fund-raisers, and advising the Bush team on major issues, particularly those relating to national security.

On one of those campaign swings, I visited Georgia with P. X. Kelley, the retired commandant of the Marine Corps. Kelley and I were "surrogates," or stand-ins, for George Bush. We spoke out against Michael Dukakis's positions on defense issues and advocated those put forward by the Republican candidate — all well within the boundaries of traditional presidential campaign practices. However, as I look back on it now, I may have offended Senator Nunn by daring to come into his backyard to criticize positions that he had helped formulate for the Democratic party's standard-bearer.

I understand that a series of speeches Dukakis made about the nation's military posture was based on material supplied to his campaign by Nunn's staff on the Senate Armed Services Committee. The points that Dukakis relied on during interviews with the news media or when taking questions from an audience also originated with the majority staff of the Armed Services Committee, which apparently functioned as a think tank for the Democratic campaign.

One assumes that a committee chairman will have a certain amount of influence on his party's presidential platform, but it seems that in 1988 Sam Nunn took a more direct role in attempting to shape, or reshape, Dukakis's positions on defense. Senator Nunn is inordinately sensitive to criticism; he fires off letters to the editor and takes to the Senate floor to answer unfavorable newspaper articles. Over the years, he had been treated gently by the Washington press and, I suspect, came to see himself as being above politics. Therefore, my criticism of Dukakis could easily have pierced Nunn's thin skin and been taken as a personal affront.

Furthermore, at the time, Sam Nunn still may have been smarting from the defeat he suffered in the summer of 1988 when President Ronald Reagan vetoed the 1989 defense authorization bill. I was one of those who advised President Reagan to reject the bill even though its terms had been agreed to in negotiations between Defense Secretary Frank Carlucci and the chairman of the Senate Armed Services Committee. Carlucci had accepted provisions that would have allowed Congress to virtually dictate future arms control policies and cut funding for the Strategic Defense Initiative by $800 million.

Although my views carried some weight with President Reagan, I certainly was not the principal moving force behind the veto. Given the political dynamics on Capitol Hill, however, with the younger, more conservative Republicans on the Armed Services Committee in open revolt against their ranking member, Senator John Warner, who was cooperating closely with Nunn, there was talk that I was instrumental in rallying the opposition to the bill. As one observer put it, "This was a done deal until Tower got involved. The veto means that he is still chairman of the Armed Services Committee." And if I heard comments like that one, I'm sure Sam Nunn did, too. Hence, I was probably not welcome in Georgia during the campaign, or four months later in front of the Senate Armed Services Committee as defense secretary designate.

The vice president had inherited the legacy of what had come to be called the Reagan defense buildup. It is an accurate, though misleadingly bland, description. After a decade of neglect under previous administrations, with the leadership of Ronald Reagan we undertook to complete a process of refurbishing, modernizing, resupplying, and improving the training, compensation, and morale of our armed services in the face of unprecedented Soviet military expansion. Without this effort, I am convinced, there would be no *glasnost,* no *perestroika* today.

President Reagan's veto of the 1989 defense authorization bill gave George Bush a valuable opportunity to round on the Democrats and hit them again and again for passing what he called "this misnamed defense bill that would redirect us only to weakness, tying the hands of the president at the negotiating table, trying to establish all foreign policy objectives in this mishmash of congressional legislation." It allowed Bush to define the differences between the Democratic and the Republican approach to defense, and in so doing helped us reverse Michael Dukakis's huge lead in the public opinion polls.

My critics accused me of never meeting a weapons system that I didn't like. As chairman of the Senate Armed Services Committee from 1981 to 1984, and as a member of the panel for twenty years, I met quite a few weapons systems; some of them were not cost-effective, did not meet a valid requirement, or were obsolescent. As a result, those were the ones that stayed on the drawing boards or were canceled, including the A-7 aircraft, for example, which would have meant jobs for Texans and profits for a Texas company.

The same glib one-liner, turned and applied to Michael Dukakis — he never met a weapons system he didn't want to cut — made my task easier as a Bush-Quayle defense and foreign policy adviser. And we enjoyed a hearty laugh at Dukakis and his tank ride. The press dubbed it "Dondi Goes to War," after the waif in the comic strip, and the free TV spots were worth thousands of dollars in political advertising to us.

I also enjoyed beating Dukakis's campaign manager in a footrace to the press room after the first of two presidential debates. The Bush "spin team" had a room just down the hall from the Dukakis people. When the debate ended, there was a mad dash to see who could be first to get to a network TV reporter. Susan Estrich is fleet of foot, but I am still a pretty fair sprinter when properly motivated.

The spin team is the latest variation on an old political game: emphasize the positive, deemphasize the negative. Both campaigns had teams of senior advisers with issues expertise ready to put the right spin on the candidates' statements; hence the name "spin team." We would watch the debate on TV, commenting aloud on the pluses and minuses. When it ended, we would quickly review the proceedings, and each team member would suggest the right line to take on the issue that was his or her specialty.

Dukakis's gaffe in the second debate — a frigid, technocratic answer to a hypothetical question about rape and what his reaction would be if his wife, Kitty, was the victim — electrified the Bush spin team. There was no need to weigh the pluses and minuses. We just went into the press room and said what the reporters themselves had been thinking: whatever Michael Dukakis's qualifications for the job might have been, his coldness and detachment were appalling.

The substantial lead that George Bush went on to establish was reassuring, but most of his senior advisers knew that the race would tighten as it hit the home stretch. Leaving nothing to chance, the Republican candidate agreed to jettison transition planning meetings that had been scheduled for the last week or two of the campaign. He wanted to devote every minute to nailing down a victory.

I suppose the meetings would have been helpful, but after eight years as vice president, on top of his hands-on experience in Congress, as United Nations ambassador, U.S. envoy to China, and director of Central Intelligence, George Bush already had a clear idea of how he wanted to organize the new administration.

The transition was well launched with the choice of James Baker III to serve as secretary of state. In selecting a cabinet, the president and his advisers usually prepare long and short lists of candidates; occasionally, there will be only one name under consideration. Despite reports in 1980 that I was in the running for the post of defense secretary, Ronald Reagan and his advisers had earmarked the job for Caspar Weinberger from the beginning. In 1988, Jim Baker's nomination to the secretary of state's post was a foregone conclusion.

I assumed that my name was on the list for defense secretary. No matter whether it was the long or the short list, I was confident that my qualifications would be carefully considered. It was no secret that I had been interested in the job since 1980, when Cap Weinberger was tapped for the post. However, the way things turned out, with Republicans gaining control of the Senate and my move to the chairmanship of the Armed Services Committee, Reagan ended up with team players at the Pentagon and on Capitol Hill.

When the job opened up again in 1987 after Cap decided to step down, I was retired from the Senate, and having twice put my private business activities on hold to return to government service, I was lucky that it was not offered to me. I doubt that I would have accepted. Frank Carlucci, who moved over from the White House to replace Weinberger, though performing ably, always operated as a lame duck defense secretary, and there was scant likelihood that he would be retained by the next administration.

It wasn't a case of wanting to join the president's cabinet just for the honor of the thing. If I had been asked to serve as secretary of the treasury or secretary of commerce I would have turned down those positions. I wouldn't have been comfortable, and probably I wouldn't have been very good at either job. Twenty years on the Armed Services Committee, during which time I had immersed myself in the complexities of defense and national security policy, had given me the qualifications to do the job as secretary of defense. In terms of experience, knowledge, and intellectual capacity, I was ready. There are times when individuals come along who have technical expertise but not the leadership skills, or they are politically astute but lack a feel for the art and science of making war and keeping the peace. Perhaps they are trusted presidential advisers without an intimate sense of the way Washington works. But I could pull it all together, and that was what was needed. We had invested too much in the military during the Reagan years to throw it away, to let the Pentagon drift or be subjected to partisan cannibalization in the 1990s. With any luck, in two to four years, I was certain I could consolidate the gains that had been made and give the military a solid and rational foundation that would last for many decades.

With George Bush in the presidency, I saw that I could fulfill the personal goal of serving as defense secretary and close my career in public service by bringing it full circle. In 1961 I had started at the side of a man by the name of Prescott Bush, who had come to Texas to help me raise funds for a special election to the U.S. Senate. Twenty-seven years later, I could stand at the side of George Bush, Pres's son, and provide some assistance to him in his efforts to lead our country toward the next century.

The next century seemed awfully remote in 1960; for Texas Republicans, making it through the year was a major accomplishment. We were fighting an uphill battle to establish a two-party system for our state.

I know that does not sound like much of a grand vision these days, but then it was about as close as one could come to an impossible dream without being written off as a mindless crank.

In fact, we were dismissed as naive visionaries and worse. The idea that the entrenched Texas Democratic party would ever be forced to share political power was considered by the experts to be about as foolish a notion as "a dog's walking on his hind legs," to use the phrase of ridicule that Samuel Johnson, the eighteenth-century English writer and sage, hurled at the heretical thought that women would ever be allowed into the pulpit to preach the Gospel as ordained members of the clergy.

History proved Samuel Johnson wrong. And history has been just as emphatic in its judgment of another Johnson — Lyndon Baines Johnson — the man I was fighting to unseat from the U.S. Senate, a man so supremely confident of his right to power that he was running for two federal offices at the same time. As John F. Kennedy's vice-presidential running mate, LBJ was hedging his bets by also standing for reelection to the Senate.

Naturally, I tried to make the most of what I conceived to be Johnson's presumptuousness and arrogance during the campaign. And naturally, as any wise, experienced politician would do, he ignored my attacks and my invitations to debate the issues.

I had been learning the rules of this rude and rambunctious game — in Texas, politics really is a contact sport — since childhood, and so Johnson's tactics were no surprise. As the chairman of the committee on education and research, which was basically the Republican party's propaganda arm, and having served as the platform committee chairman at the state convention in 1958, I was regarded as an articulate spokesman for the party's positions and philosophy.

The Republican party felt it had a moral obligation to run a candidate against Lyndon Johnson even though there was little chance of success.

Bruce Alger of Dallas, who was our sole Republican congressman from Texas, declined to run; Bruce wanted to stay in the House. Thad Hutcheson, who had made a bid for the Senate in a special election two years earlier, wasn't interested in trying again.

The leadership figured that since I had been publishing the party newsletter and making a lot of speeches that articulated the party line on the issues, I might be a good campaigner; and so it was agreed I would be the nominee.

Obviously, they were pretty hard up for candidates to turn to a thirty-four-year-old college professor who had run for office only once before and had been swamped in the process. You practically had to hold a gun on somebody to get him to run as a Republican.

They didn't need a gun with me. I guess I was too young and idealistic to know better. At the time, the job seemed similar to that of quarterback for a scrappy, underdog football team: move the ball forward, get a first down, gain experience, and make a respectable, credible showing that would one day yield touchdowns and victory.

Those sports metaphors were comforting; they helped to blunt the sharp edges of reality. They were better, in a way, than the biblical imagery that my father and grandfathers, all Methodist preachers, might have offered me; better to think in terms of the gridiron and the pigskin rather than the sacrificial lamb.

On May 30, 1960, I was nominated by the state Republican convention in McAllen, Texas, to challenge Johnson for his Senate seat. We didn't have primaries in those days, so the gatherings were always industrial-strength, undiluted politics. They were not stage-managed, orchestrated-for-TV affairs. But they were carefully worked out in leadership caucuses — smoke-filled rooms — which were congenial and fun.

A few months later, LBJ went on the national Democratic ticket as the vice-presidential candidate. Since he was the Senate majority leader and running for two offices at the same time, our contest began to attract national attention. The big-time media people from Washington and New York became aware that some little college prof from Wichita Falls was running against Lyndon and decided to send a few reporters down to take a look. The first on the scene was a young correspondent for the *Wall Street Journal* named Robert Novak, who would go on to become a respected syndicated newspaper columnist and TV commentator.

Shortly after I was nominated for the post of secretary of defense, Ernest B. Furgurson, now a columnist for the *Baltimore Sun*, recalled those days on the campaign trail:

The first time I laid eyes on John Tower was September 28, 1960. We were in an old Lockheed Constellation, Henry Cabot Lodge's vice presidential campaign plane, bouncing across Texas.

One of my irreverent colleagues glanced at the short young fellow with the slicked-down hair, his feet hardly touching the floor below his window seat. "Who's that little twerp over there?" the reporter asked.

"Oh, he's a teacher at some cow college up north who thinks he's going to take Lyndon Johnson's seat in the Senate," one of the Republicans aboard said. He laughed along with us, and as I recall, nobody bothered to interview the brash little assistant professor about his prospects.

Not long afterward, John Tower surprised us for the first, but not last, time.

But just having the likes of Ernie Furgurson, Bob Novak, and the other members of the national news media tagging along helped provide name recognition and exposure that normally would not have fallen to a long-shot candidate. Even so, it was a grueling, shoestring campaign. There wasn't much money. Many people were reluctant to give to a losing cause. Often I was forced to fly around the state on my own, rent a car at the airport, and drive from town to town.

It was worth it, though. I managed to make points with a slogan that capitalized on a well-known chewing gum jingle and on the peculiarity of the Texas ballot, which required the voter to cross out the names of the candidates that he or she opposed. I always got a laugh with "Double your pleasure, double your fun — scratch Lyndon twice."

Lodge's Lockheed Constellation was better than a rental car, but there was real luxury when Richard Nixon's entourage swept into the state. I traveled on Nixon's plane and shared campaign appearances with the Republican presidential candidate, making the most of the reflected glory of being on the same platform with the vice president of the United States.

I can't say that Richard Nixon and I became best friends during those campaign swings. There wasn't much time for get-acquainted conversation when you were leapfrogging around a huge state like Texas. He was not one for small talk, and neither am I. But we did share an interest in foreign affairs and in the nuts and bolts of domestic politics.

Much of the 1960 campaign was focused on national security issues. There was an almost palpable sense that we were on the threshold of a new and dangerous era and that what we said and did during those arduous days on the campaign trail would profoundly shape the future.

The vice president seemed to thrive on the long hours, unlike his running mate, Henry Cabot Lodge, who struck most of us as operating on autopilot whenever he campaigned in Texas. After a couple of those visits, a few senior Texas Republicans discreetly advised the Nixon campaign that Lodge's time might be better spent somewhere else.

Despite Nixon's love for political combat, he was showing signs of wear and tear. His pledge to visit all fifty states forced the campaign to spread its resources too thin. In one two-week period Nixon covered fifteen thousand miles. By the end of September, I could see that he had lost weight and was looking a bit haggard. After the first televised debate, on September 26, I was concerned, like many of those who knew Nixon personally, that his endurance was flagging. Still, measuring in terms of the substance of the debate, I was convinced that Richard Nixon had won it.

I freely confess that I was out to hitch a ride on Nixon's coattails. He had a better-than-even chance of winning Texas, thanks to a serious split between the conservative and liberal wings of the Democratic party. The so-called Shivercrats, led by Governor Allan Shivers, had refused to back Adlai Stevenson in 1952. Shivers endorsed Eisenhower, did it again in 1956, and chaired the Democrats for Nixon Committee in 1960.

His support was almost enough to win Texas and the White House for Richard Nixon — almost, but not quite. Some Republicans believe to this day that the election was stolen in Texas and Illinois. In his memoirs, written nearly twenty years later, Nixon offers this assessment:

> There was no doubt that there was massive vote fraud in 1960. Texas and Illinois produced the most damaging, as well as the most flagrant, examples. In one county in Texas, for example, where only 4,895 voters were registered, 6,138 votes were counted. In Chicago a voting machine recorded 121 votes after only 43 people had voted. I lost this precinct 408–79.

Nixon was urged to demand a recount in Texas and Illinois. The margin nationwide was only 118,000 votes, the closest presidential contest since Benjamin Harrison–Grover Cleveland, in 1888. A shift of one half of 1 percent per precinct would have changed the outcome. Even President Eisenhower wanted to challenge the results, but in the end Nixon did the right thing. He advised party leaders of both states to accept the original tally. Nixon knew that a recount would take weeks and that the uncertainty would do untold damage to the country. And practically speaking, recounts rarely make a difference; anyone unscrupulous enough to rig an election the first time around is more than likely to rig it again when the votes are counted a second time.

As for my own contest, although I lost to Johnson, I was satisfied, if not overjoyed, with the numbers. I had polled almost a million votes, a respectable showing of nearly 42 percent of the vote. A political reporter for the *Houston Chronicle* described it as an "astounding" result, given the Democratic party's apparently "unassailable" position. Most of it was an anti-Johnson vote. I'd like to think that there was an enthusiastic 42 percent vote for John Tower, but in reality there was a backlash against Lyndon for playing around with the election laws so that he could run for the two offices, and for what was viewed by many as his marriage of convenience into the Kennedy family, whose brand of liberal politics didn't go down well with Texans.

I would imagine that the charges of vote fraud against the Kennedy-Johnson ticket made LBJ more than a little uncomfortable. The last thing the new vice president elect needed was to be reminded that back home he would always be remembered as "Landslide Lyndon."

It amazes Texans to learn that the details of LBJ's 1948 primary election "victory" still come as news to most of the rest of the country. Author Robert Caro is the latest to uncover an episode that had already been thoroughly reported by Texas journalists and scholars, right down to the Wild West–style showdown between the legendary Texas Ranger Frank Hamer and a bunch of gunslingers in front of the courthouse in the town of Alice, Texas.

What brought Hamer, the lawman who led the posse that ambushed Bonnie and Clyde, to Alice was a dispute over the outcome of the 1948 Democratic Senate primary contest. Lyndon Johnson had been declared the winner, and that was tantamount to election to the U.S. Senate.

To summarize a very complex incident, this is what apparently happened: five days after the primary, a "correction" of 201 votes was reported in the Thirteenth Precinct of Jim Wells County, one of the South Texas counties that were the domain of Democratic political boss George Parr. Allegedly, those 201 votes were added to the precinct's tally sheet on orders from Parr, who was acting at the behest of someone in the Johnson camp (LBJ was trailing at the time). The correction gave Johnson a statewide margin of 87 votes — and his enduring nickname.

Johnson's opponent, Coke Stevenson, inspected the polling sheets at the courthouse in Alice, the county seat, accompanied by Frank Hamer, who actually had to reach for his holstered revolver to clear the gunman from the doorway. Stevenson then disputed the results in federal court. The legal process ended, however, when Hugo Black, the former Democratic senator from Alabama and an associate justice of the Supreme Court, ruled that the matter was one for the Democratic party of Texas to decide.

The saga of box thirteen — the ballot boxes were numbered according to county precinct — is often cited as a vivid example of the abuse of power by the all-Democratic courthouse cliques that had become routine in Texas by 1948.

*   *   *

After having spent more than a year on the campaign trail hammering away at LBJ and the issues, I was no longer the unknown, underdog college professor. With the victory of the Kennedy-Johnson ticket in November of 1960, I simply continued my campaign for the Senate, knowing that with my organization already in place, good name recognition throughout the state, and just enough money left to keep the lights burning in our headquarters, I would one day be recognized as a serious contender.

It seems peculiar now, but the idea that LBJ would ever leave the Senate for the vice presidency, a job then considered inconsequential, seems not to have crossed the minds of the Democratic party's leadership.

Governor Price Daniel, Sr., named William Blakley to fill LBJ's Senate seat for the five months until the special election in May 1961. Blakley was a Dallas millionaire who had served as interim senator once before, when Price Daniel resigned his seat. He had not run in the ensuing special election but, later, challenged incumbent Ralph Yarborough in the Democratic primary for the 1958 general election. He was soundly defeated. The assumption in 1961 was that he would step aside once a stronger candidate emerged. However, Blakley assumed differently; he decided he wanted to stay on for the balance of the term.

Predictably, there was chaos. I expected former governor Allan Shivers to run, but he was a good soldier and reluctant to oppose Blakley, who was technically the Democratic party's standard-bearer, since he occupied the post already. Shivers deferred to Blakley. It was a lucky break for me. I probably would have lost if I had gone head-to-head with him. Not only was Shivers popular with conservative Democrats, he had been a strong backer of both Eisenhower and Nixon; Shivers would have cut into my small but crucial Republican base.

With Allan Shivers out of the race and Blakley in, there was a free-for-all. Since the filing fee was only a modest fifty dollars, seventy-one names went on the ballot for the first round of the special election. Six were considered serious candidates, and four of those were elected officeholders: State Senator Henry B. Gonzalez, Attorney General Will Wilson, Congressman Jim Wright, and State Representative Maury Maverick, Jr.

Wright called himself a "progressive moderate" and set out to attract a broad base of support. If he had succeeded, he probably would have made the most formidable candidate of all. But Will Wilson was able to neutralize Wright by calling on his statewide followers and portraying himself as a middle-of-the-road Democrat. Gonzalez lost his clear shot at the liberal wing of the party when fellow liberal Maury Maverick jumped into the race. Maverick was double trouble for Gonzalez because he also appealed to Texas history buffs as a descendant of Samuel Maverick, one of the patriots who signed the Texas Declaration of Independence, in 1836.

The Democratic establishment, including Lyndon Johnson, rallied around Blakley. The *Dallas Morning News* and other major newspapers, most of them conservative, endorsed the unelected incumbent.

John Knaggs, in his book *Two-Party Texas,* analyzes the political situation this way: "In the spring of 1961, the New Frontier helped polarize Texas politics. 'You're either for or against the Kennedys,' was often heard around the capital city, 'and anybody out in the middle of the road will get run over.' "

This gave me an opportunity to continue to exploit the resentment that many Texans felt toward LBJ and his alleged sellout to the Kennedys. I could portray Blakley as Lyndon's handpicked candidate, even though Price Daniel had done the picking. Meanwhile, I was able to zing the liberals for being liberal and go after the moderates either for being too fuzzy on the issues or for rubber-stamping the Kennedy administration's policies.

When the votes were counted after the first round, I led the field with 325,000 votes, or 31.5 percent. Blakley came in second, with 18.3 percent. Wright had 16.4 percent, and Gonzalez, Wilson, and Maverick divided up the remainder with about 9 or 10 percent each.

At first glance the figures looked good. But if you combined the Blakley-Wright-Wilson totals, or worked up any other logical combination of numbers, I was in deep trouble — a long shot.

Divide and conquer was the only viable alternative.

Our strategy involved holding my conservative base while continuing to paint Blakley — who was just as conservative as I was — as an ally of the Kennedys. This forced Blakley to run against his own president, and that in turn alienated moderate and liberal Democrats.

It was not going to be easy, but I got a helping hand from an unlikely source. Senator Ralph Yarborough, a liberal Democrat who specialized in making trouble for his party's ruling elite, told the press that as far as he was concerned, "the two [candidates] were in competition as to who could denounce the Democratic administration the hardest." The statement was read as a signal that Yarborough had no intention of actively supporting Blakley.

Liberals did not need much encouragement to jump the fence. One did not have to be a political genius to realize that the best hope of wresting control of the Democratic party from the conservative establishment was to induce restive conservative voters to cross over and join the Republican party. The theory was that a two-party Texas would be built around a conservative Republican party and a liberal Democratic party. Therefore, this was a strong incentive for liberals to swallow, if not their pride, at least their ideology, and vote for John Tower. Many reasoned that I would be easier to beat in 1966 than an entrenched conservative Democrat; thus the liberals would have the opportunity to field a viable candidate in the 1966 Democratic primary and beat me in the general election.

The favorite catchphrase of the runoff was "Gone fishing," and it meant that otherwise good and loyal Democrats would sit out the election rather than make a damned-if-you-do/damned-if-you-don't choice between a conservative Republican and a conservative Democrat. And many liberals had the courage not to go fishing but to go to the polls and vote for me.

My college teaching experience had taught me a few things. The daily grind of lectures, often capped with a barrage of probing questions, had trained me to think on my feet and to talk at length, if need be, without notes. As a former Midwestern State University faculty member, music teacher, and church organist, my wife, Lou, was also adept at the spontaneous give-and-take that accounts for much of the daily routine of a political campaign.

We made a good team, and with the assistance of our three young daughters — Penny, Marian, and Jeanne — the Tower family hit the campaign trail and hit it hard.

When I look at the old photos from 1961, I realize that Lou and the kids did much to get me elected to the Senate. The girls, then ages four, five, and six, were so dear in their best Sunday dresses and curls; Lou was the model helpmate, to use a word that the newspaper feature writers were fond of back then. She could have stepped off the cover of the *Saturday Evening Post*. We exploited the photo opportunities in the best campaign tradition. Mom and Dad Tower reading to the kids; Dad driving his brood to school. It was good imagery. Poor Bill Blakley — some of the wags had started calling him "Dollar Bill" because of his wealth — couldn't match it.

The campaign, and the three others that followed at six-year intervals, provided me with more than just votes and a job in the U.S. Senate. My daughters grew up campaigning. They were little ones in 1961, all squirmy and giggly. By 1978, my final reelection bid, I had three intelligent, beautiful, vivacious women at my side. They were with me for the good times and the bad. In the winter of 1988–89, during the worst of the tempest that surrounded my nomination to serve as secretary of defense, they were still there, offering support, affection, and strength during what was, for all of us, a gut-wrenching experience. The relentless day-to-day battering, the lies, the ridicule, the character assassination, took a terrible toll on my daughters. But they rode it out with stamina and spirit. Their courage inspired me and gave me reassurance when I needed it the most, and it will abide with me always.

Television and the airplane began to come into their own as political tools in the early 1960s. I recognized that both gave me the means to overcome, or at least compensate for, the Republican party's major weak point. Having never held power, we lacked the vast network of local functionaries — courthouse cliques — needed to keep the political machinery in operation. They are the ones dispensing favors, rewarding friends, and punishing enemies. In a state the size of Texas, the average voter has minimal contact with state or national party figures. The relationship between the public and the politicians is a local affair.

By the very nature of its long hold on power, the Democratic party had an effective, old-fashioned organization in place all over Texas. In many small towns, Republicans had little or no presence. But by using airplanes, I could drop into those tiny "blank spots," let the folks see and hear me, make a few converts, and move on.

Bear in mind that Texas is the size of eight medium-sized American states put together. There is a lot of ground to cover. The Democrats could get along by merely visiting the key population centers and regional strongholds. I needed, as the saying goes, to mount up and ride off in every direction.

We take the jet plane for granted these days, but Richard Nixon and John Kennedy were the first presidential hopefuls to transform the old concept of whistle-stop campaigning into the brutal airborne "death marches" that now compel candidates and their entourages to slog from coast to coast and back again within a few hours. Theodore H. White noted the development in *The Making of the President 1960:*

[Kennedy] took off by chartered jet from Friendship Airport in Baltimore on Friday afternoon, September 2nd, as if he meant to swallow the country at a gulp. Friday evening he campaigned in Maine; by Saturday noon he was campaigning in San Francisco; Saturday night he flew to Alaska and then, with only four hours' sleep, turned the big jet back to the continent and urged it on all day to Detroit, where on Monday, Labor Day, he would officially open his campaign.

Kennedy racked up seventeen thousand miles in the first ten days of the campaign. Dick Nixon visited twenty-five states in his first two weeks on the road. I lost track of my mileage early on, and I was doing it the hard way, without a *Caroline,* the name JFK had bestowed on his chartered 707, or an *Air Force One.* Pierce Langford, a friend from Wichita Falls, was the pilot of a single-engine Beech Bonanza that carried me around Texas in my final blitz.

Some blitz. At one point, during a violent thunderstorm, Pierce was forced to land on a farm road in Central Texas. I did not wish to squander any opportunity. We taxied the aircraft into Ammannsville, found the local watering hole, where the good old boys were drinking Shiner beer and playing dominoes, and hustled for votes. I bought a couple of rounds, took a few turns with the dominoes, and after a while, when it was apparent that the storm would persist, borrowed a car to drive on to Austin. I carried Ammannsville, and the folks there have never forgotten me.

The Texas newspapers added a new word to their vocabularies in the spring of 1961: "fluke."

As far as they were concerned I was a political accident, a fluke that had resulted from a confluence of mistakes, misjudgments, and mishaps. The editors and publishers had to console themselves someway. Out of about five hundred Texas newspapers, counting the dailies and the weeklies, only fourteen had endorsed my candidacy.

There was a large portion of crow on the plate. "Fluke" probably made it a little easier for the press and the Democratic establishment to swallow it.

But on the night of May 27, and into the small hours of the next morning, months of exhausting effort, sleepless nights, and enormous tension erupted into the damnedest election-night celebration I've ever seen — or will ever see. By 10,343 votes, I went over the top and into the United States Senate.

To say that the victory margin was close would be to push the boundaries of credible understatement to the limit. A total of 886,091 ballots had been cast. Therefore, I'm talking about squeaking by with a margin of just over 1 percent of the vote.

The almost obsessive emphasis on the closeness of the election was one way for the Democrats to pretend that everything was all right. Their attitude was understandable in view of the shock that my victory had administered to the Texas political elite. But it also reflected the reality of the situation. I knew that although we had won the special election, the Republican party was still a beleaguered minority. There was a lot of work to be done in order to turn a temporary coalition of Republican loyalists, disaffected conservative Democrats, and maverick liberals into a permanent alliance. Years of effort would be needed before this peculiar mixture jelled.

Indeed, in the last few days of the 1961 campaign, it appeared that while all the right ingredients were at hand, we still lacked the right recipe for success. Democratic intraparty bickering had died down, and the party pros were working feverishly to salvage a lackluster Blakley campaign. I played down the fact that I was a Republican and appealed directly to the conservative instincts of the average Texan. I asked Senator Barry Goldwater to campaign on my behalf. Barry went all out, and I still owe him a great debt for the long hours and days he put in stumping across the state. The Goldwater magic was potent in Texas, and conservatives — no matter what their party affiliation — responded, even if the candidate in question had been described by House Speaker Sam Rayburn as a "pipsqueak."

To cover my left flank and appeal to the moderates, I invited Senator Prescott Bush to come down from Connecticut to help out, and thanks to the good offices of his son George, he accepted.

Pres was a marvelous campaigner, thoughtful and dignified without being stuffy. His support gave me a link to the Republican establishment and negated the allegation that I was some kind of right-wing kook who would be shunned and ineffective in the Senate.

One of the possibilities that had been raised by the news media during the special-election campaign was that a Tower victory could advance by ten years the timetable for dismantling the conservative Democratic party and lead to GOP congressional seats in Houston and other Texas cities, which was exactly what happened when George Bush won his U.S. House race in 1966.

And so much for the "fluke" of 1961.

When I agreed to help the Bush-Quayle ticket, I did not say, "I'm ready, but here's my price . . . I want to be secretary of defense." That is not my style, and I think George Bush appreciated that there was no pressure or IOU involved. Contrary to some press reports, I *never* lobbied Bush or any of his associates for consideration as secretary of defense during the course of the campaign.

On the Saturday following the 1988 presidential election, I read in the *Washington Post* that the president-elect was being urged by some of his advisers to appoint a "manager" to run the Pentagon, "over a political figure like former Senator John G. Tower."

I interpreted the story as an indication that the normal give-and-take of any transition was under way. It quoted David Packard, a former deputy secretary of defense in the Nixon administration and prominent industrialist, who was planning to meet with Bush to discuss his views on who should be nominated to oversee the Defense Department.

I was not particularly alarmed at the prospect of the meeting, and one reason was that the story helped make the case for my nomination:

> Packard and others, sources said, are contending that the new defense secretary must know both government and industry so that he can bring the Pentagon under control during the expected "honeymoon" at the outset of the Bush presidency rather than take a year to learn the intricacies of imposing reforms on the twin bureaucracies of government and contractors.

Paul H. O'Neill, president of Aluminum Company of America, was identified as Packard's choice for the post, but while O'Neill is a first-rate corporate manager, ALCOA is not the Pentagon. ALCOA's defense-contracting work is only a very small part of the corporation's many business activities, and its contribution to the overall military posture is limited and specialized.

But the essential point that came through loud and clear was that a year or so of on-the-job training for a new secretary of defense in the ways of Washington, the Pentagon, and Capitol Hill would be detrimental to the Bush administration.

The press, if read closely, acts as a political early-warning system. Obviously, "managing" the Defense Department was a theme that was being pushed within the transition operation; I quickly learned that it came primarily from Robert Teeter and Craig Fuller.

The two men were codirectors of the Bush transition team. Fuller had served as the vice president's chief of staff, and Teeter is a skilled public opinion pollster. Within the following week, I arranged to meet directly with George Bush to discuss my ideas for managing the Pentagon.

The vice president's office was in the West Wing of the White House, near the Oval Office, with windows overlooking West Executive Avenue and the Old Executive Office Building, the neo–beaux arts structure that once housed the State and War departments. The West Wing is cramped and crowded. Only the president gets to have a modicum of elbow room and luxury, although when the Oval Office is compared with the lavish suites of rooms provided to most other heads of state, and some corporate CEOs, for that matter, it too is extremely modest. But White House officials would sooner squeeze into tiny West Wing cubicles than be exiled to the comfort of the Old Executive Office Building, referred to as the OEOB, with its chandeliers, wood paneling, and marble staircases. And some manage to have it both ways, keeping one foot in the West Wing and maintaining satellite offices in the OEOB. Ever since I first arrived in Washington, proximity to the Oval Office has tended to reflect power and influence, in the context of who sits where in the West Wing. In those terms, George Bush's no-nonsense, utilitarian corner office was a significant measure of his close working relationship with Ronald Reagan. It wasn't a showplace, but the core of a working vice presidency and, in November 1988, the focal point of a historic transition of power.

When I walked into the office, George Bush looked like he was enjoying the job, which was, under the circumstances, understandable.

The door was open, but the president-elect was finishing another meeting. As I stepped back to wait, he called out for me to come right in. George Bush is not one to fuss about the protocol of having a secretary announce and escort each visitor into the inner sanctum. There was no need to offer him congratulations; I had done that in person on election night. There was a moment or two of small talk about the few days of rest in Gulf Stream, Florida, that the president-elect had managed to slip in after election day, but every minute counts during a transition and I quickly moved to my agenda.

I was prepared to discuss and outline a series of recommendations that aimed at getting the most defense out of the fewest dollars. I stressed that the Pentagon could be managed in a way to yield enough savings to keep overall expenditures in balance. The point, in so many words, was that John Tower was not planning to be a big spender, pushing reflexively for every major weapons system that came along. I knew there would be budget constraints on the military in the future, and I wanted George Bush to know that I understood it.

I also stressed to him that priorities had to be clearly defined and carefully reconciled on the basis of roles and missions required to implement strategy, and not on the basis of perceived requirements by the individual uniformed services. To achieve that objective I proposed to apply a team concept to administer the Pentagon that would override the traditional rivalry between the services. Clear lines of control and authority running downward through the system and commensurately clear lines of responsibility and accountability running upward would have to be established, with the ultimate responsibility devolving on the secretary of defense.

The president-elect sat on the couch, comfortable, legs crossed, but listening intently. He asked several questions and looked down occasionally at a pad to make notes.

I was determined that we should no longer have a Pentagon at war with itself. My concept of melding the deputy secretary, the undersecretaries, and the service secretaries into a management team with a unified front had never before been suggested. The secretaries of the Army, Navy, and Air Force have ended up as salesmen and political advocates for their service's point of view. Bush seemed to react favorably to my proposals.

I asked to be considered for the post of defense secretary, although I did not press for a decision, and assured him that whomever he chose, he could count on me for support and cooperation.

The president-elect told me that my ideas were interesting, and as I expected, the job was not formally offered. However, after close to thirty years in Washington and dozens of meetings with presidents, starting with Lyndon Johnson, I knew that often it is what happens after the meeting that can be of far more importance than what happens during a meeting. The follow-up, the phone calls, the orders that are issued, mean that the words will be translated into action.

After I left the office, Bush moved quickly. He immediately contacted Jim Baker to suggest that senior transition-team officials also hear my proposals on management reform for the Pentagon. The next day, Baker apprised me of the president-elect's reaction to our conversation, and we arranged a time and a place for the meeting. Naturally, I was happy to oblige. The quick follow-up indicated to me that the president-elect had no major misgivings about offering me the post, and he seemed to be signaling his advisers that I was at the top of the only short list of candidates that really mattered — George Bush's list.

TWO

A PUBLIC SERVANT AND A PRIVATE LIFE

LOU BULLINGTON TOWER was my wife for twenty-four years. We were married on March 21, 1952. Since it was a leap year, our wedding day was the first day of spring.

The divorce that ended the marriage was finalized on December 27, 1976. Hubert Humphrey once said that the job description for a U.S. senator should carry the bottom-line warning "Hard on marriages."

Dr. Edward Elson, the Senate chaplain in the 1970s, took note of the number of failed marriages clustered around the Ninety-fifth Congress and called it an epidemic. The list of casualties was a long one. My name was on it, along with those of Lowell Weicker, Herman Talmadge, Donald Riegle, Alan Cranston, Dick Clark, Floyd Haskell, Ed Brooke, and Paul Laxalt, nearly 10 percent of the Senate, not counting several other members who had been divorced earlier in their careers and remarried.

I cannot speak for the others, but Lou and I, after the children had grown up and gone off to school, began to drift apart. There was nothing sensational or dramatic, just a slow, steady deterioration.

Our daughters sensed this fairly early in the process. Marian, who was about twenty years old at the time, talked to me about it. She urged us to consider a divorce and separate lives, rather

than stick with a marriage that left us both miserable and unfulfilled.

It was sound advice, and when we parted it was amicable. There
had been infidelities on my part, but extramarital affairs are rarely
the cause of a failed marriage; they are the surface manifestations
of deeper currents.

Beryl Goodwin Tower, my mother, lived alone in a log cabin in
Cass County, Texas, until she was in her eighties — formidable,
intelligent, and feminine. In the midst of the confirmation agony,
I remembered a poem she wrote for her collection, *Poesy and
Mirth:*

> *Pain has its moments of ecstasy*
> *When white hot, searing,*
> *It burns away the dross of life,*
> *Leaving only the real*
> *Without mystery.*
> *The vision clears*
> *As in the exaltation of strife.*

It would be difficult — impossible, really — not to be profoundly influenced by a woman who could make the pain of living
yield a clear vision of "the real." She was a pioneer woman. Her
world, at once hardscrabble and Victorian, the world she and my
father shared as they moved from Methodist parsonage to parsonage around East Texas, is gone. And it was going, evolving, even
as I was growing up. The strict prohibitions against drinking and
divorcing fit the time and the place. I did not rebel against the
Reverend and Mrs. Joe Z Tower with drink and divorce so much
as live in my own time and in my own place.

I married Lilla Burt Cummings in May 1977. A Washington lawyer with a good eye for real estate investments, she had a sharp
mind and a blunt, outspoken personality. We were divorced ten
years later. The final decree was handed down in September 1987.
Fourteen months later, and a few days before I had my first meeting of the transition with George Bush, material from an interrogatory filed by Lilla during a property-settlement dispute found its
way into the *Atlanta Constitution:*

In a divorce petition filed in Washington, Lilla Burt Cummings Tower accused Mr. Tower, 63, of 'Marital Misconduct.'

She requested depositions from three women, including a Texas socialite, a Dallas television personality and a maid hired by the couple in Geneva, Switzerland, where Mr. Tower was a member of President Reagan's strategic arms negotiation team.

Mr. Tower was granted an uncontested divorce. . . . Although District of Columbia Superior Court records do not disclose the details of the settlement, Mr. Tower reportedly agreed to pay alimony and withdraw his claim for a share of his wife's property, which Mr. Tower had estimated at $2 million.

The Towers married in 1977 and separated in 1985. It was his second marriage, her third.

There is no way to determine whether Lilla leaked the material to damage my reputation. The papers are public records and available to the press. Indeed, stories on the matter had appeared months earlier in two Dallas newspapers. All a reporter had to do was go to the courthouse and search through the files.

The headline on the *Atlanta Constitution* story — "TOWER: TOO HOT FOR BUSH TO HANDLE?" — was the first of the many sensational flourishes that the news media indulged in at my expense. At the time, although it was annoying, I didn't worry about the story's damaging my chances for obtaining the nomination. A divorce proceeding, with maneuvers and countermaneuvers for legal advantage, statements and accusations to achieve tactical objectives, and one-sided presentations of events to influence a financial settlement, should have no bearing whatsoever on whether an individual is qualified to serve as secretary of defense.

The story also dredged up and mangled previous accounts that had appeared in the press about the disposition of funds left over from my 1984 reelection campaign — a campaign that never happened, because I decided to retire from the Senate, even though there was little doubt I would have won a fifth term.

A total of $1.53 million had been raised for the campaign. My staff contacted contributors to determine if they wanted the money returned. Many of them gave us discretion on the disposition of the funds, and the lion's share was donated to Republican candidates for office. Under the law that was in force at the time, I was entitled to keep the funds and spend them in any way I chose, as long as I reported and paid income taxes. However, I did not do that. None of the funds were expended for personal use. One hundred thousand dollars was provided to Southwestern University, in Georgetown, Texas, where I earned my bachelor's degree, to partially defray the cost of establishing a research repository for the more than six hundred cartons of papers and other material accumulated during my twenty-four years in the Senate. Travel and office expenses, staff salaries, and the overhead of keeping speaking commitments and dealing with a backlog of correspondence during the transition from one phase of public life — the Senate — to another phase of public life — chief negotiator for the Strategic Arms Reduction Talks — quickly exhausted the remaining balance.

A January 25, 1985, letter from the Senate Ethics Committee, following my appointment as START negotiator, stated that the appointment allowed me "to use contributions to defray any ordinary and necessary expenses you incur in connection with that office."

There again I did not expect trouble. And I was right. The Senate Armed Services Committee was fully satisfied with the disbursement of the funds and our accounting. The subject came up only briefly at the confirmation hearings, and when it did, Chairman Nunn said, "There was an extensive amount of work done on it in the executive branch and also on our Committee, and I think there are no outstanding questions now."

The Federal Elections Commission, the Senate Ethics Committee, and the IRS all reviewed the expenses and the documentation and found them to be satisfactory. Even so, the *Atlanta Constitution*'s treatment of the subject seemed to be deliberately inflammatory: "According to reports filed with the Federal Elections Commission, Mr. Tower used some of the funds for personal air travel, banquets, expensive gifts and contributions to his college alma mater and favorite candidates."

With the benefit of hindsight, and despite the subsequent comment at the hearings, I now realize that I probably should have noted the place of origin of the story — Atlanta — and read it as an indication that the senior senator from Georgia, the chairman of the Armed Services Committee, Sam Nunn, or his subordinates were beginning to organize a political offensive against the nomination, even before the president-elect had made a final decision.

A few days after my meeting with President-elect Bush, I received the invitation to get together with a few senior members of his transition team. Robert Teeter was not there, unfortunately, but the hour and a half or so that I spent with New Hampshire governor John Sununu, who had been chosen to serve as White House chief of staff, and Secretary of State designate James Baker more than made up for his absence. I like Sununu. He is not afraid to step on toes, if necessary, to get things done. We have that trait in common. Sununu's selection for the top White House staff position had been one of those satisfying Washington "bombshells." The pundits, assorted expert observers, and well-informed sources had all decided that Craig Fuller would get the top staff job and that there would be some sort of power-sharing arrangement with Bob Teeter. That all went up in smoke when George Bush decided he wanted John Sununu, who had been instrumental in Bush's victory in the crucial New Hampshire primary, to come to Washington and ramrod the White House.

I gave Sununu and Baker an outline and overview of my discussion with the president-elect. Given Bob Teeter's preference for a manager at the Pentagon — and he seemed to be the one who was pushing the idea the hardest — I pointed out that I had a reputation as a people manager. Selecting the most effective members for a team, motivating and coordinating their activities, setting priorities and achieving goals, had always been some of my strengths. I managed the Eisenhower campaign in twelve northern counties of Texas in 1956, which covered a lot of territory and involved a lot of people. Over the years, my own statewide Senate campaigns amounted to massive enterprises that made the day-to-day activities of a large corporation look tame by comparison. In addition, as chairman of the Senate Armed Services Committee, chairman of the Republican Policy Committee, and chairman of the Housing Subcommittee (Banking), I was simultaneously directing three major entities that were responsible for important legislative and political functions. Programs that accounted for roughly one quarter of the federal budget came across the desks of my Armed Services Committee staff, and those highly professional men and women earned well-deserved reputations for skill and dedication. Likewise, those I recruited for positions on my personal staff and the Banking, Policy, and Select Intelligence committees went on to key roles in business and government. Although I left the Senate in 1984, I did not leave behind my eye for talent or the ability to lead an effective organization, as demonstrated by the success of the START negotiating team and the President's Special Review Board on the Iran-contra situation.

As I had with George Bush, I stressed to Baker and Sununu the concept that at close-knit team composed of the defense secretary, deputy, the undersecretaries, and the civilian chiefs of each of the military services could bring unity and coherence to the Pentagon. They listened closely to my presentation and peppered me with questions. We were friends and political allies, but Baker and Sununu pressed hard to satisfy themselves that I was on the same wavelength as the president-elect on the entire range of important issues that would face the Defense Department, including management and procurement reform. They gave me a thorough going-over.

The meeting went well, and a few days later Governor Sununu was quoted as saying "It looks like John Tower" when he was asked who would be named to the post of defense secretary. Considering the authority of the source, I assumed it unlikely that anyone else was being seriously considered. The tight external control of my emotions gave way to inward elation. My spirits soared. Having weathered criticism and controversy, I emerged with fulfillment within my grasp.

The following Tuesday, November 22, the *Washington Post* decided that its original approach to who would be sent to the Pentagon needed to be updated:

> Former Senate Armed Services Committee Chairman John G. Tower (R-Tex.) appears to be the choice of President-elect George Bush for secretary of defense and could be named to the post early next week, according to informed transition sources.
>
> Industrialist David Packard, who headed a major study on Pentagon procurement and reform, met with Bush yesterday and said afterward that Bush promised to appoint a "strong team" to lead the Defense Department but was still mulling over who should be secretary. Packard has said publicly Bush should seize the opportunity to achieve major reforms in management of the huge department.
>
> Other sources said Tower appeared to be Bush's choice over several other alternatives who have been brought to the vice president's attention, including Paul O'Neill, chief executive of the Aluminum Co. of America, and former defense secretary Donald Rumsfeld. "It's jelling that way," one in-

formed transition official said of Tower's expected appointment. "There's not a clear second" choice.

Presidents and presidents-elect must cast a wide net to gather information and advice. George Bush's meeting with David Packard was part of that process. As chairman of the Packard Commission, established by President Reagan to review Pentagon procurement procedures and recommend reforms, Packard was extremely influential. Based on the press reports, it appeared that he was pushing Donald Rumsfeld, who had served as secretary of defense during the Ford administration.

Rhett Dawson, the Packard Commission's executive director and my former staff director on the Senate Armed Services Committee, had dinner with Packard the night before he met with the president-elect. They discussed the Pentagon, and when my name came up Packard suggested that I would be a rubber stamp for the military. Rhett took the opportunity to offer him a few of the many examples of pork barrel and "pet rock" programs that I had opposed as chairman of the committee.

There was a flaw in the logic of David Packard's advocacy of selecting a manager from private industry, which surely did not escape George Bush. Packard had served as deputy to Defense Secretary Mel Laird, a former Republican congressman. Together, the two men — one with a business background, the other a skilled political operator — made for an effective leadership team. The combination had worked well during the Nixon administration; there was no reason it shouldn't work twenty years later.

In seeking advice from friends and colleagues about the defense secretary's post, I consulted Mel Laird early on. He urged me to make every effort to do my own recruiting for senior positions within the Pentagon hierarchy. Top officials with divided loyalties can undercut a defense secretary's authority, which must flow directly from the president and then downward through the chain of command. Back-channel relationships with members of the White House staff or power factions on Capitol Hill create tension and incoherence.

Laird's advice was sagacious. But like many things that happen in Washington, it was easier said than done. The day after the *Washington Post* noticed that there was no "clear second" choice for defense secretary, the newspaper discovered that "former

Senator John G. Tower (R-Tex.), President-elect George Bush's apparent first choice as Secretary of Defense, is involved in a complex negotiation with the Bush transition team over how many top appointments he would control in taking over the Pentagon, according to informed sources." It continued:

> More than a week ago, Tower was told by a close Bush associate that he could name the three service secretaries — for the Army, Navy and Air Force — but that Bush would select the no. 2 Pentagon appointee, the deputy secretary of defense, and the two undersecretaries who direct acquisition and administer defense policy issues.
>
> Behind the maneuvering is concern among top Bush aides that Tower, a former chairman and longtime member of the Senate Armed Services Committee, has a large coterie of acquaintances and former aides who are experienced in defense matters and could fill all the top slots, thereby making the Defense Department less responsive to White House direction than they would like, sources said.

The story overstated the situation to a considerable degree. A "complex negotiation" was not under way. In discussing my views on the way I would organize the Pentagon's leadership structure, I had made it clear that I intended to recruit several former Senate committee aides and staff members. Although I did not go into specifics until after my nomination was announced by the president-elect, my plans were to move Rhett Dawson from the Reagan White House, where he was serving as presidential assistant for administration, to the post of Army secretary. Jim McGovern, the acting Air Force secretary, who had served as the Armed Services Committee's majority staff director, would stay on as Air Force secretary. And I intended to urge the president-elect to retain Will Ball, my former administrative assistant in the Senate, as secretary of the Navy. All of those posts required Senate confirmation.

Dawson, McGovern, and Ball were the nucleus of the so-called Tower Mafia. A more accurate term would be Tower Alumni. Over the years I always encouraged my staff to seek out promising opportunities in the executive branch of the federal government and in private industry. In 1980, after President Reagan captured the White House, his talent scouts raided my Senate office and minority committee staffs for subcabinet personnel and other senior positions.

I have been kidded for setting out to "infiltrate" the top echelons of government and industry with my former associates. The only credit that I will accept for their accomplishments, however, is that I recognized it would have been a mistake to hire any staffer who would be content to find a niche in the Senate and stay there for an entire career. It is advisable, indeed essential, to have a few old hands around in senior positions, like Bill Hildenbrand, the veteran secretary to the Republican leadership, a proven expediter who could provide an institutional memory. But most Senate aides should move onward and upward, before they begin to regard their jobs as sinecures or think that they constitute the permanent Senate and that the men and women elected to the body are only transients.

The proper role of the Senate staff in the legislative process is a subject of considerable importance. In meetings, when one of the newcomers to my staff would start misusing the first-person pronoun *we* — *we* have to develop legislation . . . *we* must answer . . . *we* should . . . — I would wait for an opening and ask, "How much did *we* win the last election by?" The point usually hit home.

Curt Smothers, in the mid-1970s my chief staffer on the Church Committee, which was investigating alleged abuses by the intelligence community, was extremely forceful and aggressive. He enjoyed tangling with members of the committee, particularly when off-the-wall notions would come up, like holding committee hearings in Europe to interrogate the CIA's clandestine operatives — guaranteeing, of course, that the witnesses would be marked for death. Curt would go on the attack, and I would have to say, "Curt, you must remember that you are not a member of the U.S. Senate!" He'd back off for a little while, but not for long.

Today, Curt is a successful lawyer and businessman in San Francisco. He has served as role model and mentor for young black attorneys. I am proud of him and the other members of the Tower Alumni. The point is, however, that when those men and women were on my staff, they were always answerable to me. All too often some members of the Senate allow their aides — and I'll use a favorite phrase around Washington — to go into business for themselves.

*   *   *

Washington always shuts down over the Thanksgiving holiday, transition or no transition, but I decided to stay in town to monitor what was likely to be a stormy confirmation. I had no way of knowing how agonizing that storm would be.

Over the years, I have missed my share of family holidays. My daughters were a little disappointed that I wouldn't be home. But they were aware of how much I was preoccupied by the process and probably realized that I would be distracted and a bit uncommunicative, which I have to admit happens to me when I am intently focused on a subject. Although they had misgivings about the prospect of yet another round of government service with long hours, high pressure, and severe financial constraints, Penny, Marian, and Jeanne were supportive.

My daughters are in their thirties. Though only twenty-six months apart from eldest to youngest, they have very different personalities. Penny, the eldest, is a self-assured, take-charge sort. Given the chance, she would reorganize an anthill. Marian is mild-mannered, sophisticated, and tough-minded. Jeanne is intense, sharp-witted, and as the shrewdest politician in the family is somewhat of a reflection of me. The girls are very close-knit, strongly family-spirited, good-humored, and fun.

The holiday was low-key; Dorothy Heyser joined me in Washington. We had lunch and dinner with friends on Thanksgiving Day; the other guests discreetly avoided asking about the Pentagon, and I steered the conversation toward other subjects whenever it seemed that my nomination might come up as a topic.

Dorothy and I are both in our sixties, so it is somewhat difficult to describe us as girlfriend and boyfriend, but I guess I can accept the terminology.

We have known each other for several years. She is a widow and would appear to be the Texas socialite mentioned in the *Atlanta Constitution* as having been named in my former wife Lilla's interrogatory. Dorothy was an innocent bystander to the divorce and unfortunately got hit in the cross fire. We had known each other casually in that period, and she insisted before we began dating that my separation from Lilla be permanent.

Dorothy gets along well with my daughters. We all spend a lot of time together. Occasionally Lou, the girls' mother and my first wife, joins us for a birthday party or a holiday celebration. Marian sardonically describes us as a "typical family of the 1980s."

Thanksgiving, 1988, was not quite a typical all-American celebration, however. Unfortunately, Andrea Mitchell came to dinner. Not literally; Andrea crashed the party with her television battering ram.

On Wednesday, November 23, this NBC reporter aired a piece on the evening news that rehashed the *Atlanta Constitution* story. My private life, fact and fiction, was broadcast coast to coast. Fiction, as it turned out, predominated. In the shorthand that TV reporters use to compress an eight-hundred-word newspaper story into a ninety-second broadcast, the terms "marital misconduct" and "questionable use" of campaign funds made it sound as though Andrea were a judge pronouncing the verdict and handing down the sentence.

After seeing the broadcast, I asked Martha Kirkendall, my Dallas office manager, to fly to Washington, and the two of us spent a good portion of the long weekend going through our files to account for every penny of the leftover campaign funds. The official report issued by the Senate Armed Services Committee on my nomination included nearly fifty pages of records showing where the money went and why.

One of the more frustrating things about dealing with the press is that only one side of a story is told. The corrections, the elaborations, the other side, never catch up to the initial distorted accounts. As Mark Twain said, "A lie goes half way around the world before the truth even puts on its boots."

The FBI field investigation into my background began December 1, the day after I was called to the White House by C. Boyden Gray, the president-elect's counsel, and given a set of financial-disclosure forms and other material relating to my business activities, medical history, tax records, and the like. At that point, having been through two similar investigations, I thought I knew what to expect. As had been done when I was asked by President Reagan to serve as the ambassador in charge of START in Geneva, and again when he invited me to serve on the President's Foreign Intelligence Advisory Board, the agents, I figured, would round up "the usual suspects," ask the usual questions, and record the usual answers.

This assumption was borne out — initially. My first interview, conducted by two agents from the Dallas office, followed the pattern set by the others. One difference, however, was that the details of my divorce from Lilla (it had not been finalized until September 1987) were not a major component of the background checks conducted before the PFIAB appointment. After the first few questions, I could see that Lilla's interrogatory was setting the tone and the shape of the agents' approach to their assignment.

Still, I was not alarmed. It was perfectly understandable that the FBI would pick up the trail, so to speak, where the footprints were the freshest. I was familiar with the interrogatory — a series of questions; not direct allegations, but full of innuendo and implication. I rebutted them point by point.

The phrase "marital misconduct" has a portentous resonance, and Lilla and her lawyers were careful to be oblique about what they said. Proving that I had been unfaithful to my second wife would not have been possible, because it never happened.

By proposing to embark on a fishing expedition against the women named in the interrogatory, Lilla, it seemed to me, was threatening to embarrass them in the interest of achieving the financial objectives she was pursuing in the final divorce settlement. Rather than allowing that to happen — why should they suffer because of my divorce? — I gave way to some of Lilla's demands, to expedite settlement.

But since I had not responded to the questions posed in the interrogatory, they stood as the last word, and that was where the FBI started its investigation. I was put in the position of having to prove a negative, and as any logician knows, that is an extremely difficult feat. Proving that one committed an act is always easier than proving that one did not. It is the reason that in our system of justice an individual is presumed innocent until proven guilty.

I urged the FBI to talk to the women involved, reasoning that their denials of any romantic relationship with me during my marriage would be the ultimate refutation of any suggestion of marital misconduct. I continued to take this approach throughout the investigation. As the wildest allegations surfaced, those who might have had direct knowledge were sought out to provide evidence, and time after time the charges could not be substantiated.

A few words about the FBI's role. I have been asked whether in light of my experience I believe it is inappropriate to use the FBI to conduct background checks on individuals who are being considered for important positions in the federal government. On the contrary, the FBI must investigate those under consideration for posts involving sensitive national security matters. There is no other mechanism available.

The fact that a field inquiry is being conducted, however, does not mean it should be allowed to degenerate into open season on the candidate for high office. The material that is collected — most of it unevaluated — has to be held in the strictest confidence within a limited circle of those charged with weighing the potential nominee's fitness for the position. In my case, leaks abounded. Misstatements, lies, gossip, half-truths, and personal opinion were jumbled together and disseminated by the news media, and in turn served as fuel for another round of misstatements, lies, gossip, and personal opinion. This whirligig spun out of control, and it became a perpetual-motion machine pumping poison into the political process.

Each person has a history, created minute by minute, day by day. Mine involves twenty-four years in the Senate, thousands of pieces of legislation, hundreds of close professional relationships with men and women, innumerable personal contacts with foreign leaders, and enough miles on the road to evoke a suggestion from Bob Hope that I be given the Rand McNally Award. To dissect my history (or anyone else's), to pull it apart and examine it from every angle, would take another twenty-four years, if not longer. An FBI investigation cannot be permitted to drag on past a reasonable length of time. Determining what is reasonable depends on the good judgment and goodwill of those who are directing the investigation.

And those two essential ingredients — goodwill and good judgment — unfortunately were lacking throughout the process. In terms of good judgment, the White House probably should have insisted on more stringent guidelines before agreeing to continue the investigation, confining it to charges of criminal wrongdoing or to allegations for which there were credible supporting witnesses. And as for goodwill, if the FBI field investigations are politicized, we have forged a dangerous weapon. Sam Nunn used the FBI inquiries to discredit me and to strike at the president of the United States. The essential chain of good judgment and goodwill broke down during my confirmation process. I think many Senate Democrats knew what was happening and why, but lacked the will to stop it.

*   *   *

Some commentators say that my nomination was damaged because
it "twisted slowly in the wind" between election day and December
16, when it was finally announced. I disagree.

The Defense Department was going to be one of the hot spots
of the new administration. Discussion and an examination of alternatives were entirely appropriate. George Bush would have been
faulted for rushing to fill the defense secretary's post and practicing
Pentagon business as usual if he had moved within the first days
of the transition.

The old Washington practice of sending up a trial balloon was
involved as well. As could be expected, my nomination drew an
abundance of hostile fire. I have made many friends over the years,
but I also have opponents: disgruntled aides to Democratic members of the Senate Armed Services Committee who thought their
toes had been stepped on by my staff, conservative Republicans
who thought I was soft on SDI or despised me for my pro-choice
position on abortion, liberals who resented me for helping to bring
about the defense buildup.

Yes, there was opposition; but as one member of the Bush transition team put it, the charges were not news. Throughout, the
only debate about my nomination among the president-elect's advisers was focused on my commitment to reforming the Pentagon's
procurement procedures and holding the line on excessive defense
spending in an era that was shaping up as one dominated by a
need for austerity.

The time that elapsed between the first report speculating about
my nomination and its official announcement amounted to roughly
four weeks, certainly not an inordinately long period. But my critics made use of the time, and during the news vacuum created by
the Thanksgiving break, the will-he-or-won't-he-nominate-Tower
story gave members of the news media something to write about.

The *Los Angeles Times* got in on the act this way: "Tower, according to unsubstantiated stories, is a womanizer and has a drinking problem. The tales were inspired by Tower's recent
divorce. . . . One particularly wild — and wholly unfounded —
story has Tower barred from Australia because of a drunken spree
there."

There you, the reader, can see a major national newspaper traf-
ficking in what it openly acknowledges to be "unsubstantiated,"
"wild," and "wholly unfounded" stories. Journalists are proud of

their high standards. They talk about the four *w*'s: *who, what, when, where*. And, even when a fifth *w* is tossed in — *why* — there does not seem to be room for a sixth and seventh; i.e., *wild* and *wholly unfounded*.

We rely on the press for news about our world. There is a need for information to make sound judgments. But when fact is mingled freely with gossip, it is impossible to sort out what is meaningful from the dross. At best, the news media, disclaiming their responsibility, seem to be saying, "Here, you figure out which is which — we can't do it." At worst, they have adopted the standards of sleazy scandal sheets. In either case, the implications are serious. How can we conduct our democracy, dependent as it is on the free flow of information, without a reliable source of information?

The Ill Wind scandal, a series of cases that came to light in the spring of 1988 involving allegedly corrupt relationships between some Pentagon officials and private defense consultants, had made the FBI particularly skittish about anything related to Defense Department personnel matters. The bureau did not want to be accused by its detractors of sloppy screening procedures. By the same token, the members of the Senate Armed Services Committee, who had confirmed Mel Paisley as assistant secretary of the Navy in the Reagan administration only to see him become one of the principal targets of the Ill Wind investigation, wanted to show that they were eagle-eyed and vigilant when it came to scrutinizing the backgrounds of Bush administration nominees.

Another element that related to the pace of the FBI investigation was the president-elect's determination to make ethics in government a central theme of his first one hundred days in office. The ethics issue made Washington's elected officials nervous. Aside from flagrantly indictable conduct, unethical behavior does not have a black-and-white definition. The gray areas are danger zones, but as former associate justice Potter Stewart said about the difficulty of defining pornography — "I know it when I see it" — by the time the politician starts seeing gray, he may already be in trouble. Especially if the rules of ethical conduct are constantly shifting with little or no warning.

When George Bush seized on the ethics issue, Democrats shuddered. House Speaker Jim Wright's conduct already was being criticized; they took the attitude, in a figurative sense, that they would kill or be killed on the ethics question, and they attempted to establish themselves as ethics vigilantes. The motto became Do unto Others Before They Do unto You.

As a result, the FBI background checks, a routine part of the presidential-appointments process, were blown out of all proportion in determining the fitness of any given nominee. These checks were never intended to be exhaustive, all-encompassing evaluations. Nor were they intended as a means for Congress to pursue its own investigation, which is precisely what happened in my case. When the initial FBI file was shown to Senator Nunn, in early January 1989, he immediately came back with additional questions and lines of inquiry that he wanted the agents to pursue. Later, Nunn actually took to calling the FBI directly with his instructions, ignoring the fact that the bureau was supposed to answer to the White House.

The FBI files became the rope, and the ethics vigilantes fashioned it into a noose.

As for Jim Wright, to whom this metaphor also applies, his fall was not Republican revenge for what happened to me. He wandered into the ethical gray zone — maybe he was wrong; that's not for me to say — but for his alleged sins he was tried, convicted, and strung up by the press. Only resignation saved Jim Wright from being cut down and hanged again by his House colleagues, many of whom were practicing holier-than-thou orthodoxy to prove that their own ethics were above reproach.

It was an ugly spectacle and a sad end to the career of a dedicated public servant.

Given the climate, the Bush transition team and the FBI went the extra mile to ensure that my background check was thorough. The bulk of the report was not completed until the middle of December, and there was no pressure exerted on the FBI to take shortcuts so that the president-elect could answer the charges that he was "drifting" by not naming a defense secretary.

To dramatize their stories, the news media have a tendency to impose deadlines for action. Thus, the pressure mounts on officials to make a decision, even though the deadline is artificial and without relevance to the circumstances under which they are working. There is always a source willing to play the deadline game. The *Washington Post* found one on November 26:

President-elect George Bush, facing the need to cut $8 billion to $10 billion from the fiscal 1990 defense budget, is preparing to launch a major review of the U.S. defense strategy as a first step toward bringing the Pentagon budget under control, according to informed sources.

As part of this plan, he reportedly wants to have the top three members of his national security team — the secretary of defense, national security adviser and director of central intelligence — in place by next week so that they can begin the review with Secretary of State-designate James A. Baker III, the sources said.

The readers of the *Post,* and that includes most everyone involved in the work of the federal government in Washington, were led to believe that my nomination had to be announced within a few days, or else the president-elect's review of the Pentagon budget would be stymied. John Sununu, then a novice in the ways of Washington, was quoted in the piece as saying, "I think next week you'll see action in a couple of areas associated with defense and probably over the next two weeks we'll fill that out. . . . Now where . . . the secretary and deputy secretary fall into the timing I can't tell you."

A newcomer, but catching on fast, Sununu left room to maneuver. He tried to avoid being locked into the timing of the nomination; however, the "next week" business was still hanging there, begging to be used by reporters as a deadline. And use it they did.

Over the following two weeks the *Post* reported that my nomination had been "seriously" weakened by the "delay" and that the announcement was being "held up" while the FBI conducted "an exhaustive background investigation that one knowledgeable official called 'more thorough than any . . . the FBI has ever done.' "

I should take a moment here to explain why I am quoting so heavily from the *Washington Post.* Its location in the nation's capital gives it enormous influence. In addition to having a regular readership of officials in each branch of the government and the military, the *Post* is used by members of the news media as a "reliable source." An old editor once said, "The news is what I say it is." Today, news is what the *Washington Post* and a few other major publications say it is. Their interest and emphasis on particular issues will attract the attention of the rest of the news media.

Television is also influential and in many ways is beginning to displace some of the heavyweights of the print media in terms of shaping overall news judgment. TV's taste for the quick and the flashy has awakened an appetite for similar fare. *USA Today* indulges freely in it, and newspapers like the *Post* and the *New York Times* give in to the temptation to mimic their broadcast colleagues. Sections of the paper like the *Post*'s "Style" and the *New York Times*'s "Washington Talk" column tend to have more freewheeling journalistic standards. Unfortunately, the "Style" mentality has a tendency to creep onto the front page.

My point is that the *Post*, far more than any other newspaper, is part of a cause-and-effect relationship in Washington. By characterizing the FBI check of my background as "exhaustive," the *Post* signaled that something unique, newsworthy, unusual, was under way. Bob Woodward's byline on the story gave it an extra dimension of drama. Because Woodward is half of the Watergate reporting duo, his name always attracts interest and gives his subject matter a tinge of scandal.

This characteristic of political life in Washington was, I believe, lost on some of the more inexperienced members of the Bush transition team. C. Boyden Gray, for one, the president-elect's chief counsel, had a tendency to drop his guard around the press. I have been told that Boyden Gray's relationship with Bob Woodward was such that when Woodward was covering the transition and wrote "according to one knowledgeable official," it could be translated to read "according to C. Boyden Gray."

In my dealings with him, I have found Bob Woodward to be a responsible and fair-minded reporter, and it could be that the sources who spoke to him about the "exhaustive" FBI investigation were attempting to demonstrate that the background check illustrated the president-elect's commitment to setting high ethical standards. However, the spin on the story made it seem like there was so much smoke that a conflagration was about to erupt. To that extent, Senator Richard Shelby was right when he told the *Washington Post*, "The White House poured gasoline all over John Tower."

The FBI file — Chapter 1, as it came to be known — was ready in mid-December. President-elect Bush was briefed on its contents. Of the seventy-nine individuals interviewed for the initial report, only one, an anonymous source, alleged that I abused alcohol. Allegations of marital misconduct were not substantiated. My official conduct in the Senate, in Geneva, and while serving on the President's Special Review Board was not questioned by those who were there. None, except the same anonymous source, saw any reason that I should not hold a high government post.

George Bush saw it the same way.

> Protecting our security and promoting peace are the groundwork upon which all other national progress is laid, and they're the prerequisites for a prosperous and forward-looking nation. And if we've proven anything in the last eight years, it is that peace through strength works. And therefore it is with pride and a sense of solemn responsibility that I am announcing this morning my intention to nominate a man of great experience, expertise, and commitment to peace and freedom to be the next Secretary of Defense.

After days of speculation, the announcement came with sudden swiftness. On the morning of Friday, December 16, I had gone to the transition office at the Old Executive Office Building at 7:30, at the request of Craig Fuller, who called me the night before to arrange a meeting on Pentagon personnel matters. In the middle of our meeting, I was called to the phone: it was John Sununu. He said that to avoid news leaks the president-elect wanted to make the nomination public before noon. Sununu simply skipped over the formalities of announcing the president-elect's decision and asking me to serve. Why waste words? And so the nomination came to me without gift wrapping or adornment of any sort, a subtle and fitting rebuke to those who had attempted to undermine my chances.

Despite the wait and the battering I had taken in the news media, I was pleased. I wanted the job, I knew I could do it well, and I was, at last, getting the opportunity. I had passed muster in the face of all the crap that had been spread about me in the public domain. It was vindication. The president wanted me in his cabinet. He was satisfied.

When I got back to my office, I stood beside the desk for a moment, lost in thought. When my secretary Kim Garven walked in, I looked up; I could feel my eyes getting moist, and all I could manage was "I got the call."

I asked Kim to contact Sam Nunn's office. My intention was to advise him that the announcement would be made that morning. I wanted my successor as chairman of the Senate Armed Services

Committee to hear the news from me first. But Sam wasn't available to take the call.

The president-elect's news conference was held in an auditorium in the Old Executive Office Building. It was a full house, with what seemed like every reporter and television camera crew in town. The technicians and their equipment were crowded into the back row like an unruly firing squad. George Bush elaborated on his opening statement while I stood to one side, waiting for the inevitable questions.

> John Tower served for 23 years in the United States Senate. He was Chairman of the Armed Services Committee. He has been a top U.S. negotiator in talks on strategic nuclear arms. And he is a veteran, having enlisted in the Navy at the age of 17 and served in combat on a gunboat in the Western Pacific during the Second World War. John Tower is as knowledgeable as anyone in America about defense and national security issues, and he's a true expert on defense policy, and he understands the challenges ahead. And he's established great credibility and earned great respect both in Congress and among this nation . . . for his understanding of the fundamental truth that strength and clarity in our defense and national security policy lead to peace.

The president-elect introduced me to the gathering, and as is my custom I spoke extemporaneously, having decided in advance that I should briefly outline three or four substantive points that were likely to come up during my confirmation hearings in the Senate.

> We do have a great challenge ahead of us. The bottom line is that we must provide at least as much, if not more, defense for less money. And to meet that challenge, we must do several things. We must rationalize our force structure, we must refine and reform our management and procurement procedures, we must have biennial budgeting. All of this is going to require very close cooperation with the Congress. There is a great deal that can be achieved administratively, but, in the final analysis, the whole job cannot be done without close cooperation between the Pentagon and the Congress.

It would have been an exercise in self-delusion to expect the press to have forgotten all about "marital misconduct," "alcohol abuse," and "questionable use of . . ." and to have focused dutifully on substance. Washington reporters are in competition with each other, not only for news stories, but to prove just how tough they can be. It is a macho thing, although the women are also deadly serious. And broadcasters, possessed of a residue of insecurity from the days when the print journalists were the undisputed masters of the beat, make an extra effort to be hard-nosed. The network correspondents show up early to claim the best seats, near the front, where they can't help but be called on for questions; or they order the technicians to pile equipment on a chair to hold it for their late arrival. At times, the entire front row of a news conference site will be reserved this way, with the newspaper people pushed toward the back and deeply resenting the treatment.

NBC's Andrea Mitchell had seen to it that she was in the right location to get in the first question to the president-elect when the opening statements had concluded.

> Ms. MITCHELL — With all due respect to Senator Tower, do you feel that all of the issues that were investigated by the FBI, and that have been circulated very publicly and acknowledged by Senator Tower's own staff aides as issues that were investigated —
>
> PRESIDENT-ELECT BUSH — Are you talking about issues or rumors?
>
> Ms. MITCHELL — Well, I'm talking about subjects that were investigated, that were considered important enough for the FBI to look into. Have all of those issues weakened him in any way? Do they trouble you? Are you satisfied that he is beyond reproach, and that this will not in any way hurt his ability to carry forward your policies?

By challenging the underlying premise of the question, George Bush brought it to the surface: i.e., the mere fact that the FBI was conducting an investigation had become enough to impugn my character.

The "subjects . . . considered important enough for the FBI to look into," no matter that they would be shown to be unfounded by the same investigation, put Andrea into the position of stepping out of Alice's Wonderland to play the Queen of Hearts: "Sentence first — verdict afterwards."

George Bush refused to buy into Andrea's line.

PRESIDENT-ELECT BUSH — I am totally satisfied in that regard, because the investigation was extensive. . . . I believe
this is — this matter is totally concluded. It will be — satisfy the most inquisitive members of the United States Senate who will take a look at the — this nomination. And yes,
he not only has my full confidence, but it is strengthened,
if anything, by the process that he has gone through.

Ms. MITCHELL — But, do you think that he is at all weakened in his —

PRESIDENT-ELECT BUSH — No, I don't think so. I think he
is stronger. Anytime you get subjected to a lot of rumors
out there, and then receive a clean bill of health, why, I
think you're stronger.

Salacious gossip about Andrea Mitchell's private life had swirled
through Washington during one of the low points in the Reagan
administration; for a time, it appeared that her assignment to the
White House was in jeopardy. Frankly, I never gave the rumors
much credence; but knowing what she had been through, I expected that Andrea might have been sensitive to the damage one
suffers from such a torrent of false allegations. Instead, it seemed
that she seized the opportunity to publicly demonstrate righteous
indignation as a way of rehabilitating her own reputation.

Bush responded to several more questions on a variety of issues;
there were a few more on the FBI investigation and follow-ups on
the reports about my supposed negotiations with the White House
over who would be named to top Pentagon jobs. The president-
elect flatly denied that the transition team was in a position to tell
me who would be picked for these posts.

About midway through, another reporter who specializes in indignation, Sarah McClendon, called out for recognition.

PRESIDENT-ELECT BUSH — Go ahead, Sarah.

Ms. McCLENDON — Did you elicit any promises from Senator Tower about his personal conduct before you named
him?

PRESIDENT-ELECT BUSH — I've just expressed full confidence in that, and that's been covered. Thank you.

Ms. McCLENDON — For instance, about alcoholism? Did
you —

PRESIDENT-ELECT BUSH — I've covered that subject.

Later, after the president-elect had gone and I was fielding several more questions, Sarah toned down and asked what I meant by "force rationalization." I explained that the term refers to the process of examining what level of forces is necessary to do a job, implementing a strategy, and then acting accordingly when it is time to set priorities. She was a free-lancer, and her newspaper clients, most of them small Texas dailies, would have been interested in the question, given the number of military installations in the state. I had known Sarah for years and at one point helped her stay in business by recommending her to Texas publishers after she lost one of her biggest clients.

In another month, Sarah's conduct would remind me of the old adage and joke: Let no good deed go unpunished.

As the session wound down, I was asked how I felt about all the allegations and innuendos.

> MR. TOWER — Though it was — it was not comfortable, but I understand the process. And I understand the process has to work its way. In my particular instance, there were a number of rumors and innuendos, allegations. And it was incumbent on the Vice President to order the FBI to check out each one of these very carefully, regardless of how off-the-wall they might have been. And in most instances, there wasn't even anything in the way of circumstantial evidence to support these things. . . .
>
> Q. — Did you ever say to yourself that this isn't worth it?
>
> MR. TOWER — No, I never did because I'm something of a public service junkie. I've spent most of my adult life in public service, virtually all of it if you count the time I spent working in a tax-supported institution. And I want to serve. I think I'm . . . suited to serve in this particular capacity, and I'm glad to make the sacrifices necessary.

As it turned out, I had not yet begun to sacrifice, or to fight. But the news conference, at the time, seemed like a major hurdle that had been cleared. The nomination had been announced, I had had the first opportunity to respond to the allegations in public, and the next stop was Capitol Hill — a place that, next to Texas, I considered to be my home.

THREE

CHOPPIN' COTTON

THE DAY after the nomination was announced, I had the first of many regular meetings with Secretary of State designate James Baker and Brent Scowcroft, who had been selected to serve as George Bush's national security adviser. We had a lot to get done and not much time to do it.

Brent and I had worked together on the President's Special Review Board. I discovered then, during a most difficult period, when President Reagan's credibility was hanging by a thread, that General Scowcroft had the ideal combination of intellect, experience, integrity, and mature judgment. Today, the National Security Council is fully integrated into the day-to-day foreign policy process, without the intrigue and backstage political maneuvering that had been such a destructive and dangerous factor in the past. No more rogue elephant under Brent Scowcroft.

About a year into the Bush administration, I complimented Scowcroft on his command of the job and added, "Not bad, seeing that you wrote the job description yourself." And of course, as a member of the President's Special Review Board, that's precisely what Brent had done, by examining the NSC operation and recommending a series of major reforms to minimize the likelihood that such an affair as Iran-contra would ever repeat itself.

*   *   *

Brent Scowcroft supported my nomination from the beginning, and his advocacy helped overcome some of the doubts that had been expressed by a few members of the transition operation.

Likewise, there is a close bond with Jim Baker. We are old Texas political allies. Jim ran unsuccessfully for Texas attorney general in 1978. One of the vivid moments of the campaign, which Baker is fond of recalling, came when he and I were out shaking hands, "pressing the flesh," as LBJ used to say, at El Mercado in San Antonio. It was hot and tiring, and eventually we sought refreshment in the bar of the old Menger Hotel, where Teddy Roosevelt had recruited the Rough Riders. As we slumped in our chairs and a couple of tall, cool drinks were put on the table in front of us, I said, "Jim, this is a squalid business!"

Baker and I still have a few scars from the "squalid business" of the 1976 primary battle in Texas between President Gerald Ford and Ronald Reagan. It was a close-run thing. Reagan almost succeeded in taking the nomination away from the incumbent president. To this day, some Texas Reaganites — many of them Democrats who switched to the Republican party for the primary and stayed on — still have not forgiven me for supporting Ford. But I saw it as a duty to a sitting Republican president, who by virtue of the position was the leader of the party, even though he had never faced the general electorate. Too, I felt that for the party to dump its own incumbent was to court political disaster.

At any rate, Baker, serving as Ford's campaign manager, and I were soundly beaten in our own backyard. When Reagan was elected in 1980, Jim was the first to be forgiven, although he had been active on behalf of George Bush in the GOP primary. But in spite of his role as the new president's chief of staff, there were still a few hard feelings. I remember recommending Bill Perrin, a veteran Texas Republican, for an ambassadorial post, only to be informed by Helene Van Damm, President Reagan's secretary, that Bill was "not one of us"; he had supported Gerald Ford in 1976. I laughed and said, "Well, so did I." Helene replied coldly, "We are well aware of that, Senator."

In casting around for a villain in the first days of the Bush transition, some accounts in the news media identified Jim Baker as one of those who opposed my nomination. Washington reporters, and even some of my own advisers, probably came to that conclusion as a result of background briefings from Bob Kimmit, a close associate of Baker's from the Treasury Department and from the

State Department transition. I don't know what was said at those briefings; Kimmit denies that he criticized me, but shortly afterward reports began circulating to that effect, and they were taken as prima facie evidence in some quarters that Jim was orchestrating the opposition.

However, when the stories were published, he assured me that they were false. And I never doubted they were false. There is certainly no question that Jim Baker is an adroit political operator. But he has always been up front with me and is not the type to resort to devious means to bring down a friend. Furthermore, there was nothing to be gained. A weak and ineffectual secretary of defense would make the Bush administration — and Jim Baker — look bad. As for his relationship with the president, Baker is very secure. He knew, as did I, that his position and preeminence were unassailable.

Those were the facts. But the news media rarely let the facts get in the way of a good story. A rift between the secretary of state and the defense secretary would be a prime news item. The press was always looking for signs that Cap Weinberger and George Shultz were quarreling. Getting Tower and Baker at loggerheads early on would make for an interesting, long-running soap opera. Hence Jim Baker, the *Los Angeles Times* reported, was said to "feel threatened by Tower because of Tower's independence and his power base on Capitol Hill."

At our earlier meeting in November, I assured Baker that when disagreements developed between us, I would discuss my position with him privately, in the confines of "four walls," never in public. There would be no replay of the Shultz-Weinberger squabbles. I told him that as secretary of state, he was the administration's principal foreign policy spokesman, and that I regarded defense policy as an element of foreign policy. In turn, Baker said I would be the primary spokesman on defense issues.

This exchange may seem inconsequential to those who are unfamiliar with the etiquette of Washington. But it amounted to a handshake, a nonaggression pact. We both knew the price that would be paid for open conflict between the Pentagon and the State Department, and we were willing to work closely together to avoid it.

Brent Scowcroft, Jim Baker, and I chatted about my confirmation prospects. They offered to help in any way they could, and Baker agreed with my assessment that while there would be a few bumps along the road, confirmation was more than likely because I was a member of the Senate club. We then turned to the business at hand — reviewing the current status of U.S. foreign policy and the national security situation; determining where we stood in December 1988 and where we wanted to stand ninety days to six months later.

Christmas has always been a favorite Tower family holiday. We have a gathering on Christmas Day at my flat, which overlooks the Dallas skyline from the Turtle Creek section of the city. My celebration actually started that year at Presbyterian Hospital. I flew back from Washington and went directly to the bedside of my youngest daughter, Jeanne, to see the newly arrived John Goodwin Tower Cox. Jeanne stuck him with the full handle. The baby had been born just three days after my nomination was announced. Since I am an only son and the father of girls, my branch of the Tower line dies with me. It was a highly emotional moment for me to clasp to my breast the child who would bear my name. Men seek immortality in namesakes.

I savored the holiday as long as I could, because on the day after Christmas I was to enter Baylor Medical Center for the removal of a polyp that had been discovered in my colon. Penny, Marian, and Jeanne didn't know. I wanted them to have a good time and not worry.

Good health and a strong constitution are blessings that shouldn't be taken for granted; however, I have not been one to dwell overmuch on things like proper diet, exercise, stress reduction, and the like.

My taste in food is catholic, and I'm not particularly careful about what I eat. I have a tendency to reach too often for my cigarette case, and while I like to walk, swim, and do a little shooting, I have never met a formal exercise program that I didn't find boring or intrusive.

In the mid-1970s, as a concession to good sense, I decided to cut back on my consumption of hard liquor. I was a scotch drinker in those days; but I have tasted whiskey only once in about the last fourteen years, and that exception came when an Israeli government minister ordered me a scotch without asking what I preferred.

Since then there has been an occasional vodka or gin martini, but some wine with dinner or occasionally at cocktail parties is about the full extent of my drinking. And when I am up against an urgent deadline or in the midst of demanding work, I don't drink at all.

Drinking habits in the capital have changed since my early Senate days. But the danger of comparing old and new is that there is liable to be an exaggeration of what transpired in the past, particularly when it is examined from today's Perrier and white-wine perspective, beverages that would have been laughed out of a Washington cocktail party fifteen years ago. Washington was, and is, a hard-drinking town.

I say "is" because in 1989 it still had the highest per capita consumption of alcohol of any U.S. metropolitan area. When I arrived, in 1961, drinking was a social convention, almost a ritual, on Capitol Hill. House Speaker Sam Rayburn's "Board of Education" was still meeting, although as a freshman and a member of the Senate, I was never invited to take part. "Mr. Sam" died soon after, and those late-afternoon gatherings of Congress's most powerful members over bourbon and branch water passed into legend.

On the Senate side, Republican leader Everett Dirksen continued to preside over the "Twilight Lodge." He had a special clock with each hour replaced by the number five. No matter where the hands stood, it was always after five o'clock and time for a drink.

Ev and his colleagues on both sides of the aisle took that clock seriously and would not have been comfortable in this age of digital timekeeping. Dirksen was a man of commanding presence: he had a wavy, gray mane that sometimes fell in curls over his forehead. His voice was a throaty, mellifluous baritone, which could soothe and cajole or rage like thunder. His histrionic ability was superb, with a fine sense of timing, the essence of an actor's skill. He was a spellbinder in the nineteenth-century tradition. I'm sure he would have eclipsed William Jennings Bryan had the two been contemporaries. In addition to his oratorical skills, Dirksen was one of the great legislators and political tacticians of the era. He broke the filibuster against the 1964 Civil Rights Bill, which had dragged on for six months. Those of us who opposed the bill — and I was against it on the grounds that its public accommodations provisions were of dubious constitutionality — did not stand a chance of outmaneuvering Ev, regardless of his fondness for five o'clock and the Twilight Lodge.

And when I say "fondness" I'm not using a euphemism for dead drunkenness or outright debauchery. The meetings at the Twilight

Lodge represented the gentlemanly side of the so-called gentle-men's club that the Senate was in those days. You could go at each other ferociously on the Senate floor and, an hour later, be swapping jokes over a drink. There would be a couple of drinks after a session, and then most of us would go home. We didn't hang around. Late sessions and marathon debates were not frequent. Today, they are the norm.

Hideaway offices have also proliferated. In the 1960s not many members had them. I was in the Senate about ten years before I got one. Now, I would say, more than half the members have them; these young bucks are claiming the privileges of seniority when they've been in four years or maybe a term. If a senator has a propensity for solitary drinking, he or she can close the door and go to it, well away from the office suites that are visited by constituents. Warren Magnusen of Washington State was a solitary drinker, and we'd all know how Maggie had spent the afternoon if he was called to the floor unexpectedly for a vote. Estes Kefauver was a little more social in his habits, and the effects were more visible. But I can't say that Estes was swinging from the chandelier on this occasion or that. I didn't drink with him. As a younger member, my contact with the senior senators was in the office of Jim Eastland, the chairman of the Judiciary Committee, or in Dirksen's office, or when Mark Trice, the secretary to the Senate minority, had a get-together.

Pretty sedate gatherings, really. Ev Dirksen would say, "Boys, the bar is open," and we would go trooping back there. We'd talk a little business, although, by and large, there wasn't much heavy-duty politicking. It was a good way to size up your colleagues and get a feel for their personalities. I think there is much to be said for serving an apprenticeship in which one can sit in the background, watch, and listen, and learn. New senators don't do that anymore. They plunge right into legislating and trying to run things they don't understand. There were only about five or six freshmen when I arrived. Among the Republicans, it was Jack Miller, Caleb Boggs, and I. We were the pups. Early on, I had a talk with Senator John Stennis of Mississippi. In the most courtly way and with exquisite circumlocution, he advised me to "learn to be a senator" — in other words, to keep quiet, listen, and observe — until I had been in the Senate for a while.

Today, senators are in such a hurry that there is no time to understand. They are creatures of the media, and the institutional memory of the Senate, which was passed on in places like the Twilight Lodge, has been lost.

I learned a lot from Ev Dirksen and loved the old boy. He had a style all his own. Dirksen would walk into his office, sink into a chair, and a staff member would ask, "What'll you have, Senator?" He'd look up and ponder the question. "I think I'll have a little brandy." There would be a dramatic pause. "Yes, brandy. Winston Churchill foundered on it, and that's good enough for me."

At the 1968 Republican Convention, in Miami Beach, Richard Nixon convened a meeting of several leading Republicans to discuss vice-presidential possibilities. Senator Mark Hatfield's name was mentioned, but Dirksen turned to Nixon and said, "Mark's a nice boy. However, one is not even served a soupçon of wine when invited to his house for dinner." Senator Thruston Morton of Kentucky cut through Ev's baroque style in his own unique way by asking: "You mean he's a square?" To which Ev replied, "Yes, he's a square." And that ended the discussion of Mark Hatfield for vice president.

Many of the other giants of the Senate in those days were what we would consider heavy drinkers by today's standards. It did not appear to impair their judgment or legislative skill. Senator Richard Russell of Georgia was one of the most illustrious of all the Armed Services Committee chairmen. Sam Nunn, like most Georgia Democrats, takes care to pay homage to Russell's memory when he is out in public, campaigning for votes, but he told me once that Richard Russell had had "a drinking problem." If that was indeed the case, it was not apparent to me in the years I worked — sometimes closely — with him.

About as close as I came to observing a serious episode of insobriety on the Senate floor was the time that Senator Lee Metcalf of Montana literally had to be propped up in the presiding officer's chair to prevent him from toppling over from the effects of alcohol. Metcalf had a serious drinking problem, and I would say that every journalist assigned to the Senate press and radio-TV galleries at the time knew that. And some of those same journalists, including respected names in the news business, such as Sam Shaffer of *Newsweek,* John Averill of the *Los Angeles Times,* and Bob Baskin of the *Dallas News,* could be found after five o'clock having drinks with their "reliable" Senate sources.

I hope that I have put the question of drinking and the U.S.

Senate in perspective. After my long tenure in that institution, I can say it is no more or less a problem than it is in our society at large. And the bottom line is this: when a public servant's private life interferes with the performance of his or her duties, he or she should be replaced; and when the public perceives a deterioration in the performance of an elected official, it usually will retire him from office. I was elected four times as a Republican in a predominantly Democratic state. When I retired, I did so voluntarily, to the general surprise of my constituency.

I went into the hospital the evening of December 26. I registered as John Goodwin — a truncated name, not a false one. Twenty-four hours later, I headed home. The polyp was easily removed; only a few of its cells were found to be malignant, and the doctors described those as "well differentiated," which is typical of a cancer that has been detected in its early stages. However, in examining the colon my doctor found another, larger growth farther up the intestinal tract. Getting it out would require the surgeon to cut through the abdominal wall.

My first reaction was to wait until after my confirmation. But back in Washington, my friend Bill Narva, the attending physician in the Capitol, advised me to act quickly. I am probably the first cabinet nominee in history to show a diagram of his intestinal tract to a president-elect. George Bush told me to go ahead and have the surgery as soon as possible.

The odds were that the new polyp would either be found to be malignant or would likely become so. I reluctantly decided to go ahead with the operation, despite the disappointment I felt at being sidelined when I could have been more actively involved in the Pentagon transition and planning for the confirmation phase of my nomination.

The tendency to look back on one's life is more pronounced on the eve of major surgery. I had a night alone before the operation to do some thinking. The idea of surgery didn't bother me. I have a high tolerance for pain. But I have an aversion to anesthesia. I don't even take painkillers when I'm in the dentist's chair for root canals and things like that. It's the same way with sleeping pills and other forms of medication. I don't like to be sedated. The colon surgery was my first major operation. Aside from a bit of cosmetic surgery in 1986, I hadn't spent the night in a hospital since the day I was born.

*   *   *

In my Dallas flat, the walls of my kitchen display photographs commemorating various moments in my career. In Washington, such a collection is derisively referred to as an ego wall. But even those who mock the practice seem to have their own photo displays for moments when the urge to reminisce is strongest.

One of my favorites shows former president Eisenhower standing in front of the doorway to his Gettysburg office, hands on hips, grinning the characteristic Ike grin. I am beside him looking up and looking . . . well, young. And I was young. At thirty-five, I was the youngest member of the U.S. Senate. When I arrived in Washington, in June of 1961, it was high season in Camelot. With a forty-four-year-old president in the White House, youth was in fashion.

The industry that we know today as media manipulation was in its infancy, but Republican leaders did their primitive best to call attention to my age and the facts of my election to counter the prevailing view that the party was washed up and about to be permanently supplanted by the new "generation of leadership" that JFK proclaimed he represented.

Thus, John Tower, the "Little Giant" from Wichita Falls, rolled into Washington, D.C. — actually, I flew in four days after the election — amid a thoroughly exaggerated outpouring of hoopla and hype. Naturally, I enjoyed every minute of it. It was a heady and dazzling sensation. I could hardly believe what was happening: instant celebrity for one so recently an obscure college prof.

The visit amounted to a test run for the formal Senate oath-taking ceremony that would come later in the month. I had been invited to Washington by Republican leaders to attend a fund-raising dinner honoring former president Eisenhower at the Washington Armory. They were looking to inject a little excitement into an event that might otherwise have had the atmosphere of a wake.

After eight years of controlling the White House, Republicans were on the outside looking in, while a glamorous new president was redecorating the place and threatening to rearrange the political order. To make matters even worse, the party was steadily losing its footing in Congress as the Democrats consolidated their majority hold on the House and Senate by racking up off-year election victories that exploited public discontent with the cyclical nature of the postwar economy. Nobody objected to the upswings that brought prosperity during the Eisenhower years, but responsibility for the recessions was dumped on the doorsteps of Republican incumbents.

The fund-raiser was a way to accentuate the positive. A gathering of victorious Republican candidates for the House and Senate, optimistic rhetoric about the future, and Ike, our affable, well-loved talisman against Democratic evil, were supposed to do wonders for sagging morale. The organizers held Lou and me back from the rest of the head table so that we could make a dramatic grand entrance. When we did, the place went wild with cheering and applause. Ike came over to where we were seated and posed for pictures. Lou and I were both fairly numb from the excitement.

One of the reasons I was a featured attraction at the event was that, as just over eight years his junior, I could "out-youth" President Kennedy. (I held the distinction of being the youngest senator until Ted Kennedy came along to claim his older brother's seat, kept warm by Ben Smith until the youngest member of the clan reached the minimum age required by law of a senator.) And as the first Republican to be elected to the U.S. Senate from the Old South since Reconstruction, I could be presented to the public as a symbol of the party realignment that would transform the region from the cornerstone of the Roosevelt coalition to the cornerstone of an emerging Republican majority. If I had been elected from Ohio or Iowa, it wouldn't have been a big deal. But they fussed over me because, finally, the Republican party had cracked the "solid South." Clark Reed, the chairman of Mississippi's state GOP, referred to me as the Republican senator from the Confederacy, and others said I was the father of the Republican party in the South.

But in May of 1961, that was all just a pipe dream. Senator Everett Dirksen, as Senate minority leader, and other senior Republicans made the most out of the scanty resources they had to work with. Dirksen led a delegation of congressional elders out to National Airport to meet the Braniff flight that Lou and I had taken from Dallas. Ev, the consummate actor and "Wizard of Ooze," as he was affectionately known, laid it on thick. At one point he got so carried away with his own sonorous rhetoric that he said my election was "the most significant political event since Lincoln beat Douglas."

Everybody listened to Ev with a straight face. But he wasn't kidding when he said the victory "will have a tremendous psychological impact on the whole country." The GOP needed an antidote to the commentaries that had amounted to funeral notices for the party after the 1960 presidential-election loss. Dirksen could ham it up, but he read election statistics without missing a nuance. He noted that I had captured the state's big cities. "The Republicans lost out in 1960 in the major population centers. The Tower election shows a reversal of this trend. And it also shows a need for more organizational work by all Republicans. I believe we will concentrate more and more on that in the future," he predicted.

With that one prescient glance into the crystal ball, Dirksen pointed the way to political salvation. He knew that organization was the key to winning elections in traditional Democratic strongholds, and in the nearly three decades that have followed, the lesson has never been forgotten by Republican campaign strategists. Today, when the White House and some key Senate seats are at stake, Republicans outgun and outrun the Democrats because they do a better job of putting all the component pieces together to produce an effective political mechanism.

We taught ourselves how to beat the Democrats at their own game: today, we are better at it than they are. Thanks to the attention that Ev Dirksen called to my election, it became a template for other races in the South and Southwest, where Republicans had traditionally been locked out of the political process.

The trip to Washington, coming on the heels of our victory, was a thrill. The media made a big ruckus over Lou. She had never been to the nation's capital before, so the reporters could play up the small-town-housewife-and-mother angle. There's a photo of her looking trim in a tailored suit and pillbox hat in the style that Jackie Kennedy was making fashionable.

As for me, every story seemed to dwell on my height — or lack thereof. The term "diminutive" was firmly affixed to me in that period, and someone wrote that I often needed to stand on a wooden crate to see over the top of the podium. That isn't true, but it never stopped those who needed to fill a couple of column inches of newsprint.

"My name is Tower, but I don't" was the way I handled this less than explosive issue. I used to think that my size was a problem, and it did bother me. When you know that you have a certain amount of athletic ability but you're too small to play varsity football, or you're a good actor who is too short next to the ingenue and therefore lose the romantic male leads, it hurts. But in the

Navy I learned that there are certain advantages. As my taller ship-mates clunked their heads on the metal partitions in the passage-ways, I got to sprint along just fine.

I suppose as a result of my height — five feet five and a half inches — and the fact that I was never a brilliant student, I worked harder to compensate. When I was a junior in high school, I flunked geometry. My dad said, "Son, it looks like you're not going to learn to make a living with your head, so you'd better start learning to make a living with your hands."

Our farm in East Texas was a subsistence operation, with cotton as the only cash crop. There were chickens, hogs, cows, an orchard, and plots of vegetables. The total spread was about 770 acres, which was large for that part of the state. Within a week after I flunked geometry, Dad had me out there chopping cotton and working beside the field hands hoeing corn in the bottomlands; it was hard, physical labor. In short order, I began to think that making a living with my head was infinitely preferable.

Several years into my Senate career, I was reminded of those days in the hot summer sun. I walked off the Senate floor after a particularly difficult session, turned to Senator Strom Thurmond, and said, "There has got to be a better way of making a living than this."

Strom thought about it for a couple of seconds and replied, "Beats choppin' cotton."

And as nostalgic as I am about that old farm, I had to admit that Strom was right. Serving in the U.S. Senate beats choppin' cotton.

Despite the minor irritation of reading about the Little Giant, I have never been a politician who went out of his way either to fight with the press or to cozy up to it. I always advised my staff and campaign workers either to tell the news media the truth or tell them nothing.

The press is a political tool, but by that I don't mean to sound cynical or to imply that it is acceptable to manipulate the press. Consensus building, discussion, and debate are conducted by means of the press. Without it the democratic process atrophies. Politicians who weigh their every move, however, to determine how they will be perceived by the press make themselves hostage to the capriciousness of a very capricious institution.

In 1961, I was the pet of the Washington press corps in many ways. This clipping from the *Houston Chronicle,* written by one of the paper's Washington reporters, makes for interesting reading:

> John G. Tower, United States Senator-elect from Texas, went back home this weekend after an acclaim in Washington such as no Texan Senator-elect has ever received here.
>
> For a political unknown of a year ago to have 6000 Republicans give him a tumultuous ovation comparing favorably with that accorded Texas-born Dwight D. Eisenhower, their most popular President of recent times, approaches the unbelievable, but that is what happened to Tower here Thursday night.

The piece was displayed under a headline that fairly gushed: "TOWER CAPITOL ACCLAIM EXCEEDS ALL PRECEDENT." It can take years for a newcomer to the national political scene to realize that the press suffers from almost schizophrenic swings of mood and attitude. I suppose it stems from the desire to always be first — first with the good news, first with the bad news. And, of course, to attract the most readers or viewers, the news either has got to be very, very good or very, very bad. It would not be much of an overstatement to say that the press is either at your feet or at your throat.

My dealings with the news media remained smooth for about two years. The first real blast of vituperation did not come until 1963, in the aftermath of JFK's assassination, when the press decided that conservatives and Texans had blood on their hands.

When Lou and I returned to Washington for the swearing-in ceremony, the headlines were more restrained and realistic: "TOWER SWORN IN AS TEXAS SENATOR AT 35; VICE PRESIDENT JOHNSON GIVES OATH TO REPUBLICAN IN CAPITAL."

It was a family affair. First came the *nuclear* Tower family — Penny, Marian, and Jeanne, along with my mother and father and Lou's parents. Then there was the *extended* Tower family — about two hundred friends and campaign workers who chartered a plane and flew into Washington to celebrate and witness what just a few weeks before had been considered an absolute impossibility.

The kids were too young at six, five, and four to fully grasp what was happening. However, they had a great time riding on the mini-subway system that runs underground between the Capitol and the Senate office buildings on the other side of Constitution Avenue. The distance can be walked in about five minutes, but the small open cars zoom along like amusement park gondolas. Although at first it seems like an extravagance, the subway amounts to a horizontal elevator, quickly moving senators to and from the Senate floor for votes and other business. Over the course of a week, it can save hours of time.

The subway motorman teased Jeanne, Penny, and Marian about being the prettiest riders who had ever come aboard his train. The three of them beamed all the way from the Old Senate Office Building, now the Richard Russell Building, to the basement level of the Capitol.

The children were disappointed when I got off the elevator on the second floor. I was headed into the Senate chamber and they wanted to go with me. They and Lou, however, went up to the visitors' gallery on the third floor to watch the swearing-in ceremony.

The gallery is much like the balcony in a theater. It surrounds the chamber on all four sides, with sections set aside for Senate families, diplomats, the press, and the public. We had reserved most of the space for our friends from Texas, and it was packed, standing room only.

Most people are surprised at how small the Senate chamber seems. There are modern hotels with lobbies that could swallow it up with room left over for a cocktail lounge, coffee shop, and waterfall. With one hundred flip-top wooden desks arranged in a semicircle, it looks like an old-fashioned elementary school classroom, although most classrooms don't have thick wall-to-wall carpeting and crystal chandeliers.

Because of the size of the chamber, Senate rules are very strict about who is allowed to go onto the floor when a session is under way. Senators have to formally ask permission to bring key aides in to assist them during legislative debates. Therefore, it was a special moment for my father to be allowed to ascend the dais of the Senate with the vice president to deliver the opening prayer.

From that day on, the prayer he offered has hung on my office wall:

Our Heavenly Father, we give Thee thanks for this great nation. We thank Thee for our heritage, for those intrepid men across the years who have given their lives in war and in peace that this nation, under God, may lead the races of men out of the lowlands of despair to the mountain peaks of freedom. May we merit the love and respect of free people everywhere as we give to the world spiritual and economic leadership.

Bless, we pray Thee, this great deliberative body. May the decisions here made bring honor to our country and lasting peace to our world. May each member of this body feel the tremendous responsibility of these decisive days. With the man of God, may we remember "Righteousness exalteth a nation but sin is a reproach to any people." Give us faith and courage as a nation to face up to the need of this age.

These things we ask in the name of the Father and the Son and the Holy Spirit. Amen.

The Senate always opens the day's business with a prayer, and my father's words, which opened a quarter-century of Senate business for me, still serve as inspiration. "Give us faith and courage as a nation to face up to the need of this age."

Lyndon Johnson was in the chair as presiding officer, a vice president's one and only constitutionally mandated responsibility (other than assuming the presidency if necessary). But LBJ could have excused himself from participating in the ceremony and yielded the chair to the president pro Tempore or his designee.

The idea of his Senate seat going to a Republican must have rankled Lyndon. However, he was a good sport and didn't let it show. He was a Texan through and through. He knew how important the event was to his state, and he made it a point to personally administer the oath to me. It was a gesture of magnanimity from one Texan to another that pushed partisanship into the background.

The presiding officer's desk sits on a raised platform at the front of the Senate chamber. There are two steps, or tiers, leading to the platform. I stood on the lower one and raised my right hand. LBJ, who loomed over me when we were on an equal footing, remained on the top step, forcing me to crane my neck back to look him in the eye. It probably looked a little odd, but it didn't bother me a bit. If Lyndon had wanted to administer the oath while standing on top of the desk, it would have been all right by me.

There were a few partisan Republicans in the gallery up above, and when Lyndon and I completed the oath and he shook my hand and said, "Congratulations, Senator Tower," they erupted in cheers and applause.

LBJ went back to the chair, picked up the gavel, and said, "The rules of Senate explicitly prohibit expressions of approval or disapproval from our visitors in the gallery. However, since these are unusual circumstances, the chair will overlook the infraction."

There was a good laugh over that, but the gallery quieted down as Johnson promised me the cooperation and friendship of both sides of the Senate, Democratic and Republican, "in all matters destined to promote the good of the state and the nation."

I signed my name under the oath, Johnson signed his — the scratching sound made by the tip of the fountain pen seemed to reverberate in the hushed chamber — and it was official.

At that time, cameras were not permitted in the Senate chamber except for the biennial group portrait of all the senators at their desks. It meant that swearing-in ceremonies had to be re-created in the vice president's chambers to allow the press to record the event. Before we could do that, however, Everett Dirksen took a few minutes to tease LBJ and the rest of the Senate Democrats.

Dirksen rose to chortle about the irony of a Republican's capturing LBJ's place in the Senate only six months after a Democratic victory in the presidential election. Solemnly, with tongue in cheek, Ev asked to be pardoned for his jubilation, noting that there had been no Republican senator from Texas in eighty-four years. The honorable Morgan Hamilton, he said, had served illustriously for seven years until he had voluntarily retired in 1877.

This history lesson brought out the penchant for Texana in my colleague Senator Ralph Yarborough, who took to the floor to correct Dirksen by pointing out that another Republican, J. W. Flannigan, had been appointed to the Senate by Texas's military governor during Reconstruction.

The exchange was all tongue in cheek, but it was conducted in the lofty third-person style — the "honorable gentleman" and "my esteemed colleague" — that takes some getting used to. It was unheard-of back then and a gross breach of etiquette to refer to another senator in the second person. These days, senators will lapse into the second person, referring to a colleague as "you," and many old-timers regard it as offensive and uncivilized, a sign that the Senate is losing its unique aura. This is more than musty tradition.

The words we use are important because they help determine the atmosphere. If the Senate is to function effectively, its members must take a step back from the brink of passion and turmoil. By addressing each other in the third person during a debate, senators are reminded that they are serving a larger institutional purpose, not just talking shop or scoring partisan debating points.

Dirksen went on to accept Yarborough's addendum by conceding that he should probably read up more on Texas history. And the history books would show from now on, Dirksen said, "that the great and redoubtable state of Texas searched its soul and sent a Republican to the Senate, and every Texan should be proud of their contribution to the vitality and purpose of free institutions."

Senator Albert Gore, Sr., a Democrat from Tennessee, wasn't going to let Dirksen get away with anything, and he chimed in with "I would not distract from the jubilation. But I would admonish my friend from Illinois — enjoy it while you can." Silver-haired and immaculately dressed, Gore really looked the part of the senator; there was a hint of country canniness about the man, as if he had just bought up every mortgage in town.

Ironically, his admonition notwithstanding, about ten years later I would sit in the chamber watching the swearing in of Bill Brock, the Republican who sent Senator Gore into retirement.

But in June of 1961, I sat at my new desk in the last row and listened intently to each word. Coins of pure gold. It was as though the college professor had fallen asleep over his political science textbook and woken up right in the middle of what he had always told his students was the "world's greatest deliberative body."

After the colon surgery and a night in the recovery room, I was moved back to my hospital room. The polyp was benign, but the doctors had to remove about a foot of the colon. My physician, R. D. Dignan, told reporters that I "should expect 100 percent recovery," which gave the Texas newspapers the opportunity to publish diagrams of my inner anatomy. I didn't mind all that much, though. It was a small price to pay for the optimistic prognosis.

I immediately got on the phone to Rhett Dawson, whom I had asked to head up my Pentagon transition team. Dawson was juggling several major issues, including the talent search for a deputy secretary of defense. The selection of the deputy had figured in the press speculation before the announcement of my nomination, and I wanted to move quickly to fill the job. As I discussed the situation with Rhett, I could still feel the effects of the anesthesia. I would talk for several minutes, then drift off and fall asleep. Rhett would stop and say, "Senator . . . are you still there?" I'd wake up and start in again.

There was a steady stream of visitors, including the FBI. The two agents who interviewed me early in December came back for a few more questions. I was wide awake by then. The names, dates, and places they asked about appeared to be routine. I had been given the option of waiting until I had left Baylor to meet with the investigators, but with the first FBI file having already gone to Senator Nunn and Senator John Warner the previous weekend, I wanted to complete the background check so that the two of them would be totally satisfied before it was formally offered to the full Armed Services Committee. I was taking the situation at face value — I had seen no reason to do otherwise — and the significance of what was happening did not occur to me at the time: Nunn and Warner, upon reading the initial file, had in effect rejected it and sent the FBI back to seek answers to additional questions and to pursue other lines of inquiry. It was the beginning of a nightmare that would drag on for two more months.

In early January, both senators were attending a celebrity tennis tournament at the Gardiner Tennis Ranch, in Arizona. Sherrie Marshall, an attorney who had advised the Bush campaign on federal election-law procedures, was helping C. Boyden Gray in the counsel's office during the transition, and she was assigned the task of delivering the FBI report to Nunn and Warner. To expedite things, and to demonstrate President-elect Bush's eagerness to cooperate with the Senate, an Air Force plane was pressed into service to get Sherrie and Arnold Punaro, the majority staff director of the Armed Services Committee, to Arizona as quickly as possible.

Sherrie was highly experienced at guiding White House nominees through the labyrinthine confirmation process. She had worked in the White House counsel's office during the Reagan administration, which was kept busy with the bread-and-butter effort of preparing judicial and political appointees for their FBI background checks, conflict-of-interest questionnaires, and Senate hearings. Marshall went off to private practice and a stint at the Federal Communications Commission before joining the Bush campaign.

Boyden Gray turned the details over to Sherrie as the transition got down to the serious business of staffing the White House and the upper echelons of the executive branch. Her assumption was that the procedures for handling FBI reports would remain the same as those that had been followed by the Reagan administration. Basically, the reports went only to the chairman of the appropriate committee and the ranking minority member. Committee staff members were not in the loop.

Arnold Punaro's presence on the plane to Arizona with Sherrie suggested that he and Sam Nunn had other ideas about who would have access to the material. Sherrie made Punaro and Pat Tucker, the Republican committee counsel, who also made the trip to Arizona, wait in the hall while she briefed Nunn and Warner. Only the two senators and their aides can say for sure how much of the information was shared after Sherrie departed. But apparently the policy of restricting access to the FBI file was modified to a considerable degree, and Arnold Punaro's involvement subjected me to the possibility that there would be an element of personal vindictiveness injected into the process.

Jim McGovern, who served as my staff director during the last year that I was chairman of the Armed Services Committee, tried to work cooperatively and in harmony with Punaro, at that time the Democratic minority's chief staffer. However, there always seemed to be an undercurrent of tension. I am told that Punaro — like his boss, Senator Nunn — tends to be thin-skinned and sensitive to what he believes are slights or attempts to deprive him of his prerogatives. In short, Arnold Punaro was not the easiest person to work with, although McGovern went out of his way to keep things running smoothly.

For whatever reason, real or imagined, if Punaro bore a grudge against McGovern, one of my closest advisers, the unprecedented access to FBI files would put him in a position to do great damage to my chances for confirmation.

Ten days before the 1988 presidential election, Sam Nunn sent a letter to both the Republican and Democratic presidential candidates announcing that henceforth his committee would be guided by a set of standards that would apply to nominees submitted for confirmation as secretary of defense.

Not content with the right to "advise and consent" granted to the Senate under the Constitution, Nunn proposed in his letter to, in effect, impose criteria governing a president's selection of his own cabinet and subcabinet subordinates.

The letter, cosigned by John Warner, professed a desire to avoid "any suggestion of partisan motivation" and to "initiate an early cooperative dialogue." It was a neat bit of political positioning. No matter what the outcome of the election, Nunn would succeed in establishing the precedent that a given set of Senate guidelines would be applied above and beyond the right to advise and consent.

The vagueness of the advise-and-consent provision has always been troublesome for those who would use congressional power to micromanage the government. Traditional interpretations give presidents broad leeway for action once they consult the Senate and, when applicable, submit their proposal for an up or down vote. Aside from a professional prescreening process for judicial appointments — appropriate to the nature of a lifetime place on the federal bench and in keeping with the responsibility for peopling the judiciary that is shared by the executive and legislative branches — there is no precedent for making advise and consent contingent on "guidelines."

The Nunn-Warner letter was worded to sound like a harmless exercise in good government. Neither candidate was about to quarrel with such noble sentiments as "Nominees must be of unquestionable integrity" or "Nominees must demonstrate a commitment to emphasizing overall national security goals and commitments." And the winner was unlikely to risk a clash with the Armed Services Committee by objecting to "a more comprehensive approach to the appointment of senior Defense Department officials."

Nunn put himself in a no-lose situation. With Michael Dukakis in the White House, he would have leverage to use against his own liberal president. With George Bush there, the letter would be an assertion of a right to subordinate the president's judgment to his own in determining the fitness of nominees whose confirmation process came within the committee's jurisdiction.

The letter was vintage Sam Nunn. The Georgian's motives have always been difficult to read. During the briefing at the Gardiner Tennis Ranch, and as he studied the file, Senator Nunn never referred to the letter and its sweeping assertion of authority. In that setting, to Sherrie Marshall he must have seemed more interested in working on his serve, a man intent on vacation.

Even so, Senator Nunn's actions spoke volumes. Within a few

hours of the briefing, the White House had the verdict: the file did not completely satisfy his criteria. The FBI investigation should continue.

Arnold Punaro returned to Washington to do the groundwork for my confirmation hearings, and Sam Nunn headed off to the mountains for a little skiing.

FOUR

CROSSING THE RUBICON

CABINET nominees must make the rounds. They meet privately with each member of the committee that will consider the nomination and report its recommendations to the full Senate.

The ritual has practical benefits: the courtesy calls establish the basis for a personal relationship between members of the executive and legislative branches of government; the nominees are introduced at the outset to the subtle process of congressional supervision; and the discussion that takes place provides the White House with its first reading of the tea leaves. If the nomination is in trouble, you can usually identify your friends and adversaries.

My first meeting, January 19, the day before the inauguration, was with Sam Nunn and John Warner. It would have been a breach of protocol to start anywhere else but the chairman's office.

For someone who has never served in the Senate, the courtesy calls can be a daunting proposition. But to me the hallways of the Senate office buildings — Russell, Dirksen, and Hart — were familiar territory. Over the years, I'd been welcomed into the private offices of nearly every member of the Senate, Republican and Democrat.

I am not impressed by marble and mahogany, nor am I surprised to discover that behind a majestic facade there is a workday reality of overcrowded cubicles, piles of unfiled documents, jangling telephones, and overflowing wastebaskets.

The Senate is a very human institution. It is a place of grandeur, tradition, and some intrigue, which takes a bit of getting used to. In my case, it took about ten years before I really hit my stride, before I had the seniority to be considered a major player.

My coming of age, from a Senate standpoint, coincided with the rise and fall of the Nixon administration. Richard Nixon and the ranking Republicans on the Foreign Relations and Armed Services committees, Cliff Case of New Jersey and Margaret Chase Smith of Maine, were not on the same ideological wavelength. When it came to important foreign policy and defense issues, the White House would often ask me to rally the conservative troops or present the administration's case on the Senate floor.

During Watergate, I was serving my first term as chairman of the Senate Republican Policy Committee. Barry Goldwater and I amounted to the equivalent of the canaries that coal miners used to take into the pits to detect lethal methane gas. We were watched closely for any signs that our support for Nixon was beginning to waver, and we vigorously defended the beleaguered president until a few days before his resignation. As I saw it, without convincing evidence of wrongdoing on the president's part, he should be given the benefit of the doubt, for the sake of the country's unity and security. My staff seemed to hope each time I went to the White House that it would be the day I made the decisive break with Nixon — they were getting extremely lonely out there on the limb — but after listening to his side of the story, I would come back to Capitol Hill determined to keep fighting. My aides would sigh and dutifully go back to the thankless job of defending Nixon's conduct and their boss's decision to stick with him.

After the discovery of the "smoking gun," the June 23, 1972, tape recording that suggested Nixon was actively involved in attempting to obstruct the FBI investigation of the Watergate break-in, it was all over. One of the saddest and most dramatic moments of my career came at a Republican Policy Committee lunch when Barry Goldwater proclaimed, "This man has lied to me for the last time!" On August 7, 1974, Barry and Hugh Scott, along with John Rhodes from the House, went down to the White House to break the news to Richard Nixon that it appeared we could no longer muster enough votes to stave off an impeachment conviction in the Senate. Looking back on those days, after leaving the Senate many years later, Senator Howard Baker told me that he thinks that if it had actually gone to a trial in the Senate, Nixon would have been acquitted. And while I respect Baker's opinion and vote-counting skills, the best I could come up with at the time was fifteen or sixteen votes, and that wasn't even close.

The die was cast. On the evening of August 8, Nixon summoned to the White House the people he'd felt closest to in the Congress, both Democrats and Republicans, and the leadership of both houses. We assembled in the Cabinet Room, about forty-five of us, and he thanked us for the support we'd given him over the years and told us in a firm, unshaking, unfaltering voice of his intention to go on national television in a few minutes and announce his resignation. It was a moment of high drama and high emotion. Although it was expected, it still left us virtually speechless. The tears were welling up in my eyes, and I glanced over at John Stennis to see a tear coursing down his craggy cheek. I reflected on that gloomy November day in 1963 when Stennis and I had ridden together to Arlington National Cemetery for the interment of John Kennedy and felt a similar sense of absolute depression.

Despite my growing influence in the Senate, it would take seven more years before I moved into one of the most powerful positions of all, a committee chairmanship. The long, slow climb up the seniority ladder can be frustrating. However, the gradual accretion of experience provides one with an institutional memory, well-honed legislative skills, and a broader view of the political landscape than that which comes from a rapid ascent to the top of the leadership hierarchy.

Due to a variety of unique circumstances, the two senators with whom I met on January 19, 1989, were relative newcomers to the Senate, at least as measured by the traditional standards. John Warner was first elected in 1978 and became ranking Republican on Armed Services in 1987. It took me nearly sixteen years to get to the same position, and twenty to become chairman. After being first elected in 1972, Sam Nunn suddenly was drawn by the death and retirement of more senior members from a place far down the ladder to the position of ranking Democratic member in late 1983 and to the chairmanship three years later.

I note this to illustrate the changes in the Senate that may have affected my confirmation. I don't know if I care for the term "bonding," but an apprenticeship does tend to bond the novice to the journeyman. As the apprenticeship period is abbreviated or totally eliminated, these ties of friendship, tradition, and sheer practicality are lost. Politics, particularly Senate politics, is an acquired skill. It takes years to master. Instinct isn't enough. If Nunn and Warner had been around a few more years before assuming their positions of power, perhaps — perhaps — they would have seen the danger and done things differently.

They were waiting for me in the chairman's office, which like the lairs of most senators was cluttered with autographed pictures, plaques, and home-state memorabilia. Prosaic stuff, and enough to make a fashionable interior decorator weep with frustration. I don't remember the meeting being particularly awkward, although there was a strong element of irony at work beneath the surface. Neither Warner nor Nunn knew it at the time, but had I not announced my decision to retire from the Senate in August 1983, roughly a month or so before Senator Henry Jackson died unexpectedly of a heart attack, I would have remained in the Senate. The death of Jackson, the ranking Democratic member, changed the balance of power on the committee to such an extent that, had I the option — which I did not, because I could not in good conscience rescind my decision, given the turmoil it would have created in Texas — I would have remained as chairman and then assumed the ranking Republican position in 1987, when the Democrats regained control of the Senate. I suspect there would have been a far different relationship between Nunn and myself from what developed between the Georgia Democrat and Senator Barry Goldwater, who had succeeded me as chairman in 1985, and it probably would have somewhat diminished Nunn's prominence on defense issues. In addition, as chairman, Nunn would certainly not have been able to easily checkmate the Republican side of the committee, as he has done with John Warner in the senior GOP spot.

Cooperation is always close between the chairman and the senior minority member of the Armed Services Committee. Bipartisanship on defense issues has a long tradition. As ranking minority member, I never had to worry that Chairman John Stennis of Mississippi would fail to consult with me or not provide an opportunity for the Republican members to have input into whatever legislation was under consideration. When the Republican party took control of the Senate following the 1980 elections, I gave the same opportunity to Stennis and then to Henry "Scoop" Jackson, who replaced Stennis as ranking Democrat, and later to Sam Nunn, who assumed the post after Jackson died.

By meeting jointly with me, Nunn and Warner were carrying on the tradition. But clearly Nunn was in charge. It was his show. We chatted initially about my health. I told them that the second polyp had been successfully removed and found to be benign and that my doctor felt I had an almost 100 percent chance of avoiding a recurrence, thanks to the polyp's small size and early detection.

Nunn did not seem much more than routinely interested in the allegations about my personal life but did ask a few questions about alcohol, which at the time appeared to be put to me in a matter-of-fact manner. I pointed out that the FBI had found nothing to substantiate the charges that had appeared in the press, that several Democratic senators had been interviewed and none could recall anything untoward in my conduct during the years I had served in the Senate, and that nothing had been introduced to show that I had ever done anything illegal, unethical, or contrary to the national interest in the twenty months that I had worked as a private consultant after leaving government service.

The wisest nominee uses his ears more than his mouth while making Senate courtesy calls. By listening closely, he can hear the hinges creak and trouble crossing the threshold. I heard in the questions some expressions of legitimate concern but nothing that was particularly troublesome. There was some discussion of reforming Pentagon procurement and management practices and cracking down on waste, fraud, and abuse. Both Nunn and Warner clearly understood the reality that the Department of Defense would have to deal with reduced funding and that its resources would have to be carefully marshaled and managed.

I made clear my own recognition of that fact of life as well. In accepting the nomination to be secretary of defense, I knew that after revitalizing its defenses, the nation faced a new challenge: to preserve and enhance what had already been achieved in the face of ever more sophisticated threats while, at the same time, living within demanding fiscal restraints.

No matter who was doing the preaching, the gospel was being directed at the choir. I knew from working with Sam Nunn that we were in basic agreement on many of the issues, and he said as much in the meeting. We have some things in common: Southern backgrounds, small-town childhoods, Methodist upbringings, conservative instincts (albeit different brands of conservatism), and deep interest and a willingness to immerse ourselves in the details of military affairs.

But Nunn's early interest in defense seemed to stem more from family ties and Georgia politics than it did from an intellectual predisposition or, as it had in my case, from being saturated in the war-and-peace sagas of Texas history. I can still recite the letter Lieutenant Colonel William Travis sent out from the besieged Alamo: "I shall never surrender . . ." My World War II experience as a Navy enlisted man also contributed.

My father had served on Guam during his Navy days, and I remember his being invited in the late thirties by a service club in Beaumont, Texas, where we were living at the time, to speak at a luncheon. Instead of pursuing a spiritual theme, in keeping with his vocation as a Methodist minister, he chose to address the need for fortifying Guam and its strategic importance to the United States. It was an early lesson on geopolitics, and one I eagerly absorbed.

Unlike the isolated and comfortable rural society in which Sam Nunn had grown up as the son of a prosperous and powerful local landowner, Beaumont, a bustling and somewhat gritty port city, provided me with a vantage point from which I could observe the signs, if not the substance, of the impending conflict of World War II.

Tons of scrap metal were being loaded aboard foreign flag freighters for shipment to Japan while I was in high school. One Sunday, a couple of British officers from one of the vessels attended services at my father's church. Afterward, he chatted with them about the news of the day, and the Britons asked point-blank when the scrap metal that we were so foolishly providing the Japanese would come back to the United States in the form of bombs and other weaponry. The question was rhetorical, but my father was not one of those who would have scoffed at the idea that the United States was unwisely arming its own enemy. The question that the officers asked was finally answered, of course, on December 7, 1941, with the Japanese attack on Pearl Harbor.

In June 1943, after finishing my freshman year at Southwestern University, I signed up for the Navy's aviation cadet program and was called to active duty the next September. I wasn't pilot material; I washed out and was eventually assigned to sea duty as a deck ape aboard an amphibious gunboat in the Pacific.

Sam Nunn's military service was limited to six months of active duty in the Coast Guard, teaching swimming and physical training. To use his own words: "We fought in the Mosquito War in Cape May, New Jersey. A lot of blood flowed in that war." But Nunn's great-uncle was Carl Vinson, one of the more powerful chairmen of the House Armed Services Committee. An internship in Vinson's office gave him a taste of the political life in Washington; he ran for the Georgia House and from there challenged the incumbent Democratic senator David Gambrell, appointed by then-governor Jimmy Carter to serve out the term of Richard Russell, who had died in office. Nunn surprised most everyone by winning the primary and going on to take the general election.

As successor to Russell — who himself had stepped into the shoes of Georgia's Walter George to chair the Senate Armed Services Committee — and Vinson's grandnephew, the freshman senator Nunn was given a seat on the committee by the Democratic leadership, which was eager to please increasingly restive Southerners. (A few years before, I had waived my seniority rights on Armed Services to encourage Strom Thurmond of South Carolina to jump the fence and become a Republican without losing the seniority that he had accumulated.)

I didn't pay too much attention to Nunn at the time. In the aftermath of the Vietnam War and in the midst of détente, when the Pentagon was a popular target for those who wanted to save money or make cheap political points, Sam Nunn did not risk becoming a vocal champion of the military. It took Senator Henry M. Jackson of Washington State to make being pro-defense legitimate again among Democrats. While we were complete opposites on energy policy, Scoop Jackson and I worked together to jump start the revitalization of the U.S. military after nearly a decade of neglect by Democratic and Republican administrations. We played good cop–bad cop, even if it meant, in his case, challenging Jimmy Carter, his party's president, or in mine, questioning the wisdom of the Nixon-Ford-Kissinger approach.

Scoop's untimely death in 1983 cost me a good friend. It wasn't a tennis, golfing, or dinner friendship; it was based on mutual and strongly held convictions. We teamed up for the first time in 1969, to spearhead the fight for an antiballistic missile system. And what a fight it was. The Senate voted to authorize an ABM system by just one vote. President Nixon had asked me to be the administration's point man on the issue and later said it was the most important thing I had done as a senator. As Nixon saw it, the ABM authorization gave him the leverage he needed with the Soviets to successfully negotiate the ABM treaty.

By the time of Scoop's death, his legacy was priceless: strength and peace. He gave Democrats like Sam Nunn the cover they needed to come out in the open and say they supported a strong military. Senator Nunn got behind the military-pay-raise issue after being very lukewarm about it. He had come late to the realization that there was a lot of political capital to be made championing the cause of putting more money in the pockets of the uniformed military and their dependents, many of whom were moonlighting or on food stamps.

Scoop's death also profoundly reshaped the Armed Services Committee. If he had survived the heart attack that claimed him, he would be chairman today, and I can say with confidence that my nomination would have sailed through the committee and the full Senate. He would not have felt threatened by me at the Pentagon.

Might have been's don't count in politics, but they do make for interesting speculation. There also might have been a different outcome if John Warner had not been the ranking Republican member. John suffers from a debilitating political weakness: he wants to be well liked by everyone. As a result, he goes out of his way to be accommodating. On one occasion, as chairman, I had to watch John constantly while an important amendment that the committee leadership opposed was being debated on the Senate floor. At some point in the debate, when I left him alone for a few minutes to tend to business off the floor, he began releasing senators from their commitments to vote against the amendment, figuring, I suppose, that the margin would be sufficient. My staff director, Jim McGovern, knowing that the margin could easily disappear without a trace, came out to tell me what was going on. I rushed back into the chamber to confront the crestfallen senior senator from Virginia, who lamely explained that he thought we had it in the bag. John went back to the cloakroom like a chastened schoolboy and told one of my associates, "Boy, the chief is really mad at me!"

Even before he moved into the ranking Republican position on the committee, John Warner was known in Washington circles as "a wholly owned subsidiary of Sam Nunn." From a strictly political standpoint, it appears that Warner's eagerness to cooperate with Sam Nunn stems from his need to court Virginia's predominantly conservative and Democratic electorate. Moving in lockstep with Nunn, he can negate criticism that is aimed at him by potential Democratic rivals. By coopting Warner, however, Nunn left the other Republicans on the committee in the awkward position of either directly challenging their party's senior member, fighting a guerrilla war behind his back, or passively playing follow the leader. Frustration is one reason that Strom Thurmond, who stepped aside in 1977 to allow me to become ranking member and ultimately chairman — a gesture of friendship inspired by the seniority shuffle that occurred when he switched parties — keeps threatening to claim his rights and oust Warner from the ranking spot. Strom, despite his age (at the time of the confirmation battle he was eighty-seven), is not easily manipulated, and he is not inclined to lightly surrender to anyone when he has strong views on an issue.

John Warner, I am afraid, does not even know when he is being set up and used. At our meeting, his comments and questions closely paralleled those offered by Nunn. I was asked to elaborate on my work as a consultant to defense contractors after I resigned as chief START negotiator, in 1986. I told them that my business relationships with the defense firms and consulting operations had been severed as of December 1, 1988, the day after I had been officially informed that I was under consideration for secretary of defense. Even though this abrupt termination put a squeeze on my finances — I still had staff salaries and office rent to pay — and aside from the fact that most nominees continue to conduct their business activities until the Senate confirmation process is nearing completion, I felt it was the right thing to do.

Nunn and Warner did not suggest that conflict of interest was a problem, since I would be assuming the Pentagon post without having any ongoing financial interest in firms that did business with the Defense Department or that stood to profit by my decisions. And since that is the legal definition of conflict of interest, there wasn't much to add to or subtract from the equation, once I had notified my consulting clients that our relationships were being terminated nearly two months before the Senate Armed Services Committee would begin its hearings on the nomination. Furthermore, I held no equity in the firms, nor were there promises of a future equity position or compensation of any sort.

However, beyond the strict legality of the arrangement, the two senators were circling around another factor at our meeting. There was the "appearance" of a conflict of interest. Ideally, Warner should have taken a sympathetic line, insisting that I was observing the spirit of the law by going beyond the letter of the law. If the language of a statute is too ambiguous, Congress must act to strengthen it. The appearance issue is dangerously vague. What appears to be a conflict to one individual may seem totally above-board to another. By insisting that I had discharged my legal obligations, Warner would have built a firebreak behind me; thus, I could have moved to accommodate Nunn on the appearance issue without reinforcing the impression that I was conceding that a conflict problem actually existed.

Without a little help from my friends, I would be left in the position of appearing to be insensitive to appearances by simply declaring that I had obeyed the law — period. To avoid that trap, and to go the extra mile to prove that I would be sensitive to what might appear to be a conflict, I planned to tell the Armed Services Committee that I would recuse, or disqualify, myself from any future debarment proceedings that might be directed at my former clients, debarment being the ultimate administrative sanction. The catch-22, however, remained: if there was no conflict, those who were out to find fault could ask, why should the secretary of defense recuse himself? In so many words my answer was — to satisfy Democratic senators who have raised the appearance issue. Yet, instead of accepting that position as a workable compromise, they came back and said there must be a conflict, then, or enough of an appearance of conflict to be a serious problem, to prompt a recusal. They were upending the cause-and-effect relationship that had brought about the offer to recuse myself. The cause was not a conflict of interest; the cause was the Democrats' uneasiness about the issue. It was circular logic in the extreme and needed a vigorous counterattack, but by echoing Nunn and the other Democratic opponents of my nomination, Warner helped to undercut my chances of confirmation.

In the period between the president-elect's announcement of my nomination and the inauguration, I asked my associate Richard Billmire, an economist and former staff member of the Senate Republican Policy Committee, to make soundings on Capitol Hill. Basically, I wanted Billmire to find out what kind of reception we would get once the confirmation process got under way. His conversations with conservatives, moderates, and liberals, with Republicans and Democrats, were reassuring. As one knowledgeable

Senate aide told Billmire, "You know they're going to give him a hard time about the defense contracting, but that's manageable."

My personal life, the false allegations that Lilla was actively spreading about me to the press and in phone calls to members of the Senate Armed Services Committee, the wild exaggerations about my drinking and relationships with women, were not rated as major problems by those who talked to Richard Billmire. One conservative said to him, "Look. They [the Senate] worked with him for twenty-four years. He did his job; never showed up drunk on the Senate floor. We will have a few problems here or there, but that's not one of them."

As we had found in the early stages of the transition, when Craig Fuller and Robert Teeter were questioning the wisdom of my nomination and their reservations were focused on the manager issue, the ridiculous charges about my personal life were not a major factor. The assumption was that I would be confirmed, although Treasury Secretary Nicholas Brady apparently did warn the president-elect's top advisers that it would not be as easy as everyone thought.

Brady, an investment banker, had served briefly in the Senate as an interim appointee. He was able and respected. Brady was assigned to the Armed Services Committee and witnessed my sometimes not too gentle efforts to instill discipline among Republicans on national security issues. He had never experienced, as I had, the consequences of congressional confrontations with the president on such matters. He had seen me raise the hackles of some of my colleagues and concluded that I had few friends in the Senate. I did have friends there and still do. The Senate, however, was my place of business. I *worked* there for twenty-four years. I drew my friends from a wider circle of acquaintances. Like many people, I kept my social life separate from my professional life.

The Senate has undergone a transformation in the last ten years. There has been tremendous turnover. Strom Thurmond, Claiborne Pell, Robert Byrd, and Quentin Burdick are the only current survivors of my first year in the Senate. Half of the members of the Senate Armed Services Committee have joined the panel since I retired from the Senate. In the process, traditions that once endured from one generation to the next have been swept away.

Twenty or twenty-five years ago, for example, when the chairman of the Armed Services Committee brought a defense authorization bill to the Senate floor, he was rarely second-guessed by colleagues. The 1966 defense authorization bill was passed in one day, with no floor amendments, and by a unanimous vote. In 1984, the year I retired from the Senate, the 1985 defense authorization bill took ten days, with several of the sessions running far into the night; there were 107 amendments offered from the floor.

Is it any wonder that a responsible committee chairman ends up stepping on toes if he wants to get anything done?

The Senate has become more like the U.S. House of Representatives. In recent years, there has been increased cross-pollination between the two bodies, as House members have succeeded in overcoming the disadvantage of serving a single congressional district, which deprives them of statewide recognition and leaves them vulnerable to governors or other officeholders with a broader base of support in a contest for the Senate. Those former House members bring with them a more casual and strident, more hit-and-run, parochial attitude. The Senate, as a result, is less deliberative; it tries to do too much in too short a time frame; partisanship intrudes into areas that were once off-limits to political infighting. In an effort to keep up with the incredible output of the House, the Senate has adopted the ethos of a legislative assembly line.

At one time, what the Senate did not do was as important as what it did do. The Senate was intended by the founding fathers to act as something of a brake on the more impetuous lower house of the U.S. Congress, which because of its size and the two-year election cycle tends to react to the slightest changes in the political climate.

These changes also affected the personal relationships between members of the Senate. The after-five-o'clock camaraderie in hideaway offices does not take place to the same degree, the mentor-protégé dynamic between the senior and junior members is gone, and the social interaction between senators and their families is severely curtailed by long hours and grueling schedules, which keep members on the road raising funds and fulfilling an endless round of political obligations.

Yes, it is not surprising that Nick Brady said I had few friends in the Senate. The Senate isn't a very friendly place anymore.

Over the years I have attended seven presidential inaugurations, counting the swearing-in ceremony for Gerald Ford in the East Room of the White House, which ended the "long national nightmare" of Watergate. Six presidents in all.

Nothing captures the essence of democracy better than the exquisitely simple act of a man (and perhaps one day a woman) placing his left hand on a Bible, raising his right hand, and swearing to uphold the Constitution of the United States. In less than sixty seconds, the complicated business of transferring power, or reinvesting that power — which in many societies comes about only after violent internal struggle — is complete.

Since Ronald Reagan's first inaugural, in 1981, the ceremony has been held on the West Front of the Capitol Building. It is a magnificent setting. The Lincoln and Jefferson memorials, the radiant obelisk of the Washington Monument, the White House, and the Mall form a backdrop to the proceedings that is so rich with historical association and meaning as to be almost hypnotic in its effect.

Those of us who were sitting on the upper terrace near the podium where George Bush would take the oath of office at high noon on January 20, 1989, had the full benefit of this panorama.

The nominees for the president-elect's cabinet had choice seats. We were grouped to the right and slightly behind the row where George and Barbara sat with the rest of the Bush family. The cabinet designees, the Senate and House leadership, and the Supreme Court — the representatives of the three coequal branches of the government — were placed at the center of what amounted to concentric circles of power.

From where I sat, what with the tiers of VIP seating, camera platforms, press stands, and network anchor booths perched on towers, the whole thing looked like a football stadium that had suddenly sprouted up at the apex of the triangle where Pennsylvania and Independence avenues converge.

One disadvantage of being a cabinet designee is that you are on your own. I couldn't share the view with the rest of my family. They were relegated to a standing-room-only area. Every four years, there is a scramble for inaugural tickets. The incoming administration is deluged with requests from friends and supporters. It is a major undertaking to ensure that tender egos are not damaged by seat assignments that seem incompatible with an individual's own sense of importance and esteem.

Complicating this ticklish diplomatic assignment was that with the Bush-Reagan transition, the outgoing administration was also interested in fully participating in the event. Not since 1929 had presidential power passed between members of the same party after a general election. The losers didn't pack up and leave town. Everybody was a winner and stayed around to celebrate.

We were all justifiably proud of the continuity. George Bush had been elected in his own right, but it was also a vote of confidence in the eight years of Ronald Reagan's presidency. Dwight D. Eisenhower had been the last president to serve two full terms in office. Although John Kennedy's election captured the White House from the Republicans, Eisenhower left office without being scarred by the traumatic consequences of events like Vietnam, Watergate, and the Iran hostage crisis. The nation wasn't angry or frustrated when JFK took the oath of office, and I think it had a lot to do with the high hopes and goodwill that launched his presidency. Similarly, George Bush was the beneficiary of Reagan's effective leadership. For the first time since 1961, the power of the presidency that was being transferred wasn't damaged merchandise, something suspect and troubled. Finally, as a nation that depends so heavily on its president to provide vision and direction, we were back in business.

Traditionally, there is a luncheon in the rotunda of the Capitol Building hosted by the congressional leadership after the president takes the oath of office and delivers his inaugural address. Cameras and the press are excluded; it is a time to step out of the spotlight and begin the process of interaction between the two branches of government that is essential to the effective functioning of the country.

As we were waiting to be seated, Senator John Warner approached me to discuss our previous day's meeting with Sam Nunn. "I had some doubts before yesterday, John," he said. "But I think you've crossed the Rubicon."

At the time, I took the comment at face value. Later I wondered if I should have read more importance into it. Warner seemed to be saying that he regarded Nunn as a problem. When one crosses the Rubicon, as Julius Caesar did when he returned from Gaul to enter Rome and assume power, there is no going back. Warner's metaphor, I think, was meant to convey that he thought that I had cleared a significant obstacle by satisfying Sam Nunn and that I would be confirmed. But I did not regard Nunn as an obstacle. And that was a fatal misreading of the situation. I had crossed the Rubicon; there was no going back. What lay before me, however, was not confirmation as secretary of defense, but a political killing field prepared by the chairman of the Senate Armed Services Committee.

Dorothy and I had seats together on the presidential reviewing stand in front of the White House, where we spent the rest of the afternoon watching the inaugural parade. George and Barbara Bush appeared to be enjoying the event enormously. If anybody deserved the right to have a few hours of uncomplicated fun, clapping to the beat and waving at the bands that marched by and giving the thumbs-up sign to the equestrian units prancing along Pennsylvania Avenue in high Texas style, it was the president and First Lady. They had earned it the hard way.

The press, as always, grumbled about the parties and the limousines that rolled into Washington for the event. But it's phony to pretend that an inauguration should be all solemnity and no fun. It is a national party. And, as far as I am concerned, the mix of glitter, sophistication, and casualness of the 1989 inauguration accurately reflected the man we elected to be the forty-first president of the United States.

I completed the courtesy calls to the Democratic members of the Senate Armed Services Committee on Monday and Tuesday, January 23 and 24, following inauguration weekend. Two senators, John Glenn and Alan Dixon, told me not to bother stopping by their offices. Both indicated that they were comfortable with my selection as secretary of defense, that they knew my record, and that there was no need to pose any questions before the hearings.

With the others, I made it a point to say that, since there had been so many misleading accounts in the press about my private life, I would be happy to answer any questions along those lines. Not one of those senators took me up on the offer. They waved me off, saying they were not deeply concerned about the allegations. Carl Levin of Michigan said he would leave questions about the allegations to Sam Nunn. Shelby of Alabama was very supportive, and it was in this meeting that he made the comment to the effect that he saw nothing wrong with a man who had an affinity for women and alcohol, which I would recall the day my nomination was rejected by the full Senate.

Senator Levin had sent me a long list of questions about various defense-related issues that he wanted answered before my hearings began. Levin is a very intelligent and aggressive lawmaker who styles himself as the Senate's resident prosecutor of the Defense Department. Like most lawyers, he apparently sees the process of government as one that primarily involves drawing up a set of rules and regulations. If there is a problem, the solution is to enact more legislation. The end product is a Gordian knot of red tape. For most monies authorized and appropriated, there are often narrow and arbitrary statutory constraints.

The practice of posing written questions to a nominee is part of a game that Democrats started to play with the nomination of Walter Hickel to be interior secretary during the Nixon administration. The former Alaska governor was a controversial figure, and the Democrats set out to hedge him in by forcing him to answer in minute detail questions about nearly every aspect of Interior Department policy. Hickel tried to be responsive to the senators, but he fell into the trap of being too specific in relating what he would and would not do about environmental, land use, and natural resources leasing policies. After he was confirmed, the Democrats used the record as a club, and they bashed Hickel over the head with it every time he strayed, or seemed to stray, from the precise commitments he had made during the hearings.

Ever since, congressional committees have attempted to run the cabinet-level departments by "hickeling" the nominees for the top posts. It is a way for the Democrats to compensate for their inability to capture the White House and exercise executive authority.

I pulled Levin's list of questions from my briefcase and told the senator that with the hearings about to open, there was not much time to answer in detail. He seemed surprised by the list, as though it were the first time he had seen it. Levin asked for the sheaf of papers, looked them over carefully, and then underlined several questions that he was most interested in having addressed. It was still an unreasonable number — several pages, detailed in nature and dealing largely with procurement and "waste, fraud, and abuse" issues.

Nunn had also sent me a list of questions to be answered in writing, and like Levin, he had seemed to be unfamiliar with the material. In both cases, I suspect, the questions were the work of Senate staffers, and I was seeing the effects of the infamous "autopen." The autopen, which can be used to duplicate a senator's signature, is employed by Senate aides to magnify their influence and to distort the legislative process to such a degree that, in some instances, relatively inexperienced and unelected men and women are wielding power inimical to the proper functioning of representative government.

Using a computer to generate a letter in response to a constituent inquiry is legitimate. Thousands of pieces of mail arrive at a Senate office each month. The sheer volume makes it impossible to personally answer each one. In my Senate office, we developed a system in which my position on a specific issue was boiled down to a paragraph. Each paragraph would be coded, so that if we received a letter asking about oil import fees, farm price supports, and SDI, for example, the computer would print out the three appropriate mini-statements.

My hard and fast rule was that every letter that came in was answered. The ones that required individual attention, like tracking down a lost Social Security check or a hardship discharge from the armed services, were turned over to caseworkers for follow-up.

The system worked reasonably well. Occasionally, there would be backlogs because a hot issue generated a sudden flood of letters. And I'd always hear about it on my trips back home: "Why haven't you answered my letter?" It was a sure sign that the mail room was swamped, and I would have extra people assigned to help bail it out.

But turning over legislative supervision, including the Senate's constitutional obligation to offer advice and consent on presidential nominations, to a computer and a Senate aide is a practice that I strongly condemn. Even granting that it is proper for a member of the Senate to delegate responsibilities to his subordinates, the tasks assigned must not be allowed to usurp the legislator's own role in the process.

There is nothing inherently nefarious about asking an aide to gather information. However, when the questions and answers become legislative ends in themselves — which is what happened to Walter Hickel — the Senate is in danger of becoming a rubber stamp, a front behind which members of the staff individually or collectively pursue their own agendas. The lists of questions handed to me by Nunn and Levin were examples of this. Senate aides, not senators, were driving the process.

The day before I met with Nunn and Warner, I spent two or three hours with Arnold Punaro and other members of the Armed Services Committee staff going over the financial information and other background material that I was providing to the Senate. The purpose of a meeting like that is to ensure that the committee gets the data necessary to evaluate a nominee's compliance with legal requirements to organize records and statements in a coherent, accessible manner. Punaro and the other committee staff members were painstakingly thorough. The Democratic staff director kept coming back to my military records, looking for indications that my activities in the Navy reserve had been padded to create pension benefits. I finally was able to produce documentation to show that whatever active-duty time I served after my discharge at the end of the war did not enhance my government pension.

Punaro then became interested in awards and decorations that were presented to me at the time I retired from the Senate. He wanted to know if I was really entitled to them.

"Look," I finally said in frustration. "If there is any question about this, I'll return them to the Department of Defense, at whose initiative they were presented. I've never sought awards that I was not entitled to."

Beyond the nitpicking, the meeting was somewhat strained anyway. Punaro knew that my staff and I suspected him of making critical comments about me to the press and of leaking unfavorable bits and pieces of the FBI report soon after it had been delivered to Nunn and Warner at the Gardiner Tennis Ranch. Punaro's reaction was to blame it all on the Tower Mafia. He told me, "Jim McGovern has been spreading the word that I'm doing the leaking, but that's just not true." I think it really irked him that McGovern was sitting over at the Pentagon as acting Air Force secretary while he was shuffling papers on Capitol Hill. It's that kind of personal rivalry and animus that can drive Senate staffers into attempting to one-up the executive branch by micromanaging policy implementation, which, under our system of government, is not a function of congressional staff.

As I left the session, one of my aides who knew Arnold Punaro well summed it up. "Remember, Senator, Arnold is a little man in a large job."

Large or small, Punaro was Sam Nunn's man. As chairman of the committee, Nunn did not give his staff director much latitude. I had the impression that Arnold was always on probation and that he needed to prove himself to Nunn.

One of his colleagues on the committee staff told me that Punaro was "too smart to get caught leaking information to the press . . . it would be too easy to trace it back to him." Nevertheless, there was a visible trail, and even the news media were willing to follow it back to its source. John M. Broder of the *Los Angeles Times* saw where it led as early as December 7, 1988:

> The source of these tales is often obscure, but those close to the transition process believe that some are coming from aides to Sen. Sam Nunn (D-Ga.), the current chairman of the Senate Armed Services Committee and the Democrats' leading expert on military affairs.
>
> Although there is no evidence that Nunn himself is responsible for the campaign, he stands to benefit from Tower's distress. If Bush backed away from Tower and brought in an outsider as defense secretary, Nunn would have no credible rival as Washington's foremost spokesman on defense, at least for the year or two it takes for the new secretary to learn his way around the Pentagon and Capitol Hill.
>
> "Sam Nunn does not want to have a guy with the stature of John Tower at the Pentagon," said one Tower partisan. "He [Nunn] is running for President. That's what this is all about. He would love to have an industry guy [as defense secretary] so Nunn . . . can dominate national defense issues."

At the time the article was written, Sam Nunn was on a fact-finding mission in Africa. An aide denied that there was an attempt to scuttle my nomination. The negative comments from Nunn staffers were, he said, "unauthorized and certainly not directed by Sen. Nunn. I'm certain they do not reflect Sen. Nunn's position." The aide was not certain enough, however, to allow his name to appear in print, just in case he was misreading Nunn's position.

Another possible source of the leaks noted by Broder was, unfortunately, closer to home:

> Other anti-Tower reports are believed to be coming from old Tower congressional staff foes who have no hope of winning good defense jobs if Tower is named secretary and are trying to push another candidate or another agenda. Several of Tower's favored committee aides have moved on to senior jobs at the Pentagon and are expected to prosper if Tower moves into the secretary's office.
>
> "There are big stakes here, obviously, and there's always evil afoot," said a former Tower aide who would like to see

his former boss get the job. "Mostly, somebody else has a candidate and wants to trash someone along the way."

Broder concluded with a quote that became one of my favorites of the confirmation period: " 'He's a Texan, make no mistake, and he's no angel,' said one Tower supporter."

Preparing for the hearings while overseeing the Pentagon transition was already consuming most of my attention. Rhett Dawson, whom I had asked to be the director of my transition team, went through nearly four linear feet of briefing books prepared by the Pentagon bureaucracy on key issues that were likely to come up at the hearings. Rhett and his assistant, Ken Krieg, gave me a couple of loose-leaf binders highlighting the essentials. After reading through the material, I began drafting my formal statement, which would be introduced into the record. I intended to open my testimony with extemporaneous remarks drawn from a few notes and then take the committee members' questions.

As this preparation regimen was under way, I was also involved in a series of briefings that were intended to bring me up to speed on Pentagon procedures. The chain of military command that leads down from the president is very intricate; the public and most members of Congress are not aware of how it works. Even though I was still only the defense secretary designate, I had to be totally familiar with the responsibilities that went with the job in case of an emergency a few minutes after I was confirmed and sworn into office.

In this nuclear age, on-the-job training for a defense secretary and, for that matter, the president and his entire national security team is a perilous proposition. Given his own high level of government experience, President Bush saw the need for seasoned national security professionals in the top Pentagon, State Department, and National Security Council positions. We all knew the territory and could hit the ground running. By January 20, 1989, he had selected, I would say, some of the most knowledgeable foreign and defense policy advisers to serve any president in the postwar period.

One of the themes that had been emphasized by Robert Teeter during the transition was "new faces." As an experienced pollster, Teeter knew that this was a concept that could be packaged and sold to the public and the press. Teeter's credibility was also reinforced by having helped the Packard Commission as a public opinion research adviser. His surveys found that since the complexities of Pentagon procurement were lost on most people, the six-hundred-dollar toilet seat had become the symbol of government ineptitude and waste. Therefore, the solution to the problem had to be equally symbolic and simplistic — new faces.

Fortunately, President-elect Bush wasn't about to buy the *whole* package. At a meeting on January 17, he signed off on my plan to move Rhett Dawson from Pentagon transition director to the post of secretary of the Army. I had to sell Rhett a little bit, though. The president had heard stories around the White House that there had been a "Dole Mole" among the Reagan staff slipping inside information to Senator Bob Dole during the primaries; somebody had apparently fingered Dawson as the culprit. I assured him that Rhett's loyalty was beyond reproach. But Jim McGovern and Will Ball, respectively the acting secretary of the Air Force and the Navy secretary, fell into the twilight zone: they were neither new nor old faces. Both men had put in time at the Defense Department during the Reagan administration after leaving Senate staff jobs. Ball, who had served as legislative affairs officer for both the State Department and the White House, moved into the Navy secretary's job in 1987. McGovern, the undersecretary of the Air Force, had been temporarily filling the secretary's slot since December 17, 1988, the day after Edward C. Aldridge left office. After hearing the talk about new faces and Tower's Mafia, the president-elect was leery about keeping them on, but I convinced him to go for a trial period. After all, I pointed out, both of them had helped me develop the comprehensive plan that I had brought to him in November for reforming and managing the Pentagon. Bush said I could use McGovern and Ball for a few weeks, and I was certain that their performances would persuade him to make the appointments permanent. They were being given a chance to prove themselves. I knew they could and would.

By delaying a final resolution, I also knew that since Teeter had turned down John Sununu's offer to make him deputy White House chief of staff, his influence would not be as significant in a month or two.

Just as the president must have an experienced cadre of senior national security advisers, the defense secretary depends on subordinates who can move quickly to staff, set priorities for, and energize the massive military bureaucracy. Dawson, McGovern, and a couple of other old Washington hands assisted me in the primary objective of coming up with a short list of candidates for the post of deputy secretary of defense. I told them I wanted someone with strong managerial credentials, preferably with some defense industry experience.

Dawson found that some of the candidates on the list were not interested in making such a drastic change in career. Government service can entail a severe financial sacrifice. At $89,500 a year, the salary was a fraction of what a chief executive would earn at a major corporation. An additional complication is stock options and pension plans that cause conflict-of-interest problems. When he became deputy secretary of defense during the Nixon administration, David Packard lost millions of dollars — I've seen estimates as high as $35 million — by disposing of his holdings in Hewlett-Packard to comply with the regulations. Congress has imposed restrictions on the business activities that former Defense Department officials may engage in after they leave the Pentagon, and that has also discouraged many people from taking on government assignments, for fear that they won't be able to return to their chosen professions once they reenter private life. Rhett was careful to be discreet. When in doubt, he made inquiries through second and third parties before I approached a prospective candidate, and even then some of those begged off before we got to the interview stage.

I set up shop in room 4E830 at the Pentagon, on the floor above the secretary of defense's offices, which Frank Carlucci had vacated to make way for his successor. I would have been criticized for moving into the secretary's office — as it was, I was being sniped at for even daring to set foot in the building — and the temporary quarters were appropriate and perfectly adequate.

We had three rooms: a reception area, my private office, and what came to be known as the bullpen, where the professional staff worked. I tried to keep my door open so that my aides would have no inhibitions about entering to discuss the ongoing business of the moment.

I think Sam Nunn disapproved of this casual style and of the rapport I created with my staff. At one of our meetings he asked, "Is it true that you have been seen balancing an empty wineglass on your head?"

"Yes, I do that every now and then when I'm with friends or staff. Over the years I have balanced an empty coffee cup on my head in the mornings and walked out to my secretary's desk for a refill. It was simply inner-office levity, a running gag." Sam fails to comprehend that kind of thing; there is no place for levity in his office.

When I interviewed Don Atwood for the job of deputy secretary of defense, we spent about an hour and a half digging into the substantive questions on Pentagon management. I liked his responses, and my last question was "Don, one more thing: do you have a sense of humor?"

Atwood is a quiet man of serious, businesslike demeanor. As vice chairman of General Motors, he had a reputation for being a decisive, gutsy executive with a solid engineering background. He smiled and said, "Yes, I do have a good sense of humor."

"Fine. You're going to need it around this place."

FIVE

BAPTISM OF FIRE

I HEARD Sam Nunn rapping the gavel — quick, impatient strokes. The photographers, elbowing and jostling each other for position, a rugby scrum equipped with heavy-caliber Nikons that clicked and flashed like automatic weaponry, broke and fell back from the witness table where I was seated. Nunn rapped the gavel again for good measure. "The committee will come to order."

There was a moment of eye contact between us, just a fraction of a second. Nunn looked down at his script and began to read. "The committee meets this afternoon to begin our hearings on the nomination of the Honorable John Tower to serve as secretary of defense." Hunched forward, his elbows on the green felt cloth that covered the long, lozenge-shaped table dominating the front of the cavernous Senate caucus room, he read the words off the page. "On behalf of the entire committee, I extend a warm welcome to our former colleague, and to our present colleagues who are here to introduce him."

Senator Robert Dole, the Republican leader, was seated to my right along with Senator Phil Gramm of Texas, the Republican senator (formerly a member of the House) who had been elected in my place after I decided not to run for reelection. Senator Lloyd Bentsen, the senior senator from Texas, was on the left. The home-state senators usually show up at the opening of confirmation hearings to vouch for a nominee; Bentsen's presence was also a subtle gesture of solidarity that was not lost on those who had been working to undermine my confirmation prospects. As chairman of the Finance Committee, he matched Nunn in power and prestige. And Dole's appearance before the committee was a generous extra dimension of support from my party's leadership that I deeply appreciated.

It seemed as if I had been waiting for months to hear the sound of Sam Nunn's gavel open those hearings. Actually, only thirty-nine days had elapsed since George Bush announced his intention to nominate me for the post of secretary of defense. But those thirty-nine days had been difficult — "a death of a thousand cuts," as one friend described it. Traditionally, cabinet nominees are expected to suffer in silence until the time comes for them to testify before the committee that has jurisdiction. Despite the temptation to launch a major public relations offensive in the face of the barrage of allegations, rumors, and innuendos about my business activities, Senate record, and personal life, I kept my contacts with the press to a minimum. On the day President-elect Bush announced my nomination, I agreed to tape an interview with Leslie Stahl of CBS that would be broadcast on Christmas Day. Shortly after making the commitment, I was advised by the transition office that, as a matter of policy, I should not be talking to the press or become actively involved in a public relations effort to promote the nomination. However, since I had already given a promise to Stahl, I stood by my word. In the interview, I denied the charges that had been leveled against me but generally tried to keep the discussion focused on the substantive issues that I would be dealing with at the Pentagon.

One television interview, however, could not begin to repair the damage that had been done. If there is a lesson to be learned from the experience, it is that future presidents-elect must move expeditiously to name their cabinet secretaries and top officials. Between election day and December 16, when George Bush announced my nomination, we were vulnerable to attack from all sides. The constraints on what one can and cannot say are bad enough for an official cabinet designee, but those of us like Louis Sullivan, Richard Thornburgh, and Jack Kemp, who had been identified as front-runners for administration posts, had to endure enormous pressure while we waited to be brought aboard.

Every day that went by seemed to bring another news story

about the "problems" that were "delaying" the nominations. And every nomination that was announced reflected on those that were still pending.

On the Monday before Thanksgiving, when John Sununu told reporters "It looks like John Tower," my friends immediately started getting calls from members of the press who wanted to know when the announcement would be made. We were left without an answer. Richard Billmire took to saying, "Well, it's Thanksgiving week . . . these things take time. The president-elect is deliberating."

It sounded awfully lame. At the same time, George Bush, Jim Baker, and Sununu were all out of town for the holiday. There was a news vacuum. But some opponents of my nomination were around to talk to the press and fill that vacuum.

George Bush does not like news leaks, and neither do I. And it's not just a matter of keeping a secret. We both know how disruptive leaks can be to orderly decision making and to the policy formation process. I told my people that, as a preventive measure, they were not to reveal the meeting with the president-elect that took place on November 17; they were also ordered not to tell reporters that I had been called to the Old Executive Office Building on November 30 to pick up the various forms that would be needed for an FBI background check, a sure sign that I was the only candidate for the defense secretary's job. Had we disclosed this information, a lot of the speculation about my nomination — particularly the business about opposition within the transition team and "second thoughts" — would have been dampened. However, at that juncture the inaccurate reports amounted to a minor annoyance, not worth countering if it meant infringing on the president-elect's prerogatives to control the pace and timing of the cabinet selection process.

President Bush was wise to insist on a careful and close evaluation before my nomination was announced, in light of the charges about my fitness to serve. If he had moved much earlier, there would have been criticism of George Bush's blind loyalty to a political crony and of his failure to await the outcome of the investigation of those charges.

To protect future presidents from being caught in this dilemma, it might be wise to announce the cabinet all at once. There would be inevitable speculation and rumor in advance, but no one would be left dangling. By setting a certain date for the announcements, perhaps January 1, the FBI would have a deadline to work against in conducting its background checks without becoming bogged down in the sort of open-ended investigatory process that damaged my nomination. The press, meantime, would not be able to second-guess and prod the president-elect into taking action just for the sake of taking action.

Despite the difficulties that I had experienced, I was confident as the Senate hearings opened on January 25 that the worst was over. The first few paragraphs of Nunn's statement included oblique criticism of my stewardship of the Armed Services Committee:

> The committee initiated improvements in our confirmation procedures at the beginning of the 100th Congress. We directed the formulation of new procedures for handling background investigations and financial matters; required additional certifications and material from the executive branch and implemented a detailed questionnaire for each nominee covering, in particular, conflict of interest matters.

Embarrassed by the Ill Wind bribery scandal, the committee had "initiated improvements in . . . confirmation procedures." I had been chairman when Mel Paisley's nomination for assistant secretary of the Navy was submitted by the Reagan administration. A senior Boeing executive and World War II combat pilot, Paisley appeared to be well qualified. Furthermore, his nomination had the strong backing of my Democratic colleague Scoop Jackson. The hearings were routine, nothing out of the ordinary turned up, and he was confirmed. Subsequently, when Paisley was implicated in Ill Wind, there was a scramble to find a scapegoat. The Democrats tried to pin the blame on our confirmation procedures, but we had inherited the formula from previous Democratic chairmen.

Ill Wind gave Sam Nunn an excuse for second-guessing the FBI and the White House:

> The committee role is then to review that process and the documents to determine which need clarification or supplementation and to apply our own standards and procedures to the material and determinations provided by the executive branch. We also look to ensure conformity with existing rules, regulations and laws. We conduct our own investigations to supplement these as necessary.

The preceding paragraph of Sam Nunn's opening statement put the Senate Armed Services Committee into the business of conducting investigations. In case there were qualms about this, Nunn suggested that the FBI needed his help.

> When Senator Tower's nomination was announced on December 16, 1988, the FBI report was not complete. At that time, the FBI had completed what they termed a "Summary Memorandum containing the partial results of the investigation of John G. Tower."
>
> That summary is now called Chapter 1. Chapter 2 was completed on December 23, and Chapter 3 was completed on January 6. On that day the transition office informed Senator Warner and I [sic] that the FBI report was available for our review, and we reviewed the report on the next day, that is, January 7.
>
> Since then we have worked with the FBI, the White House, and our staff to obtain additional information to clarify certain information, to conduct our own review and investigations. Any other matters that may come to our attention during these hearings, or any additional information that may be needed on certain issues, will also be thoroughly reviewed.

Behind these bland and ambiguous phrases, Sam Nunn was sharpening the cutting edge of a powerful political weapon that could possibly cripple or destroy the confirmation prospects of any nominee singled out by the chairman of the Armed Services Committee.

As for my exact fate — crippled or destroyed — I'm not sure that even Sam knew at that point. The Senate does not easily turn on one of its own.

> I want to emphasize that throughout this process, we had excellent cooperation from the transition office and excellent cooperation from Senator Tower and members of his staff.
>
> Senator Tower is well known to the members of this committee, having served on it with distinction 20 years, including 4 years as chairman. Beyond his congressional experience on national security issues, Senator Tower's qualifications are strengthened significantly as the chief START negotiator and by his chairmanship of the Tower Board during a very difficult period for our country.

Senator Tower, as Secretary of Defense, all of your experience and expertise will be put to the test as the Bush administration and the Congress together deal with the significant opportunities and challenges confronting our Nation as we enter the 1990's.

Nunn did not read the letters he had sent to the Democratic and Republican presidential candidates informing them of his committee's new approach to reviewing nominees for senior Defense Department posts; those went into the record without comment or fanfare. Almost as an afterthought, given the significance of the nine-point set of guidelines that he was imposing on the executive branch, the chairman had presented the letters to the committee for a belated review and endorsement *after* the letters had been sent out to the candidates.

John Warner, who had cosigned the letters as the committee's senior Republican, thereby committing himself to the dubious venture, was the next to speak.

The chairman and I have worked as a team on every aspect of the nomination thus far. The staff has been directed to operate jointly on all matters, and they have done so. We have been given access to all information, have participated in all meetings, and have been involved in all decisions about how to proceed with the nomination.

In short, the minority has been afforded a greater role in preparation for this nomination than has been the case in any previous nomination in the 10 years that I have been privileged to be on this committee, and more than likely in the history of the committee.

Second, there may be some question in the minds of some on the manner in which we have conducted the hearing thus far. I believe the chairman and I have done everything possible to see that the elements of fairness and thoroughness have been done.

Behaving like a hostage who had become psychologically dependent on the goodwill of his captor, Warner was unable to see that he was unwittingly providing Nunn with the nonpartisan camouflage he needed to conceal his partisan objectives. The minority, or opposition party — and the Republicans are the opposition party in Congress — must never be seduced into losing sight of its own objectives. Warner was so eager to gain Nunn's respect and approval by embracing his seemingly high-minded rhetoric that he completely forgot that his job as the Republican leader on the committee was to see to it that a Republican president, not a Democratic senator, got to choose the members of his cabinet. By being unwilling to assert himself, Warner was easily manipulated.

And now that I have harshly judged Senator Warner in retrospect, I will offer him the benefit of the doubt. While he is an experienced enough politician to know that you always keep your back to the wall — and Warner did not do that — none of us realized how vulnerable we were at the time. As a former committee chairman, I was aware that when a chairman goes all out to block a nomination or oppose legislation, and if he is determined to use the full resources at his command, there is very little that can be done to stop him.

The only counterweights to the power of a committee chairman are the traditions and institutional dynamic of the Senate itself and the goodwill of the individuals involved. The rhetoric of nonpartisanship has such an appeal because it does, indeed, lubricate the political mechanism. Factionalism can paralyze the system, as it did before the Civil War, when both sides saw their causes, states' rights and abolition, as bigger than the need to maintain the integrity of the republic and the existing process of government. In this case, Sam Nunn, the partisan Democrat, the ambitious politician seeking a route to the White House, saw his cause as bigger than the Senate, bigger than a two-hundred-year tradition that holds that the president selects his cabinet subject to the advice and consent of the Senate — consent normally withheld only in extraordinary circumstances.

To repeat that important phrase: the advice and consent *of the Senate,* not the advice and consent of an individual committee chairman. I believe that if the entire Senate had been free to vote according to conscience and personal inclination, I would have been confirmed. But once the power of Sam Nunn's chairmanship had been brought to bear against my nomination, my chances were slim indeed.

Determining exactly when he decided to oppose me is a matter of conjecture. Only Sam Nunn knows. My assessment is that he was dissatisfied with the nomination from the beginning. He staked out his turf by sending the letters to George Bush and Michael Dukakis. He, or his minions, circulated the rumor that the president-elect had offered him the defense secretary's job (which is pure fantasy; it never happened). It certainly seemed to me that he either encouraged his committee staff to launch a whispering campaign to impugn my character or failed to discourage them from doing so. George Bush was supposed to get the message: back off and select someone more to Sam Nunn's liking.

On January 25 Sam Nunn, it seems to me, was still straddling the fence. He wanted to oppose me openly but was still afraid of the consequences. His carefully cultivated statesman's image could be badly smudged in the confrontation. He could beat me, but it might be a Pyrrhic victory. I sensed his reservations about me, and therefore my objective as the hearings began was to convince him that I would be a closely cooperative secretary of defense — and I thought I could do it.

"When I first considered the matter of appearing before this committee, I thought John Tower really did not have to be introduced, having been its distinguished chairman from 1981 to 1984." Senator Lloyd Bentsen got us off to a good start.

> But in checking on this committee, I find that approximately a third of the committee came to the Senate after John left the U.S. Senate. So to each of you, I want to assure you that I feel John Tower is strongly qualified to be Secretary of Defense.
>
> He was an enlisted man in the Navy during World War II, with four decades of service in the Reserves; in addition to that, he served in the U.S. Senate . . . with a very primary interest in the defense of our country.

By linking my Navy service with my interest in national defense, Bentsen made an important connection, one that explains a lot about why I was sitting in the Senate caucus room and why I aspired to be secretary of defense.

One phrase, and there are many, that rolls off the tongues of contemporary defense analysts is "force projection capability." I have used it many times myself, but when I do, the abstract and academic quality of the jargon gives way to a far more concrete manifestation of the underlying concept. The hull is battleship gray and she rides through the deep swells of the western Pacific. I think of the USS *LCS-112*, an amphibious gunboat.

I keep a model of her behind my desk in Washington. *LCS-112* was unglamorous and ungainly; 150 feet fore and aft, 30 feet at the beam, flat-bottomed, she was known as the seagoing bedpan. Despite her ugly-duckling quality, for those of us who went down to the sea in that particular ship to fight that particular war, *LCS-112* was just fine. She took us out there and brought us home in one piece. And while there were tense moments standing beside the after-starboard 20-millimeter machine gun, where I served as gun captain, unfortunately for the purposes of memoir writing some forty-five years later, I wasn't thinking deep thoughts about war and peace or geopolitics; I was concerned about getting my butt shot off. I like to think that the experience of this elemental pragmatism, a common trait among combat veterans, would have served me in good stead as secretary of defense.

After the battle for Okinawa, which *LCS-112* supported, enduring, along with the rest of the U.S. invasion fleet, 1,900 Japanese suicide attacks along with another 3,900 conventional aircraft sorties, my ship was assigned to one of the flotillas earmarked for the invasion of Japan. I have never had any trouble choosing sides in the debate over whether President Harry Truman was justified in ordering the atomic bombs to be dropped on Hiroshima and Nagasaki.

When *LCS-112* was anchored off Saipan, I would cheer along with the rest of the crew as the B-29s flew over us on their bombing runs against Japan. The *Enola Gay,* the plane that dropped the bomb on Hiroshima, came from Tinian, the neighboring island, but of course we had never heard of the A-bomb and could not comprehend its destructive force. We did, however, based on our experience at Okinawa, understand the kamikaze tactics and fanatic tenacity with which the Japanese would defend the rest of their home islands. At Okinawa they sank 36 American vessels. About 5,000 Allied sailors were killed. Our total combat casualties amounted to more than 12,000 dead, 38,000 wounded. The Japanese paid an even higher price, with 110,000 killed and 8,000 aircraft destroyed. If the Japanese could not be bombed into submission, Japan would be taken only at an enormous cost in American lives. At Saipan we were installing extra machine guns wherever there was available space aboard the ship to provide us with additional firepower for the invasion.

The bombs, when they were dropped, appeared to foreclose that prospect and promise an imminent end to the war. Forty years later, during my tenure as strategic offensive arms negotiator, I couldn't help bristling at the suggestion of my Soviet counterpart that the A-bombs had been dropped only to intimidate the USSR.

Without doubt, World War II had a major impact on my views of national security issues. Twenty years later, when as a junior member of the Senate Armed Services Committee I made my first of many visits to Vietnam to get a close look at our combat operations, my observations and judgments were tempered by an enlisted man's perspective and a political scientist's insights.

Lloyd Bentsen was kind enough to mention my World War II service, but in his comments to the committee he also referred to more contemporary events in which I had played a role.

> I believe his chairmanship of the Iran-Contra affair [the President's Special Review Board] demonstrated his toughness and his independence of judgment. . . .
>
> As I said when he retired, John Tower is too much of a conservative to turn a blank check on the Treasury over to the Pentagon, even if that blank check is to pay for national defense.
>
> John, I do not really envy the job that you have ahead of you, because you are going to have to squeeze more of the waste out of the Defense Department, and some corruption that we have been finding.
>
> But I believe that very reputation for toughness and fairness should permit him to do that job with skill and with success, and I hope that this committee, after giving the witness his baptism of fire, will approve him.

By expressing that sentiment, Lloyd Bentsen was honoring me, but he was also keeping faith with a set of values that are grounded on the belief that national security issues are too critical to our welfare to be politicized. "John Tower is a partisan," he noted.

> He makes no apologies for that. He is formidable on the campaign stump. I had that brought to my attention a couple of times last year during the campaign. But that political contest is behind us, and he understands that national defense is a concern of all Americans. I believe he will be a very able Secretary of Defense, and that his nomination deserves bipartisan support.

My nomination was also commended to the committee by Senators Gramm and Dole, but I could see from the reaction of the senators arrayed to the left and right of Sam Nunn that Lloyd Bentsen's endorsement was warmer than expected — more than pro forma. The automatic winders on the photographers' cameras clattered as Bentsen left the hearing room.

The chairman asked me to introduce my family. They were seated behind me, in the front row of the spectators' area: Penny Tower Cook, Marian Tower, and "Jeanne Tower," whose married name, of course, is Cox. (How could I have lapsed on the introduction of my youngest but first-to-be-married daughter? She, of course, graciously forgave me.) And then Lou. Lou Tower rose from her seat and nodded, as she had done with modesty and poise on so many occasions as we campaigned together around Texas. Having her there meant a lot to me. I had not asked her to come; it was her idea, and a generous one. Our marriage had ended some twelve years earlier, but our friendship has endured.

Lou has said that the best period of our marriage was the year we spent in England while I was studying at the London School of Economics and Political Science. It was just the two of us. We had been married for only a few months when I decided to take a leave of absence from my teaching post at Midwestern State. I borrowed three thousand dollars to underwrite the traveling expenses, pay the rent on a flat in Montagu Square near Hyde Park, and cover the day-to-day miscellaneous costs of living overseas. In the summer of 1952, we set sail from New York for Plymouth on the majestic old ocean liner *Ile de France*.

In many ways, our life in London was much like a long honeymoon. I hit the books hard — immersing myself in diplomatic history, geopolitics, and the British parliamentary system — but there was also time for weekend and recess travel around the British Isles. I combined business and pleasure by doing the field research on a thesis that involved what was then regarded as an anomaly: the British Conservative party's ability to attract support from working-class voters. I saw the subject as an opportunity to pursue my own academic and practical interest in the mechanics of building a broad-based political movement.

I bought a little Austin, and we drove all over, stopping in cities and villages to conduct interviews. Many times Lou had to sit outside in the car while I went into the labor halls and clubs — territory that was off-limits to "ladies."

From the first, I made it a point to seek out young British conservatives. Those friends and acquaintances have lasted me a lifetime. A few went on to serve in Parliament, the Foreign Office, and the Civil Service. Their counsel and companionship draw me back to Britain several times a year. On a visit in the sixties, I was introduced to an extremely impressive and promising member of the House of Commons by the name of Margaret Thatcher, and from her I received one of the first letters of congratulations from a head of government after my nomination to be secretary of defense was announced.

Next to Dallas (and every other Texas city), London is my favorite city. I wouldn't say that I'm an out-and-out Anglophile, but I did develop a taste for a few things that have since typed me as such. I wear British-cut suits (although it was years before I could afford to go to a Savile Row tailor to have one made), prefer dress shirts with detachable collars, and smoke a brand of British cigarettes. Lou and I shipped the Austin back home to Wichita Falls — probably one of the first foreign cars in Texas. I wish I still had it. And there are old friends who kid me about wearing a homburg for a while after I returned.

The bomb damage from the war was still to be seen throughout London in the early 1950s; luxuries were in short supply, many of the necessities were still being rationed, and making ends meet for the average Londoner wasn't easy. The Labour party's answer had been a strong dose of socialism. The opportunity to personally experience the grim, stultifying inadequacy of the welfare state gave me abundant political insight and ammunition to use during my years in the U.S. Senate.

After Lou and our daughters were introduced, Sam Nunn then worked his way down the committee's membership roster, calling on each senator in order of seniority, alternating between the Democrats and Republicans. James Exon of Nebraska was the next to speak, followed by Strom Thurmond, Carl Levin, and William Cohen. Edward Kennedy was introduced next. Unlike Exon, who had referred to "some questions raised that must be clearly aired," Kennedy did not beat around the bush.

I too want to welcome the former chairman of our committee back to the Armed Services Committee. We did not always agree on the issues, but I respected Senator Tower as a chairman, and I look forward to working with him as Secretary of Defense.

I might add a personal word at the outset. Ordinarily, the Senate confirmation process is the major ordeal that a nominee endures.

Senator Tower also has experienced another ordeal in obtaining the nomination, and I think I speak for many Senators on both sides of the aisle in saying we deplore the unseemly treatment he has received. It was unfair, but he endured it with characteristic determination, and he deserves credit for prevailing.

I read the comments of Senators Bentsen and Kennedy as a strong indication that bipartisan support was shaping up in support of my nomination. In that first round of statements Exon was true to form: he barely touched on issues of substance. Levin, his polar opposite intellectually, sought to demonstrate a lawyer's mastery of the technical aspects of defense policy. If I had to rate their votes at the time, I would have said that Exon would go the way the wind was blowing — an aye. Levin would probably vote no to show that he had serious reservations about the new administration's approach.

Once the preliminary statements were out of the way — and since there were TV cameras and microphones present, each member could be counted on to exercise his right to be heard — Nunn asked me to begin my testimony. Because most members of the committee had had a chance to read through my written statement, I asked permission to submit it for the record and make a few additional remarks before taking questions. I won't repeat the entire presentation here, but there are three short extracts that addressed major points which should be included.

First, I set out to make it quite clear that I was not about to carry any grudges with me to the Pentagon.

I want to thank the chairman, the ranking member, other members of the committee, and the staff, for the thoroughness with which they have gone about the processing of this nomination.

I think that it is essential that, in a position of this sensitivity, thoroughness be dictated. And although I may have suffered a little discomfort from time to time, by virtue of things that appeared in the media, I think it was incumbent on this committee and on the administration to conduct a very, very thorough field investigation inquiry, and I commend you for a job well done.

Second, I needed to show my critics and potential opponents they were wrong to conclude that as defense secretary I would give the military free rein on spending.

I understand that we must live within constraints. I am not such a mindless hawk that I would come to you and ask you for a substantial increase in defense expenditure when I know that is not going to happen.

However seized of conviction I may be, I am at once a realist. And I know that we have to operate within restraints.

And you know, on reflection, Mr. Chairman, members of the committee, maybe it is good that we are compelled to go through this exercise. Perhaps it will give us the discipline that we require to do things in the executive branch that perhaps we should have done long ago, and perhaps even do things in the Congress that perhaps the Congress should have done long ago.

One of those things to which I was referring is biennial budgeting, a key recommendation of the Packard Commission. I have been advocating such a reform since before I retired from the Senate. The burden of annual budget making preoccupies the time and attention and resources of Congress to such an extent that other matters of crucial importance are crowded off the calendar entirely or given short shrift. Number crunching has become the primary legislative activity for many members of the House and Senate for months at a time.

In addition, a one-year budget cycle makes it difficult to pursue coherent long-term planning at the Defense Department. The fluctuation in spending levels can mean that this year's politically popular program winds up on the chopping block next year, wasting the money and the effort that have been expended in the interim.

Biennial budgeting would not foreclose the possibility of eliminating programs and weapons systems, but the two-year time frame allows for at least some of the anticipated benefits to trickle down the pipeline. Ideally, Congress would finish work on the budget within nine or ten months and then have more than a year to devote to other business.

I was also referring — without being overtly confrontational — to Congress's propensity to use the military budget as a political grab bag, or pork barrel. When defense spending is increasing every year, the temptation is irresistible to add a few million here to satisfy favorite special-interest groups, and a few million there to please others. Soon, as Everett Dirksen quipped, it adds up to real money. It is a luxury that we have never been able to afford, even when budget deficits were relatively modest in size. In 1983, as chairman of the Armed Services Committee, I sought to control the rate of increase in military spending while fending off those who were demanding deeper and more damaging budget cuts. Periodically, another member of the Senate or the House would try to win political points by calling for one more pound of flesh from the Pentagon. My response was to send out a letter to all senators requesting specifics on what military program or project located in their state could be eliminated from the budget. Not surprisingly, I did not get a very enthusiastic response.

The third topic that I wanted to raise at the outset of the hearings was the state of relations between the United States and the Soviet Union.

> Mr. Chairman, I think we are all encouraged by the recent progressive steps taken by General Secretary Gorbachev. We look forward to a thawing of the cool relationships between the United States and the Soviet Union.

> But we must not luxuriate in wishful thinking. The world is as it is, not as we would like it to be. And in spite of the progressive moves of Mr. Gorbachev, in spite of the very intense and, I am afraid, all too effective public diplomacy campaign of his, there is still a formidable threat that confronts the United States and the free world.

> That threat has not diminished yet through the era of perestroika and glasnost. And it is incumbent on us to maintain the strongest possible defense commensurate with the threat that confronts us.

I finished my opening remarks by acknowledging that questions had been raised about my business dealings as a private consultant. I saw no point in sitting there and waiting for someone else to bring up the issue. The facts were that I had formally ended my retainers and contracts more than two weeks before the announcement of my nomination.

As I have noted earlier, conflict of interest arises from an ongoing and continuing financial relationship. I had none when I faced the committee. To clear the books, I returned $16,667 to one of my clients, the balance of a retainer for the months of December and January.

I sent out letters submitting my resignation and firmly closed the door on a brief period in my life — roughly two and a half years out of thirty-seven years of public service, if I count my time as a teacher.

At sixty-three years of age, I was willing to take on heavy responsibilities that could, at the president's discretion and the continuation of the voters' mandate, obligate me for as many as eight years. In so doing, I was also voluntarily committing myself to forgo a demonstratively lucrative career as a defense contractor when I returned to private life. Nonetheless, I looked forward with enthusiasm to the challenge that lay before me.

Much of the work of a confirmation hearing is carried out in the question-and-answer sessions between the nominee and the members of the committee. But in my first day of the hearings — actually an afternoon session — the questions did not break any new ground. Pentagon management, the Cold War, MX, burden sharing, conventional force modernization, were some of the issues raised. Carl Levin aggressively pursued a line of questioning about a comment I had made in the early 1970s that decisions vis-à-vis defense spending must be made independently of economic and budgetary considerations. Like a prosecutor, he was looking for an inconsistency.

> SENATOR LEVIN — Today your testimony is somewhat different from that, saying that we must live and operate within fiscal constraints. I am wondering whether you could explain your change in your thought processes on that. There has been a clear shift —
>
> MR. TOWER — I am not sure my thought processes have changed, Senator. As I said earlier, I am a realist.
>
> SENATOR LEVIN — You were a realist in 1973, I think too —
>
> MR. TOWER — 1973? Well, times have changed —

SENATOR LEVIN — In 1983, I think you were a realist when
you said we should not allow economic conditions at home
to dictate defense.

MR. TOWER — Well, let me state it this way. And that is, I
believe that you must size your defense establishment to
requirements that are driven by an external threat. And that
is something over which we have very limited control, virtually no control. If you continue to simply base your
dedication of defense resources on perceptions of afforda-
bility — and ignore the threat — then I think we do so at
our peril, if I can state it in perhaps a little bit more sophisticated way than I did at the time.

The only member of the committee to adopt an openly antag-
onistic attitude toward me during the first day of the hearings was
Senator Robert Byrd of West Virginia. Byrd fancies himself a student of constitutional theory, and he chose to quarrel with a thesis
that I had expounded on, in a speech at Georgetown University in
1988, on the strained state of relations between the executive and
legislative branches. Byrd cited several excerpts from this speech,
including "The executive branch is in danger of becoming so constrained by Congress that its ability to formulate and implement a
coherent, reliable foreign policy is seriously threatened." Apparently, to Byrd, I had committed sacrilege. He entered the entire
text of the offending speech in the printed committee record.

Byrd has a tendency to resort to a flatulent indignation, which
alternately amuses and annoys his Senate colleagues:

I must say that I was somewhat astonished in reading this
statement which indicates to me that in your individual thinking, your intellectual scope of the relations between the executive and the legislative branches, especially after you served
in the Senate all these years and as chairman of this committee — a very strong chairman, a very strong advocate of whatever you believe in — that I was rather astonished to see what
I felt might be a visceral inability on your part to accommodate yourself as Secretary of Defense to what I conceive as
being a role in which we are going to have to work together
and should work together in constructive harmony.

I assured Byrd that I would not and could not be confrontational
with Congress.

Yes, I made those criticisms. I made them pointedly and emphatically, and perhaps harshly. I still intellectually believe that. Let me note that Congress is not monolithic on foreign policy issues. . . .

Congress does, from time to time, change its mind, which is very good on domestic matters, but it adds an element of uncertainty when you are trying to formulate long-term reliable foreign policy. . . .

I revere the Senate, as do you, Senator Byrd, and I served here with those great men like Senator Russell, Senator Harry Byrd, Everett Dirksen, Mike Mansfield, men that I really looked up to.

The fact is, one of the problems I have with Congress is we do not have a smaller group of people imposing some discipline on the legislative process as we did in those days. If we did, perhaps this problem would not be present.

I was not deliberately presenting an indictment of Byrd's years as Senate majority and minority leader. But it wouldn't surprise me to discover that he took the comments as a personal affront.

Much of the second day of the hearings was taken up by consideration of my business activities. Over the course of twenty months, my firm, John Tower & Associates, had seven major clients (defense industry–related) and earned just under $750,000. The committee members could see from the records I had turned over to their staff that I had completely severed my connection to the defense contractors, but Sam Nunn went ahead and focused on the "appearance of a conflict of interest":

How would you answer the question from just an ordinary member of the public who writes in and says, how can Senator Tower be objective after receiving from three quarters of a million to $1 million in fees from these defense contractors over the last two years? How can he then be objective in protecting both the national security and taxpayers' interest?

I suppose the objective of the question was to make me squirm with embarrassment. But I had nothing to be embarrassed about. My firm had been well paid for its services, which consisted mainly of information gathering, analysis, and advice, commodities that are very much in demand these days. The compensation was well within the norm of what is charged by Washington consultants and law firms. Many of them bill clients at a rate of $250 an hour. Using that figure as a benchmark and spreading our small client base out over a two-and-a-half-year period, deducting professional salaries, clerical wages, rent for office space, and overhead, the net income was entirely reasonable.

Why would I favor a former client any more than an attorney or a businessman who had left a lucrative position in a private firm to serve in Congress or the executive branch would favor his former clients? Generally, the experience has been that those who are carefully selected for high posts in government have placed duty above personal enrichment. The relatively few who have abused their positions for private gain are exceptions; they are not typical. Without a presumption of honesty and goodwill, we are reduced to forbidding government employment to anyone with the very range of professional and occupational experience that would aid them in the performance of the duties and responsibilities of government service. Nunn's reasoning seemed to be inconsistent with his letter to Bush and Dukakis setting forth the attributes he expected in a nominee. He made clear that such experience was virtually essential in meeting his criteria of qualifications for a senior defense nominee. "Nominees must have substantial experience and expertise within their proposed areas of responsibility" was the standard set forth in the letter, which went on to assert with finality, "There is no time for on-the-job training in the DoD."

There is immense hypocrisy involved when any member pontificates on the earning and professional pursuits of former senators and representatives. Few of them have any intention of returning home, like the late senator George Aiken did, to pick up where he left off with his wildflower nursery and farm in Vermont. Most former members of the House and Senate settle permanently in Washington, and they are so numerous these days they could form a subchapter of the District of Columbia Bar Association.

Is there one standard for lawyers and another for the rest of us? In my response to Sam Nunn, I tried to note that the appearance of a conflict of interest could also reflect negatively on Congress:

> As you pointed out, we are going to have people there [at the Pentagon] who have been associated with the defense industry, just like Members of Congress are suspect from time

to time on the part of the public because of various financial contributions that are made to political campaigns.

I can remember that from my own experience in getting angry mail from some people saying, "We know who you received campaign contributions from, and you are unduly influenced by them." I don't believe that's true.

I was seeking to caution the members of the Armed Services Committee that they could go only so far on the conflict-of-interest issue before they bumped into their own appearance problems. Those who were making the most of the issue failed to get the message. They kept returning to the issue throughout the rest of the day, but by late afternoon it seemed that their momentum was spent. Nunn noted that I planned to spend the weekend in Munich, West Germany, at the annual Wehrkunde defense conference, where I intended to present a major position paper, the first such statement of the Bush administration:

> CHAIRMAN NUNN — Express my greetings to many of our mutual friends. I know it will be a meaningful conference, because it is a time when an awful lot of things are happening and a lot of —
>
> MR. TOWER — It should be very interesting.
>
> CHAIRMAN NUNN — . . . so have a good weekend, and we will be back on Tuesday with outside witnesses.
>
> At that time, we will hear from Mr. Paul Weyrich, National Chairman, Coalition for America.

SIX

A MAN
OF SOME DISCIPLINE

THE OFFICIAL RECORD of the Senate Armed Services Committee hearings on my nomination to be secretary of defense runs to 553 pages. It's a hefty paperback book in a pale green cover, but not one that I would recommend for light bedtime reading. The plot never seems to thicken. The personalities and texture are lost under the weight of all the verbiage.

The made-for-TV version is far more revealing. The videotapes come closer to capturing what was actually happening in the hearing room. On the page, the exchanges between the members of the committee and myself seem somewhat more contentious than they were in reality. I am, perhaps, not the best judge of what was happening during that initial two-day period. But just before Sam Nunn rapped his gavel to adjourn the meeting for the weekend, a *Time* magazine correspondent slipped a note to Ben Schemmer of the *Armed Forces Journal* that said, "Tower has the committee in full retreat."

A bit of hyperbole, but it was reassuring. Although I had sparred with a few individual members of the committee, they did not appear to be interested in doing serious damage to my confirmation prospects. Even Nunn, after harping about the appearance of a conflict of interest, conceded that impropriety on my part was not the issue. He said, "I know you, and I know you to be an honest person."

The tone of the hearings prompted *Washington Post* columnist Mary McGrory to comment, a trifle sarcastically, that I had undergone "a miraculous personality change" and had been found to be "something of a saint and surely a martyr" by my former colleagues. McGrory continued in the same vein:

> Albert Gore (D-Tenn.) observed wistfully that he had not had the "opportunity" to serve with Tower when he was chairman of the committee, and predicted, with monumental inaccuracy, that "there will be tough questions."
>
> "Who better," asked Trent Lott (R-Miss.), "to keep an eye on the foxes than the fox?"
>
> Senators are notoriously soft on former fraternity brothers who come before them for confirmation for higher office and, against Tower, who was, additionally, a former chairman, they had no defenses whatever. When the question of conflict of interest arose, they apologized for bringing the matter up, and Chairman Nunn ventured the thought that the danger might be not that Tower would tilt toward his erstwhile clients, but that he would lean over backwards to avoid the appearance of evil.

I would never classify Mary McGrory as a sympathetic journalist, and that is precisely why her column strikes me as being valuable supporting evidence as to the temperature and tenor of the hearings:

> There was never any question about Tower's ability. He was manifestly the smartest man in the room at his hearings, and by far the toughest.
>
> There was also no question about his confirmation. The senators fell all over him as if he were already installed in the Pentagon and they were defense contractors, anxious to ingratiate themselves. With the flap over the congressional pay raise and continuing revelations about the fat fees they rake in themselves for spending time with corporations, they are not in a majestic position on the conflict-of-interest issue.

After those two days of hearings, I felt that I had succeeded in neutralizing the conflict-of-interest issue and pushing the false allegations about my private life into the background. The lead story in the *New York Times* on January 27 gave only three paragraphs out of twenty-five to my work as a consultant (and those were at the bottom of the story), emphasizing instead a comment I had made about the Strategic Defense Initiative to the effect that I believed it would be impossible to devise an umbrella that could protect the entire American population from nuclear incineration. It was hardly an earthshaking comment and certainly not front-page news.

As a candidate, George Bush had taken a position on SDI that was generally more modest and realistic than the grandiose vision of a nuclear umbrella offered to the American people by Ronald Reagan. I was also on record as advocating a more realistic approach to SDI. At the 1988 Republican platform hearings, I urged the hard-liners to pursue what was feasible from a technological and political standpoint rather than insisting on a defensive system that posited complete invulnerability as its central feature.

This heretical notion — heretical to many of the far-right fringe groups that made Washington their New Jerusalem during the Reagan years — put me at odds with a small number of individuals who, while allied to the Republican party, are quick to attempt to demonize and destroy those who don't totally subscribe to their views on litmus test issues.

SDI was one such issue; another was abortion. I believe that Paul Weyrich's testimony on January 31 was prompted largely by my position on the latter of those two subjects, and not by his "serious reservations about [my] moral character."

Richard Billmire warned me about Weyrich. Rhett Dawson and Jim McGovern were also concerned when they learned that the Armed Services Committee was scheduled to hear testimony from him and a few other individuals who portrayed themselves as leaders and representatives of legitimate groups.

Billmire has impeccable conservative credentials. As an economist and political consultant, he stays in close touch with that side of the political spectrum. Richard knows, in my opinion, how to distinguish between real conservatives and the counterfeit variety. Some of them in the mail order fund-raising business, dependent upon remaining highly visible, frequently pursue agendas that are inimical to a philosophy based on the principle that individual freedom is of paramount importance. These people, who exploit deeply held convictions for financial gain, proclaiming themselves to be the New Right, give the right a bad name. Their objective is to impose and enforce a set of social and ideological values on the rest of us. Anyone with the temerity to resist is branded as immoral.

My pro-choice position on abortion has subjected me to criticism and, in some cases, vilification. At the Texas Republican state party convention in 1978, anti-abortion demonstrators were out in full force. There were signs and shouts of "Baby murderer!" when I appeared at one point.

I have refused to be shouted down on this issue, just as I refused to be silent on McCarthyism. Hysterical, anti-communist witch-hunting did great harm to innocent individuals. It hurt the Republican party and the conservative cause.

We must not allow extremists of the left or the right to hijack our political process. Compromise and conciliation drive American democracy. But I am afraid that Sam Nunn allowed the extremists to get behind the wheel of the Armed Services Committee and to take the Senate on a wild, destructive ride.

Paul Weyrich was the designated hit-and-run driver. Nunn and his staff knew that Weyrich would oppose my confirmation. The word around the conservative community was that at a meeting of the more extreme representatives of the New Right, convened to discuss what they perceived as their lack of influence on the president-elect and the impact it was having on their fund-raising prospects, Weyrich had vowed to bring down a Bush cabinet designee. As national chairman of the Coalition for America, a catchall organization that purports to represent several conservative groups, Weyrich needs high public visibility in order to raise funds to sustain his operation. Therefore, boasts about bringing down cabinet designees should be seen in the context of self-promotion and hype. Such braggadocio was intended to shake the green leaves off the money tree.

Thus we see a mixture of volatile ingredients: Sam Nunn's political ambitions; Paul Weyrich's need to demonstrate clout; the New Right's zealous enmity toward opponents.

My associates and I briefly considered whether it would be advisable and possible to head off Weyrich by objecting to his inclusion as a witness. In no way could he be considered a genuine representative of the conservative movement. But Senate committees have wide latitude in selecting witnesses. Generally, the leaders of groups with an appropriate interest and level of expertise who seek to offer their views on presidential nominees are given the opportunity to be heard.

Several prominent conservatives were ready to testify on my behalf, but I was anxious to avoid needlessly prolonging the hearings. In addition, I did not believe that Weyrich's testimony would have a detrimental effect on my chances. On the contrary; just as it is possible to judge someone by his friends, it is equally valid to judge him by his adversaries. As I saw it, being opposed by the likes of Paul Weyrich was the equivalent of receiving the *Good Housekeeping* Seal of Approval.

In his opening statement on January 31, at a public session I did not attend, Weyrich told the Armed Services Committee that he had "grave doubts" about my suitability to serve as secretary of defense, doubts that stemmed, he said, from my "moral character." He continued:

> The old saying that "Where there is smoke, there is fire" must give one pause in this case. The smoke surrounding the nominee's personal life seems rather intense. I have made enough personal observations of this man, here in Washington, to have serious reservations about his moral character.
>
> By the way, I might add that were he nominated for some other position in this administration, that is, like Secretary of Transportation, I would not be here. But I think the Defense Department is a different situation.

The witness capped this detour into the thicket of conditional morality with the assertion that "the transition team of the new administration received hundreds of letters opposing [the nomination] . . . and some of them contain specific allegations of moral impropriety on the part of Mr. Tower, impropriety which, in the view of those writing the letters, makes him unfit for this high position."

If Weyrich and his friends had been sending "hundreds" of missives of that sort to the Bush transition offices, they must have been mailed to the wrong address. A subsequent search of the incoming correspondence turned up a handful of letters from cranks, and a few of the allegations were turned over to the FBI for investigation, but no substantiation was found.

It was all hearsay. Unfortunately, Sam Nunn was in the mood

to take it at face value. Personal allegations about nominees are generally heard in closed sessions and not aired in public testimony before a Senate committee. And they certainly weren't when I was chairman. Yet Nunn saw the advance text of Weyrich's remarks and allowed him to proceed.

Later, under questioning, Nunn invited the witness to elaborate:

> CHAIRMAN NUNN — During the last several weeks we have had a surplus of rumors concerning the nominee, and a shortage of witnesses with personal testimony and personal knowledge. You state here you do have personal knowledge of, I assume, defects in personal behavior, is that correct?
>
> MR. WEYRICH — Well, Mr. Chairman, I do not frequent the social activities of Washington. In fact, I avoid them because I find it is good for family life. And so, if I encounter somebody then my presumption has to be that probably there is a problem because, first of all, I do not seek such information on anybody, and, second, I do not go to enough activities that I would be inclined to encounter somebody who was occasionally having a problem.
>
> And, over the course of many years, I have encountered the nominee in a condition — lack of sobriety — as well as with women to whom he was not married.

Weyrich went on to add that since he had spent eleven years as a Senate employee, he could recognize my wife — a statement that astounded Lou, who had never before laid eyes on the man. At that point, Nunn decided that the committee should hear the rest of Weyrich's testimony in closed session, anticipating the objections he was about to hear from the Republican side, and (John Warner, as usual, being painfully slow on the uptake) they came first from Malcolm Wallop:

> I guess I have as much of a heavy heart as you . . . profess to have after having heard your testimony this morning, especially that dealing with intimations of moral misconduct, turpitude, because it was possible, I think, to give those in detail in an executive session of this committee.
>
> The cameras are on. The innuendos have been made, the insinuations are on the table. Whatever comes out this afternoon will not be heard, and I personally find that troublesome.

And he bore down on Weyrich's suggestion that the fees my firm earned for consulting work with defense contractors constituted a bribe paid for services I had rendered as a senator, or services I would render as defense secretary. Senator Wallop noted that former defense secretaries Harold Brown and Caspar Weinberger had entered the private sector after public service, adding:

> I think it is important to point out . . . Mr. Carlucci's first press statement saying he was leaving was that he was going to the boards of some ten companies. Did anybody suggest to him that that was payment for what he did as Secretary of Defense?
>
> And yet, we have heard here intimations that what Senator Tower did by going to the private sector was in fact perhaps a payment for what he had done or what he might do. Presumably, somebody knew that Mr. Bush was going to be elected and that [Senator Tower] was going to be nominated and would come back.
>
> Now, I just have to declare my lack of comfort with things so vague as that while television cameras are on, and while no standing proof, no name, has been attached to any of the charges of innuendo or of moral turpitude. You may have them and you may provide them this afternoon. I do not know. I will wait to see.
>
> But I am very uncomfortable about choosing the open session to provide the intimations and then letting us be the judge of whatever may happen in the closed session.

Senator Wallop went on to challenge comments made by another witness, William E. Jackson, Jr., an assistant professor at the University of Alabama:

> I think it is unfair. Lord knows, I am a friend of Senator Tower's, have been for a long time. I have traveled with him to the Soviet Union, I have seen him in Geneva. I have traveled with him to Germany and France. I have traveled with him in Texas, I have traveled with him to Pascagoula.
>
> I have not been with him all of his adult life or all of his life around here. But I have not seen these kinds of things. . . .
>
> There is something really wrong in the country, it is my belief, when experience and knowledge and competence is viewed as a disqualifying factor and that inexperience or lack

of experience is viewed as somehow or another a guarantor of moral success.

A few minutes later, James Exon conceded that 90 percent of the accusations leveled at me was "pure garbage." In closed session that afternoon, the witnesses who had impugned my character before the TV cameras were asked to corroborate their allegations with specific details and instances of impropriety. All they provided was a regurgitation of that initial round of hearsay, innuendo, guesswork, and personal opinion.

After the closed session, several members of the committee told me that Weyrich's and Jackson's testimony lacked merit. Senator John McCain had asked Weyrich to be specific. What was Tower doing that seemed improper? He was "coming on" to a young woman, Weyrich said. "What do you mean by 'coming on'?" McCain demanded. The best that he could do was to say that I had held the woman's hand. McCain was flabbergasted: "You mean holding somebody's hand is immoral behavior?"

Repeatedly, Weyrich had been pressed to say when and under what circumstances he had seen me demonstrating a "lack of sobriety." After Weyrich assured the committee that he was a family man and did not travel in the same social circles that I had, the validity of his observations about my conduct were highly suspect. Ultimately, his answers did not go beyond the generalities that he had presented in his public testimony. Jackson was equally vague and, as it turned out, was forced to withdraw a claim he made in open session to the effect that he had a source in Geneva who could verify my supposedly improper behavior.

The best that I can say about the two men is that they have a right to their opinions about me. But the point of the confirmation process is to examine and evaluate a nominee's qualifications for high office, not to substitute the opinions of Paul Weyrich or William Jackson — individuals who are unknown to all but a tiny minority of Americans — for the opinion and judgment of the president. I think most members of the committee agreed with my assessment. Nonetheless, the charges were fodder for the news media, and the story was that much easier to tell because the complicated part — the rebuttal and demolition of the charges — happened out of camera range, behind the closed doors of the hearing room.

*   *   *

Rhett Dawson, Richard Billmire, Dan Howard, and I watched the
TV news shows on the set in my Pentagon office. Dan had been
appointed assistant secretary of defense for public affairs during
the Reagan administration, and he was helping us deal with the
press during the confirmation. We discussed reconsidering the
original decision to forgo the opportunity to call friendly conservative witnesses. There was no doubt that the Heritage Foundation
and the American Enterprise Institute would be more than willing
to send their top officers before the committee. But here again, I
felt that Weyrich's statements were so flimsy and so transparently
self-serving that they would be written off by the members of the
committee and the full Senate. And after the committee met in
closed session, I was told by Republicans and Democrats that
Weyrich and Jackson had wasted their time with charges that could
not be substantiated.

Billmire contacted several prominent conservatives, urging them
to talk to the press and explain that Weyrich was not speaking for
the conservative community. Persuading the TV networks to put
Weyrich into perspective was a lost cause, but we were able to
make headway with a few newspapers. The Wednesday morning,
February 1, edition of the *Washington Times* reported, "Even after
the closed hearing, Tower's approval seemed sure."

After taking Mr. Weyrich behind closed doors to hear more,
members of the Senate Armed Services Committee emerged
unimpressed and today are expected to unanimously approve
Mr. Tower's nomination to head the Pentagon.

"I heard nothing you didn't hear in the open session. I
didn't hear anything persuasive to me," said Sen. Malcolm
Wallop, Wyoming Republican, who earlier had complained
about "innuendos . . . and insinuations" against the former
Texas Senator.

"Beyond statements of seeing Senator Tower on a couple
of occasions carrying a little more alcohol than he should
have, he hasn't been able to add anything specific that wasn't
hearsay," agreed Sen. Pete Wilson, California Republican.

Sen. Alan Dixon, Illinois Democrat, added: "As an old trial
lawyer, I would say that most of what I heard has to fall into
the hearsay category, even given the high motives of the witness."

The *Washington Times* also focused on comments gathered from conservative spokesmen:

> David Keene, chairman of the American Conservative Union, complained that Mr. Weyrich testified as spokesman for the Coalition for America. . . . "We are listed as members of the Coalition, but he overstepped his bounds in giving the impression he represents our viewpoint," Mr. Keene said.
>
> Brent Bozelle, executive director of the Conservative Victory Committee, said: "Anyone who believes that [he] is speaking for the sentiment of the conservative community is mistaken. He's speaking for Paul Weyrich. We issued a press statement today endorsing Tower. My goodness, if we are going to judge a man by those standards, there are plenty of people on Capitol Hill that we have chosen to overlook."
>
> Phillip Truluck, executive vice president of the Heritage Foundation, said: ". . . We don't have any problem with John Tower."

Our efforts at damage control seemed adequate, and on February 2 the *Washington Times* and other newspapers were also carrying my first public comment on Weyrich's smear. The previous day I had testified before a closed session of the Armed Services Committee in committee chambers, mostly concerning my activities as a private consultant. Afterward, the hearings resumed in the Senate caucus room, with the press and the public in attendance. After a few preliminary questions on conflict of interest, Senator Nunn referred to Weyrich and Jackson's allegations and raised the subject of alcohol and its abuse:

> CHAIRMAN NUNN — Senator Tower, there were allegations made in public session yesterday. You may have read the news clippings and may have even observed some of the proceedings. I would like you to tell this committee and the American people your own attitude toward the consumption of alcohol if you are confirmed as Secretary of Defense, while you are Secretary of Defense.
>
> MR. TOWER — I think that it is essential that the Secretary of Defense be at all times capable of exercising the duties and responsibilities of his office. . . . And therefore I think that there should be zero tolerance of anyone as Secretary

of Defense or in any other sensitive job in the Defense Department who has an alcohol problem.

CHAIRMAN NUNN — You have assured us privately, and I would hope you would also give us in public your own view toward alcohol and whether you yourself have any alcohol problem?

MR. TOWER — I have none, Senator. I am a man of some discipline.

I have been told that that comment was a mistake. Perhaps it was. The *Washington Post* described my choice of words as a "cocky denial." I did not intend to sound smug or arrogantly dismissive. At the time, the comment seemed appropriate, and in fact it was accurate. I gave up scotch in the mid-1970s. I don't miss it. Even the smell of it bothers me these days.

The moment of truth that I can identify as having convinced me of the need to go easier on my consumption of alcohol occurred when Lilla, my second wife, told me flatly one day that it was time to make a choice — her or Johnnie Walker Black. When I put it in those terms, it sounds more dramatic than it really was. My drinking throughout the sixties and early seventies had probably been on a gradual upward trend. Lilla is a lawyer, and she fancied herself an expert on medicine because of a few malpractice suits that she had handled. She was always second-guessing her doctors, and she got the idea that if I kept drinking I'd destroy the neurons in my brain or some such thing.

Lilla didn't get any argument from me. I knew that excessive consumption of alcohol can lead to physical dependence, and I wasn't about to let that happen. It was time to cut back. I'm not a procrastinator; I make a decision and I follow through on it. From that point on, my drinking was primarily limited to wine.

Alcohol abuse is an occupational hazard for a politician. A senator's workday does not end at five o'clock. It continues well into the evening hours with social events, where, with few exceptions, wine and spirits are served.

If I had been going home to suburban Bethesda each night to Lou and the girls, drinking wouldn't have been an issue. But in the first ten years that I was in Washington, Lou and I had a live-in housekeeper to look after our daughters, who otherwise would have been left alone most nights because of my demanding schedule. Sadly, it was not a normal family life. Penny claims that she and her sisters learned how to be independent and how to cook as a result of our absence. She is a good sport, but I suspect it wasn't much fun for the girls to be on their own that much. It probably helps explain why the three of them prefer Texas to Washington. When we were back home, I spent more time with them around the house in Wichita Falls. Even then, though, I tended to be preoccupied with Senate and political business. The kids learned to cope with that by coming over to me, putting their hands on my cheeks, and saying, "Daddy, are you tuned in to what I'm saying?"

Probably every politician has a few least-favorite photographs. One of mine was snapped as I left Love Field, in Dallas, one day just as I put a cigarette between my lips; I got a letter from my mother on that one with a long lecture about the evils of tobacco. She is also a teetotaler, as was my father, who would admit to having had alcohol only once, when he was in the Navy in 1919. Dad spent a few days campaigning with me in 1966 as I ran for reelection the first time. I banned alcohol from the bus that was taking us around East Texas, and there was much grumbling about it from the hard-drinking press corps. One reporter commented acidly, "It's nice to know that God is on John Tower's side, but I'd just as soon not have God on the bus."

I am not a solitary drinker. Sneaking off to a hideaway office in the Capitol and belting back a few drinks, as a few senators routinely do, is not my style. There was a wet bar in the office, but I preferred to have drinks with friends over dinner.

If there was ever a time that I did noticeably demonstrate a "lack of sobriety," it was one evening at the Monocle restaurant, about two blocks north of the Capitol, where many senators and their aides have lunch or dinner when the Senate is in session. It was summertime, our families were out of town on vacation, and Hubert Humphrey and I got to the Monocle at about the same time. He invited me to join him at his table; we started talking and swapping stories as Connie Valanos, the restaurant's owner, kept our glasses filled.

We had just come in from a Senate floor fight — of course, the two of us had been on opposing sides of the issue. Anybody who knew Hubert Humphrey can testify that he loved to talk politics, and so you can imagine that we were at it for a long time. Despite Humphrey's liberalism, he was on the best of terms with his conservative colleagues in the Senate. He once got us laughing by telling Barry Goldwater, "You're so handsome, Barry, you ought to be in the movies." Hubert paused for effect and added, "Yes sir, the movies — Nineteenth Century Fox."

Washington does not have a professional baseball team, but it is a big-league city when it comes to gossiping. A few glasses on a senator's table are soon exaggerated into out-and-out inebriation. It is one reason that politicians are so jumpy about what they do in public. The halo has got to be in place at all times.

As far as I am concerned, the job of being a senator is hard enough without having to pretend that you are a saint. I frequently dined at the Monocle, and many times there was one or more female staff members with me. Automatically, to the gossips, this translates as "booze and broads."

Unlike Sam Nunn, who has a reputation for being distant and disdainful toward his staff, I treated my aides with friendship and respect. In return, I got tremendous loyalty and extended effort. It was not at all unusual to punctuate a long, stressful day with a break at the Monocle.

My daughter Penny, in exasperation during the confirmation fight, told a television interviewer that she felt like wearing a sign reading "I'm his daughter!" whenever we were out together in Washington. And I probably should have put a sign over that table in the Monocle — "She's a professional Senate staffer!"

There is a double standard that I refused to buy into when I was in the Senate. Two men can have a working lunch; a man and a woman, in the same circumstances, are presumed to be having a romance. The lesson is clear: to be safe, a politician must not be seen in public with "women to whom he is not married." The professional exchanges that are important elements in effectively doing a job and advancing a career are thereby denied to women. The men and the women on my staff got equal treatment and equal opportunities. The Senate was my life, and just as I shared that life with the men on my staff — the travel, the long hours, the seemingly endless meetings — I shared it with the professional women. When I hired someone, I knew that I would end up working closely with that individual, and I never said to myself that it would look better if I gave the job to a man. To silence the gossipmongers, I could have surrounded myself exclusively with men, and many senators have done that. Until recently, most of the top Senate staff jobs went to men. I broke precedent by hiring Carolyn

Bacon to be my administrative assistant (the person who runs a Senate office). Carolyn was at the time the only female administrative assistant in the Senate. Until that point women did most of the hard labor in a Senate office — scheduling, research, the all-important constituent casework — but the men were given the impressive titles, along with the salaries that went with them.

I also integrated the Senate old boy's club by hiring women to be my legislative assistants. I put Nola Smith in charge of my reelection campaign in 1972, and that made history because no woman had ever managed a U.S. senator's campaign before.

During the confirmation process, I tried to keep from getting angry at what was being said. I could handle the allegations about the drinking, but the claims of womanizing were disturbing since they demeaned every woman that I had worked with, and that really made me angry. Sam Nunn broached the subject in the next question that he asked after inquiring whether I had an alcohol problem:

> CHAIRMAN NUNN — I would like to ask you a question about your attitude as Secretary of Defense toward the treatment of women in the military, and particularly whether you would tolerate any sexual harassment or any abuse of power regarding women and whether you would stand for equal treatment of women in the military?
>
> MR. TOWER — I will answer again with the term zero tolerance for discrimination against women, for sexual harassment of women.
>
> I believe that professional women should be afforded the respect and the deference that they deserve. I believe they should be given equal opportunities for advancement. I will say that I do not believe that women should serve in combat slots, but I believe, in every noncombatant position that is open to women in the service, that they [must] be treated equally with men.

I have thought long and hard about the womanizing issue. Although I have been married and divorced twice, that's not unusual these days. What is unusual, though, is that I *like* women. Some men don't. They'd prefer to be out with the "guys." But I enjoy the company of women, and what has apparently intrigued the Washington gossips is that I am willing to actually be friends with women, and to conduct the friendship in public.

What does not occur to the Paul Weyrichs of the world is that not only could the woman they see me with be a member of my staff, she might well be an important Texas political ally. My home state has a long tradition of political involvement by women. Anne Armstrong, former ambassador to Great Britain, and former congresswoman Barbara Jordan are two examples drawn from opposite sides of the political spectrum. Texas women have made sure that politics isn't exclusively a male prerogative.

Another factor is that I have three beautiful daughters. Rose Narva, the former manager of the Jefferson Hotel, where I stayed during the confirmation proceedings, told me that one night she was being badgered by a reporter who wanted tidbits about my personal life. Rose assured the man that I was behaving myself. As she spoke, I emerged from the hotel's dining room arm in arm with Marian and Penny. "Look at that," the man proclaimed in triumph.

"For God's sake . . . they're his daughters," Rose snapped back at him.

The residents of every capital city, from Austin to Albany to Washington, D.C., tend toward cynicism. This cynicism is the dark shadow of ambition. Those who congregate near the seats of government, be they politicians or pundits, seek to share the power that is centered there. But like an ocean wave, power is all substance and no form. There is motion and movement, sound and force; in the end, it seems to be all salt spray, foam, and nothing. The wave looks as if it has had no effect on the shoreline, just as the day-to-day ebb and flow of power in Washington appears to have little consequence. Limousines come and go, gavels rap for order, memos are exchanged. Yet those are all trappings of power — form without substance. The ambitious soon begin to wonder if they are not wasting their lives in pursuit of such ephemera. They comfort themselves with a blanket of cynicism.

Tennyson advised his readers to "cleave ever to the sunnier side of doubt." But the cynic is trapped in his own shadow, and to break out — to reclaim a semblance of equilibrium — he mocks the world in which he lives, a world peopled by poseurs and posturers, in which nearly everything and everyone is corrupt, or corruptible.

These outbursts seem to sweep over Washington with more frequency now than they did in the past. The cycles of satisfaction and frustration have increasingly shorter duration, and the effects are more destructive. Why does one generation tolerate, even lionize, someone like Jimmy Walker, the celebrated New York mayor whose nightlife seemed to have more resonance and significance than his political accomplishments, or ignore the long-running sexual relationship between Franklin Roosevelt and his secretary, while another generation professes to be shocked when a former U.S. senator is seen in a hotel lobby with his daughters?

The cynicism that I refer to is certainly a by-product of disillusionment, and I would say that the early 1960s was the age of unparalleled "illusionment" for Washington and many Americans. In his book *Mafia Kingfish*, John H. Davis addresses this phenomenon:

> A considerable body of myth has sprung up about the character and style of the Kennedy administration. It was the historian and admirer of the Kennedys, Theodore White, who first invoked the Camelot image in an article he wrote for *Life* magazine in 1964. He quoted Jacqueline Kennedy's wistful characterization of the Kennedy White House as having resembled the mythic palace, court and realm of King Arthur and his knights known as Camelot. The analogy gave rise in the public consciousness to the notion that under Kennedy the White House had been a seat of unparalleled splendor, sweetness and light.

The Kennedy White House was indeed glamorous. When I arrived in 1961, Washington was captivated by the man and his family. Even the Bay of Pigs fiasco, "the worst disaster of that disaster-filled period," in the words of Kennedy's biographer and speechwriter Theodore C. Sorenson, could not dent the president's popularity. An invasion force of fourteen hundred Cuban exiles, recruited, trained, armed, transported, and directed by the CIA, was left on the beach without air support or naval cover, to be killed, wounded, and captured in less than three days. JFK's ratings in the public opinion polls leapt to record highs after he acknowledged that "victory has a hundred fathers and defeat is an orphan." The president said, "I am the responsible officer of government and that is quite obvious." Sorenson recalled that while Kennedy was willing to accept blame, he felt that others merited a fair share of it as well:

As we walked that Thursday morning, he told me, at times in caustic tones, of some of the other fathers of this defeat who had let him down. By taking full blame upon himself, he was winning the admiration of both career [civil] servants and the public, avoiding partisan investigations and attacks, and discouraging further attempts by those involved to leak their versions and accusations.

Kennedy's political instincts were at odds with his carefully nurtured image. John Davis further examines these anomalies:

His inner circle — the Arthurian Knights — perpetrated a nasty secret war against Cuba, the violent overthrow of the Diem family in Vietnam, and an often vengeful campaign of questionable tactics aimed against the mob and their pawns in organized labor. And although John and Robert Kennedy possessed extraordinary leadership qualities and a high degree of political responsibility, there was a secretive, reckless side to both brothers' private and public lives that bore little resemblance to the chivalric spirit of the legendary Camelot.

The President had a propensity to enter into *liaisons dangeureuses* that, in retrospect, were so dangerous as to strain credulity. His most reckless extramarital adventures were with the starlet Judith Campbell, who was also a Chicago Mafia boss's girlfriend, and with the actress Marilyn Monroe. The attorney general proved equally reckless in entering into a relationship himself with Marilyn Monroe, at a time when agents of Jimmy Hoffa were keeping the actress under close electronic surveillance.

I first learned of John F. Kennedy's relationship with Judith Campbell in 1975, when I was vice chairman of the Church Committee — officially called the Select Committee to Study Government Operations with Respect to Intelligence Activities. Senate Republican leader Hugh Scott asked me to take the assignment and act as "damage control officer" on the committee. Vietnam, Watergate, news reports about "black bag jobs" and wiretapping, and other allegations of improper activity by the FBI and CIA had inspired the Senate's liberals to launch a crusade against the U.S. intelligence community. Frank Church, the new committee's chairman, also had his sights set on the White House. In many ways it was an extension of the Watergate hearings — for better and for worse. Sam Ervin and his people moved out of an old Senate auditorium that had been converted into office space, and we moved in.

It would have been preferable to have had a breathing spell instead of going from one supercharged set of hearings to another. Scott and I saw the need for a thorough investigation and the enactment of appropriate reforms, but we were concerned that the barn burners would destroy the edifice to drive out the rats.

It was not an enviable assignment, and at least one member of my Senate staff advised that I decline. I was less than three years away from a reelection campaign — one that proved to be the most difficult of my career. I already had a full plate as chairman of the Republican Policy Committee and as ranking member of the Committee on Banking, Housing, and Urban Affairs. A potentially bitter, high-profile investigation of U.S. intelligence activities could strain our resources and possibly put me on the wrong side of an issue that would come up during the campaign. I was already tagged in the news media as a Nixon diehard, and it wouldn't require much literary license to distort even the most innocent of comments about the need to be cautious and prudent in our investigation into some sort of blanket endorsement of Big Brother and unbridled government snooping.

In the end, I decided that I did not have any choice in the matter. I am a team player. Scott wanted me on the committee, and as a senior member of Armed Services, which until then had held jurisdiction over the CIA and military intelligence, I felt it was my duty to serve. As it turned out, the hearings helped put me on the map, so to speak, as a major Senate player. Until that point the press had periodically written about the "great unrealized potential of John Tower."

I had good backup from Barry Goldwater and Howard Baker. Barry did not mind being a lightning rod, and Howard had earned a surplus of credibility as ranking Republican on the Ervin Committee. He had challenged Scott for the leader's post in 1972, and we kidded Baker about how Hugh was getting revenge by handing him two back-to-back dirty jobs.

We did succeed in controlling some of the damage; however, the repercussions of the Church Committee's misguided zeal are still being felt today. The committee's inquiries severely shook the confidence of allies who had cooperated with us in intelligence-gathering activities and caused many of them to reassess their relationship with the U.S. intelligence community. They feared that the precedent of allowing congressional investigations of the CIA would lead to the exposure of their own intelligence sources and methods. In private conversations with officials of friendly intelligence agencies, I have been told that the Church Committee raised doubts about the wisdom of cooperating with the United States in the future. Such concerns have also adversely affected our cooperation with countries that for political reasons take a publicly hostile attitude toward the United States but that privately cooperate with us on some matters of mutual interest. They were alarmed at the prospect that the publicity generated by congressional investigations would expose what was essentially a private relationship and lead to unfavorable domestic political consequences for them. It is such a sensitive area that to this day I've got to be extremely circumspect about what I write. Morale was shattered, dedicated intelligence professionals felt betrayed, and there were many resignations from the CIA and other agencies.

From the beginning, it seemed that Frank Church thought that alleged improper and illegal intelligence-gathering activity began with Richard Nixon. The Democratic committee staff spent a lot of time investigating the Huston plan, a lengthy memorandum prepared by a Nixon White House aide that proposed a unified, government-wide approach to intelligence gathering. They also focused on the United States' role in the downfall of Salvador Allende, in Chile. Both were legitimate subjects for inquiry. Church was fascinated by Cuba, a subject that he probably considered sufficiently remote historically as to be relatively safe from a political standpoint. But, in the process, he bumped into the aforementioned Judith Campbell.

A coincidence first alerted the committee staff to a possible link between Campbell, organized-crime figures, and John F. Kennedy. A routine check of the White House visitors' logs indicated that she had been there frequently around the same time that we suspected assassination plots against Fidel Castro were taking shape. A committee investigator checked with JFK's former secretary, Evelyn Lincoln, who told him that Campbell was a "campaign worker."

It was decided that the best course of action would be to try to contact the woman. At the same time, an effort was under way to reach another individual who was suspected of being involved with the Mafia. The staff was sharing close quarters in the old auditorium in the Dirksen Building, so that when the same lawyer responded to our inquiries on the same day on behalf of both Campbell and the person with possible ties to the mob, the bells started to ring.

Under the committee's rules, a subpoena could be obtained only if both the chairman and the vice chairman signed off on it. The one exception was if either was out of town; then only one signature was necessary. Frank Church, it turned out, was back in Idaho, and I authorized the subpoena. Campbell was interviewed by the committee's staff on a Saturday morning. Majority counsel F.A.O. "Fritz" Schwarz conducted the questioning. It had been agreed in advance that if Campbell's relationship with the president proved to be purely personal, then the matter would be pursued no further.

Campbell acknowledged being "friends" with President Kennedy, as well as with Mafia kingpin Sam Giancana and another organized-crime figure, John Roselli. Both Giancana and Roselli were involved with CIA attempts to assassinate Castro. It was obvious that a euphemism was being used and equally obvious how it translated. Schwarz apparently was satisfied that the relationship was a personal one, and therefore he concluded the interrogation. But my chief staffer, Curt Smothers, was far from satisfied. He felt we should explore the possibility that Campbell's relationship with the president also included the role of liaison between the White House and the mobsters. He believed it was a major piece of the puzzle that would help explain both how the nation's intelligence apparatus had been misused and the extent to which it had been corrupted by involving it with gangsters who were able to get access to the White House through the president's "friend."

Smothers, however, was overruled. The members of the Church Committee had no stomach for dredging up the martyred president's indiscretions. The line of inquiry was terminated, and all eleven of us voted not to disclose Campbell's name or sex. Fifteen years later, the carefully worded report dealing with the episode is still startling:

As elaborated in the previous sections of this report, all living CIA officials who were involved in the underworld assassination attempt [on Castro] or who were in a position to have known of the attempt have testified that they never discussed the assassination plot with the President. By May 1961, however, the Attorney General and [FBI Director J. Edgar] Hoover were aware that the CIA had earlier used Giancana in an operation against Cuba and FBI files contained two memoranda which, if simultaneously reviewed, would have led one to conclude that the CIA operation had involved assassination. There is no evidence that anyone within the FBI concluded that the CIA had used Giancana in an assassination attempt. The Committee has uncovered a chain of events, however, which would have given Hoover an opportunity to have assembled the entire picture and to have reported the information to the President.

Evidence before the Committee indicates that a close friend of President Kennedy had frequent contact with the President from the end of 1960 through mid-1962. FBI reports and testimony indicate that the president's friend was also a close friend of John Roselli and Sam Giancana and saw them often during this same period.

On February 27, 1962, Hoover sent identical copies of a memorandum to the Attorney General and Kenneth O'Donnell, Special Assistant to the President. The memorandum stated that information developed in connection with concentrated FBI investigation of John Roselli revealed that Roselli had been in contact with the president's friend. The memorandum also reported that the individual was maintaining an association with Sam Giancana, described as a "prominent Chicago underworld figure." Hoover's memorandum also stated that a review of the telephone toll calls from the president's friend's residence revealed calls to the White House. The President's secretary ultimately received a copy of the memorandum and said she believed she would have shown it to the President.

The association of the president's friend with the "hoodlums" and the person's connection with the President was again brought to Hoover's attention in a memorandum preparing him for a meeting with the president . . . on March 22, Hoover had a private luncheon with President Kennedy. There is no record of what transpired at that luncheon. According to the White House logs, the last telephone contact between the White House and the president's friend occurred a few hours after the luncheon.

Four days before the Church Committee released its report, the *Washington Post* published a story revealing the connection linking President Kennedy, his friend, the two underworld figures, and assassination plots against Castro. Remarkably, given the controversial nature of the material, the story ran on page A6, with the headline "PROBERS DOUBT KENNEDY KNEW OF POISON PLOT AGAINST CASTRO." But the story identified Judith Campbell as the president's friend, and once the implications had been sorted out, there was an outburst of sensationalism.

The shattering of the Camelot image and the resulting disillusionment was compounded by the strong suggestion, if not the inescapable conclusion, that J. Edgar Hoover, who had been feuding with JFK and his brother Robert, used his knowledge of Kennedy indiscretions as leverage to maintain his hold on the FBI. Hoover, it has been documented, also attempted to damage Martin Luther King's reputation by circulating material gathered during surveillance operations that his agents conducted against the civil rights leader. The information was obtained by the Church Committee during the course of its COINTEL investigation, in which it examined allegations that the intelligence community had improperly conducted operations within the United States against groups and individuals engaged in legitimate political activities. One member proposed that transcripts of the tapes be included in the public record, an idea that outraged Barry Goldwater. He declared that he wasn't going to be a party to destroying King's reputation and, rising painfully onto his arthritic hip, hobbled out of the committee room. Barry's protest injected some common sense into the proceedings; I moved to table the idea, and the electronic surveillance transcripts were kept out of the record.

In the final analysis, though, we weren't just protecting King's reputation. We were defending the viability of his ideas and the cause that he represented. Not that I agreed with everything that he said or did. There was a larger principle involved. Those who sling mud usually proclaim that they are only serving the public's right to know. And that's nonsense. They are serving their own ends. Destroy King's good name and you have destroyed, or damaged, a political and social movement. The members of the Church Committee didn't need to be told that they were acting in their own self-interest when they voted to withhold the transcripts. Our ideas and our causes were as vulnerable as King's if we succumbed to the temptation to allow the irrelevancies of a person's private life to outweigh all that is truly relevant and important. King's sex life had no bearing whatsoever on the service that he provided to the country.

Hoover's conduct vis-à-vis the Kennedys and King is profoundly disturbing. He misused his investigative powers and in so doing contributed to the opening of a Pandora's box, which awakened a public appetite for scandalous revelations about the private lives of public men. To some it was titillating, to others revolting. There was deep disappointment and disillusionment. Ultimately, it demonstrated the ease with which careers and reputations could be destroyed and the political process manipulated.

By 1989, the shadow, not the substance, of allegations about my private life was sufficient counterweight to thirty-six years of public service. After Paul Weyrich's testimony, the cynics and their shadows were mobilized against me.

SEVEN

ENLIGHTENED SPECULATION

MY FINAL APPEARANCE before the Senate Armed Services committee, on Wednesday, February 1, was preceded by a brief executive, or closed, session. Much of what transpired could just as easily have taken place in public.

As I have already recounted, Sam Nunn asked about Weyrich's allegations, and I denied them. And I should add at this point that Weyrich was virtually a stranger to me; I think I had seen him once before, and I'm not even certain of that. Without the benefit of the TV news clips, I still would be unable to pick the man out of a crowd, which seems curious for an individual who claimed to have observed me closely over the course of many years.

Aside from Nunn, the rest of the committee members were more interested in cleaning up the miscellaneous details pertaining to my business activities. At the conclusion of this session, the committee's Democratic staff director, Arnold Punaro, handed Sherrie Marshall a note. She and I were standing together in the anteroom when Punaro walked over to us. It was a classic good news–bad news situation. The good news, as Punaro informed us, was that the committee staff had prepared a favorable report on my nomination, the strongest possible indication that there was every likelihood I would be confirmed. The bad news was contained in the note, which said that a woman had phoned the committee with allegations of sexual harassment and driving under the influence of alcohol. Sherrie and I read it simultaneously.

To summarize, I was being accused of twice driving my car into a gully beside the apartment building where I had lived on Cathedral Avenue in Washington. The gully in question is more like a deep ravine, and if I had driven my 1972 Dodge Charger into it, the Green Bullet, as I call it, would have been reduced to a pile of junk and I would probably have been seriously injured. The Green Bullet and I are still going strong; the story was patently false. There was no police report, repair record, or insurance claim to sustain it.

Additionally, the accusation stated that I sexually harassed female members of my staff. The only substantiation that was offered was from the caller, who said that she had once hosted a TV talk show and that women had called in and made that charge. When the FBI investigated, there were no names, no specifics, and no tapes of the calls to back up the accusation.

One upshot of the note was that Sam Nunn later accused Sherrie of breaching confidentiality by "showing me" the note. She did not show me anything. Punaro brought it over to the two of us and did not indicate that I was not supposed to be informed of the contents.

As a White House counsel, Sherrie was functioning as a liaison between me and the committee. Her job was to facilitate the confirmation of the president's nominee. Apparently, Sam Nunn saw the role differently. Marshall was to remain neutral and serve only as a conduit for delivering the committee's requests for more material from the FBI — at least, that is how I read his attitude. But under that kind of an arrangement, I would be deprived of counsel. If the White House was not going to act on behalf of my interest (and the president's), who would? Throughout the confirmation process, Senator Nunn bristled whenever President Bush or a White House official dared to speak on my behalf. It was permissible to attack John Tower, but not to defend him.

The episode involving the note was the first of a series of run-ins between Sherrie Marshall and Sam Nunn. The treatment that she received was probably not atypical of the way Nunn dealt with his subordinates generally and could well have reflected some of the hostility he felt toward me, which he was reluctant to express in our face-to-face dealings. One does not carelessly make enemies in Washington, since the consequences can be unpleasant, and had

I been confirmed, Sam Nunn probably would have been dismayed to discover that Sherrie was to be my choice for general counsel of the Defense Department.

The note and its groundless accusations represented a major setback and gave Sam Nunn an excuse to delay a vote. Alone, Weyrich's hearsay was not sufficient to justify reopening the FBI investigation; but the woman who called the committee with her absurd tales was just what Nunn needed to force a postponement. If the informant had been offering direct evidence and knowledge of the alleged improprieties, it would have been one thing; but she had provided nothing more than hearsay.

I was not in a position to object, and neither was the White House. If we had, Sam Nunn would have made us look as though we were trying to hide something by insisting that the committee hold to its scheduled vote on my nomination the next day.

Nunn apparently saw an opportunity to whipsaw the nomination between two issues — allegations of personal impropriety and the appearance of conflict of interest. Carl Levin took the lead on the latter when the committee resumed its public hearings. Levin opened the line of attack by suggesting I had done something wrong by resuming my consulting business after I resigned as the chief START negotiator in April 1986:

> SENATOR LEVIN — After your resignation you began to advise clients on the probable outcomes of those ongoing talks as it might affect the product developments of those clients. . . . I believe there is an appearance [of a conflict of interest] there that we should address in law and in some way.
>
> MR. TOWER — Let me say, Senator, that was all enlightened guesswork on my part.
>
> SENATOR LEVIN — It was enlightened?
>
> MR. TOWER — Yes, it was enlightened.
>
> SENATOR LEVIN — And the appearance issue is that the enlightenment was based on what you knew in your position as the ambassador to those talks or as the chief negotiator. There is an appearance that you were profiting by giving advice based on the information relative to those ongoing negotiations that you had access to which was not publicly available. I think that would be a commonly acknowledged appearance problem.

MR. TOWER — I did not convey anything to them that was not already in the public domain, Senator.

I assured Senator Levin that I had never revealed classified information to unauthorized sources under any circumstances. The Democrats in the Senate know that, and they also know that they don't have to look any further than their own colleague, Patrick Leahy of Vermont, to find someone who did expose classified information on television, in the midst of the *Achille Lauro* affair. But Levin was looking to score political points. The purpose of the questions was to lock me into a position as secretary of defense from which I would be unable to oppose moves to restrict government employees from retiring to jobs in the private sector that had even the remotest connection to their previous responsibilities as public servants. I was getting impatient, but I tried to keep it under control. I gave Levin a few examples of what could happen if Congress overreacted to the appearance issue:

> You might precipitate an exodus, say, of nuclear engineers from the Navy . . . that would leave the Navy before the effective date of the legislation or something like that. I think you have to consider the impact on the ability of the Government to recruit talented people, particularly people that are relatively young, say in their 30's or 40's, who might not want to make a career of Government, but spend some time in Government, but still have a lot of career time left after they get out.

Each senator gets a limited amount of time for a round of questions. Levin came to the end of his and had to give way to other senators, but when his turn came up again he returned to appearances:

SENATOR LEVIN — In that situation, without suggesting an impropriety in actuality, without suggesting in the slightest that you advised them of confidential or privileged information, just the fact that you were advising them on probable outcomes of those talks, don't you see an appearance problem there? That is my question.

MR. TOWER — I do not see it, Senator, because the question has never been raised until now. Nobody has ever questioned me on that before now, and I have not really seen any press commentary on that.

In that exchange, Levin, I believe, demonstrated that the Democrats were so eager to create an alternative issue to satisfy senators who had reservations about the character assassination under way that he was willing to engage in legal sophistry to the point of acknowledging that there was no suggestion "in the slightest" that I had advised my clients of confidential or privileged information. Hence, Levin was forced to frame his argument in such tenuously abstract terms as to make it meaningless.

Only Levin, with some help from Sam Nunn, seemed deeply interested in the line of questioning, and in a few minutes it ran dry.

> SENATOR WARNER — Senator Tower, we want to thank you for your cooperation, the clarity and precision of your responses to the inquiries of the committee.
>
> MR. TOWER — Thank you. Mr. Chairman and Senator Warner, I want to thank you for the very professional way in which this whole matter has been handled. I think it is in the public interest that everything relevant to this nomination be thoroughly considered and dealt with by the committee. I admire the professional way you have gone about it, and I thank you for your cooperation.
>
> CHAIRMAN NUNN — Thank you, Senator Tower.

And so what was probably my last appearance before a Senate committee came to an end. When I look at the final words that I uttered there, I wouldn't mind requesting the right to "revise and extend" my remarks, to use the phrase that is employed so often by members of Congress when they wish to include additional material in the *Congressional Record*.

My exchange with Carl Levin left a bad taste; it reminded me of why I decided to retire from the Senate in 1984. Levin and many of his colleagues invariably seek to impose institutionally rigid "solutions" to problems that, while serious, are either temporary in nature or require utmost flexibility to avoid creating a chain of malfunctions leading toward government paralysis. To put it in plain English, they solve one problem by creating two others.

Nowhere is this propensity more evident, wrongheaded, and dangerous than in the field of national security policy. Congress must of necessity take a tactical approach when enacting domestic legislation, since passage of those laws is achieved by constantly shifting coalitions. The overall effect is a body of legislation adopted piece by piece by a changing majority of legislators. The end product reflects the consensus of various political alliances. If mistakes have been made along the way, corrections can be made. Housing subsidies, for instance, might be found to be inadequate and adjusted upward the next year.

The piecemeal approach works, after a fashion, when we set out to enact a domestic agenda, but it does not lend itself to the formulation of a long-term, coherent foreign policy. Our errors can be costly. The off-again, on-again coalitions that form around shortsighted legislation may alienate a friendly government, with years elapsing before the damage is undone and the losses recouped.

In the first year of the Reagan administration, for example, the pro-Israel lobby came close to severely damaging U.S. relations with the Arab world at a time when we were still struggling to stabilize our position in the Persian Gulf and the Middle East in the aftermath of the Iran hostage crisis. At the request of Saudi Arabia, President Reagan agreed to sell the Saudi military several airborne radar command posts, known as AWACS, air warning and control systems. The deal was announced in April, but in short order Senator Robert Packwood, a Republican from Oregon, working with the American Israel Public Affairs Committee, had 54 senators and 224 members of the House ready to oppose it.

Howard Baker, the Senate majority leader, persuaded the White House to postpone a vote from April until October. Lobbying in the meantime was intense. We whittled away at Packwood's 54 votes, one by one. To do it, however, the White House had to attach restrictions on the Saudis' use of the AWACS. For instance, they could not share intelligence gathered by the system with other countries unless Washington approved of the transfer. As in the Jordanian HAWK missile deal in the 1970s, the Saudis were being forced to accept humiliating conditions. In the end, the deal was approved, 52 to 48.

But as a consequence, AIPAC redoubled its efforts to influence Congress. In 1985, AIPAC and its allies lined up 74 members of the Senate to oppose a $1.5 billion arms package for Jordan, which Ronald Reagan had personally promised to King Hussein. Reagan was forced to renege. Another weapons deal, this one for the Saudis again, ran into congressional resistance. King Fahd was eager to buy additional F-15 jets from the United States, but the climate was so hostile he took his business to Britain. By that time, I had retired from the Senate and one of my consulting firm's clients was British Aerospace. President Reagan asked me to return to Capitol Hill to help with the lobbying effort to save the deal. I ended up actively working against my client's best interest by assisting the administration. Even so, I willingly agreed to help — because it was in the best interest of my country. And when the opponents of my nomination to be secretary of defense wondered whether I would be tempted to put my previous business relationships ahead of what was beneficial to the country, they ignored the actions I took in 1987 on the Saudi arms deal.

Eventually, the Saudis got some of the weaponry. It took Secretary of State George Shultz to engage in personal negotiations with AIPAC's executive director. The lobbying group agreed not to oppose a scaled-down Saudi arms package. By that point, though, Congress was so riled up it rejected the deal anyway, and the president got it through only by vetoing the disapproval resolution and persuading the Senate to uphold the veto after he dropped eight hundred Stinger missiles from the package as a sop to the opponents.

As a postscript to all of this, British Aerospace ultimately concluded a multibillion-dollar deal with the Saudis for the Tornado fighter aircraft, yielding a loss of American jobs and influence.

At this point, I should make it clear that I regard Israel as our principal strategic partner in the Middle East. It is in our national interest to lend whatever assistance we can to the protection of the political and territorial integrity of Israel. In addition, I feel strongly that we have a moral obligation to that embattled state.

We should never pressure Israel into accepting political arrangements that would seriously threaten its ability to defend itself. But there are some instances in which our perception of the national interest is in conflict with what the Israelis perceive to be of paramount importance. Sometimes, by virtue of greater objectivity, our view of what is in Israel's best national security interest may be more enlightened than theirs. I believe that regional stability is of primary importance to every state in the Middle East. To that end, it is critical that the United States be in a position to talk to all sides and be an active and effective player in Middle East diplomacy. We must be mindful of the security needs of the Gulf states and Jordan, which are currently more concerned about present and potential threats from other states in the region than they are in mounting a punitive war against Israel.

This does not mean, however, neglecting our commitments to Israel. On the contrary, arms sold by the United States — including those that go to other powers in the Middle East besides Israel — carry with them some restraints on their use. Arms are available from some major exporters of military hardware who do not share our level of concern for the security of our friend and ally. Politically motivated congressional meddling militates against our ability to maintain a balanced policy in the region.

The foreign policy process involves an aggregate of separate bilateral and multilateral relationships that interlock into a comprehensive scheme designed to promote the long-term national interests. With a grand design in mind, those who carry out foreign policy can respond to changes in the international environment, substituting one tactic for another as it becomes necessary but retaining the overall strategy.

When 535 members of the House and Senate with different philosophies, parochial interests, and constituent concerns find it difficult to even deal with some of the less demanding domestic problems that we face, forging and articulating a unified foreign policy that reflects the interests of the United States as a whole is virtually impossible. Similarly, negotiating with foreign powers, or meeting the requirements for diplomatic confidentiality, is well beyond the capabilities of the legislative branch, as is the ability to take quick, decisive action in response to changes in the international scene.

Truman instituted the Berlin airlift, and Eisenhower sent the Marines into Lebanon. If Congress had interjected itself into the process, both of those crises would have been exacerbated.

The constantly shifting coalitions of Congress, which serve to build our highways, regulate our financial institutions, and protect our environment, are not well suited to the day-to-day conduct of external relations. An observer has compared the conducting of foreign relations to a geopolitical chess game. Chess is not a team sport.

Throughout the 1970s, as a member of the Armed Services Committee, I watched as Congress attempted to reinvent the rules of the geopolitical chess game. The decade was marked by a rash of congressionally inspired foreign policy initiatives that limited the president's range of options. More than 150 separate prohibitions and restrictions were enacted limiting executive-branch authority to formulate and implement foreign policy. The thrust was to curtail the president's ability to dispatch troops abroad in a crisis and to proscribe his authority in arms sales, trade, human rights, foreign assistance, and intelligence operations. Not only was much of this legislation poorly thought out, if not actually unconstitutional, it has in a number of instances been detrimental to the national security of the United States.

Starting with the Cooper-Church amendment, in 1971, my Senate colleagues went on a legislative binge. They proposed, and in many cases adopted, acts that aimed at forcing the United States into an early withdrawal from Southeast Asia. Cooper-Church cut off funds for U.S. troops, advisers, and air support in and over Cambodia, regardless of the consequences to Indochina — and we know now how gruesome the consequences were. McGovern-Hatfield, in 1971–72, set deadlines for American withdrawal from Indochina; the Eagleton amendment, in 1973, called for American withdrawal from Laos and Cambodia. Could there have been any doubt on the part of the North Vietnamese leadership that Congress intended to eventually legislate the United States out of Vietnam? The administration lost credibility, leverage, and flexibility in the peace negotiations it was attempting to conduct. By making it clear to the North Vietnamese that Congress was determined to prevent the president from using military force as a means of compelling the other side to negotiate in good faith, or from enforcing the eventual peace, Congress sent a clear signal to our enemies that they could win in the end. The North Vietnamese were encouraged to stall in the Paris peace talks, and once an agreement was concluded they moved with impunity to throttle South Vietnam.

On July 1, 1973, any hope of survival for South Vietnam was lost. The Fulbright amendment to the Second Supplemental Appropriations Act for Fiscal Year 1973 prohibited the use of funds to "support directly or indirectly combat activities in . . . or over Cambodia, Laos, North Vietnam and South Vietnam."

As I warned the Senate at the time it debated a forerunner to the Fulbright amendment, we were in effect telling North Vietnam, "You may do whatever you please. Having concluded the agreement at the Paris accords, we intend to walk away from it, and we don't care whether you intend to violate those provisions or not."

I believe then and still believe that our failure to enforce the Paris accords was a principal contributor to the Communist victory in Indochina and the resulting horrors we have seen since in Laos, Cambodia, and Vietnam. Reasonable men may argue about whether we were right in being in Vietnam in the first place. I remain convinced that we made many mistakes that led us there and that our direct involvement was ill conceived. But to deny a president the military means to enforce a negotiated agreement guaranteed that all the sacrifices that came before it would be in vain. We bought a settlement in Vietnam with more than fifty thousand American lives that gave South Vietnam a chance to survive — a chance that was thrown away when we refused to be guarantors of that settlement.

The War Powers Act is probably the most potentially damaging of the 1970s legislation, although we have yet to experience a crisis in which its effects are felt. Congress's frustration with the war in Vietnam and a desire to prevent such a situation from ever happening again gave birth to the War Powers Act. President Nixon vetoed the act on the grounds that it was unconstitutional. The House and Senate voted to override.

The act provides that before American troops are introduced "into hostilities or into situations where imminent involvement in hostilities is clearly indicated by the circumstances," the president is to consult with Congress "in every possible instance." The president must notify Congress and submit a report within forty-eight hours after armed forces are deployed abroad, "setting forth the circumstances necessitating the introduction of U.S. forces" and the estimated scope and duration of the hostilities or involvement. After this initial two-day period, the president has sixty days to withdraw those forces or receive congressional authorization for an extension, or a declaration of war.

This act inhibits the president's ability to respond quickly, forcefully, and, if necessary, in secret to protect American interests abroad. It increases the likelihood of delay and indecision and thus may even invite crises. Although the act does not specify whether the report to Congress must be unclassified, there remains the possibility that a confidential report would become public knowledge. In many cases the more urgent the requirement that a decision remain confidential, the greater the pressure for disclosure. Therefore, by notifying Congress of the size, disposition, and objectives of U.S. forces dispatched in a crisis, we run the risk that the information will get into the public domain and into the hands of our military adversaries. The results could be disastrous.

By using Vietnam as a precedent to establish Congress's "right" to interpose itself in the process of formulating and executing foreign policy, members of the House and Senate now routinely make legislative demands that severely proscribe the president's ability to build and maintain bilateral relationships. Starting in 1974, the first in a series of Nelson-Bingham amendments required the president to give advance notice to Congress of any offer to sell foreign countries defense articles and services valued at $25 million or more. Congress was empowered to disapprove those sales within twenty calendar days by concurrent resolution. Two years later, the law was tightened to require advance notification of any sale of "major" defense equipment totaling more than $7 million, and Congress gave itself thirty days to exercise its legislative veto power.

As a consequence of these laws, every major arms-sales agreement is now played out amid an acrimonious national debate, blown out of all proportion to the intrinsic importance of the transaction in question. Often the merits of the sale and its long-term foreign policy implications are ignored, since legislators end up posturing for domestic political purposes. The intense media attention provokes members of Congress to make rash statements and take positions before there is an opportunity for informed deliberation. Such behavior by legislators makes it difficult to forge compromises. Meanwhile, the debate diverts the president and Congress from focusing on vital internal matters.

Presidents Nixon, Ford, Carter, and Reagan all faced prolonged and bitter struggles with Congress over arms sales to Middle Eastern countries. Our ability to provide creative, farsighted leadership in that part of the world has been hampered by the controversies. We have yet to completely repair the damage done to relations with King Hussein in 1975, when a humiliating compromise was necessary to get Congress's approval of a deal to sell HAWK surface-to-air missiles to Jordan. Ostensibly to prevent the Jordanians from moving the missiles to the front lines with Israel, we took the wheels off the missile carriers. Everyone involved knew that King Hussein could easily buy the wheels from other sources if he chose to, but the gesture was what counted — a gesture of contempt toward Hussein and a political gesture to score points for members of Congress with special-interest groups.

The Turkish arms embargo is another case where Congress tied the president's hands in negotiations and did lasting damage to U.S. security. After the Turkish invasion of Cyprus in 1974, the State Department immediately began diplomatic efforts to reconcile Greece and Turkey, both NATO allies. But Congress did its own thing. With a close eye on Greek-Americans, who constitute a sizable block of votes in some parts of the country and who make hefty financial contributions to political campaigns, it introduced resolutions calling for a total Turkish troop withdrawal from Cyprus.

The administration was justifiably concerned that the congressional pressure would make it harder for Turkey to follow a conciliatory policy and thus would destroy any hopes of a negotiated settlement. At one point, Prime Minister Bülent Ecevit of Turkey privately communicated his willingness to settle on terms that would have gone beyond the existing status quo, which at the time meant that the Greek Cypriots might have regained lost territory by diplomatic means. White House officials invited members of Congress to a briefing and showed them the evidence that the negotiations, if left unimpeded, would probably result in improving the Greek position. Nonetheless, these congressmen continued to push for an arms embargo, and the negotiations collapsed. Ecevit's moderate government was ousted from power; a month later Congress imposed the arms embargo; and in a chain reaction, Turkey responded by putting all U.S. bases and listening posts on provisional status. On July 27, 1975, two days after the House rejected a motion to partially lift the embargo, Turkey announced that it was shutting down all U.S. installations on its territory.

Instead of reaching agreement with the moderate Ecevit government when it controlled only one quarter of Cyprus, the United States had severely strained relations with an angry Turkish military government, which had ousted Ecevit and went on to take control of two fifths of the island. Furthermore, the aid cutoff weakened Turkey militarily, jeopardizing the southern flank of NATO and putting at risk our strategic listening posts in that country.

Playing politics with our foreign policy is a grave mistake. In his memoir, Harry Truman contended that the creation of the United

Nations, the Marshall Plan, NATO, and other crucial projects "would have been hampered, if not blocked completely," without the bipartisanship shown by Senator Arthur Vandenberg and Congressman Charles A. Eaton, both Republicans, who helped convince their colleagues that politics stopped at the water's edge. That is not to say that the issues are too important to be debated. We can and must examine alternatives and air our views. As a member of the Senate, I never tried to use leverage on a president on important foreign and defense policy questions. But I would have little reservation about doing so on a domestic matter of critical interest to my state where no national security or foreign policy issues were at stake.

In the late seventies, when a bipartisan Senate coalition opposed ratification of the SALT II treaty, President Carter was duly warned by senators of both parties that the pact was flawed. If that treaty had been approved by the requisite two-thirds majority of the Senate, it would have become the supreme law of the land, binding future presidents and exerting long-term influence on our defense posture. There wasn't any horse trading back and forth between the Hill and the White House. The Democrat-controlled Armed Services Committee determined that the treaty was "not in the national security interest of the United States" by a vote of 10 to 0, with 7 abstentions. Jimmy Carter marked time for a while, and when the Soviets invaded Afghanistan he withdrew the treaty himself.

Now, contrast that situation to Senator Robert Byrd's mischief making in 1990, when he blocked urgently needed aid to Panama and Nicaragua to retaliate against President Bush for opposing an amendment to the Clean Air Act that the West Virginia Democrat was sponsoring. Byrd was looking out for a few coal miners in his home state; never mind the consequences in Central America. It was a vivid display of one senator's willfulness and small-minded disregard for the best security interest of the United States.

The authority to conduct external relations should not vacillate between the president and Congress as a result of personal pettiness, narrow-gauge legislative initiatives, or dubious ideological presumptions that may be temporarily fashionable. The whole point of a written constitution and body of judicial opinion is to establish a consistent mechanism for apportioning or limiting authority. Whereas the Constitution confers on the Senate the duty of advise and consent in the making of treaties, on Congress the power to appropriate monies for armed forces and to declare war, along with special authority in trade matters, it confers on Congress no other special right in the field of external affairs.

This comes, I am sure, as a frustration and disappointment to someone as bright and aggressive as Carl Levin. It seems so much easier and more glamorous to conduct our foreign policy than to attempt to cope with the country's seemingly intractable domestic problems. Bashing Arabs or Turks, second-guessing arms sales, raising the ante on U.S.-Soviet troop cuts, make for bold headlines and catchy sound bites on the evening news. But do they move us forward toward a realization of our national objectives?

Senator Levin's fixation with the conflict-of-interest question, for instance, would be considered a sexy issue by his media advisers, since it hints at corruption in high places and at waste, fraud, and abuse. The idea is to simplify a complex and emotional subject. And in defense of simplicity, I can say that those who serve the public interest must be held to a high standard of ethics, morality, and accountability. However, while instances of true corruption are extremely disturbing and must be prosecuted to the full extent of the law, equally troublesome is the increasing trend toward a political climate where candidates and public servants are judged less on the quality of their views and commitment to issues of public policy than on whether they have lived their entire lives free of blemish.

We must not confuse behavior that truly betrays the public trust with the reality that American politicians reflect the spectrum of society that they have been elected to represent — sometimes including that spectrum's most visible flaws.

To insist that elected officials or public servants meet an unrealistic standard that very few Americans can approximate will render public service an office to which many otherwise highly capable individuals will no longer be able to aspire. The true losers in such an environment will be the American people.

Can we trust our leaders to protect and promote the national interest? This, it seems to me, is the question of overriding importance. Although the way they conduct their private lives may be an important predictor of how they will conduct the nation's business, much of the debate overlooks the central point: the moral fiber of our leaders must be judged on the basis of their depth of commitment to the articles of faith, embodied in the Declaration of Independence and in the Constitution, that long have formed the common moral consensus of our nation and that govern our lives today. Judgment of an individual's suitability for public office must rest, then, on the quality of his or her performance with respect to the most important of our society's values — protection of individual rights, religious and racial tolerance, love of country and what it stands for.

The values that Carl Levin was seeking to superimpose on the confirmation process had nothing to do with these essentials. Curiously, I was repeatedly assured by Levin, Nunn, and others that my character and honesty were not the issues. And nearly every member of the committee praised my credentials and qualifications. Yet they couldn't resist hefting the stones and toying with the thought that maybe those who cast the first ones would be regarded by the public as being without sin.

Despite the news media's periodic accusations of great moral lassitude at all levels of government, personal experience has led me to believe that the vast majority of our national public officials are dedicated to high standards of conduct. Their jobs are difficult ones that often require negotiating a perilous path, balancing narrow constituent interests against the larger public interest. More often than not, they do it well.

Indictments, prosecutions, and convictions of former officials do not necessarily indicate that we are awash in corruption. Abuse-of-power and conflict-of-interest cases litter the past. Those who stand before the American public fairly accused of criminal wrongdoing do so because the system works. Although the number of such incidents has increased, this can be attributed to more state and federal law enforcement machinery, which is being used effectively to expose that which often remained hidden in the past.

The proposition that we must go to new and extraordinary lengths to "solve" the conflict-of-interest problem will lead us deeper into a bewildering legislative maze. There is so much to do and so little time in which to do it. Can we afford to explore every blind alley to satisfy our self-righteousness when we have yet to confront the task of reconciling our national security needs with the just allocation of our financial resources?

First things first. And as a member of the Senate Armed Services Committee I always felt that my colleagues, with their wisdom, experience, and farsightedness, put the country first. The committee was one of the anchors that helped stabilize the Senate in periods of turmoil. Chairman John Stennis was a Democrat, yet he

was so trusted by Richard Nixon and the rest of us in Congress
that the president proposed turning the Watergate tapes over to
him to determine the legal relevance of their contents. Furthermore, the committee seldom went through each defense authorization request meticulously, line by line, imposing the Senate's
judgment on the military. Stennis, Richard Russell (I could reel
off a long list of names), weren't looking for a chance to grandstand on every issue. But after my four days of testimony, I left
with the feeling that the anchor was dragging.

On my way to the door of the caucus room, I shook hands with
Sam Nunn and several other senators. The photographers bunched
up in the front of the room for a last flurry of picture taking.
Arnold Punaro followed me out to the adjoining anteroom, and it
was at that point that he hit me with his good news–bad news
combination. I was relieved to learn that a favorable report was
already in the works. It was apparent that Sam Nunn believed a
majority of the committee would vote to recommend to the full
Senate that I be confirmed as defense secretary. A favorable report
would accompany the recommendation, explaining and elaborating
on the majority's viewpoint. It did not necessarily mean that there
wouldn't be some members of the committee who would oppose
me. I did not expect a unanimous endorsement, but it was reasonable to assume that by volunteering the information, Punaro was
carrying out Nunn's instructions. I could have been left guessing;
instead, I was being told — in so many words — "You're in." I
read it as a gesture of goodwill on Sam Nunn's part.
    But the bad news was depressing. It was certain to delay a vote,
and there was nothing I could do. I was scheduled to have lunch
with Dorothy at the Jefferson Hotel, and it should have been a
celebration, but I was glum. I had gone directly back to the hotel
from Capitol Hill. She was a few minutes late, and as I waited I
took stock of the situation. Although I was seeing light at the end
of the tunnel, I didn't like the idea of those two wild allegations
that had been phoned in to the Armed Services Committee offices.
    After we moved into the dining room, Dorothy could see that
I was distracted. She patted my knee and asked, "Would it cheer
you up if I fondled your knee?" I smiled and lightened up a bit.
Dorothy always has a cheery disposition and never says anything
pejorative about anyone. Just having her at the table brightened
my mood.

EIGHT

FRIENDS AND FOES

KIND AND CHEERY WORDS were in short supply the next day. I usually do not read the *Washington Post* "Style" section. Its excess of gossip and glitz is not to my taste. Unfortunately, though, "Style" is must reading for many Washingtonians. And this is what they saw:

> What would John Tower have done if New Right activist Paul M. Weyrich had been lunching at the Jefferson Hotel yesterday? Weyrich had questioned the defense secretary-designate's social activities Tuesday before the Senate Armed Services Committee when he made references to Tower's drinking and socializing with women other than his wife. Tower is now divorced from his second wife. Yesterday he completed his testimony at his confirmation hearings, where Weyrich's accusations were raised, and then went to the Jefferson Hotel for lunch.
>
> Tower waited there alone until his girlfriend Dorothy Heiser [*sic*] showed and then they moved to an intimate area of the dining room and sat next to each other on a banquette. Obviously, unconcerned with what Weyrich thinks or says, Tower suddenly, playfully lunged at Heiser, his arms reaching toward her under the table, and said, "I'm going to fondle

you!" She gave a little shriek and jumped slightly and said, "Don't you do that!" He stopped and they resumed eating.

Over the course of my long career in politics I have become accustomed to being the focus of attention when I am out in public. Although I have given up a significant measure of personal privacy, the sacrifice comes with the job. I suppose that, being a clergyman's son, I learned early on that my father's conduct, like that of a public-office holder or any other prominent member of the community, would be under constant observation and evaluation. When I was a boy, my friends were anonymous for the most part, while any youthful indiscretion committed by Joe Z's son did not go unremarked.

Therefore, decorum is second nature to me. I am never loud or boisterous. I never lunge at anyone, even in jest (nor does Dorothy ever shriek). However, I do try to lead as normal a life as possible despite the scrutiny; otherwise I could never enjoy a meal in a restaurant or an evening out with friends. From the morning of the "Style" piece on, I realized that my conduct was being subjected to an extraordinarily close examination and that the most misleading, unfair, and untoward interpretations were being applied.

The news media had staked out the Jefferson Hotel so thoroughly that my every public moment was under the tightest surveillance. Unless I resorted to calling room service and becoming a prisoner in my room, I was vulnerable at mealtime, and to be on the safe side in the dining room, Dorothy and I kept to ourselves, away from the other patrons. However, a couple of *Washington Post* reporters were having lunch there on the afternoon of February 1. They were a good twenty or thirty feet away and not nearly close enough to gain an accurate impression of what was happening at our table. The "fondling" story — written by yet a third reporter, Chuck Conconi, who was not there — was the result.

At the time, it irritated me to see it in print, but measured against the horror stories I had been reading regularly in the news media the article seemed trivial. Several weeks later, I learned that Arnold Punaro was telling associates that Sam Nunn was furious about the "Style" item. In Nunn's eyes, the report of my lunch with Dorothy — one that was inaccurate and, what's more, the work of the newspaper's gossip columnist, not a legitimate journalist — was an example of John Tower flaunting his indiscreet life-style and defying the committee.

I understand that there are those at the *Washington Post* who believe that the resulting piece of "Style"-page fiction was what scuttled my confirmation. They give themselves too much credit; however, I have to say it did hurt. My public image and reputation had been mangled to such an extent that any additional item would have been bound to have an exaggerated impact.

Yet there is a danger of making too much out of the story. After all, on page 1 of the same newspaper (in typical Washington seesaw fashion, which first humiliates you and then sends your hopes soaring again), a headline announced "COMMITTEE VOTE DUE TODAY." The *Post*'s Senate correspondent, Helen Dewar, wrote that "the committee was expected to approve Tower's nomination," although, she added,

> some members, including committee chairman Sam Nunn (D-Ga.), continued to express concern over "appearances" arising out of Tower's private life and his work as a consultant to major defense contractors. "I am weighing all of that and my final judgment will have a lot to do with that . . . I have had and continue to have concerns . . . I'm wrestling with them," Nunn told reporters after concluding four days of hearings in which Tower was questioned about allegations of drinking, conflicts of interest and other problems.
>
> While he had no doubts about Tower's competence or ethics, Nunn said, he was concerned that Tower . . . could suffer from an "appearance problem" in attempting to restore public confidence in the Pentagon.

Nunn had picked up on Carl Levin's line of attack. Even so, Punaro's statement about the favorable committee report convinced me that Nunn was simply trying to position himself should any future questions arise on the issue. He could in the meantime fuss about appearances, try to make President Bush uncomfortable, and then vote for the nomination on the grounds that he had no doubts about my competence or ethics.

There was no mention of the allegations that had been received by the Armed Services Committee. I was hoping we could avoid a delay by moving fast to shoot down the false charges. "Here they go again" is the way I greeted my Dallas office manager, Martha Kirkendall, when I got through to her on the phone. I asked her to check with my insurance agent in Wichita Falls to obtain copies of any claims that had been filed on the car. Martha also talked to Lou, who did not remember any such incident but recalled the names of some of our old neighbors in the apartment building on Cathedral Avenue. One of them, the former president of the condominium association, told the FBI that he would have heard about a car being driven into the ravine and that nothing of the kind had ever occurred. He also denied that my drinking had created problems in the building or that there had been a move to have us evicted. We also contacted former members of my staff to determine if they could provide information. The most that we could come up with was a couple of minor fender benders. One of them had occurred at the apartment building when I backed out of my parking place one morning and scraped a rear fender against a column. The claim for those damages showed up in the insurance agent's file, along with another, for a stolen spare tire and wheel. There was also a bill for a couple of hundred dollars in bodywork to repair the car I kept in Dallas after Phil Charles, then an aide in my Senate office in Texas, took a sudden right turn while we were driving to a midmorning appointment and collided with a Volkswagen. I must add that, even though Phil was driving, the accident was my fault. I said "Turn here," indicating the intersection that we were just entering. Phil, as befitted a former Army sergeant, responded to the order immediately. Luckily, nobody was hurt and the damage wasn't serious.

Pulling together close to twenty years of insurance records took time, and in the end there was nothing to show that the car had plunged down a steep, heavily wooded embankment. Despite Martha Kirkendall's fast work — she's a one-woman quick-reaction force — there was no way to tie it all up in one day. Furthermore, the FBI wasn't going to be rushed, and I didn't blame them.

"NEW ITEMS PUT TOWER VOTE ON HOLD" was the way *USA Today* handled the story:

> Senate leaders abruptly postponed plans to vote Thursday on former Sen. John Tower as Defense Secretary to review new charges about his personal conduct.
>
> "Certain new items that have come up" will be investigated by the FBI, said Sen. Sam Nunn, D-Ga., Armed Services Committee chairman.
>
> Nunn refused to say who provided the information about

more incidents of drinking and womanizing by Tower, a former senator from Texas. It surfaced since Paul Weyrich . . . told the committee in public and private sessions about other incidents.

Senators said the incidents raised questions about Tower's judgment. "There were two separate matters . . . I don't think we ought to categorize them," Nunn said.

Two things were starting to happen: one, the press feeding frenzy was resuming; and two, senators were beginning to move from what appeared to have been a position of neutrality or perhaps support into opposition. The senators who were quoted as questioning my judgment were not named, but often it is the case that someone who is holding a "for attribution" briefing, as Nunn had done when he announced the postponement, will go on background to provide additional material without attaching his name to the comments. The circumstantial evidence points to Nunn and probably also to John Warner, who appeared with him.

Notice, as well, that the allegations had become "more incidents of drinking and womanizing." The presumption of innocence had been obliterated.

Simultaneously, "sources" began to surface who volunteered everything from "the administration is looking for alternatives to Tower" to "former Tower aides are under investigation for selling information to defense contractors" and "Tower chased his secretary around the desk in Geneva."

It was as if I had been attacked by a swarm of hummingbird-sized mosquitoes that I had to slap at so hard and so fast that I was in danger of giving myself a concussion.

The nomination was in trouble. I could see that, as could most halfway attentive observers of the political scene. But we still had more than a reasonable chance of an early and favorable vote. President Bush agreed with this assessment. He and I were in regular contact. On a few occasions, White House strategy sessions would be moved to the Oval Office or into the Bush family living quarters so that the president could participate in the discussion. Nobody was panicked. We were still able to crack a few jokes about the situation. John Sununu kidded me one day about the FBI file that had just been received. "Wait until you see the pictures," he said, rolling his eyes and chuckling.

A brief postponement of the Senate Armed Services Committee vote was not necessarily fatal. When the FBI resumed its investigation, on Thursday, February 2, the agent in charge indicated that he would probably be ready to deliver a report by the following Tuesday. If there were no new and shocking revelations — and since it was my life under investigation, I was not worried on that score — then we could probably ride out the delay.

In viewing the confirmation battle in retrospect, however, there is some validity to the view that if we had gone on a public relations offensive over the weekend, our chances of prevailing might have been enhanced. The *Washington Post*'s Bob Woodward remarked to one of my associates that had we called in the press and laid out all of my potential liabilities and embarrassments, the situation could have been turned around. But the problem with that theory is it assumes I was aware of the imaginary skeletons being dragged out of the closet. The chilling thing about the allegations that were made to the FBI and then leaked to the news media was that I was hearing about them for the first time. I was not permitted to confront my accusers, nor did I have direct knowledge of the accusations — for that I had to rely on the press.

How could I have laid it all out, as Bob Woodward suggested? For example, there was an allegation that I had gotten drunk and obnoxious on a transatlantic flight to London. Anyone who has traveled with me on overseas flights knows that I tend to catch up on my reading, drink a glass of champagne or wine, and sleep for most of the duration of the flight. It is a pattern set by years of air travel and the only way to rest or get any work accomplished. Anticipating that particular allegation would have been impossible (it came from an anonymous flight attendant who could not remember the date, the flight number, the destination, any other passengers, or the names of his fellow crew members); and once it had been made, the press would have said, "See, he didn't come clean," thereby dismissing the good intentions of the public relations effort.

Doing something — anything — as opposed to doing nothing is one of the strongest, and I would say most dangerous, impulses that politicians must learn to control. As professionals, we are action-oriented. The thought of waiting, biding one's time, seems unnatural. Over the years, I have taught myself patience. If you stampede with the rest of the herd, there will be so much dust that you won't see the edge of the precipice until it is too late.

I felt that there was too much of a risk in going on the offensive. If Sam Nunn had in fact ordered the committee staff to write a favorable report, I could antagonize him by appearing to be partisan and pushy. As a former chairman, I knew Nunn was of a sensitive and prerogative-conscious nature. Personally, he is proud and quick to react to small slights. If he got his back up, there would be big trouble.

It was better, therefore, to discreetly work the margins. I discouraged Rhett Dawson from immersing himself in the confirmation battle, since I needed him to ramrod the Pentagon transition along with Don Atwood, the new deputy secretary designate; we had the largest department of the federal government to staff and run. Dan Howard agreed with me on the need to keep a low profile with the press. He would continue as our "Dr. No," denying the allegations as they surfaced. Richard Billmire also handled questions from the press and worked the conservative network on Capitol Hill, keeping tabs on a few Senate aides who were hostile to me for a variety of reasons. The wing nuts, as they are called, were capable of zealous opposition to me because of my pro-choice position or for my work to achieve a strategic arms control agreement with the Soviets.

Everyone got the word to be cautious — except for one of my friends, who ended up doing more damage than a battalion of enemies.

Earlier in this chapter I refer to my long experience of air travel. In my twenty-four years in the Senate, just going back and forth between Texas and Washington I probably logged millions of miles, and that's not counting the mileage racked up within the state once I got there.

Having won my first election by only 10,343 votes, I could take nothing for granted. I returned home whenever I could get away from the Senate floor, and frequently that meant waiting late into the day for a vote and then boarding a plane for an evening flight that got me in after midnight. On top of that, I was in demand as a speaker for Republican candidates and organizations all over the country.

Juggling those demands was difficult. I did a lot of wheel spinning for the first year or so. Since then, I have watched many other new senators go through similar adjustment pains. It is not easy to identify priorities, adjust the right mix of personalities and

capabilities needed to staff offices in Washington and your home
state, and come up with an administrative routine that can
smoothly handle everything from a lost pension check to screening
appointees to the federal bench.

In 1965, I hit on an excellent combination by asking Ken Towery,
my press secretary, to take the post of administrative assistant in
the Washington office. Ken, a Pulitzer Prize–winning journalist
who had worked for the *Austin American-Statesman,* agreed to
make the move. The best candidate to take over responsibility for
the news media was Jerry Friedheim, a bright young journalist
from Missouri. Together, Towery and Friedheim shifted the operation into high gear. Towery was familiar with Texas politics,
and with his amiable personality and strong conservative convictions he was ideally suited for the top position. Friedheim, who
eventually went on to be assistant secretary of defense for public
affairs, laid down a barrage of press releases announcing awards of
federal contracts and projects in Texas, establishing in the public
mind that I was responsible for them, even though there was a
Democratic administration in the White House and an overwhelmingly Democratic Texas congressional delegation.

More often than not, freshman senators get off to a slow start.
Washington can be confusing and distracting. The sudden transformation of an airline pilot, the owner of a grocery store chain,
or, as in my case, a college professor into one of only a hundred
members of the United States Senate does strange things to one's
equilibrium. Overnight, it can turn Aesop's ant into a grasshopper.

Not only did I need to consolidate my political base in Texas
and make a name for myself in the Senate, but I wanted to play a
part in the conservative movement that was gaining momentum
nationwide. I was on the road constantly. When I think back and
try to remember where I was when certain important historic
events occurred, it seems I was almost always making a speech
somewhere. The Cuban missile crisis broke while I was campaigning for Jim Broyhill in North Carolina. The tension and the dramatic denouement, with Soviet cargo ships steaming toward the
U.S. blockade and turning back at the last minute, had Washington
and the rest of the country on edge. But the potential for nuclear
war has been exaggerated by Kennedy iconographers. A few weeks
before JFK issued his ultimatum, many of us in the Senate feared
that the White House would find a way to rationalize acquiescence

to the presence of Soviet offensive missiles ninety miles from Florida. In a speech on the Senate floor I said flatly and accurately that the Russians would not risk a thermonuclear war to protect Fidel Castro. Those who spoke out were accused by the White House of playing politics with the crisis. Ironically, though, it was Kennedy who scored all the political points. By standing firm, as we had advocated, he was lauded for going eyeball to eyeball and forcing the Russians to "blink."

I was asked to visit Indiana during the crisis to help Senator Homer Capehart, who was campaigning for reelection. I phoned back to Washington and told Ev Dirksen, "Homer's supposed to win easily out here . . . take it from me, he's in trouble and this missile thing isn't helping." The wave of Kennedy adulation cost Capehart and many other Republicans their seats in Congress. Barry Goldwater summed it up at the time: "We were Cuber-ized."

A year later, I was called forward to the cockpit as my plane landed in St. Louis, where I was scheduled to make a presentation to the Midwestern State Republican Conference on behalf of the Republican Senatorial Campaign Committee. There was a passenger-service agent waiting to escort me to a telephone; I was to call my office immediately. As we hurried through the crowded terminal he told me the news: the president had been shot in Dallas.

John F. Kennedy's assassination changed everything. Washington went into mourning, and those who lived and worked there seemed to be gripped by a heavy depression and despair that lingered for years. The traumatic loss, combined with LBJ's unique style of leadership, required an adjustment, and there were some who were unable to make the transition.

I went from being ignored by the White House, which didn't have much use for a freshman Texas Republican, to being a welcome visitor. To say that LBJ never forgot his Texas roots would be an understatement. He stayed in close touch with the members of the Texas congressional delegation, and as the war in Vietnam escalated there were late-night phone calls, briefings, and occasional offers of flights on *Air Force One* back home to Texas. Once, following a holiday period, when I was preparing to return to Washington with my family from our house in Wichita Falls, Lyndon called to offer me a ride. "Mr. President," I said, "I appreciate the offer, but I've got a wife and kids and a dog to transport back there." There was a slight pause while LBJ did some fast figuring.

He must have pulled the phone away from his ear, but I could hear him holler to an aide, "Make some room on the plane for Tower's three girls and Lou . . . and a dog."

Johnson was hard on his staff, but his style was to kill another politician with kindness. He wanted your vote and went out of his way to get it. He never threatened me or twisted my arm — just the opposite. Johnson would look for a way to do a favor and pick up an IOU in return. He was still at it the day he left office. We had met about three days before he was due to step down from the presidency at a reception that was held in his honor by some of his old Senate pals. As we chatted, Johnson said he was looking forward to being a neighbor of mine in the Austin federal building, where the General Services Administration was fixing up a suite of offices for his use in retirement. One of my three state offices was in the building, and I knew all about it. "I want you to come up and have a drink with me, John," LBJ said. I accepted the invitation but added, "I'd be glad to, Mr. President, if I can find a parking place." He gave me a puzzled look. I explained that the GSA had appropriated our parking spots along with those allocated to my Senate colleague Ralph Yarborough. Nothing more was said, but an hour before he left office, as I was preparing to go out to the East Front of the Capitol for Nixon's inauguration, LBJ called me. "I wonder what this is all about," I thought to myself when the secretary told me who was on the line. I picked up the receiver and LBJ said, "I've looked into that parking situation . . . and I don't want to get crosswise with you and Ralph. I've ordered the GSA to give those spaces back."

In the darkest days of the Vietnam War, Johnson paid me what was, for him, the ultimate compliment: "John, I get more loyalty and support from you than I do from the members of my own party."

Before we got to that crossroads, though, I had to survive the disastrous 1964 presidential election and my own reelection campaign two years later.

Nineteen sixty-two was a year of measured growth for Texas Republicans. We had hoped to consolidate the gains that we began to make two years earlier. But our candidate for governor, Jack Cox, was up against John Connally, LBJ's protégé, and while Cox was an attractive, spirited campaigner, Connally was a political heavyweight who was quick and deadly when it came to one-on-

one slugging. It occurred to me that should he be elected, he would probably serve four years as governor and then challenge me for the Senate seat in 1966, a contest I might not survive. After Connally's initial bid for statewide office, however, our timetables never coincided. Connally served three two-year terms as governor and returned to Washington as treasury secretary in 1971. He ultimately switched parties and ran unsuccessfully for the Republican presidential nomination in 1980.

Despite Connally's effectiveness. Jack Cox refused to roll over and play dead. His principal campaign strategy was to exploit the LBJ issue, and he used the slogan "Lyndon's Boy, John" to describe Connally. Cox kept hitting Connally for his close ties to Johnson and, by extension, his connection to the Kennedys. LBJ and Lyndon's boy, John, "had sold out the South," he declared at every opportunity.

It was gutsy, but not enough to change the outcome. And Kennedy's soaring popularity after the Cuban missile crisis made matters worse. Still, Cox ran strongly enough to give some help to other Republicans on the ticket. None of our statewide candidates survived, but six of the Dallas County state legislative seats went Republican. Bruce Alger retained his place in the U.S. House by twenty thousand votes, and Ed Foreman scored a major breakthrough by taking the Sixteenth Congressional District in West Texas. In addition, we picked up a few county offices.

While our gains were modest, they were not insignificant. Our base with Anglo voters in major urban areas was beginning to shape up, but I could see from voting patterns that we needed to make further inroads in the Mexican-American community and the rural areas. It was obvious to me that by combining conservative Anglos and Hispanics — who shared a devotion to family, religion, and hard work — we could begin to break the Democratic hold on Texas.

I also knew it was not a process that could be accomplished overnight. My election to the Senate had jump started the Republican party in Texas, and now we needed something to get us up to speed. Peter O'Donnell, the newly elected state party chairman, decided that the something was a someone by the name of Barry Goldwater. O'Donnell became the national chairman of the Draft Goldwater Committee, an unauthorized ad hoc group that was trying to whip up a grass-roots movement to stop Governor Nelson Rockefeller of New York from taking the 1964 Republican presidential nomination. In later years I discovered that Nelson was a pretty good guy, and not nearly as liberal as he felt he had to make himself out to be to please his New York constituents. But in 1962, from our perspective in Texas, he looked like the arch-enemy.

Goldwater's powerful appeal to conservatives in the South, Southwest, and West crossed party lines, and it make perfect sense to energize Texas Republicans by going all out for Barry. Abstract conservative principles are one thing, but a real, live, hell-for-leather candidate of Goldwater's caliber made it a lot easier to build a strong party with focused resources, funding, and themes.

Barry was like the genie that popped out of Aladdin's magic lamp. He gave us three wishes. We asked for financial contributions — and the money rolled in; we asked for energetic campaign workers — and volunteers came out in droves; and, as our final wish, we asked for a young, attractive, articulate, energetic candidate for the U.S. Senate to run against the liberal Democratic incumbent, Ralph Yarborough. By 1963, we had funds, manpower, and George Bush.

John Kennedy died at Parkland Memorial Hospital in Dallas on November 22, 1963. I got back to Washington from St. Louis that night. The Senate had gone into recess. All we could do was wait for the funeral. Long lines of people encircled the Capitol as mourners came to pay their respects to the fallen president, whose flag-draped casket sat on a black catafalque in the middle of the great rotunda. A sad and dispiriting moment.

In the next year, Lyndon Johnson became a veritable dynamo of political energy. He adroitly converted the nation's grief over JFK's tragic death into a reservoir of political capital, and he spent it methodically. The flame that burned at Kennedy's grave site became a symbol for a sweeping social agenda, which Johnson devised and implemented, using his enormous skills as a legislative tactician. Those of us who opposed the headlong rush to create the Great Society were at a marked disadvantage, given the circumstances.

The emotions generated by Kennedy's assassination were such that criticism of LBJ's approach was translated as an attack on the Kennedy legacy. The hate mail and threatening phone calls in the immediate aftermath of the assassination were of considerable volume and intensity. As a precaution, on the recommendation of the

FBI, I sent my wife and children to stay with friends in rural Maryland. Dallas was denounced as a city of hatred; conservative nuts were blamed for inflaming murderous passions; and John Kennedy's prominent political opponents were accused of indirect complicity in the murder.

Some of these denunciations were aimed at me. My election to the Senate had propelled me into a high-profile role in the conservative movement, and I had been active in the early stages of Goldwater's bid for the 1964 Republican presidential nomination. Suddenly, I went from being something of a favorite with the national news media — a regular on the talk shows and frequent subject of profiles in major publications — to an extremist. And there is no label more deadly in American politics.

I could have headed for the sidelines and waited it out. However, Johnson was pushing for his Great Society programs and for the enactment of the 1964 Civil Rights Act. I joined the filibuster against the act because I felt that its public accommodation provisions were unworkable and unconstitutional. I was wrong about that, and would vote differently today.

The struggle lasted for six months; it paralyzed and polarized the Senate. In terms of the end of a historic epoch, the experience, I would imagine, was akin to being a deckhand on one of the galleons in the Spanish Armada. It was the last great massing of old-fashioned Senate power. At the time, the rules were written to protect the minority's right to delay final action on a deeply controversial and emotionally charged issue. A vote of two thirds — two thirds of the senators present and voting, rather than of the entire body — was necessary to invoke cloture, or cut off debate.

Those who were filibustering needed to have at least one of their number present on the Senate floor at all times to keep talking and to object to any unanimous-consent requests to bring the motion in question to a vote. The verbal marathon went to ridiculous lengths, with senators reading page after tedious page out of the *Congressional Record* just to kill time. To wear down the opposition, the leadership scheduled round-the-clock sessions, which meant that one of us had to be up and talking all night. I remember discussing with my colleagues the stratagems for answering the call of nature when one was alone on the Senate floor (alone in the sense of being the only opponent of the bill; the presiding officer and at least one representative of the Democratic leadership were always present) without yielding the floor. Senator Russell Long told me that his father, Huey Long, used to wear a dark suit so that he could relieve himself on the spot during a Senate filibuster without anyone noticing. Others advocated the use of a catheter and a bag that strapped on under the trousers. And Strom Thurmond went without consuming liquids for hours, deliberately dehydrating himself, before his turn at leading the filibuster. Strom recalled that during one "extended debate," as they were euphemistically termed, he had clocked up several hours of talking when Senator Wayne Morse strolled over and put a pitcher of cold orange juice on the desk in front of him. "Isn't that thoughtful," Strom said to himself. "He's on the other side and is still willing to bring me some refreshment." He caught himself reaching for the pitcher just in time.

In the end, the filibuster was broken by Johnson's ability to persuade his old friend Everett Dirksen to make a separate peace. Dirksen siphoned off enough Republican votes to give LBJ the two thirds he needed for cloture.

Lyndon Johnson was unstoppable. As the 1964 elections neared, we concentrated on building firebreaks to save what we could. George Bush was an ideal candidate. He was pressing hard at the heels of Ralph Yarborough. In one of those amusing quirks of fate, my first participation in politics was when I handed out Yarborough leaflets as a small boy. When I got to the Senate, I mentioned my youthful indiscretion to Yarborough, who, of course, subsequently delighted in telling everybody that he gave John Tower his political start in life. I respected Ralph, and we had a friendly and cooperative relationship, but from an ideological standpoint he and I were about as far apart as two people could be and still remain in the same solar system.

Yarborough was a capable politician, and he was worried about Bush. He hit back with full-page newspaper ads that screamed "Vote Against Extremism!" and "George Bush's expensive advertising campaign conceals one crucial point: his alliance with the extremist Goldwater-Tower–John Birch wing of the Republican party." This was capped off with a call to "Vote for Sane Government . . . Vote for Lyndon Johnson and Ralph Yarborough."

George Bush has been criticized for keeping at arm's length from the Goldwater-Miller ticket. The criticism is unfair. Bush endorsed Goldwater early on, but he had to run *against* Yarborough, not *for* Goldwater. His strong showing pulled more votes than the combined total of those cast for Bill Blakley and myself in the special election of 1961. But Bush was defeated, and there was nearly wholesale carnage among the other Republican candidates, because Barry Goldwater was overwhelmingly rejected by Texans and the rest of the American people. Barry has described the experience of running for the White House as similar to "trying to stand up in a hammock."

Because of his blunt and sometimes brash way of stating his views, Barry was publicly perceived as an extremist and dangerously belligerent toward America's adversaries. In addition to emphasizing the president's popularity at the time, LBJ's managers exploited and heightened those perceptions with some of the toughest and most creative negative advertising that we'd ever seen in a presidential race. In addition, the Goldwater campaign was monumentally inept. It had a penchant for putting the candidate in the wrong place to say the wrong thing at the wrong time.

The result was one of the worst political blowouts in American history. The Texas Republican party was in shambles. All of our statewide candidates went down to defeat. Bruce Alger and Ed Foreman lost their U.S. House seats. Ten of the eleven Republican legislative seats were lost, with the Dallas delegation being totally wiped out. Only a handful of local officeholders pulled through. The political pundits were quick to point out that I was extremely vulnerable and predicted that I would join the list of casualties in 1966.

A few days after the election, Peter O'Donnell convened a small group of prominent Republicans at the old Commodore Perry Hotel in Austin. The day was cold and damp; clouds had rolled in from the coast, and we were as gloomy in spirit as the weather.

There were no recriminations, excuses, or apologies. I have always believed that a wise politician starts from a worst-case scenario and thoroughly examines all the possible pitfalls before contemplating the benefits and rewards of victory. Long before the first vote was cast, I had looked squarely at the downside possibilities. It didn't make the defeat any easier to bear. If you can get off the tracks, seeing the train coming is helpful, but we had no place to go.

My press secretary, Ken Towery, was in a position to say "I told you so." Right after John Kennedy's assassination he advised me and other senior Republicans that it would be more pragmatic to pull back and allow Nelson Rockefeller to take the nomination.

Ken said that any Republican was bound to be defeated by LBJ and that by insisting on Goldwater and linking our survival to his, we were risking a disaster. I disagreed on the grounds that it is impossible to know when lightning may strike and that the party should always go with its best candidate. Ken had been right, but he was thoughtful enough not to rub it in.

O'Donnell called the meeting to order and gave me the opportunity to speak first. Since our purpose was to look to the future, rather than to refight the last war, I started by offering to step aside in 1966 if a stronger candidate could be found. I said that the Senate seat belonged to the Republican party, not to John Tower.

Ken Towery has accused me of being a "moody" campaigner. In other words, if everything was going well — a nice airplane, good crowds, effective advance work — then I could run forever. However, if things got out of joint, I'd start wondering why I wasn't back in the classroom teaching comparative European political systems to a group of upperclassmen. He apparently thought I was letting my mood get the better of me. And I have to admit that the overwhelming losses we had suffered were demoralizing. In my head, I could sort out the technical factors that had conspired against us, but in my heart, it seemed as if the conservative movement had been repudiated. Maybe it was mood, or perhaps — and I am not sure that I know for certain to this day — I was trying to remind the group, in as dramatic a fashion as possible, that we had to rebuild brick by brick. Under the circumstances, I was just about the only brick left.

In any event, O'Donnell and the others immediately agreed that the first priority was my reelection. I think Pete's first words were "Hell no, John . . . you're all we've got!" As we discussed the situation, it became clear that the objective was to avoid the destructive infighting between pro- and anti-Goldwater factions that was occurring in other states by uniting the party behind my candidacy. Volunteers and contributors who had supported Goldwater and George Bush would be channeled into the Tower campaign. All other races were to be subordinated to the goal of retaining the U.S. Senate seat, to the point that Republican candidates would not be encouraged to run unless they could demonstrate that they had a good chance of winning or unless a token candidate had to go on the ballot.

It was a risky, all-or-nothing strategy. There were those who doubted its prudence and wondered where the Texas Republican party would stand in two years if the gamble did not pay off. But a general whose troops are encircled must break out. If he hedges the bet by dividing his forces, he risks not having enough strength in any one place to prevail. I had a lot more life left in me than the legendary El Cid of Spanish folklore and Hollywood epic, whose corpse, borne into battle on horseback, galvanized the desperate Castilians into a victorious attack on the Moors; in effect, though, I was being tied into the saddle in full regalia, visor down, lance at the ready, and sent out to rally the army for a last charge.

I won reelection to the Senate in 1966 by nearly two hundred thousand votes.

The first battle, and it may have helped win the war, was the one that I fought in Washington to get on the Senate Armed Services Committee. The committee assignments that had been handed to me in 1961 were Labor and Education, and Banking and Currency. Ev Dirksen had honored his campaign promise to Texas voters that if elected I would get a powerful committee slot. Dirksen came through by giving up his seat on Banking. I was deeply grateful. However, my other committee assignment, Labor and Education, was a different matter. The Labor Committee was dominated by liberal Democrats. There was little chance that I would ever have much influence. Successful political careers are not built around naysaying, and if I had stayed on the committee, most of my energy would have gone into opposing rather than proposing.

Even so, the Labor Committee assignment gave me the credentials to speak out against the proposed repeal of Section 14(b) of the Taft-Hartley Act. The Johnson administration was committed to eliminating 14(b), which permitted states to enact "right to work" laws. Johnson's allies in organized labor wanted to establish exclusive union shops on a nationwide basis, forcing workers to join the union or, if they refused, do without the job. Right-to-work has always been a popular issue in Texas, and I was its champion in the run-up to the 1966 election.

The Senate Republican leaders recognized that I was in a difficult position. Dirksen could see that Armed Services would give me a stronger platform from which to run for reelection, and he knew that I had worked hard for the party since coming to Washington. It wouldn't surprise me to learn that my more senior Republican colleagues, those who could have outbid me for the coveted vacancy on Armed Services, agreed to step aside without having to endure any real arm-twisting by Ev. We were a small, closely knit group, and nobody needed to be reminded that the vacancy would simply reopen in another year if the predictions of my political demise, widely circulated in the Texas press at the time, proved correct.

The move was pivotal to my career. By transferring to the Armed Services Committee in 1965, while retaining my seat on Banking, I was able to gain visibility on defense issues at the time the Vietnam War was beginning to escalate. It gave me a forum and the opportunity to travel across Texas visiting military installations, talking to local leaders, and immersing myself in the substance of what was a crucial factor in the state's economic well-being.

Several pages back, I mention the grasshopper and the ant of Aesop's fable. I think that Ken Towery, who was so helpful to me in putting down a solid political foundation, would probably agree that I was something of a grasshopper until I got on the Armed Services Committee. I was so frustrated and dissatisfied on Labor and Education that I really didn't work very hard at it. Banking wasn't much better initially, although something clicked when I was named to the panel's housing subcommittee, and from then on I was fully engaged.

Unfortunately, the grasshopper image stuck with me for several years; it was, after all, Washington's first impression of the junior senator from Texas. I do not consider myself an ant by any means, but I worked hard on the Armed Services Committee. The issues were fascinating, challenging, and important. I found my niche and myself.

The Gulf of Tonkin incident occurred in August 1964. I voted for the resolution that endorsed LBJ's decision to respond by dispatching American bombers on reprisal raids against military targets in North Vietnam. I do not believe that President Johnson deliberately deceived Congress or intentionally exaggerated what seemed to be premeditated North Vietnamese torpedo-boat attacks on two U.S. Navy ships, the USS *Maddox* and USS *Turner Joy*. The administration made a powerful case; there were only two dissenting votes in the Senate for a resolution that called on Congress "to approve and support the determination of the President as Commander in Chief to take all the necessary measures to repel any armed attack against the forces of the United States to prevent further aggression. . . . The United States regards Vietnam as vital to its national interest and to world peace and security in Southeast Asia." The House adopted the resolution unanimously, 416 to 0.

I did not regard the resolution as a blank check. And those who maintain that Congress should have been asked to approve a declaration of war fail to consider that we were assisting an ally and honoring existing treaty commitments. Whatever the provocation in the Gulf of Tonkin, it was not sufficient to justify an all-out declaration of war. And, too, there was the question of whether we could declare war against a political entity whose de jure existence we did not recognize. No matter what the formal legal status of the conflict, throughout it President Johnson operated within his authority as commander in chief. Congress, in turn, exercised its responsibility by authorizing and appropriating funds to carry out the necessary military operations.

In my conversations about the war with Lyndon Johnson, I came away with the correct impression that his sole interest was in helping South Vietnam preserve its independence and in protecting U.S. interests in the region by applying the minimum amount of military force necessary to do the job. He gradually escalated our participation in the war, searching for that necessary minimum. We discovered, too late and after too much bloodshed, that the maxim attributed to Pliny the Elder — "Fortune favors the brave" — is, indeed, correct. Johnson's innate caution, which served him so well as a politician, deprived him of the ability to strike hard and fast and decisively in the early stages of the conflict.

This predilection for caution was reinforced by the advice he received from Secretary of Defense Robert McNamara. For some reason, LBJ was fascinated, almost mesmerized, by McNamara. At a White House reception, the president took me aside — he loved to maneuver me back into a corner and trap me there, leaning down and jabbing at my lapel to make his points — and as we talked, McNamara passed by. He pointed at the cabinet secretary. "There goes the smartest man in Washington," Johnson said.

McNamara thought he was smarter than all the generals and all the GIs. He attempted to quantify the unquantifiable, to fine-tune war, the crudest of all enterprises. McNamara thought like a technocrat and business executive. There were statistics and computer readouts to justify every move. Anecdotal evidence, like reports from the field that the rules of engagement were permitting the enemy to operate out of sanctuaries off-limits to U.S. bombers, was discounted as being without scientific merit.

I made my first official visit to Vietnam in the spring of 1966 and returned six times. I'll never forget sitting at a battered mess table in Danang one evening with Marine Lieutenant General Lew Walt. We were looking at reconnaissance photos and talking about the war. Walt got angrier and angrier as he discussed the rules of engagement imposed by McNamara until he was crying with rage and resentment that his Marines were dying and he was being denied the discretion and flexibility to effectively suppress the warfighting capability of the enemy.

I told President Johnson about Lew Walt's anger and tears. He always listened closely to the briefings I gave him after my fact-finding missions to Vietnam. Ironically, unlike McNamara, he was very interested in the anecdotal evidence, particularly when it came from the combat troops who were doing the fighting and the dying. On my visits to Southeast Asia, I always broke away from the official briefings as quickly as possible. I couldn't describe the decor of General William Westmoreland's private office, although I was there several times, but the hootches, the makeshift command posts, the firebases, and the jungle clearings remain vivid.

I recall talking to Major General James F. Hollingsworth, the deputy commander of the "Big Red One" — the 1st Infantry Division. I asked him what he needed the most. He pointed to an M-16 rifle, a weapon originally called the AR-15 that had been designed as a survival weapon for aircrews downed in hostile territory. A light, rapid-firing, stubby rifle, it was ideally suited to jungle warfare. It was already standard issue to the air-mobile 1st Cavalry Division, which had seen so much of the early fighting in Vietnam. The standard-issue M-14 was hardly a full generation removed from the World War II–vintage M-1 and had been designed for European battlefield conditions. The M-14 was too heavy and unwieldy for Vietnam, the ammo added extra weight, and to lighten the load as they traversed rugged jungle terrain, GIs were carrying the bare minimum number of rounds, which often wasn't enough to get them through a firefight. To my dismay, as I talked to Hollingsworth and his combat soldiers, I learned that rather than shipping M-16s to Vietnam, where they were needed, we were about to close down the production line for the weapon.

Back in Washington, I told Johnson about the grunts' preference for the newer weapon, and I included it in my report to the Armed Services Committee. Fortunately, that piece of anecdotal evidence was not ignored. The production line was held open, and soon our troops were armed with M-16s.

Between 1966 and 1974, I made more visits to Vietnam than any other member of Congress. But observing a war is a far different matter from fighting one, and I will not presume on the sacrifices and courage of the men and women who served in Vietnam by telling war stories based on a relatively limited exposure to the conflict.

I attended long hours of briefings and watched senior officers stab at maps with their pointers and turn the pages of many a flip chart. I got out in the field as much as I could, accompanied most of the time by a single escort officer, who was instructed to advise the commanding officers of the units we visited that I did not expect formal military honors or special treatment; they were to go about business as usual. The press was never invited.

By keeping the visits on a strict, serious, and businesslike basis, I gained valuable insights that would not have been available to me by staying in Washington. On one occasion, I was invited to go through a booby trap course that simulated the hostile jungle environment. I was "killed" or "maimed" several times, and left the base with a keen awareness of the dangers our troops faced with every step they took, no matter how innocent the situation seemed. Similarly, as I prepared to stay overnight at a remote base, the instructions I received on my perimeter defense assignment to a Browning automatic rifle position should we be attacked after dark were a reminder that despite B-52s and sophisticated weaponry, the Vietnam War was also being fought at ground level, face-to-face with a determined foe.

As I said, though, the story of the Vietnam War belongs to those who served there.

One of those who served was Phil Charles, a member of my Senate staff. He came into the office one morning, put the draft notice on the desk, and said, "Senator, they're trying to draft me." I looked the document over. It was the real thing, complete with the traditional salutation — "Greetings . . ." I remembered the lyrics of an old song and said to Phil with a smile, "There's something about a soldier that is fine, fine, fine!"

Phil became an intelligence NCO in the 1st Cavalry and on his return to civilian life took over as my principal traveling aide whenever I returned to Texas. We spent hundreds of hours together flying and driving from town to town. There never will be an adequate substitute for that kind of campaigning, and I believe it was crucial in helping me win my first race for reelection to the Senate, in 1966.

In that contest, and again in 1972 and 1978, I put particular emphasis on spending time with Mexican-Americans. The numbers don't sound very impressive today, but when we pulled two hundred South Texans, many of them Hispanics, to a barbecue in Duval County, solid Democratic territory, I knew we were making progress. A few weeks later a hundred Duval County Democrats switched to the Republican party.

We had what the press called a "cow county" strategy. I visited the rural counties in 1965, making friends and showing the flag. The next year I worked the major population centers. In that way, I was able to make inroads into the rural Democratic bastions without neglecting my urban base.

Texas attorney general Waggoner Carr, whom I had drawn as an opponent, played to the party faithful in order to combat the defections. One of Carr's themes was that he could be more effective in Washington, where Democrats controlled both Congress and the White House. But by coming on strong against repeal of Taft-Hartley's right-to-work provision and by supporting the Vietnam War, I had undercut Carr's appeal to conservative Democrats. He was further weakened by the liberals in his party. Once again they were out to make trouble for the Democratic establishment.

By June 1966, the momentum seemed to be going my way. And then I opened my mouth and inserted my right foot. It happened at an 11:00 A.M. news conference in Houston. My managers had made the mistake of scheduling the session at the Houston Country Club, where I was to address a luncheon; it was not the ideal setting, given the subject matter that was bound to be raised. Our second mistake was to permit the news conference to drag on too long. After forty-five minutes of fielding questions on a variety of other issues, I was asked about melon pickers in the Rio Grande Valley, who were seeking a minimum wage of $1.25 an hour. The issue had come up many times before, and I had addressed it without incident. However, this time I was careless. The existing wage was 85 cents an hour, and I said, "The question is not just the adequacy of the wage but also the economics of the melon business. If wage costs go too high the business will simply move south of the border and the pickers in the valley will lose their jobs and, after all, eighty-five cents an hour is better than nothing."

Predictably, the next day the newspaper headlines screamed, "TOWER SAYS 85 CENTS AN HOUR IS BETTER THAN NOTHING." The stories described the country club setting of the news conference, reinforcing the perception of a "let them eat cake" attitude.

Survival in politics is often a matter of making fewer or smaller mistakes than your opponent. Carr made one late in the campaign that obliterated any memory of my gaffe. The restive farm workers in the valley struck and organized a march on Austin to demand redress of grievances — a movement called the Huelga. Governor Connally decided to intercept the march in New Braunfels, fifty miles southwest of Austin, and warn the strikers that invading the capital would serve no useful purpose and that they should return home. Carr accompanied the governor and was confronted by one of the leaders, a Father Gonzales, who brandished a crucifix in his face. The widely circulated picture of the incident was indeed worth a thousand words and an incalculably greater number of votes lost to my opponent.

The Democrats tried hard to get out the vote by making it a strictly and starkly partisan contest. I decided that I could use television effectively to reach across party lines. On election eve, back home in Wichita Falls, I brought the campaign to a close with a speech that was filmed in our living room:

> Foremost in my reasons for seeking reelection is my love for our state and my desire to serve our people as unselfishly as I know how.
>
> Since boyhood, I have been impressed with the fierce native pride of our Texan people and with the profound love of liberty that was manifest in our state's infancy when Colonel Travis with his sword drew a line in the dust of the Alamo and invited all those who were prepared to stand and face almost certain death to cross the line. One hundred eighty-three men crossed the line and, after three assaults from a vastly superior force, on a bleak day in March in 1836, laid down their lives because they had resolved that they had rather die as free men than live as slaves.
>
> It is for our generation of Texans to carry on this magnificent tradition. The preservation of our free institutions

should and must be our constant concern. I pledge myself to that pursuit. In good conscience, I earnestly ask for your support at the polling place tomorrow, and I do not fear the judgment of the people.

Good night and God bless you.

A few minutes after the broadcast, Waggoner Carr went on the air with a huge Democratic rally. I had charged that "Carr can't stand on his own two feet in the political arena," and there he was, surrounded by prominent politicians who seemed to dwarf the candidate as they lavished him with praise.

The next day, I made history again, as the first Republican in a century to win statewide in a general election. I won between 30 and 35 percent of the Hispanic vote. About four hundred thousand Democrats and Independents gave me their votes, and I carried sixteen counties that had never before voted for a Republican, not even Eisenhower. Waggoner Carr even lost his home county of Lubbock.

We gained several more seats in the state legislature, put a Republican in the state senate for the first time since 1927, and — certainly more than a historical footnote or postscript — George Bush took the Seventh Congressional District in Houston and went to the U.S. House of Representatives.

The victory was deeply gratifying, but by no stretch of the imagination could I conclude that I had secured permanent tenure as U.S. senator. Nothing could be taken for granted. The weekend trips from Washington to Texas and back to Washington were still part of the routine. By 1978, my travels had taken me to all 254 Texas counties. Frank Tolbert, the Texana writer for the *Dallas Morning News* and world-class chili aficionado, was the only other person to hold the distinction, and Frank died a few years ago. As my traveling aide, Phil Charles may come in a distant second in the number of counties visited, but he missed a few because on some trips I would instead take a staff specialist in a particular area. In the mid-1970s, among those who pinch-hit for Phil was Larry Combest, a young man destined for the U.S. House of Representatives.

It was Larry who on his own tried to lend a hand with my confirmation, and it was Larry's well-intentioned initiative that boomeranged.

NINE

A PUFF OF SMOKE

SAM NUNN'S INTERVIEW with Congressman Larry Combest was little more than an afterthought. Following the confirmation hearings, Combest called the Armed Services Committee offices to volunteer to help "set the record straight." He said that he had traveled with me in Texas and could provide information that would put allegations about my drinking into the proper context.

The offer was not given top priority by the committee's Democratic staff — probably because Larry, as a Texas Republican and former Tower aide, was considered biased in my favor. I understand that on Friday, February 3, after the telephone call from Combest, a member of the minority staff mentioned to Chairman Nunn that a congressman wanted to come by and talk about his experience traveling around Texas with John Tower in the 1970s. Nunn was apparently in a typical Senate Friday mode; he wanted to get out of the office as early as possible, and he indicated to the staffer that since it was probably going to be a quick and routine matter, the best course of action would be to ask Combest to come right over. "We might as well go ahead and talk to him" was the way Nunn's attitude was described to me later. At the time, I had no knowledge of Combest's offer to meet with Nunn, nor did any of my associates.

I would guess that with a favorable committee report on my nomination already in the works, the Armed Services Committee staff had little interest in processing an additional piece of pro-Tower material. However, the order, no matter how offhand, had come from the chairman, and Nunn's secretary put in a call to invite Combest to a meeting. John Warner was also summoned.

The three of them — Nunn, Warner, and Combest — spent only about fifteen minutes in the chairman's office. No one else was present. When Larry left, Arnold Punaro and Pat Tucker were called in. Nunn and Warner were both clearly upset by what they had heard.

I wasn't there, of course. At that moment I was conducting a meeting of my Pentagon transition team. I have tried to piece together what happened. Larry's subsequent statement to the FBI has been helpful in that regard, as was a telephone conversation I had with him sometime after he spoke with Nunn and Warner. Still, I am not certain that I have a clear picture of what transpired.

The Nunn-and-Warner version of events has never been communicated to me directly, nor was it included in the official public record, and therefore I have had to rely on secondhand and thirdhand accounts like this one in the *Washington Post:*

> The young congressman spilled out a portrait of Tower as a man who, during the 1970s, consumed a bottle of Scotch a night several times a week and who had to be helped out of his detachable shirt collars and into bed.
>
> Combest apparently drew this grim portrait — some believe it was deliberately exaggerated — to emphasize to Nunn and Warner how much progress Tower had made in the years since, how he had progressed from a serious problem drinker to relative sobriety. But Combest's account, according to one senator, conveyed a quantity and frequency of Tower's drinking that exceeded anything investigators had heard.

Nunn and Warner quickly dictated a memorandum based on the conversation. It was soon circulating around the Senate. "It was the most damning memorandum that I've ever read," one of my former Senate colleagues told reporters. When I heard about it, I called Combest. "What on earth did you tell those guys?" I asked. Larry seemed embarrassed and crestfallen. He told me that he was trying to help by showing the old John Tower versus the new John Tower. Larry said that he didn't mean to imply that I had consumed a whole bottle of scotch by myself, but that a few people would gather in my hotel room to discuss the day and would collectively consume the bottle. In a conversation with Richard Billmire, who was understandably irritated by this turn of events and didn't attempt to hide it, Combest said that he had "screwed up" by not clarifying what had gone on nearly fifteen years earlier.

Larry also gave Nunn and Warner the impression that he had traveled with me extensively. As I have said, Phil Charles was the staff member who did most of that sort of work. In statements to the FBI and in a letter that was read on the Senate floor, Charles said that my behavior in that period did not bear the slightest resemblance to that which had been described by Larry Combest. Phil was even willing, on my behalf, to make a disclosure in his letter to Senator Pete Wilson about an aspect of his own private life that most people with a similar background would just as soon not see published in the *Congressional Record*:

> As an individual who had a longer and closer relationship with him of any of the staff, both as a legislative assistant and principal traveling aide, I feel competent in addressing the notion of alcohol abuse which has figured so prominent in the debate over Senator Tower's fitness to serve.
>
> Without belaboring the point, I state simply that I am unaware of any instance when Senator Tower's judgment or ability to render reasonable and cogent decisions on matters of import was impaired owing to alcohol abuse or dependency. My observations in that regard are from the perspective of a recovering alcoholic who sought treatment for my alcoholism in 1979 at the insistence of Senator Tower and who has maintained sobriety since that time. In my view, Senator Tower does not now, nor did he in the past, manifest those characteristics of dependency which typify the alcoholic.

While it is true that I drank, and I drank scotch in the 1970s, neither Larry Combest nor any other member of my staff put me to bed drunk. As Larry and I talked, and the enormity of what he had done began to sink in, he was very distressed about it. At John Warner's suggestion, Combest was interviewed by the FBI. His statement to the agents was significantly different than the one he gave Nunn and Warner. He explained that hotel managers and friends would leave a bottle of scotch in my room, which served as a kind of command post and central gathering place. Over the course of an evening, people would be coming and going through there and the scotch would be consumed in the process. He said that he had observed me drink to excess on perhaps one or two occasions and that my use of alcohol did not interfere with my ability to walk unaided or to dress or undress myself.

Although the FBI interview was provided to the Senate, Combest's original, hasty, muddled account made more interesting reading. Larry even went back to Nunn and Warner to clarify his statement, but they waved their original memo under his nose and demanded to know whether or not it reflected what he had told them. Larry was stuck. He couldn't recant; those were his words. The wrong words, but his nonetheless.

By nature, politicians are opportunists, constantly on the lookout for anything exploitable in the pursuit of a political objective. Larry Combest turned up, and Sam Nunn saw that he had a validation of his reservations about my nomination. To have opposed confirmation based on Paul Weyrich's flimsy testimony or Lilla's whispering campaign against me would have subjected Nunn to the charge that he was simply seeking excuses to justify opposition to a nomination that would otherwise meet all reasonable standards of fitness. But Combest could be packaged as a credible witness: he was a member of the House, a former Tower aide, and an individual who seemed to have no special interest in providing highly negative information to the committee.

Combest was an opportunity, yet Nunn was cautious. He is known around the Senate as a man who rarely gets out in front on an issue prematurely; he takes few stands, because in doing so he would run the risk of losing. Those who have worked closely with him say that Sam Nunn hates to lose to the point that he feels it is better to keep a low profile than to risk defeat and criticism.

When the chairman of the Senate Armed Services Committee left the office for the weekend, he reiterated his order to the staff to continue to prepare a favorable report on my nomination. Opportunity had knocked, but Sam Nunn apparently needed a little more time to ponder the risks and the rewards before throwing open the door.

The meeting with my Pentagon transition team consumed most of Friday morning. With Don Atwood, the deputy secretary of defense designate, aboard, we could get down to the urgent business

1961 campaign: Penny, Marian, and Jeanne (*left to right*), with Mom and Dad and Senator Barry Goldwater.

With his father, Dr. Joe Z Tower, and Sport and Mike at the Anchorage, the Tower family farm, near Douglassville, Texas, in 1966.

Discussing jungle warfare with General James F. Hollingsworth, deputy commander of the 1st Infantry Division (*center*), and the commanding officer of the Australian Regiment, in Vietnam in 1966.

Debriefing President Lyndon Johnson in 1966 following a return from Vietnam.

With President Richard Nixon at a White House reception for congressional leaders.

Above, the National Chili Cook-off, a friendly rivalry.

Left, with President Gerald Ford in the Oval Office, 1975.

With Senator Hugh Scott
and Golda Meir, prime
minister of Israel.

Conferring with Chancellor
Helmut Schmidt of West
Germany, 1981.

Below, with Sultan Qabus
of Oman, 1981.

Sharing a lighter moment with Senator Henry "Scoop" Jackson.

Meeting with President Ronald Reagan, 1984.

Below, the Senate Armed Services Committee in 1982.

Above, being sworn in as U.S. negotiator in 1985 with Max Kampelman (*center*) and Maynard Glitman; Chief of Protocol Selwa Roosevelt is at left, Secretary of State George Shultz at far right.

Left, with Ambassador Viktor Karpov before a weekly plenary session in Geneva.

With Senator Sam Nunn at a reception at the U.S. mission in Geneva, 1985.

President George Bush arrives at the Pentagon in March 1989 for briefings and to meet with the Armed Forces Policy Council. *From left:* William Howard Taft IV, acting secretary of defense; Admiral William J. Crowe, Jr., chairman of the Joint Chiefs of Staff; Senator Tower, secretary of defense designate; President Bush; and General Brent Scowcroft, national security adviser.

With Dorothy Heyser, Mrs. Bush, and President Bush at a White House reception honoring the chiefs of mission of the diplomatic corps and their wives, 1989.

Delivering his statement at the Pentagon following the Senate's vote on his confirmation as secretary of defense.

With his daughters at the Pentagon in March 1989 (*left to right*): Penny Tower Cook, Marian Tower, and Jeanne Tower Cox.

Tower today, at his Washington office.

of reorganizing the management structure of the Defense Department, selecting the right people for the top jobs, and developing a budget. I had told Rhett Dawson to put out the word that we were going to make major personnel changes and that all political appointees were to submit their resignations as per the instructions issued earlier by the Bush transition operation. I did not want to leave the impression that Pentagon officials were exempt from the order. Some individuals had been maneuvering behind the scenes to keep their positions, and Rhett reported on a meeting he had held with politically ranked deputy assistant secretaries and deputy undersecretaries to inform them of the plans.

Not surprisingly, there had been hard feelings. Robert Costello, the undersecretary of defense for acquisition, had many friends within the conservative community who were eager to see him remain in the position. They were conducting a campaign in the press, emphasizing Costello's relationship with Vice President Dan Quayle. Although Costello had been brought in after the Ill Wind scandal broke, the acquisition post was too sensitive politically to go to a holdover from the Reagan administration. I made sure that Rhett had informed Costello that he was being replaced.

Atwood had already begun to look at existing procurement practices and management procedures. This was preparatory to a full-scale management review assigned to Paul Stevens, a lawyer assisting the transition, who had served as general counsel to the Packard Commission. We were to prepare a comprehensive outline of the review, submit it to the president for his approval, and, pursuant to his okay, begin work.

Although at the time I did not visualize the magnitude of the reductions ultimately to be imposed on military spending, I was anxious to develop a plan that would allow us to use shrinking dollars in the most rational and effective way.

Consistent with the national security positions articulated by President Bush and his surrogates during the campaign, Brent Scowcroft was moving to direct a comprehensive strategic review. Ideally, such a review, when completed, would provide the guidelines for determining what military roles and missions were most essential in implementing the overall strategy, thus enabling us to rationalize force structure and prioritize spending. Brent and I agreed that the review should go forward under the direction of Paul Wolfowitz, the new designee for undersecretary of defense for policy.

The strategic outlook was changing. The Intermediate-range Nuclear Forces Treaty, eliminating a whole class of intermediate-range nuclear weaponry, had been concluded; strategic offensive and defensive systems negotiations were ongoing, and the talks on conventional force reduction in Europe were about to begin. Simultaneously, Gorbachev was pushing Soviet internal reforms, political and economic liberalization in Poland and Hungary was evolving, and the establishment of improved lines of communications and steps toward confidence-building measures between the superpowers was being undertaken. Seen in the broadest context, there was a relaxation of tensions and a perceptible thaw in the Cold War.

Nonetheless, the potential threat posed to the West by the enormous military power of the USSR, while it appeared less menacing, had not significantly diminished. If anything, the Soviet military machine was even *more* capable, by virtue of continuing refinements, improvements, and new weapons systems incorporating the latest technological developments. The West must take great care to continue the balance of power vis-à-vis the East while moving with it to reduce offensive military power. Headlong rushes to unilaterally take positions we consider desirable do not ensure that the Soviets will keep pace.

In their eagerness to celebrate the thaw in the Cold War, some seemed to forget that the defense modernization program and the collective demonstration of political will by the NATO nations helped convince the Soviets that the West could not be intimidated by their relentless military buildup of the 1970s, achieved at enormous cost to the Soviet economy. Without that pressure, there would be no certainty that the Kremlin would continue to be as restrained in its deeds as it had recently been in its words.

Each of us on the transition team was well aware that countervailing pressure of a twofold nature was being brought to bear on the Bush administration to reduce U.S. military spending. There was internal pressure generated by the federal deficit's effect on the allocation of resources, which was being intensified by the financial community's nervousness about the federal government's inability to control spending; and external pressure brought about by the diminishing prospect of East-West armed conflict. The U.S. defense budget had been decreasing in real terms since 1985, and we were prepared for the trend to continue.

I told my staff that our job was to take initiatives to manage change in order to meet our most urgent national security requirements for fewer dollars. We would not merely acquiesce to those who believed that wishful thinking is enough to defend the country and protect our global interests.

Throughout the weekend, Dan Howard was kept busy fielding questions from reporters on a new spate of rumors about my private life generated by the postponement of the Armed Services Committee vote. It is a given that one sighting of a flying saucer prompts another, just as kidnappings, serial murders, and other sensational crimes tend to be reproduced by unstable individuals swept up in the sensational publicity, drama, and emotion sparked by the original act of violence. Psychologists do not completely understand the cause of this phenomenon, but as I worked with the transition team on Friday and Saturday, I saw that Dan Howard was getting an education in its effect.

Phone calls were going to the Armed Services Committee, the FBI, and the White House. Some of the allegations were almost immediately leaked to the press, and often that was our first indication that yet another piece of slander was in circulation. Dan was caught in a difficult spot. As soon as he denied a rumor, his denial gave the news media an excuse to run the story without the need for a second source, substantiation, or a detailed rebuttal, which naturally wouldn't have been available until the investigators were sent out to conduct interviews, a process that could take days. The rush was on to get a piece of the John Tower story, no matter how flimsy and specious a piece it might have been. One of the very worst examples of irresponsible journalism came from the *Philadelphia Inquirer* on Sunday, February 5, under the headline "TOWER BACKED ARMS-TALKS AIDE FOUND TO BE A SECURITY RISK":

Defense-secretary designate John G. Tower and other top American officials went to bat for an Air Force colonel in a sensitive diplomatic post whose adultery and mishandling of classified materials made him a security risk, according to federal investigative files.

Even as investigators closed in with evidence that Col. Robert L. Moser Jr. had an affair with a woman with Soviet-bloc connections, that he purchased drugs, improperly copied classified documents and sexually harassed his secretary, Tower wrote a glowing letter of support for the colonel.

Moser, a top-ranking staffer at the U.S.-Soviet arms control talks in Geneva in 1985 and 1986, worked closely with Tower, who was a leading U.S. negotiator.

"I do not believe that the allegations against Col. Moser are warranted," Tower said in a March 1986 letter "to whom it may concern." The letter was written two months after Moser was recalled to the United States.

I am not pleased that I have to reprint the *Inquirer*'s story, or many of the other press clippings in this book, but without offering them to the reader, I would be presenting only one side of the record. There would be no basis for intelligent comparison. You would have to take my word that the press account was distorted or biased. Better to see this stuff for what it is. And what it is, in the case of the Moser story, is an exercise in guilt by association. Lieutenant Colonel Robert Moser did provide certain administrative services for my negotiating group. He was not on my staff, but on that of Ambassador Max Kampelman, who was in charge of the support personnel for the three groups that composed the American negotiating effort. Moser was his executive secretary. Like Kampelman and Ambassador Maynard Glitman, my two counterparts at the Geneva arms talks, I wrote Moser a letter of commendation for his professional performance based entirely on my working experience with him.

The *Inquirer* went through grotesque contortions to link me to Moser and a situation to which I did not have even the slightest association. And the *Inquirer*'s lurid sex-drugs-and-espionage summary of the case, in fact, misrepresented the final outcome: the action taken by the Air Force was limited to putting a letter of reprimand in Moser's personnel file. He was not prosecuted in any way, as the *Inquirer*'s headline ("FOUND TO BE A SECURITY RISK") implied. "A glowing letter of support for the colonel" written "even as investigators closed in," as the newspaper phrased it, is melodramatic nonsense that would be laughable if it weren't so malicious.

The president was aware that the situation was deteriorating. Another round of denials from Dan Howard would not have been sufficient. To keep the balance from tipping against my nomination, we needed to bring presidential weight to bear, and George Bush was ready for action. Even though it was a Sunday, the White

House was in full operation. Administration officials had been working on a plan for dealing with the savings and loan crisis. The president was eager to launch the proposal. He called a news conference, knowing full well that the S & L bailout would not be the only subject pursued by the reporters.

Q. — You have placed considerable stress in these early days of your presidency on ethics and propriety, yet in recent days there's this controversy on Capitol Hill concerning the propriety of Senator Tower's alleged behavior, and questions raised over the weekend about the financial arrangements on the private funds of the man in charge of ethics, your counsel Boyden Gray, and other questions involving members of the administration or members-to-be of the administration. . . . What's happened here? Is it too harsh behavior on our part, too lax behavior on your part? What?

PRESIDENT BUSH — I don't think anything has happened. I learned long ago in public life not to make judgments based on allegations. . . .

And we are in a new era on these matters; matters that might have been approved and looked at one way may have a different perception today. And, so, what I want to do is finalize our standards and then urge everybody in all branches of government to aspire to those standards.

But I do think that it's fair that we not reach judgment on Senate hearings before the Senate hearings are concluded, because it's very hard to filter out fact from fiction, spurious allegation from fact. And I am not about to make a judgment based on a sensationalized newspaper story. . . . That wouldn't be fair, and I'm not sure how ethical it would be. So let's wait and see. . . . The Tower matter. . . . has been looked at by the FBI. The committee now has that. They have the responsibility to make a determination. And I'll be very interested to see what they say. But I am not going to . . . jump to conclusions based on stories that may or may not have any validity.

Q. — Even if, as your spokesman says you do, you continue to back Senator Tower for the position, there are those . . . who say that the best thing he could do for you is to step aside because, even if confirmed, he then would become "damaged goods," weaker in administering a very,

very tough job in your behalf. How do you respond to that
suggestion?

PRESIDENT BUSH — Well, I think people would not want a
person to step aside, given rumor, particularly if the rumor
is baseless. . . . The problem is the process is taking a little
longer than I would like, and yet, I think the Senate has
got to do what they're doing, looking at these allegations
very carefully. . . . If these allegations prove to be allegations without fact behind them, I think the people are
going to say, "Wait a minute. What went on here? How
come it was all this — we'd read this one day, and then
kind of a puff of smoke the next?" And, so, I don't
think . . . if the Senate committee gives its endorsement to
the senator, particularly after all of these allegations, that
there is any danger at all of damage to his credibility or his
ability to do the job.

The president was trying to immunize us against two viruses:
first, the allegations that seemed to be multiplying in an uncon-
trolled chain reaction; and second, demands that the nomination
be withdrawn. His statement warned the Senate that it would be
held accountable by the public if the allegations turned out to be
"a puff of smoke." It was a sound approach to take, and one that
would not have been lost on experienced politicians. Fair play is a
basic tenet of American life, and treating every outrageous accusation seriously regardless of its source would soon be seen as man-
ifestly unfair. As for withdrawing the nomination, President Bush
refused to accept the premise that I was "damaged goods." He
foresaw the possibility, I believe, that there would be some administration allies who would rather avoid an all-out confrontation
with the Democrats in the Senate over my nomination, which
might sour the mood of his first few months in office. Although
he did not flatly rule out the possibility of withdrawing the nomination, by dismissing the questioning in the way that he did the
president was telling his friends that he felt my nomination and
effectiveness had not been irreparably harmed.

In reviewing the statement, however, one clause does stand out
as subject to damaging misinterpretation: "If the Senate committee
gives its endorsement to the senator, particularly after all of these
allegations, [I don't think] that there is any danger at all of damage
to his credibility or his ability to do the job." I don't know how

Sam Nunn read that. Did it point out to the chairman of the Senate Armed Services Committee that it was within his power to inflict grievous damage to my ability to function as defense secretary, damage that would lead the president to withdraw the nomination? There really isn't a satisfactory answer, unless Sam Nunn provides one. I do know that George Bush was not leaving himself an out, as amply demonstrated by his subsequent actions.

And I know one other thing: on Monday morning Sam Nunn was in open opposition to my nomination. As a courtesy, Senator Alan Dixon of Illinois had notified the Senate Armed Services Committee staff that he planned to announce his decision to vote for my nomination. When Nunn got the message, I have been informed, he called Dixon and warned him that he had better read the Combest memorandum before talking to the press. Dixon wasn't born yesterday; he must have known that Nunn, who immediately sent the memo off by courier, was also sending the signal that he was committed to blocking confirmation. As the newly elected assistant Democratic whip, Dixon was in the uncomfortable position of opposing a senior member of his party's leadership on a key vote. He immediately began rethinking his position, and as he later told a writer for the *Washingtonian* magazine, "I began to think, when you depart from the leadership to vote on someone, it should be for someone who you really want in the job, 'cause this is a biggie."

In addition to the Combest interview, the rash of new allegations over the weekend, including the Moser story, probably had an influence on Nunn's decision to openly oppose the nomination, and most likely it contributed to pushing Dixon over the edge as well.

Another damaging factor was the news coverage given to Senator Alan Simpson's appearance on NBC's *Meet the Press,* which Washington insiders watch, along with the other network political talk shows, with religious devotion. This is how it was represented by the *Los Angeles Times:*

Senate Minority Whip Alan K. Simpson (R-Wyo.) said Sunday that he sees "more of a conflict" in Defense Secretary-designate John Tower's receipt of more than $750,000 from Pentagon contractors than in allegations about the nominee's personal life.

"That's heavy bucks, and people just don't understand that

part," Simpson said of Tower's lobbying and consulting fees from six defense contractors from 1986 through 1988.

Simpson's comments . . . are significant both because of his Republican leadership role and his friendship with President Bush, with whom he went fishing shortly after the election.

Alan Simpson's remark, taken in the context of his observation "That's heavy bucks, and people just don't understand that part," was a valid assessment of the political realities of the situation. No politician in his right mind says, "Conflict of interest? Hey, no big deal!" Simpson was taking basic precautions. Like the rest of us, he saw a cloud on the horizon but had no idea that in the equivalent of a few seconds a tornado would rip through and blow the roof off. Through no fault of Simpson's, the *Los Angeles Times* story, by placing undue emphasis on his friendship with the president and on Simpson's position as assistant Republican leader, was distorted into one that incorrectly suggested that both George Bush and Senate Republicans were having misgivings about my nomination.

A pattern was forming: whatever was said on my behalf — or even neutral comments that were presented to explain or to contextualize — was twisted and used against the nomination.

At the same time, the newspapers were reporting that two defense industry publications, the *Army Times* and *Defense Weekly,* had called for the withdrawal of my nomination. Both newsletters were indulging in intramural back-stabbing by going after me, since I was the former chairman of a competing publication, *Armed Forces Journal International.*

Taken in one lump, all of these developments were a powerful incentive to draw Sam Nunn into direct conflict with the White House over my nomination. By heading off Alan Dixon's attempt to endorse me, Nunn was moving to form a united Democratic front. He had to keep the more independent-minded members of the committee, like Dixon, Edward Kennedy, and Richard Shelby, from straying. The Combest memo was a valuable tool, as was the suggestion that Republicans were beginning to have second thoughts.

At this point, I am convinced, we could still have kept Sam Nunn in check if it hadn't been for the actions of C. Boyden Gray and John Warner. First, Gray. The president needed an emissary to the Senate Armed Services Committee who could deliver clear, unequivocal signals; unfortunately, he turned to his White House counsel, who at the time was not well versed in the subtleties of congressional protocol. I understand that Gray shocked both Nunn and Warner by making derogatory comments about me during a private meeting with them. My personal behavior and life-style, he said, reflected a "Napoleon complex." I imagine that Gray thought he was making a favorable impression on the two senators by being so forthright, but I've been told that the impact on them was adverse.

The error had to help convince Sam Nunn that the nomination was vulnerable, at the very least. He would have also been justified in concluding that Boyden Gray, widely known as a close personal friend of the president's, may have been reflecting George Bush's attitude.

John Warner's conduct was a departure from what is normally expected of the ranking member of the president's party on a Senate committee. Outright partisan bickering between the majority and minority is the exception, not the rule. You can disagree without being disagreeable. John Warner didn't seem to be able to grasp the basic concept behind that maxim. His instinct was to avoid disagreements at all costs. To keep on good terms with Sam Nunn, he ceded the rights of the Republican minority to object to a course of action that was inimical to its best interests. His passivity and lack of focus had been handicaps since the beginning of the confirmation process; by countenancing the drafting and the circulation of the Combest memorandum, Warner became Nunn's accomplice. Any Democrat would have seen it as an open invitation to launch a frontal assault on the nomination.

On Tuesday, February 7, just in case his Democratic colleagues had overlooked the obvious, Sam Nunn, I was informed, attended the regular weekly Democratic caucus and indicated that he would oppose my nomination and that John Warner would also cast a no vote. I say "indicated" because it is unclear whether he stated flatly that he had a commitment from Warner. A Democratic senator who was there told one of my associates it was plain to him that Nunn was out to block the nomination and that the chairman thought he was going to be able to bring Warner along to provide nonpartisan camouflage.

Given Sam Nunn's predisposition toward caution, I would assume that he equivocated in some way. Even so, he was edging farther out on the limb, and for him it was a bold move even to suggest that he was considering such action. Therefore, what happened a few hours later must have come as an extremely unpleasant surprise. Without warning, John Warner sawed about three quarters of the way through the limb on which Nunn had risked his precious reputation.

By noon Tuesday, the FBI had completed its investigation, but the file was still being typed and reviewed. To expedite the process, the White House counsel's office offered to give the members of the Senate Armed Services Committee a briefing on the file's contents and findings. Nunn refused. He wanted the report itself. Since the Republican Policy Committee held its weekly luncheons on Tuesday, Sherrie Marshall was dispatched to Capitol Hill to answer any questions that the GOP senators might have on the status of the FBI investigation.

The intention was not to give the Republicans a sneak preview or to thwart Nunn's desire to see the written report. After a weekend of rumor and allegation, the Republicans were understandably eager to get an update from the White House, and the policy luncheon was the logical forum.

There were many questions. Sherrie fielded them with her characteristic incisiveness. The Republican senators weren't about to beat around the bush. They wanted to know whether the FBI file, which would be delivered to the committee in a few hours at most, was good news or bad news. Sherrie told them that the FBI found no evidence to substantiate the allegations that had been phoned in to the Armed Services Committee offices. The source of the allegations (the one about my driving my car into a wooded ravine and another regarding my sexual harassment of women in my office) had been relying on secondhand accounts of my supposed indiscretions, and the principal secondhand account — attributed to the caller's husband — could not be corroborated, not by any available evidence or by the man himself, who seemed less than thrilled that his wife had gotten him involved with the FBI and my confirmation. The FBI couldn't even find a secondhand or thirdhand account on the sexual harassment charge.

The news media were waiting outside in the hallway. When the senators emerged after lunch, they deferred to John Warner, as the ranking Republican on the Armed Services Committee. The reporters wanted to know about the FBI report. Warner noted that the written report had yet to be received and added, "It provides, in the judgment of the White House counsel, no basis on which senators can find a factual situation that would amount to any disqualification." He went on to tell the press that he would urge Sam Nunn to call the committee into session to accept the written report from the bureau, "if necessary, in the early evening," and to hold a vote on the nomination.

Suffice it to say, Nunn did not call the committee into session that evening. The word quickly spread that he was furious at Warner and the White House. Warner was faulted for violating an agreement that the two men were said to have concluded that all news conferences and statements about the nomination were to be handled jointly by the chairman and the senior Republican on the committee. Furthermore, Nunn charged, speaking through the Democratic committee staff, the White House was guilty of partisanship by discussing the FBI's findings with Senate Republicans.

The reaction was totally out of proportion to the provocation — unless Nunn suspected that he was being double-crossed by Warner. It is entirely possible that Nunn had convinced himself that he was in a no-risk, no-fault position, that he could block the nomination without paying a price. This strategy would have had to hinge on John Warner. By using Warner as the Judas goat, he could attract enough Democrats and Republicans to his cause to persuade President Bush to withdraw the nomination. Thus, Sam Nunn would have won a major victory over the new administration without exposing himself to a bruising political battle.

On its face, Warner's statement was innocuous. It could even have been read as indicating that he had doubts. The *New York Times,* for instance, seized on his use of the word "disqualification":

> Senator Bob Dole of Kansas, the Senate minority leader, was asked if there was any significance to Mr. Warner's saying only that the report does not "disqualify" Mr. Tower, which seemed short of a complete exoneration.
>
> Mr. Dole hesitated. Then he was asked if he agreed with that characterization. "I think that's about right," he replied.
>
> Republican aides declined to elaborate on Mr. Warner's comments.

It was not the last time that Bob Dole would have trouble with Warner's circumlocutions. In this instance, Dole also found himself in the position of being asked to agree or disagree with an ambiguous "characterization" posed by the reporter. Was he agreeing with the characterization that the FBI report did not disqualify me, or the characterization that Warner's comment stopped short of a complete exoneration? The Republican leader was walking through a verbal minefield. The function of the FBI was to investigate, not to pass judgment. The investigation found no evidence to substantiate the allegations, but by framing the question in terms of exoneration, the press was implying that there was guilt because the bureau had not done something that was in fact beyond its scope and its responsibility. I think it was at about this point that Bob Dole stopped trying to be subtle. As one of my staunchest advocates, he could see that subtlety was lost on Sam Nunn and the news media.

But semantic subtlety was not the major consideration for Nunn, who had put himself in jeopardy at the Democratic caucus. His colleagues had barely had enough time to digest the import of the news that he brought them (i.e., that both the chairman and the ranking Republican on the Armed Services Committee opposed the nomination) than Warner threw everything into doubt by calling for an immediate vote on the nomination.

John Warner had unwittingly broken up Sam Nunn's play. Nunn was forced to improvise. His first reaction was to go after Sherrie Marshall. Nunn blamed her for violating the ground rules by briefing the Republican senators and permitting John Warner to speak to the press. Sherrie was to be the human sacrifice, and the White House offered her up to propitiate Nunn. She was pulled off the assignment and stashed away in an office lest the sight of her offend the chairman of the Armed Services Committee.

Nunn's quarrel should have been with John Warner, who should have known whether the luncheon briefing violated his commitments with the chairman. What's more, Sherrie could not have prevented a U.S. senator from talking to the press.

Nonetheless, the White House was well advised to move Sherrie out of the line of fire if there was any chance of soothing Nunn's hard feelings. In the end, just a single vote counted on the Senate Armed Services Committee, and it belonged to Sam Nunn. I knew that if he went into open, full-scale opposition, it would take a miracle to save my nomination.

By midafternoon, with rumors ricocheting around Capitol Hill like shrapnel, there was only one person who could stabilize the situation — George Bush.

Nunn and Warner were invited down to the White House to

meet with the president; his chief of staff, John Sununu; and National Security Adviser Brent Scowcroft. I am told that the president made it absolutely clear that he was not going to withdraw the nomination. Nunn said he was still concerned about the allegations that had been made against me. He was obviously beginning to lean the wrong way, but he stopped short of informing the president, face-to-face, that he would oppose the nomination. Instead, he relied on the newspapers to deliver the message. The news summary that George Bush found on his desk the next morning had this story culled from the *New York Times:*

John G. Tower's chances to become Secretary of Defense were further damaged today when the two top Democrats on the Senate Armed Services Committee turned against his nomination.

Senator J. James Exon, the second-ranking Democrat on the committee, said he and Senator Sam Nunn of Georgia, the chairman, now felt they would change their minds only if they learned something new to ease their doubts about reports of Mr. Tower's drinking and his behavior with women.

The story made it clear that the message was being read loud and clear in the Senate:

A Republican senator confirmed that Mr. Nunn was prepared to vote against Mr. Tower. He described the Georgian's decision as "an incredible event" that put Mr. Tower's nomination in considerable doubt. Even if Mr. Tower were to somehow win confirmation in the full Senate, the Republican said, he might be so damaged as to be "useless" as Secretary of Defense.

Despite a strong effort by the White House and Senate Republicans to force a vote on the nomination, there was also a deepening partisan cleavage on the committee and Senators said information was coming to light about Mr. Tower that would require further Federal investigation.

Another allegation had been received by the White House, a few hours after Nunn and Warner met with the president, which amounted to an accusation that my Senate campaign committee in 1984 had accepted an illegal contribution from a former official of a defense-contracting firm involved in the Ill Wind scandal. The

FBI report would go to Capitol Hill the next day as planned, but the Senate would be informed that the investigation would continue. At that point, Boyden Gray made a serious miscalculation by requesting that the Armed Services Committee delay its vote, which I had hoped would take place Thursday or Friday, before the Senate went on a ten-day recess. Gray's request came just as the Republicans in the Senate had made their first concerted effort to bring pressure to bear on Nunn to act on my nomination. After temporizing for so long, John Warner was finally exercising some leadership. The White House counsel pulled the rug out from under him and the other Republicans. The most recent allegation was not significant enough to warrant a postponement of the vote at such a critical juncture, given the source and his motivation — plea bargaining. The fact was that the FBI had already concluded I was not connected in any way to the Ill Wind scandal.

I was dismayed by this turn of events. The first postponement of the vote had been bad enough; it triggered a burst of new allegations about my private life. A second could be as bad or worse and would probably fatally weaken the chances for confirmation. Eventually, if the open-ended investigation-allegation-investigation cycle continued, enough mud would be thrown on my reputation — for whatever reason, be it malice, politics, kookiness, the vindictiveness of an ex-wife — that it would be impossible to scrape it off in a month or a year or a lifetime.

If common decency had eroded to that point, I was defenseless. But I could not bring myself to believe that after twenty-four years in the U.S. Senate, friends, former colleagues, and those who had come to the institution after my retirement would judge me by standards that were so flagrantly at odds with a respect for decency, honor, and fair play. What was happening to me could have happened in an evil, Kafkaesque society. It couldn't happen in the United States. It couldn't happen in the U.S. Senate. Those people knew me. And when I added up my sins and transgressions against them — yes, I caught George Mitchell pretending that he was more sophisticated than he really was about strategic doctrine and I pointed it out on the Senate floor; I successfully opposed Nunn on some defense micromanagement issues; I outmaneuvered senators, one of them in my own party, who tried to grandstand on the waste-fraud-and-abuse business; I probably offended Nancy Kassebaum, who didn't like it when Kansas firms lost a defense contract; and I was hard-nosed in defending authorization bills in

conference and on the Senate floor — I could find no act so despicable that I deserved to be burned at the stake. Yet Sam Nunn
was piling up the kindling at my feet.

This man was not for burning, at least not if I could help it. I
arranged to meet with Nunn and Warner on Wednesday, February
8; I thought I might be able to soothe Nunn's ire, answer his
questions, and mollify his concerns.

TEN

UNTO THE BREACH

SAM NUNN'S DISPLAY of temper and the leaks to the news media prompted the White House to issue what amounted to an apology. On February 8 the president's spokesman, Marlin Fitzwater, told reporters at his daily news briefing that there had been "mistakes" and that the nomination had been "mishandled."

The statement was intended to appease Nunn and to give him an escape route — should he desire one — from the impasse. If there were no more mistakes and mishandling, Fitzwater's choice of words suggested, then the misunderstanding could be resolved without damaging the nomination. The Bush administration would take the blame on itself, and, indeed, a measure of blame did legitimately fall on White House Counsel C. Boyden Gray. (I am told that after hearing about the Russian-ballerina allegation, Gray's first reaction was to immediately call the committee to inform Nunn about it, as though the smoking gun had been found at last. A quick look at that absurd fabrication should have convinced anyone with experience that it was too wild a story to hold up under even the most cursory examination. The Russian-ballerina allegation deserves a thorough review, and I will come back to the subject in a later chapter.)

In response to the tension and anger that were becoming palpable on Capitol Hill, Boyden Gray made it a point to personally deliver the FBI report to Sam Nunn and John Warner. The objective of the gesture was to demonstrate that the White House was not attempting to obstruct the legitimate work of the Armed Services Committee. But it also served to call special attention to the report, which, unlike the one that accompanied my nomination when it was first sent to the committee, read like a police dossier of a criminal investigation. Instead of recording general comments about the interviewee's opinions on my fitness to hold office, the FBI was pursuing specific allegations by using the techniques normally employed to track down an alleged drug dealer or Mafia hit man. As a result, the tone of the report was far different from that of the earlier version. With its typographical errors, misspellings, and snarled grammar, it read like the first draft of one of Mickey Spillane's Mike Hammer novels.

Bear in mind, however, that my description of the report was set down on paper for the first time almost a year after it was delivered to Sam Nunn. On February 8, 1989, I did not know the report's tone or contents. The pile of documents, roughly eight inches high, that sat on my dining room table in Dallas while I wrote this book was the product of a Freedom of Information request that took seven months to be processed by the Justice Department. In a criminal-law proceeding, the accused has a right to be fully informed of the allegations against him and a right to confront his accusers; witnesses must give sworn testimony and therefore face the penalties of perjury; and all evidence is provided to the defense. In my case, the identity of the accusers was withheld, and neither the committee nor the White House would reveal to me the details of the allegations. Therefore, I had to guess at what I was being accused of by analyzing either the questions that were asked by the FBI or the leaks to the news media.

Throughout the photocopies delivered to me in September 1989, the names of many of the FBI's respondents were blacked out, and properly so, since it had been a confidential investigation. But in a courtroom, the testimony would have been ruled inadmissible as hearsay or as secondhand or circumstantial evidence. Of those few who were willing to speak to the FBI without requesting anonymity, I could identify old political enemies with a score to settle and past acquaintances with some smoldering hostility; the rest were publicity seekers, crackpots, and busybodies. There also appeared to be cases of mistaken identity or false impressions. None of the statements was given under oath.

                              *   *   *

I could think of only one sure way to determine whether the president's intervention and the efforts of Marlin Fitzwater and Boyden Gray had succeeded in dousing the fire: I needed to personally take a temperature reading of the situation. It was at this point that I requested a late-afternoon meeting with Nunn and Warner to follow the delivery of the FBI report.

When I arrived at Nunn's office, his secretary informed me that the chairman and Senator Warner were still at the Armed Services Committee rooms reviewing the FBI material. I sat there and cooled my heels for an hour.

When they finally arrived, Nunn's demeanor did not suggest that he was incensed or alarmed by what he had just finished reading. He asked me about two or three of the allegations, and, essentially, I repeated the statements rebutting the charges that I had already given to the FBI. Warner tossed in a few additional questions, usually as a follow-up to a question from Nunn.

To disprove the allegations that I had a drinking problem, I gave them a quick summary of my medical condition and suggested that I would allow my physicians to be interviewed by any experts that Nunn might want to designate. I did not offer to undergo a medical examination, because I had already authorized release of my medical records to the FBI, which sent out agents to review the material and interview my doctors. When I had inquired of Dr. William Narva whether it would be advisable to submit to medical tests to demonstrate that I was not alcohol-dependent, he told me that it was a complex and lengthy procedure that might drag on for weeks. Therefore, I felt that providing the records and making my physicians available were the only reasonable alternatives.

Warner, as I recall, tried to make a joke about how glad he was that his personal life was not being examined as rigorously as mine. But the mood was not at all light. I wanted to get an indication of where Nunn stood on the confirmation. I thought I would smoke him out by stating that I intended to give up drinking spirits while serving as secretary of defense, but even that failed to produce a definitive reaction. The reading was frustratingly inconclusive. Judging by his comments, Nunn seemed to be straddling the fence, which I could live with as long as he stayed there and permitted the Democrats on the Armed Services Committee to vote their consciences and personal judgment. His reaction to my comments about the allegations and to my willingness to cooperate with outside medical experts was bland. The most vivid statement made by Nunn during the session was also ambiguous: "Tower, I'll say this for you — you have a bellyful of guts."

In the end, however, Nunn and Warner could beg off. Their excuse was that since another allegation had been raised, judgment must be reserved until the FBI looked into it. As the nominee, I could not say what had to be said to get us off dead center. And John Warner was incapable of it. I needed a Barry Goldwater or a Strom Thurmond to be there in that office to needle and prod Nunn until he scheduled a vote. "Let's move it, Sam — end the process here" was all that needed to be said.

When I left the meeting I had to run the gauntlet of cameras and reporters. An old Texas friend saw the videotape that evening on the network TV news and later told me that I looked very worried. She was right — I was worried.

During the drive downtown to the Jefferson, I told Dan Howard, "I've done everything I can to satisfy Sam's concerns. On the drinking thing, I told him I would not consume spirits while sitting as secretary of defense." Dan inquired about Nunn's reaction. I replied: "He didn't seem to be concerned about that [the spirits]. But I answered his questions about my consultancies. I answered every question that he had. Now let's wait and see what Sam does. We'll know more later."

The next morning, the *Boston Globe* managed to capture and summarize what I was most anxious about in this front-page article:

> For the first time since President Bush nominated him as secretary of defense, John Tower is in real trouble.
>
> President Bush yesterday reaffirmed his support for Tower in no uncertain terms, but he is increasingly becoming a lone voice.
>
> Sen. Sam Nunn (D-Ga.), the chairman of the Armed Services Committee, said yesterday he has so many "serious concerns" about Tower's personal and professional conduct that he would oppose Tower's confirmation if a vote were taken now.
>
> "There are new allegations of a financial nature which are now being checked in the Tower nomination," Nunn said. . . .
>
> Sen. James Exon (D-Neb.), a conservative and the

second-ranking member of the committee, seconded Nunn and added that the two senators were not alone. "Two days ago," Exon said, "there were probably the votes to report out his nomination in committee and to approve it on the floor. . . . Today, I couldn't say there are the votes on the committee. There may be, but I couldn't say."

A House Republican with close connections to Bush said of the nomination: "It looks to me like it is going sour fast. He may be beyond rescuing. . . ."

But Bush told reporters yesterday, "I have seen nothing, not one substantive fact, that makes me change my mind about John Tower's ability to be secretary of defense and be a very good one."

Dismissing allegations as "rumor and frenzied speculation," the president said: "There's always some other allegation and . . . each of them has been reviewed and shot down in flames. . . . Let us be fair enough that we do not deal in rumor after rumor."

Bush said the Justice Department "has an obligation" to look into any new charges, but he added, "What's gone too far is allegations that the senators themselves would agree are totally unfounded to have been floated around for a long period of time and damage the integrity and honor of a decent man."

The "obligation" to investigate the allegation that the president referred to in his news conference was sapping the strength from my nomination. Simply by trying to be aboveboard, notifying the committee that new charges had been received, and suggesting a postponement of the vote, as Boyden Gray did the evening of February 7, the White House was unwittingly giving ammunition to my opponents. Again, the *Boston Globe:*

On Tuesday night, Sen. John Warner of Virginia, the Armed Services Committee's ranking Republican member, told reporters that still further charges had come to the attention of the White House and that a vote to confirm Tower should not take place until the FBI had time to investigate them.

This announcement came just a few hours after Warner emerged from a meeting with White House officials and said the FBI report contained nothing to disqualify Tower. Warner then said the vote should take place at once.

[Sen. James] Exon said he thought Warner's turnaround led to the shift in sentiment on Capitol Hill. "The actions of the White House last night — when they said, 'Don't vote, we want to check into these new facts,' after saying 'Let's vote now' — this has to have some people around here wondering, 'What's going on?' " Exon said.

After my meeting with Nunn and Warner, with Nunn's position uncertain, I had to make a worst-case assumption that he would vote against my nomination. The impending congressional recess meant at least another two weeks would go by without a vote. Those two weeks would give Nunn the opportunity to twist the arm of every wavering Democrat on the committee as he feigned neutrality and claimed he was just waiting for the FBI to finish the investigation. And as it turned out, the bureau made short work of the Ill Wind allegations. Within a few days, the attorney general was able to report back that there was no evidence to support the allegation that my campaign committee had received illegal contributions from a defense contractor. Apparently, the man who was the source of the allegation was plea-bargaining by dragging my name into his problems in the hope of getting a better deal from the prosecutor.

On Thursday morning Sam Nunn had breakfast alone with the president. The meeting was not reported in the press at the time. A few hours later, Nunn told reporters that if he was forced to bring my nomination to an immediate vote, he would cast his vote against confirmation.

When I saw the wire-service accounts of Nunn's news conference, I told Dan Howard, "Well, from here on out my chances are very slim."

The Senate went into recess on Friday, February 10, with my nomination hanging in limbo. Almost simultaneously, Lilla struck again.

I had suspected that my former wife was instigating some of the more lurid allegations, a suspicion that was widely shared, as confirmed by this report in the *Los Angeles Times*:

Many of the most bruising wounds involve his second wife, Lilla Burt Cummings, from whom he won an exceedingly bitter divorce in 1987. Through friends in Washington society and the news media, she has spread a trail of stories about

Tower's alleged "marital misconduct" and close relations with defense contractors.

She raised the question in divorce papers as to whether Tower had carried on extramarital affairs with three women.

Tower's friends deny he had affairs with any of the three.

One of Lilla's conduits was Sarah McClendon, a reporter who free-lances for some small newspapers. McClendon showed up at the White House briefing on Thursday to pounce on Marlin Fitzwater after he finished telling reporters that the president was firmly committed to my nomination:

Ms. McClendon — Well, Marlin, why is it that the president will not take the word of a woman who was married to Tower for ten years and says he is an uncontrollable alcoholic?

Mr. Fitzwater — Well . . .

Ms. McClendon — Now, the president certainly has access to that information, it's in the FBI report. He knows Mrs. Tower, and Mrs. Bush knows Mrs. Tower. Why can't they believe her? She's not telling a lie.

Mr. Fitzwater — Well, we have to examine this matter . . .

Ms. McClendon — And there are White House staffers, right today, assistants to the president, who have said they know Tower, and they know that he is an alcoholic, and they know that he has done nothing to cure his alcoholism. Why doesn't the president believe that?

Mr. Fitzwater — Well, we have to take information from a number of sources, but these matters are all looked into by the bureau. All of these people, including Mrs. Tower and others, have been interviewed, doctors, other people who have relevant information. And we are persuaded by the conclusions of the bureau investigation checks.

Sarah has been notorious since her earliest days in Washington. John Kennedy tongue-lashed her at a televised presidential news conference for asking a question that sounded as if it had been torn out of one of Joe McCarthy's witch-hunting notebooks. She has specialized ever since in making outrageous statements and hanging question marks on the end to preserve the fiction that she is actually seeking information.

During our marriage, Lilla routinely struck Sarah's name off guest lists that included the Texas press corps. In those years, whenever Lilla had anything to say about it, Sarah McClendon was persona non grata around my Senate office. Their reconciliation and alliance struck me as most bizarre.

Even more bizarre was the alliance between Sam Nunn and Lilla. Sarah McClendon's railing about alcoholism at the White House briefing helped keep the issue alive among that influential segment of the Washington press corps. Lilla's telephone calls to Nunn assisted in fueling the conflagration on Capitol Hill.

On one occasion, Nunn invited John Warner over to his office to participate in a three-way conference call with Lilla. The speakerphone was switched on, but when Lilla was told that Warner was on hand, she refused to talk to him. Despite Nunn's entreaties about the need to be bipartisan, she refused to budge. Lilla didn't like Warner, and when I was in the Senate she went out of her way to let him know it. Apparently, the hostility was based on what Lilla thought was the shabby way Warner had treated his former wives, including Elizabeth Taylor. Her revenge in this case was to force Warner to sit in silence beside Nunn's desk and listen to the diatribe against me.

The main feature of this conversation was the outrageous lie that, late at night, when Reagan's defense secretary Caspar Weinberger would call to consult with me as chairman of the Armed Services Committee, Lilla would refuse, she said, to put the calls through because I was too drunk to be allowed to talk with Weinberger.

To Sam Nunn's credit, much of what Lilla told him was not given a lot of credence. Nunn had served with me long enough in the Senate to know about Lilla's reputation: her temper tantrums, verbal abuse of my staff, scenes in restaurants that were fairly frequent and ugly to the point that we were no longer welcome in some establishments. As Senator John McCain told one of my associates when they were poking through the wreckage after the nomination was rejected by the Senate, "I don't know how to explain Lilla except to say that great men sometimes have great flaws. And Lilla was John Tower's great flaw." Senator McCain and I traveled many miles together in Europe, the Middle East, and Asia when he was the Navy's Senate liaison officer, and so he knows enough about my private life to speak with authority. And I believe he would agree that I bear the ultimate blame for Lilla's conduct. She became a major problem during my reelection campaign in 1978, made life hellish for my staff and friends, and, worst of all, strained the relationship between me and my daughters. She criticized them constantly and made Penny, Marian, and Jeanne feel unwelcome. I was blind to all of that misery until Penny came to me sometime in 1985 and said, "Daddy, tell me that she'll be gone someday . . . tell me that you're not going to stay with her forever."

I first met Lilla in an elevator in the Capitol Hill Club. I was on my way to make a speech, and we were introduced by a mutual acquaintance. She wrote me a note a few days later saying how much she was impressed by the speech. I followed up by inviting her to lunch.

My marriage to Lou Tower was in its terminal stages. Our daughters were grown and back in Texas. I was in my fifties, and, having spent more than a decade and a half in the Senate, I was beginning to take stock of my life and examine the future. I suppose the psychologists would call it a midlife crisis. I am not sure that I buy that as an explanation. In any event, I was attracted to Lilla for her deep intellectual capacity, her mastery of the English language, and her strong personality. We shared many interests and philosophic views, and a lively appreciation of the fine arts.

A divorce, no matter how amicable and ultimately beneficial to both sides, is personally traumatic. But Lou and I got through it relatively well. Even so, divorce is a liability for any politician, and it had an impact on the prospects for my reelection in 1978. To put the situation into perspective, however, I must roll back even further.

In 1972, my reelection campaign had been hard fought. It was the first time that I could not count on the disaffection of liberals for the Democratic candidate. They rallied behind Harold Barefoot Sanders, one of LBJ's protégés and a former state legislator.

The Democrats had demonstrated unusual harmony in 1970, when George Bush, running against Lloyd Bentsen for the U.S. Senate, and Paul Eggers, our gubernatorial candidate, were defeated. Bush had been counting on running against Ralph Yarborough, who was vulnerable to a conservative challenger. But Yarborough was so vulnerable he was picked off by Bentsen in the Democratic primary. In the general election, Bentsen moved to the right and cut into George's natural base. Eggers was nickeled and dimed to death in the cow counties by Preston Smith, who ran well in the traditionally Democratic rural areas.

I could see that I had to get busy, and get busy early. Nola Smith, my campaign manager, and I organized a fund-raising dinner in 1971 at the Fairmont Hotel in Dallas and tied it in to the tenth anniversary of my original election to the Senate. We called it the Decade of Service dinner, charged $150 a plate, and raised $250,000, which made it one of the most successful fund-raisers for a Republican in Texas history. It demonstrated that I was no longer dependent on an inherently shaky liberal-conservative Republican coalition. After ten years, I had finally become the candidate of the Texas political establishment.

My political evolution turned out to be perfectly timed because 1972, as a presidential-election year, the first that had coincided with one of my reelection campaigns, was going to serve an especially difficult combination of issues and complications. The Vietnam War had become unpopular, and Nixon was being faulted for not moving fast enough to get the country out of the quagmire. Forced busing, as a panacea for correcting racial imbalance in public schools, was also becoming an emotional issue. The president tried to defuse it by making a number of antibusing statements, but it was easy for voters to take out their frustration on the administration in Washington. In the past, I had always been the beneficiary of low voter turnouts, and there was a danger that a fired-up electorate would mean that our smaller Republican base would be inundated.

On top of that, Republicans were feuding among themselves. Hank Grover won the gubernatorial nomination and, consistent with his style as an outspoken maverick, demanded the ouster of the party chairman. Cooler heads prevailed, but the last thing I needed was a divided party.

Having John Connally as Nixon's treasury secretary muddied the waters as well. Connally was still nominally a Democrat. One of his associates, Joe Kilgore, established a Democrats for Nixon committee and made it clear that its activities were on behalf of Nixon only, not for John Tower. My staff did a lot of wheel spinning on symbolic matters, like whether it would be Connally or I who emerged with Nixon from *Air Force One* when he visited the state.

Nixon's people were so obsessed with rolling up a huge victory margin in 1972 that they kept the president at arm's length from any Republican candidate who was not a guaranteed shoo-in for reelection. I was considered vulnerable, and as a result there was little cooperation from the White House, to the point that Nola Smith had to obtain bootlegged film of Nixon and me in the Rose Garden after the president's staff refused to provide it. After the footage aired on Texas television, Nola got a call from presidential assistant John Ehrlichman, who wanted to know how it had been obtained. Nola politely told him it was none of his business.

These contortions were unnecessary, of course, thanks to George McGovern. I served with George, and he was an effective senator. We rarely agreed on the issues of the day, but he was not the wild-eyed extremist that he was made out to be. Unfortunately, Mc-Govern had to identify with the far left of his party to obtain the nomination, and there was no way to get back into the middle of the road, where all presidential elections are fought and won. I linked Harold Sanders to McGovern whenever I could. For good measure, I hung Ramsey Clark around his neck. Clark was an old associate of Sanders's and had made a two-thousand-dollar contribution to the Sanders campaign. "I'm glad," one of my standard zingers went, "that Ramsey Clark is supporting my opponent, an old crony of his. . . . Frankly, I don't welcome the support of anyone who goes to Hanoi and condemns our country."

I won over Sanders by better than 310,000 votes. It turned out to be the high-water mark of my political career. In 1978, I scraped by with a 12,227-vote margin. The divorce and the lingering bad blood generated in the 1976 Ford-Reagan primary battle put me at a disadvantage. I don't think that most Texans held it against me that my marriage had failed. But it gave my opponent in the general election, Congressman Bob Krueger, a handle on an issue that I had never confronted before. Krueger made the rounds of church suppers, and when he was sure that the press wasn't around to catch him at it, he would start reciting the old gossip about John Tower's private life. By keeping the attacks out of the news media, Krueger avoided being charged with mudslinging. But some of his comments got back to us and into the papers. One of them particularly angered me. Krueger suggested that I voted for a congressional pay raise — which wasn't true, for starters — so that I could pay for my daughters to shop for expensive clothes at Neiman-Marcus.

A wise incumbent ignores his opponent. However, I was not going to let Krueger's personal taunts go unanswered. I swung back at Krueger, branding him as "a lame duck Congressman and a dead duck politician. His campaign is foundering for lack of public support, so he is resorting to personal attacks and mudslinging."

Krueger was also targeting Lilla. He demanded that we disclose her financial holdings. The press picked up on the issue, even though I explained that we had agreed to maintain separate estates and that Lilla was entitled to her privacy. I hit back at Krueger, who was a bachelor at the time, by saying that he knew "little about marriage, and knows nothing of the sensitivity involved in a marriage between two people with children by previous marriages and long-standing careers." I denounced him as "this little Lord Fauntleroy, a beneficiary of inherited wealth," who was unfairly attacking my wife. "When a woman marries a man, she doesn't give up her rights to privacy even if she marries a senator."

By going after Lilla on the finances, Krueger was reminding voters indirectly that I was divorced and that Lou, who had become popular throughout Texas for her warmth and friendliness, was no longer at my side. The newspapers found the issue irresistible. The *Houston Post* was on to the story first.

> The flap over John G. Tower's refusal to make public his wife Lilla's finances is rooted primarily in her opposition to doing so, according to several sources. . . . It is just another example, the sources claim, of why grumbling continues within the Tower camp about her role in the Texas Republican's reelection effort. The senator obviously regards his wife as a political asset and indeed she appears to have been an unqualified hit on the campaign trail. Even critics acknowledge her genuine charm and her abilities as a polished speaker. But behind-the-scenes, she has crossed swords numerous times with Tower aides over strategy, personnel and other matters.

The *Dallas Times-Herald* got into the act several days later with a piece from the paper's Washington correspondent reporting that Carolyn Bacon, my administrative assistant, had "abruptly left her post." The next sentence made the Lilla connection, and unfortunately it was accurate: "Sources said Ms. Bacon, an eleven-year veteran of Tower's Washington office, was forced to resign her job because of pressure from the senator's wife."

Lilla also persuaded me to replace Robert S. Heller, who had handled the advertising for my campaigns since 1961. I shouldn't have acquiesced to her, but I did. As a consequence, uncertainty and instability undercut the effectiveness of my campaign. Carolyn Bacon was a major loss to the Washington operation, and without Heller our initial ad campaign was a flop. I had brought Ken Towery back, as campaign manager, and his relationship with Lilla deteriorated to the point that they stopped speaking to each other.

Towery, however, held things together. In many ways, the 1978 Senate race was a classic contest between new- and old-style politics. Krueger's campaign managers were young, very aggressive, and highly proficient in the latest techniques of media manipulation. The Krueger campaign even circulated material ridiculing me for being a lowly Navy enlisted man rather than a commissioned officer. That was too much for Ken Towery, who spent most of World War II in a Japanese prison camp. He blistered Krueger with a speech that he delivered himself in San Antonio, noting that my opponent had never served in any branch of the military and had spent "his time hiding out in academe, studying poetry, while his peers were called" to serve their country. Towery suggested that if any physical impairment had prevented Krueger from enlisting, "he could have at least joined the USO and gone abroad to entertain the troops with poetry readings."

The blast succeeded in putting Krueger on the defensive. He issued a statement that an asthma condition had kept him out of the military. We also scored with a second round of TV ads, which homed in on Krueger's congressional attendance record. "How would you like to show up for work twenty-five percent of the time and still get paid $57,500 per year . . . one hundred percent of the time?" was the not so subtle way we phrased the question.

Krueger's hired political guns, who included Gary Mauro, a former McGovern operative; Roy Spence, the adman behind Walter Mondale in 1984; and Pat Caddell, the pollster for Gary Hart and Joe Biden, shot back. My opponent circulated the reprint of a newspaper column written by a controversial Tennessee journalist. It slammed an unnamed U.S. senator for drinking and womanizing. At the top of the column there was a note that read: "Dear Editor: Thought you might be interested in this unusually candid description of Bob Krueger's opponent in the U.S. Senate race, John Tower." Krueger later admitted that Mauro had made the decision to distribute the material and said it had been a mistake.

With less than a month to go before election day, Bob Krueger and I appeared together at a Houston Press Club luncheon. My

opponent strolled over to my table and offered to shake hands. I
refused and turned away. The sequence was caught by a *Houston
Post* photographer — Krueger offering his right hand, John Tower
turning back to his salad plate with disdain. There was a mixed
reaction to the episode. Some people thought I was entirely justified. Others felt that I was being a poor sport.

This latter, adverse reaction was most pronounced in media markets where the newspapers neglected to explain the circumstances
and provide background on Krueger's circulation of the newspaper
column. We issued a written statement to put the incident in
proper context:

> For months, my opponent has continued a campaign of un-
> abated distortion and deception. I think he has engaged in
> scurrilous campaign activities which Texans do not admire.
> He is a man who has no loyalties and no convictions. As many
> others have observed, including newspaper writers, he seems
> to be a man who is fired only by personal ambition, and will
> do or say anything to achieve that ambition. . . . I was
> brought up to believe that a handshake was, and is, a symbol
> of friendship and respect. I was not brought up to believe
> that a handshake is a meaningless and hypocritical act done
> for public display. . . . I think under the circumstances that I
> should not have dignified him by shaking his hand after what
> he has been engaged in.

Several polls put the race as running dead even, and the day after
the above statement was released, one survey gave Krueger the lead
by four percentage points. My campaign tracking polls, nightly
telephone surveys, showed that our support had gone soft in West
Texas and in the Dallas–Fort Worth area. My pollster, Lance Tarrance, warned that we would have to prevent Krueger from making
inroads in the southwest Houston area; otherwise I would not be
able to win statewide. On October 25, with twelve days to go,
Tarrance said, "The election today hangs in the balance between
defeat and victory."

I had time for one last roll of the dice. Houston and Dallas–
Fort Worth were major media markets that could be reached by
television. Likewise, the most effective way of getting to the voters
in West Texas that late in the game was through TV. Thus, I ended
up at a production studio on the Hemisfair grounds in San Antonio, not far from the Alamo, standing before a camera and

holding up a copy of the *Houston Post,* which bore a large picture of Bob Krueger offering to shake my hand. "Perhaps you've seen this picture of my refusal to shake my opponent's hand," I said as I tossed the newspaper aside. The camera moved in for a tight shot as I continued: "I was brought up to believe that a handshake is a symbol of friendship or respect. Not a meaningless, hypocritical gesture. My opponent has slurred my wife, my daughters, and falsified my record. My kind of Texan doesn't shake the hand of that kind of man. Integrity is one Texas tradition that you can count on me to uphold."

When we completed filming the ads, and as I left the studio, one of my aides held up a sign that proclaimed "Once More unto the Breach," the famous line from Shakespeare's *Henry V* that I had used to open all my reelection campaigns. We hit the road again with a final bus tour through the Hispanic areas of the lower Rio Grande Valley.

To borrow a line from another master of the English language, Charles Dickens, the 1978 campaign was the best of times and the worst of times. The Republican party finally captured the Texas governorship. Bill Clements ran a superb campaign. Our political game plans dovetailed nicely. Clements had concentrated time and resources on the rural areas, and my solid base in the urban areas assisted him. A most satisfying development was that my strength among Hispanics had helped me beat Krueger by twenty thousand votes in his home district.

The downside was that we had run a terrible campaign, making, along the way, just about every mistake imaginable. Plus, the viciousness and personal nature of the contest were thoroughly repugnant to me. Until 1978, my record and the stands that I took on the issues had been the focus of my campaigns, but I had been forced to endure a ferocious personal assault during that last one.

Sam Nunn and John Warner agreed to tell neither the Democratic nor Republican staffers about the phone call with Lilla. But Nunn drafted a memo about the conversation that ended up in the hands of his aides, who apparently made sure it made the rounds. The one-sided flow of information forced the Republicans to go to John Warner to ask him about the phone call. Only then did my allies realize what they were up against.

Nunn was looking for evidence to show that I had not moderated my drinking in the late 1970s, as I testified to the Armed

Services Committee and stated to the press. Who better to dispute my contention than Lilla? After all, I had said that she was the one to persuade me to give up scotch. By fabricating incidents that only she could have witnessed, Lilla was undercutting one of my strongest and most irrefutable arguments: to wit, that my drinking had never been shown to have interfered with the performance of my duties as a senator, which every member of the Senate who had served with me knew to be true. In effect, she was saying there was a public John Tower, known to his Senate colleagues, and a private John Tower, known only to her.

I think that Sam Nunn realized he could take Lilla's statements only so far without exposing himself to the charge that he was being manipulated by an angry former spouse who was pursuing a private agenda. However, Nunn likes to recall that he had worked for years with Herman Talmadge, the former senior senator from Georgia and chairman of the Senate Agriculture Committee, without realizing the extent of Talmadge's problems with alcohol. He has regaled his colleagues and aides with the story of how he assumed that after Talmadge put in a full day in the Senate, he went home and drank eight ounces of liquor. The next morning Talmadge would be back, ready for work. The postscript is that, according to those who have heard Nunn's version of events, after Talmadge was defeated for reelection, his marriage disintegrated and there was a bitter divorce action that featured lurid accounts of the former senator's alleged abuses of alcohol. These accusations apparently convinced Sam Nunn that he had badly misread his colleague, a mistake that he was determined not to repeat in my case. I can only conclude that Lilla's phone calls seemed like confirmation to Nunn that there was some kind of pattern repeating itself. Instead of questioning her motives, he set out to prove to the Senate that there was a darker, Jekyll-and-Hyde quality to John Tower.

James Exon was Nunn's point man on the subject of alcohol, a cynical stroke of political manipulation. As he had with John Warner, Nunn took a hostage. Exon drinks, and drinks heavily. His Senate colleagues know this; many of his constituents do too. But Exon sought out reporters to provide this statement: "I'm convinced that John Tower at one time months or years ago had a serious problem with alcohol. The question on all of our minds is whether he has corrected that problem."

As far as the votes went on the committee, Nunn had little leverage with Edward Kennedy. But by nailing down Exon at the outset, he was letting him know that he would have to rethink the supportive statement he made as the hearings opened; otherwise, he would be vulnerable to the accusation that he was merely siding with another member of the Senate "playboy" club.

Exon also served the purpose of blunting Sam's priggish image. With a genuine boozer on his side, Nunn was not as likely to be dismissed for sanctimoniousness. It helped convince the press that I had a serious drinking problem if my behavior offended someone like Exon.

A few members of the national news media caught on to what was happening. An editorial in the February 9 *Wall Street Journal*:

> Just to make sure we heard right, let's run through this again: The World's Greatest Deliberative Body is going to turn down one of its former Members as Secretary of Defense on grounds of booze, sex and money? The good Senators even found a poker game in the U.S. arms-negotiating delegation; like Claude Rains in "Casablanca," they were shocked!
>
> By all means, put off the vote. The spectacle is worth another week. Especially, bury once and for all this hoary notion of "senatorial courtesy." It is terribly unfair that Senators ever enjoyed immunity from each other. Let New Right activist Paul Weyrich vet the personal morality of every future Cabinet nominee. No one in the current affair need worry. Senator James Exon, point man in the attack on John Tower, figures the FBI won't be poking into his background; clearly he assumes that for the rest of his career there will be no Democratic Presidents to appoint Cabinet members. Senator John Warner, playing both sides of the street, is a Republican, but surely he's been celibate since his divorce from Elizabeth Taylor.
>
> And let it be engraved in stone, no Senator ever shall take a consulting fee or legal fee after he leaves office. Wily defense contractors are too smart to hire former Secretaries of Defense, after all. They know where the bacon is and hire former Chairmen of the Armed Services Committee. No current Senator should face such temptation in the future.
>
> In other words, the hypocrisy meter has gone off even the Beltway scale. So far as we can see, there has been zero sub-

stantiation of any of the rumors about Mr. Tower, yet the "scandal" seems to mount. The Senators seem to have taken leave of reality and, less believably, even their personal self-interest. What in the world is going on here?

Clear as day: Senator Sam Nunn wants to run the Pentagon from Capitol Hill. President Bush offered him the chance to run it as Secretary of Defense [the *Journal* is incorrect on this point], but that would have involved being someone's subordinate. Much more convenient simply to take the Pentagon away from the President and run it to suit your own fancy. The other Senators will help, even the Republican ones.

For this scheme to work, of course, you need a "good manager" as Secretary of Defense. The perfect choice is a former defense contractor already schooled in the congressional prerogatives. The last person you want as Secretary of Defense is a former Senator. Especially a former Chairman of the Armed Services Committee. Especially a former Chairman who has proved himself a gutsy little guy. Someone who understands the system, and is bright and tough, might actually succeed in keeping the Pentagon under the Commander in Chief.

So you unleash the Beltway's all-weather guided missile, the ethics issue. Members of Congress wallowing in their PAC contributions and extorted honorariums profess a high-minded concern with personal morality. It's not necessary, of course, that anything be proved. It's only necessary to keep one fresh rumor or accusation alive at every moment to insure a permanent investigation. If drinking won't do, try sex, then try conflicts of interest, then try one of the Justice Department's runaway investigations. Go on recess, keep any decision in limbo, wait for the nominee or the President to throw in the towel.

Cooler heads in Washington recognize that this game has begun to carry an enormous overhead. "Given all the play-acting we do, Washington often doesn't know real corruption when it appears," writes Meg Greenfield of the Washington Post. Why isn't anyone preoccupied, for example, with the congressional breaches of responsibility that gave us a $100 billion savings-and-loan crisis? Instead, the political culture is preoccupied with the possibility of "alcohol abuse."

By using Exon as his stalking-horse, Nunn probably hoped to preserve and enhance his own equine status, that of a presidential dark horse in 1992. Exon would do the out-in-front dirty work, while Sam remained statesmanlike. Conservatives, who might object to what happened to me, would be encouraged to blame it on Exon; liberal Democrats, never overly enamored with Sam Nunn, would be invited to reassess the chairman's new credentials and image. To put it in the baldest terms possible: anyone who knocked off a hawk like John Tower couldn't be all bad.

Presidential ambitions were, I believe, a major factor in Sam Nunn's decision to oppose my nomination. For the most part, the Democratic party's national leadership had been decapitated by the sequence of events in 1988 that culminated in the defeat of the Dukakis-Bentsen ticket, on November 8. By systematically eliminating all of his major rivals in the primaries, Michael Dukakis left the party without alternative leadership, should he fail in his bid for the White House. Only Jesse Jackson retained enough viability and vitality to continue to attract a measure of national attention. Joseph Biden, Albert Gore, Paul Simon, and Bruce Babbitt dropped out of sight. While Richard Gephardt seized the opportunity that occurred when Jim Wright resigned the speakership by moving into the post of House majority leader, he has been submerged, predictably, in the heavy work load and Byzantine intrigue of the House of Representatives.

Both major parties have always suffered through severe difficulties in the aftermath of a presidential-election defeat. In the absence of party elders — true relics of a past age — and a modicum of continuity from one generation to the next, Republicans and Democrats alike are subjected to the recriminations and the instability that inevitably occur when they are unable to capture or to retain the presidency. After the defeats of 1960 and 1964, the Republican party went through a traumatic transformation and redefinition of itself. The same thing happened to the Democrats after 1968, when the liberal, antiwar wing of the party seized power. Its ascendancy brought on another disaster, in 1972, which opened the way for what was perceived as a more conservative element, led by Jimmy Carter, to take control. By defeating Gerald Ford, arguably the candidate of the governing establishment of the Republican party, Carter set the stage for Ronald Reagan, who was able to wrest the nomination away from more mainstream candidates (I mean the term "mainstream" to suggest that Reagan had not held national elective or appointive office and was therefore perceived as an out-sider): George Bush, Bob Dole, and John Connally.

By 1988, Sam Nunn had been in Washington long enough to observe this process at work. By boldly challenging the new pres-ident, he positioned himself to assume the leadership of the congressional wing of his party, which, after all, is its only national power base.

In my estimation, Nunn perceived it to be a no-win situation for the president, and a no-lose situation for himself. Merely by inflicting nonlethal damage on a senior cabinet nominee, Nunn could gain visibility in the news media and demonstrate his influ-ence. And once he opted to go all out to sink the nomination, he sought to damage the president's political credibility and authority, perhaps weakening the administration sufficiently to make it vul-nerable to defeat in 1992. The credit for this victory would go to the chairman of the Armed Services Committee, giving him a leg up on the presidential nomination.

Wisely, George Bush avoided the temptation of getting into a public political brawl with Sam Nunn. He kept the confirmation process on an institutional level. If he hadn't, no matter what the outcome, the press would have portrayed Sam Nunn as a political rival with enough clout to challenge the White House and get away with it.

There was one element missing, however, from Nunn's calcula-tions. He did not realize that to block my nomination he would have to expend so much of his hard-earned political capital, in-cluding the sacrifice of his scholarly, statesmanlike image. Nunn put the Senate through the wringer, and most of his Democratic colleagues did not enjoy the experience. He embarrassed Finance Committee chairman Lloyd Bentsen, who endorsed me, intro-duced my nomination to the committee, and voted for it on the floor of the Senate. Freshman Senators Charles Robb and Joseph Lieberman, two Democrats with a bright future on the national scene, were likely not at all pleased to be forced into supporting a position about which they had personal misgivings; and, ironically, many liberals, whom Nunn hoped to impress, were put off by the raw and ugly nature of the proceedings. Former senator Eugene McCarthy, for one, wrote a newspaper column in my defense. I also heard from George McGovern and from Sissy Farenthold, who in the 1970s ran unsuccessfully for governor of Texas a couple of times and was the first chairperson of the National Women's

Political Caucus — probably the only time the three of us agreed on anything more politically controversial than the time of day.

If Nunn had suspected that he would end up looking like an unscrupulous political mudslinger who would stop at nothing to achieve his objectives, perhaps he would have satisfied himself with making a few critical comments expressing whatever reservations he may have felt, even to the point of indicating that I was on probation, and then voting to approve the nomination.

But Sam Nunn was blinded by his own ambition.

ELEVEN

SHELL GAME

PRESIDENT BUSH summoned the cabinet to a meeting at the White House on Thursday afternoon, February 9. By custom, the secretary of defense sits to the president's immediate left at the long conference table that stretches the length of the Cabinet Room. Like those of his predecessors, George Bush's armchair was placed with its high brown leather back to the windows that overlook the Rose Garden, at the midpoint of the east side of the table. The president does not preside over the meeting from the head of the table, and this seating arrangement reinforces the cabinet's collegiality and encourages a free-flowing discussion.

Most cabinet meetings begin with a photo opportunity for the news media. The press was particularly interested in recording the session because it preceded the president's first address to a joint session of Congress. To visually enhance their previews of Bush's address, which would unveil the administration's new budget, the networks needed to obtain videotape of the president and his cabinet well before the late-afternoon deadline for the evening news shows. The still photos were also useful to the newspapers as illustrations for budget stories that would run in the next morning's editions.

Given my position to the president's immediate left, I ended up being featured in most of the pictures, which the news media concluded was a deliberate effort on the part of the White House to demonstrate George Bush's continuing commitment to my nomination. It was even stated that we played musical chairs so I would be at the president's side when the photographers and Mini-cam crews arrived in the Cabinet Room. Of course that wasn't true, but the photos did demonstrate that I was a full participant in the day-to-day activities of the Bush administration.

The president's address to the joint session of Congress brought to a close the very first phase of the political and administrative life cycle that began with the transition period immediately after the election.

Revising the budget inherited from the previous administration is a major item on any new president's agenda. The job is an arduous one, requiring hundreds of hours of meetings and countless decisions and compromises. Most of the officials involved are new to their jobs, and yet they must operate as though they are old hands, familiar with every aspect and policy of their department. Mistakes made during the first close encounter with the budget can be extremely costly, and it can take months or years to repair the damage.

In selecting my Pentagon transition team, I put great emphasis on recruiting senior officials with extensive experience at the Defense Department or as congressional staff members, knowing that we would be under intense pressure to make significant reductions in military spending.

Based on my meetings with President Bush and the weekly breakfast sessions that I participated in with Jim Baker and Brent Scowcroft, I had a sense that the most workable formula would be one featuring some sort of a flexible freeze on Pentagon spending. I did not object to that approach, on the grounds that a freeze can be of limited duration, and it is better than outright cuts. But a freeze, if allowed to remain in effect too long, erodes the spending power of each dollar in the budget through the impact of inflation.

In the negotiations with Office of Management and Budget Director Richard Darman, I was careful to observe a rule that many of my former congressional aides say they learned from me and still use when they are called on to haggle over the important details of a business deal or a legislative program: don't go in with your going-out position. It is a mistake to open negotiations by immediately revealing your bottom line. As chairman of the Senate

Armed Services Committee, during conferences with the House to resolve differences in legislation my first objective was to identify the other side's priorities. Once I did, I formulated my own negotiating strategy. During one particularly difficult set of negotiations, I made an offer to the House delegation that met them more than halfway by packaging many of the programs favored by a majority of the House with other items that did not have the same basis of support but that were favored by the Senate. They left the room to caucus, and I could hear a heated exchange of views in the hallway. Apparently the conservative Democrats on the panel and the Republicans were at loggerheads with the more junior liberal Democrats, led by Les Aspin. At the time, Aspin was maneuvering to become chairman of the House Armed Services Committee; to win favor with the Democratic caucus, which has the power to grant or deny chairmanships, it was essential for him to take a strict, no-compromise position. When the group returned, the senior Republican on the panel, William Dickinson, said he would have to refuse the compromise. I knew that I had met their going-out position and that Dickinson and the other senior House conferees badly wanted to accept the package. The shouting in the hallway had raised the tension level considerably. I took my time, doodled a bit on my writing pad, and then looked up. I said, "Bill, I'm reminded of that old song — 'Your lips tell me no, no . . . but your eyes say yes, yes, yes.' " Dickinson and his colleagues burst into laughter, and eventually we were able to work out a deal.

My negotiating style in conference has been denounced as "dictatorial," and one disgruntled Democratic House aide said of me, "He just has the biggest bladder in the room . . . he just sat there and sat there and sat there until, finally, he'd wear you down."

I think it has less to do with one's physiological attributes than it does with sheer patience and determination. I have always been willing to sit and listen for as long as it takes for the other side to get serious about striking an agreement. The difficulty in dealing with the House on defense issues is that individual members are allowed to hijack important pieces of legislation by adding non-germane amendments, many involving significant sums of money to benefit their constituents, which the Senate must either accept or go through protracted negotiations to remove. Some Senate chairmen find it easier not to fight these tacked-on amendments. However, as far as I am concerned, they are a waste of the

taxpayer's money and an abuse of the legislative partnership between the House and the Senate. Whenever possible, I insisted
that all but the most minor amendments be subjected to the full
legislative process in both houses of Congress.

The committee system is designed to examine the merits of a
proposal and subject it to critical evaluation from a full range of
various perspectives. If nothing else, this is an essential screening
process. By permitting its members to circumvent the process, the
House leadership is engaging in a trade-off to secure cooperation
and votes for what are deemed to be "essential" programs in return
for acquiescence to a practice that amounts to slam dunking the
Senate. As chairman of the Armed Services Committee, I insisted
that the Senate had no business accepting proposals that originated
in the House and were beyond the committee's purview. To do so
risks turning the Senate into an appendage of the House of Representatives. And my attitude led to many a long night in conference committees.

Representative Patricia Schroeder criticized me for taking advantage of the late Mel Price, the former chairman of the House
Armed Services Committee and Les Aspin's predecessor, when we
faced each other in conference. Price was quite elderly at the time,
and he was unable to manage his own delegation, the members of
which, naturally, ended up being the ones to "take advantage" of
their chairman's infirmity by pursuing their own private agendas.
I was deferential to Price, and whenever a potential conflict was
about to develop, I dealt directly with a member of the House
delegation who had a stake in the issue so that Price would not be
caught in the cross fire.

Much of the criticism that was leveled at me from the House
during the confirmation was a product of the dynamics of the
conference-committee process. Standing House committees have
larger memberships than do Senate committees. We sent all of our
members to conference, and the House Armed Services Committee
appointed an equivalent number. Hence, some House members
were left out, and the selection process was driven by seniority. It
meant that more conservative members of the House committee
dominated the proceedings, pro-defense lawmakers like Sam Strat-
ton and Sonny Montgomery. The junior members sat at the end
of the table, and there was always conflict. These sessions dragged
on for hours, days. The atmosphere was similar to an Oriental
bazaar, with endless haggling and bickering.

During the course of my chairmanship, it became customary in the House to accept amendments to the military authorization bill that were nongermane or that concerned peripheral matters that should not have been dealt with in the bill. These were riders that had little chance of passage as freestanding legislation. The obvious strategy of the sponsors was to hold critically required military legislation hostage to acceptance of those proposals, which were usually very, very liberal. House Speaker Tip O'Neill would stack the conference with the sponsors of those bits of mischief, who were permitted to act in conference when such matters were considered. On one occasion, the total number of conferees exceeded seventy House members.

It is important to understand that, to the average member of the Senate, a conference committee is an additional burden to an already overloaded schedule. At any given moment during his or her workday, a senator is probably expected to be at three places at the same time: at a committee hearing, with a constituent, or in the Senate chamber participating in a debate. This means that senators sometimes duck conference committees when possible. As chairman, I was always present and therefore the focus of any resentment or hostility generated by the process. I don't recall ever denying anyone the right to be heard or arbitrarily stifling debate. I am told, even by some who opposed my confirmation, that I was tough but fair.

It was my responsibility as a committee chairman to exercise leadership. To lead, one must be willing to "just say no." But unfortunately Congress has become a body where expediency too often dictates accommodation to ill-advised proposals that are sometimes politically, sometimes ideologically motivated. The cost is not calculated, nor is the impact on rational public policy. "No" is a word that makes enemies. With the rise of single-issue politics, members of the House and Senate are discovering that their affirmative, positive acts — hundreds if not thousands over the course of a political career — can be negated by one no on a litmus test issue. As a consequence, the tendency is to go along to get along.

In my budget negotiations, I got along well with OMB Director Richard Darman. He is cunning, quick-witted, and enormously sure of himself. A first-rate negotiator, he knows your numbers, and he knows his numbers. He is probably an excellent poker player.

Armed with the foreknowledge that the president's preference was for a limited and flexible freeze in defense spending, we were able to work up a formula that allowed the military budget to be put on hold at the current level for one year and to rise by 1 percent (after inflation) in the next two fiscal years, followed by real growth of 2 percent in fiscal 1993.

We hammered out the formula at a series of White House meetings over the weekend before the president's address to Congress. By that juncture, Darman was well along toward a final draft of the new budget, and it was our last chance to make changes in his initial figures before the final document was sent to the Government Printing Office to be set in type, printed, and bound. Richard Darman and Treasury Secretary Nicholas Brady were the principal advocates of imposing zero growth on the Pentagon for at least three years. I was teamed up with Jim Baker, Brent Scowcroft, and Admiral William J. Crowe, the chairman of the Joint Chiefs of Staff. The honest broker who mediated between the two positions was John Sununu. Crowe was present at my suggestion, and his enormous professional credibility helped to counterbalance Darman's persuasiveness and skill at juggling the numbers.

Our going-in position, which Darman must have known we weren't wedded to, was that the spending plan recommended by former president Reagan be adopted in toto by President Bush. There wasn't a chance of that, since the Reagan budget called for 2 percent real growth in each of the next three years.

It came down to accepting the concept of a freeze and adjusting its duration and the numbers. Since our going-out position was a limited freeze on spending anyway, there was not an insurmountable problem on that issue. It could be persuasively argued that a freeze lasting beyond one year would imprudently lock the administration into a spending mode before it had had time to thoroughly analyze the Defense Department's requirements. Furthermore, a two- or three-year freeze would deprive the Pentagon of the resources it needed to cover obligations it had made for weapons systems in the early 1980s, which were to come on-line in 1992 and 1993.

As for the budget numbers, based on the Reagan figures and given the fact that we were working against the ideal of a 6 percent growth rate over three years, the objective was to split the difference with the other side. In the end, we achieved a 4 percent increase over the same period, which amounted to meeting Darman *less* than halfway and tossing in the freeze for good measure.

This formula trimmed Pentagon spending by $6.4 billion for fiscal 1990. It was well within the terms of my initial analysis of what the Defense Department could sustain without affecting the performance of its mission. I saw that the military would be able to absorb a reasonable reduction in spending by cutting manpower, transferring some active-duty units to the reserves, and scaling back our military presence in the Persian Gulf region. Should the Soviets make good on their promises of troop and tank pullbacks from Eastern Europe, I felt, additional savings could be made. However, if Gorbachev changed his tune or was ousted from power, nothing would have been cut to the bone, and I would have ample justification for returning to Congress with a request for additional funds. I had told the Senate Armed Services Committee that "nothing is sacred" but cautioned that "the world is as it is, not as we would like it to be."

Responsible congressional leaders spend much of their time fighting the tendency on Capitol Hill to create a fantasy world where the tooth fairy comes along to pay the bill and solve our problems.

Since Congress's constitutional authority is grounded in its responsibility as guardian of the public purse, it is particularly vital for the budget-making process to be firmly grounded in reality. Sadly, that is not the case. In recent years, some in Congress have assumed an attitude that I can only describe as one of smug superiority toward the executive branch and its efforts to develop a comprehensive spending plan for the federal government.

The House and Senate have taken to ignoring presidential budgets — not just part of them, but whole budgets. With the Democratic party in control of the legislative branch, a barter system has developed between the White House and Capitol Hill — highly informal, politicized public negotiations — that was never contemplated by the authors of our Constitution.

The essential question that must be asked is, Does Congress have the individual and collective competence to adequately perform this role? I think not, and I base that answer on my many years of experience as a United States senator. A lack of institutional self-restraint set in, as I observe earlier, in the late 1960s and 1970s. Lyndon Johnson whetted Congress's appetite by proposing sweeping legislative programs and inviting lawmakers to help cobble together a new social order. I remember sitting in the House chamber in 1965, listening to LBJ's address to a joint session of Congress that unveiled his plans for the Great Society. As its enormity sank in, I turned to Charlie Halleck, the former House Republican leader, and said, "Oh, Lord, here we go."

Whereas the typical number of presidential messages to Congress had been three or four a month, LBJ sent a total of sixty-four initiatives to Capitol Hill in 1965. As noted by Johnson biographer Doris Kearns, the legislative torrent produced a "politics of haste." He hooked Congress on elephantine programs and grandiose political gestures; the addiction persists to this day, as does the politics of haste.

To keep tabs on the Great Society and the federal bureaucracy that it created (atop the New Deal infrastructure), Congress took a relatively basic subcommittee system and transformed it into a vast network that reaches into every nook and cranny of the government. As a result, jurisdiction is fragmented to such a degree that it is a major undertaking to accomplish the simplest task. Legislators by the dozen, each with two or three staff members in tow, are now regularly involved in matters once dealt with by one executive-branch official who rarely, if ever, was called on by a House or Senate committee to account for his actions, large or small.

In the area of national security, for example, almost every committee in the Senate has some involvement in some aspect of the subject. The interest of the Armed Services, Appropriations, and Budget committees is obvious. Consider, however, these additional players: the Foreign Relations Committee has jurisdiction over arms control, foreign aid, security assistance, war powers, and many other matters connected to the use of military force outside the United States; the Small Business Committee injects itself into the breadth of the procurement process on the basis that it is concerned about the opportunities for small business to participate in defense contracting; the Veterans' Affairs Committee has jurisdiction over a series of benefits available to those who have served in the armed forces, though this benefit package may have an impact on military recruitment and retention; the Governmental Affairs Committee asserts a claim, which I strongly dispute, that it has primary jurisdiction over procurement policy, including procurement policy in the Department of Defense; the Banking Committee has jurisdiction over the Defense Production Act, which is critical for ensuring an adequate defense industrial base, and this committee also has jurisdiction over the Export Administration Act, a primary legislative tool for stopping the transfer of militarily sensitive technologies; the Commerce Committee has jurisdiction over the National Aeronautics and Space Administration, which plays an integral role in providing access to space as well as to critical research for the Department of Defense, and it is involved with the Merchant Marine, another vital component of the national defense mechanism; the Intelligence Committee has primary jurisdiction over the gathering of intelligence, a function that is inextricably linked to military posture.

The list is illustrative of the extent to which aspects of national security are divided among a huge number of committees. In the House, I should add, the situation is even worse, with the House Energy Committee sharing jurisdiction over the Department of Energy's nuclear weapons program. What this fragmentation means is that the only committee with a comprehensive overview of national security, the Armed Services Committee (House and Senate), spends much of its time and energy negotiating sequential referrals, monitoring the activities of other committees, and acting to minimize the adverse impact of intrusive and unsound policy initiatives from those committees.

The hodgepodge of jurisdictions is, to say the least, confusing and cumbersome. But most of all it is a detriment to the social and national security objectives that we, as a nation, have determined to be vital to our well-being. The existing committees, however, have a vested interest in protecting the status quo. One committee's loss of power through the elimination of overlapping jurisdictions is another committee's gain. After much difficulty in 1974, the Senate succeeded in creating the Budget Committee to oversee the formulation and enactment of an annual resolution that fixes the total amount of federal spending and sets ceilings or targets to guide each of the authorizing committees. Although those ceilings are not mandatory, during my tenure as chairman the Senate Armed Services Committee voluntarily "reported out" authorizing legislation; that is, complied with the limits when it sent legislation on to the full Senate for final action. There was no reason that the other committees could not have done likewise.

By imposing fiscal discipline at the beginning of the budget process, it would be possible to eliminate an entire layer of the committee structure. The Senate could profit by disbanding the Budget Committee. The authorizing committees could perform both an authorizing and an appropriations function, leaving the Appropriations Committee to oversee the budget resolutions and the individual ceilings and to appropriate monies for those spending functions not requiring authorization.

Under a plan I recommended to the Senate in 1984, as I prepared to retire, the Armed Services Committee would report out the Defense Department Authorization Bill and the parallel appropriations measure, instead of forcing the Pentagon to undergo two sets of hearings, two sets of negotiations, two ordeals of number crunching, et cetera. Likewise, the Foreign Relations Committee would report out the Foreign Aid Authorization and Appropriation Bill; the Commerce Committee would report out the NASA Authorization and Appropriation Bill, and so forth.

I realized then, and I am still well aware, that the twenty-nine members of the Appropriations Committee are not about to willingly surrender their very considerable influence. The challenge is to find a balance between self-interest and the national interest. To do so may require creative solutions. One alternative is to establish a super-appropriations committee. Every senator would be a member, each with an assignment to a place on two subcommittees. These subcommittees — ten all told — would combine authorizing and appropriating functions. To increase efficiency and decrease overlap, the Budget Subcommittee, for instance, would draw its membership from the chairman and ranking minority senators of the other appropriations subcommittees and from the Finance Committee. Thus the present Budget Committee could be eliminated.

Several other panels could be dropped, but a limited number of separate standing committees would still be necessary: Foreign Relations, Finance, Government Operations, and Judiciary, to name four. Ethics and Rules, and a committee to deal with financial institutions, are also indispensable.

I don't want to belabor the issue, and perhaps I have already, but Congress must get its house in order instead of chasing after trivia or politically glamorous subjects that are beyond its capacity.

At the moment, the budget is a full-time preoccupation, almost an obsession. To participate responsibly in the budget-making process, Congress needs to rethink its roles and procedures. Yet it is too busy trying to participate responsibly in the budget-making process to take the time to rethink those roles and procedures. The quickest way to gain control of the budgetary treadmill would be through the enactment of a two-year budget cycle. Biennial budgeting would give Congress an off year away from specific programmatic decisions. There would be time for legislative supervision and the examination of larger questions of national purpose and policy. The Pentagon, for one, would benefit from the increased stability that would result in the procurement area.

There are those who oppose biennial budgeting on the grounds that it would be insufficiently flexible to meet rapidly changing circumstances. However, I think adjustments could be made by providing periodic emergency budget windows during the off year, during which Congress might choose to amend the spending plan. Biennial budgeting is certainly not a cure-all. It is, though, a start. If the system is not changed, and changed substantially, the country will be the loser because we will have — and in fact now have — a Congress that simply cannot finish its work.

My discussion of the Senate committee structure has served to remind me that I have all but ignored the twenty-four years I spent as a member of the Banking, Housing, and Urban Affairs Committee. (In 1970, the name of the committee was changed from Banking and Currency.) Certainly my first love was the Armed Services Committee; but Banking was an important assignment, which I took seriously.

I was fortunate to move rapidly up the seniority ladder. For many years, the chairman was John Sparkman of Alabama. As Southerners and conservatives, Sparkman and I agreed on a broad range of issues, even though we were members of different parties. He gave me wide latitude and authority as a result. I was able to help shape most of the public housing programs that were put in place during the 1960s and 1970s.

When Sparkman relinquished the chairmanship to William Proxmire, in 1975, my role became more adversarial, although I got along reasonably well with the Wisconsin Democrat. Many of the issues were highly technical, and, as I had with the Armed Services Committee, I made a special effort to recruit a top-notch staff, people who were on the fast track and with no desire to settle into a Senate sinecure for the rest of their career. Howard Beasley, who went on to become chief executive officer of Lone Star Technologies, was my principal Banking Committee aide during the period when I was trying to convince the Nixon administration that the time had come to abolish the wage and price controls imposed on the economy in 1971. President Nixon had started off as an

opponent of economic controls, but when the Democratic Congress went ahead and voted him sweeping authority to regulate
prices, wages, and salaries, the temptation to make use of the
power proved irresistible. By 1974, the administration had applied
four different variations on wage and price controls, and the country, I felt, was in danger of becoming habituated to them.

I urged the White House to oppose a move by Senator Adlai
Stevenson III to extend the controls, but Nixon's economic advisers were concerned that inflation would reignite. As a result, I was
fighting some officials within the administration and the Democratic majority on the issue. I ordered Beasley to work with the
Senate's legislative research service to develop alternative amendments that could be tacked on to Stevenson's bill to neutralize the
controls. We also had to prepare similar riders to block Senators
Edmund Muskie and Bennett Johnston, who were pushing their
own versions of the control-extension legislation. Beasley came
back with about 150 different amendments, each one written to
specifically anticipate the other side's countermoves. We literally
developed the legislative equivalent of a football playbook to use
on the Senate floor. Hours of preparation went into an intricately
designed orchestration of the action-reaction sequence that would
occur when Democratic leadership brought the measure up for a
vote by the full Senate. It came down to saying, "If Stevenson or
Muskie does a, then we will do b, and in turn he will respond with
c — we then hit back with x, y, z." The objective was to have an
amendment that would fit with any combination of moves by our
opponents.

I enjoy a good legislative floor fight. One of the keys to success
is being flexible and spontaneous without losing sight of the goal.
With the administration prepared to acquiesce to their plans to
extend the controls, Stevenson, Muskie, and Johnston did not anticipate our onslaught. What should have been simple for them
quickly became complex. At every turn there was an obstacle. After
we forced seven roll call votes on the first day of debate alone,
majority leader Mike Mansfield intervened to slow our momentum
by asking for the debate to be delayed by about a week. When it
resumed, on May 9, I offered an amendment that would replace
language already added to the bill to extend the controls on a
standby basis. I was barred by the rules of the Senate from actually
proposing to strike the provision, but the substitute was the next
best thing, since it was worded to reduce the controls to existing

on paper only. Muskie countered by moving to table my substitute, but he lost, 43 to 47. He tried again, by cooking up a substitute for my substitute, and was defeated, 37 to 46. Frustrated, his temper rising, Ed Muskie told the Senate that my proposal "would be an illusory promise to the American people that we were doing something meaningful about inflation." He then moved to table the entire bill.

Howard Beasley was with me on the floor, and when Muskie made his move we looked at each other in amazement. If the Senate agreed to table the entire bill, wage and price controls, which were part and parcel of it, would be dead. I jumped to my feet to support Muskie's motion, and it was adopted on a roll call vote. Several minutes went by before the other side realized what had happened. They belatedly tried to undo the damage, but it was too late. Wage and price controls were no more. As we were tying up the loose ends, Senator John Pastore of Rhode Island shook his finger at me, smiling, and said, "You little SOB, that was what you wanted them to do, wasn't it?"

It takes years to learn the rules of parliamentary procedure and the Senate's unique variations on them. Many senators are not sufficiently interested or are too impatient to undertake the necessary study. I found it, however, to be an endeavor essential to survival as a member of the minority for twenty years. Knowing the rules of the game helped even up the unfavorable odds.

A senator who was an expert parliamentarian and a superb debater was Jacob Javits of New York. My direct confrontations with him were infrequent, although we did tangle on one occasion. I was advocating a measure that would require financial service companies that issue travelers' checks to return the funds held from unredeemed checks to the states of residence of the individuals who purchased those checks. Millions of dollars were involved. Javits took a dim view of the idea, since American Express, which did most of the travelers' check business in the United States, was headquartered in New York. In that state, as in many others, so-called escheated funds (principally money from inactive bank accounts) were transferred to the state treasury. My bill pitted New York against the forty-nine other states, which would begin receiving the funds. And, of course, Texas would get a sizable portion of the revenue from the unredeemed travelers' checks.

I moved as quickly and as quietly as I could, but Javits and Pat Moynihan swung into action. I could tell that Javits was not very familiar with the details of the escheat issue. Once on the Senate floor, though, he was absorbing information with impressive speed. Jack was firing questions at me and stripping the answers down to their component parts to extract the data he needed to argue his own case. In short order, he was coming back with a counterattack that was seriously undercutting the proposal I was advocating. Howard Beasley, who was again assisting me on the Senate floor, handed me a note pointing out that Javits was starting to damage our position and urging me to hit back at him. I leaned over and whispered to Howard, "You want me to get up there and take on the smartest man in the United States Senate?" Jack, who a few minutes before had known little about escheat, was well on his way to being the most knowledgeable person on the subject in the Senate chamber. "Howard, we've got the votes. It doesn't make any sense to fight with Javits — he's just doing what he has to do for New York."

I was correct. There was no way Jack Javits was going to win against forty-nine other states. However, he probably would have found a way if I had given him enough time to organize a counterattack. I once told Jack that if I was ever indicted for a criminal offense I would want him to defend me. Javits, who was as liberal as I was conservative, responded in good humor, "I'll do it without a fee."

I was saddened when Javits was defeated by Alfonse D'Amato in the 1980 New York Republican primary. The loss ended his political career just as our party was about to capture majority control of the U.S. Senate. It must have been very painful for him to be on the sidelines watching as his junior colleagues took on the power and the leading roles that he had waited so long to assume.

After the Reagan landslide of 1980, Strom Thurmond decided that he would take the chairmanship of the Judiciary Committee, and I therefore became chairman of Armed Services. Strom was by dint of his number of years in the Senate the senior member of both Judiciary and Armed Services. But Senate rules prohibit a senator from being the chair or ranking member — a term that denotes the lawmaker who functions as leader of the minority — of more than one standing committee. Since Strom had opted several years before to claim the ranking spot on Judiciary, I served in that role on Armed Services. Strom could have pulled rank on me, but he would have had to give up the chairmanship of Judi-

ciary and the considerable political power over judicial appointments that accompanies the post.

The workings of the seniority system can result in musical chairs.
For example, I had more time on the Banking Committee than
any other Republican. But I preferred the ranking place on Armed
Services and therefore yielded to Jake Garn of Utah, who became
Banking chairman.

Fortunately, Senator Thurmond stayed put at Judiciary (he was
also a valuable member of Armed Services), so there was no need
for me to consider bumping Senator Garn and setting off an unseemly scramble for chairmanships. Even though I was busy at
Armed Services I was able to work closely with Garn and stay up
to speed on banking issues.

It wasn't all dry and technical on the Banking Committee. We
did have some fun with an amendment to allow elderly tenants in
federally subsidized housing units to keep their pets. The committee staff discovered that since there was no federal policy on
whether pets were permissible in a housing complex, most state
and local governments and private-property managers had instituted blanket "no pet" rules. This was a hardship for the elderly,
who derive comfort, love, and companionship from their cats and
dogs. There is an overwhelming amount of evidence from health
specialists and gerontologists that it is very important from a health
standpoint for older people to be able to have their pets with them.

In gratitude for my role in backing the amendment, which eventually became law, one of my constituents, a sign painter, whipped
up a masterpiece that he called "Kitty Litter," a montage of
hundreds of cats on rooftops and windowsills. The artist was
dubbed a "Picture Purr-fectionist" by the *El Paso Herald-Post,* and
I ordered the picture to be displayed in the committee office.

We sensed that we were on to a good thing. Fortuitously, Lilla's
prolific female cat, who consorted with every tom in the neighborhood, had recently presented us with another litter. I arranged
to have a basketful of them brought into our next public hearing.
I called the subcommittee to order and said, "Three weeks ago
during the consideration of the Proxmire Cat Amendment, I personally thanked Senator Proxmire and said that I would have a few
ready for adoption. I would like to announce that they are ready
for adoption, four beautiful tabbies. They wanted to be here to
personally thank Senator Proxmire, and if anyone would provide
a good home, just call Mandy, 224-2934. I emphasize, however,

they are a product of social irresponsibility." Proxmire and I couldn't resist cuddling the kittens during a break in the hearings, and photo editors couldn't resist the pictures, which ran in several Wisconsin and Texas papers.

But it was pretty tame compared with a couple of other stunts, which got slightly out of hand. One was a chili-cooking contest at the National Press Club with Senator Barry Goldwater that degenerated into a good-natured exchange of insults. Barry showed his true colors by alleging that the ingredients for Texas chili were gathered off the floor of the corral. The subsequent exchange of views is unprintable. The press made it seem as if we had declared war on each other. Of course, my chili recipe was the clear winner of the contest. Arizona chili is a contradiction in terms.

The other occasion came back to haunt me during my confirmation battle. In February of 1979, I appeared as Superman in a takeoff on the popular comic strip. The function was called the Underground Gridiron, an annual affair put on by the Dallas working press. In previous such productions I had played Peter Lorre and Gene Autry. This event provided the opportunity for Republican and Democratic politicians and the press to be convivial and civil with each other. It was always off the record — always, that is, until the night a visiting *Washington Post* photographer, not understanding the rules, took a picture that appeared in her newspaper. That opened the door for others who had taken shots during the evening to job them out to other publications (traditionally, once ground rules are broken, deliberately or in error, journalists consider it fair game to use the material without restrictions). Photos of the event appeared in *Newsweek, Time,* and *People* magazines, and in other newspapers, including some European periodicals. I even received clippings from my British pals, along with some pretty pithy comments. The pictures of me in full Superman regalia resurfaced with misleading captions ten years later as part of the character assassination campaign. Carolyn Barta, editor of "Viewpoints" in the *Dallas Morning News* (and a participant in the event), in an article critical of the "rumor-permissive climate" surrounding my confirmation, observed in a column of March 13, 1989:

The press contributed to the climate even before the hearing. I read columns about John Tower attending "boozy" parties in Dallas and cavorting in a Superman suit. As a part of those

parties for press and politicians in Dallas, I knew Sen. Tower
as an amateur thespian who loved nothing more than a good
performance. Those performances always included other politicians, both Republican and Democrat, including Gov. Bill
Clements, Congressmen Martin Frost, Jim Collins, Jim Mat-
tox, Steve Bartlett and others.

The popular image of a Senate committee chairman tends to make
those who wield the gavel seem like supermen, but the reality is
far more modest. When I was chairman, one of my principal devices for encouraging the Republicans on the Armed Services
Committee to work together on legislation was caucuses featuring
discussions about the virtues of a common position on issues that
were pending in the committee or on the Senate floor. If necessary,
I would invite individual senators to private meetings to pursue
the subject. Bill Cohen and I, for instance, talked at length about
chemical weapons, and eventually he became one of the most articulate advocates of the need to modernize the U.S. chemical arsenal as a means of deterring potential adversaries from ever
resorting to chemical warfare in the belief that we did not have an
effective retaliatory capability.

On other occasions, these discussions revealed that a senator's
legitimate constituent interests could not be reconciled with the
common position, and in those cases I would say, "Clearly, you
can't vote with us on this one." I don't offer any apologies for the
fact that I am a team player and that I expect other Republicans
to make a *reasonable* effort to support the national security agenda
of a Republican president.

The Reagan administration got off to a rocky start in 1981 with
the Senate when it nearly lost the vote to raise the federal debt
ceiling to $985 billion. Howard Baker, who was enjoying his new
status as majority leader after years in the minority, counted heads
and to his chagrin discovered that a number of freshmen Republicans were planning to defect and that he was going to be defeated.
Baker twisted arms as hard as he could, but he was getting nowhere. He asked me to talk to some of the new senators, and I got
the same negative response. Almost all of the thirteen GOP freshmen were dead set against deficit spending. It took Strom Thurmond to save the day. Baker called a Republican caucus and set
Strom loose. He told the freshmen that he had never voted to
increase the debt ceiling, but that he had never had Ronald Reagan

as president. And Strom said he was going to vote for the bill and "so are you!"

Had we been defeated on the debt-ceiling bill just seventeen days into the president's first term, there could have been a replay of the guerrilla warfare between Congress and the White House that so badly damaged Jimmy Carter's presidency. Carter suffered several legislative setbacks in his first months in office, and his energy program — the "moral equivalent of war" — was laughed off Capitol Hill, thus breaking his early momentum.

Baker's debt-ceiling victory taught Senate Republicans a valuable lesson: we controlled the White House and the upper house of Congress; we had the power to govern, and it was time to use it.

After he had been in the Senate awhile, Howard Baker told me that I had been one of his political role models — so to speak. About a month after my special-election victory in 1961, I appeared on NBC's *Meet the Press*. Howard was watching that Sunday and, as he related the story to me, said to himself, "If that little SOB can get elected to the Senate, so can I."

Baker was an effective majority leader, but by 1985 Ronald Reagan's power was facing increasing challenges from the Hill. It was inevitable. When I assumed the chairmanship of the Armed Services Committee, in 1981, I knew that the sentiment for the Reagan defense buildup was finite. Political power always ebbs and flows. We needed to move quickly after Reagan's victory, and fortunately we already had a head start in rebuilding the U.S. military, thanks in so many ways to Senator Henry Jackson's efforts late in the Carter administration. He and I had worked together to bring about increases in defense spending by the simple expedient of elaborating on the draft budgets that had been submitted to the White House by Carter's defense secretary, Harold Brown. Instead of just taking the military's wish list and the programs that various special interests were pushing, we built on Brown's generally sensible requests, requests that were being ignored at the Carter White House and Office of Management and Budget. Jackson and I, and our staffs, could see that the Carter administration was bleeding the readiness accounts — ammunition, spare parts, maintenance, manpower — to fund flashier programs (among them the B-2 bomber) and show that it was taking a tougher posture toward the Soviets as the president went into the 1980 election. It was creating a "hollow army," as General E. C. Meyer, the former Army chief of staff, called it, which looked good on paper but couldn't function to maximum effectiveness in combat. And it wasn't just the Army. The Navy had undermanned ships tied up in port. The Air Force down rate, which measures the numbers of aircraft out of service for mechanical reasons, was soaring, and the department routinely resorted to creating "hangar queens," the practice of cannibalizing one aircraft for spare parts to keep others flying.

By using the Pentagon's own original budget figures, Jackson and I had credible alternative proposals that were in line with what Harold Brown had requested, and when he appeared before the Armed Services Committee, he could only argue around the margins about feasibility and timing; the substance was his to begin with.

Having pushed a real increase in defense spending through Congress, we had a base to work from in 1981 and the makings of a pro-defense coalition. The Democrats couldn't very well back off their positions just because Ronald Reagan had replaced Carter. The Soviets were still in Afghanistan, and the Brezhnev doctrine was making itself felt in Poland, Africa, and Central America. In addition, the incoming administration did not have to start from scratch with a brand-new defense-spending plan. The Reagan transition team, working under time pressure, slapped together a Pentagon budget that was perhaps somewhat of an overreaction to the neglect of the Carter administration, but under the circumstances it was responsive to perceived requirements. Thus, a spending plan with its roots in the Jackson-Tower approach was presented to Congress.

Defense Secretary Caspar Weinberger was not well versed in defense issues when he first took the job. But what could have been a prolonged and uncertain learning process was overcome by Weinberger's quick intellect and by his willingness to listen to the uniformed military leadership and to appoint talented and experienced people to senior Pentagon positions. And Weinberger wasn't at all reluctant to raid my staff from time to time — which I, of course, considered an exercise in good judgment.

I spent much of my time as chairman shaping the Pentagon budget requests. We did not write any blank checks. In those first years of the Reagan defense buildup, we were *rebuilding*. The military was so desperately short of spare parts, adequate stockpiles of ammunition, fuel reserves, and personnel that it was imperative for us to move quickly to provide these resources.

As an old Navy man, I was delighted to support the goal of a six-hundred-ship navy during my chairmanship, although it was more than just nostalgia and parochialism that prompted my support. Since the early 1960s, the Soviets had been engaged in building an offensive blue-water naval force to spearhead the expansion of Communist influence around the world. In 1981, naval intelligence reports told us that Russian shipyards were operating at full capacity. They had their first nuclear-powered supercarrier under construction. Kirov-class nuclear-powered battle cruisers were joining the fleet. Two new classes of ultraquiet submarines were about to go into production.

With much of the free world's trade passing by merchant ships through vulnerable navigational "choke points," the United States could not afford to ignore the Soviet naval buildup. The Kremlin's ability to project itself into these vital sea-lanes significantly altered the military balance of power. Military strategists and geopolitical experts have long been concerned with the possibility that the enormous Soviet land-based military power, occupying as it does the heart of the Eurasian landmass, could be linked to a global naval capability. The combination made for an unprecedented concentration of Soviet military might.

The navy the Soviets were building was far in excess of what was required to mount an adequate maritime defense of the homeland. The Soviets have relatively secure inland lines of communications and a high level of self-sufficiency in energy and raw materials. They are not heavily dependent on the sea-lanes and external sources. As Joseph Luns, former secretary general of NATO, once said, "All they need the sea-lanes for is chocolate, bananas and a little bauxite." The United States, on the other hand, depends on external sources for energy, critical raw materials, and marketplaces, as do our allies. It is axiomatic that everything of bulk importance moves by sea. In addition, our allies are far-flung and our deployment and logistical demands are global. Our densely populated coastlines are vulnerable to Soviet submarine attack. Our safety and economic well-being are dependent, therefore, on the security of sea lines of communications. In that context, the force-projection capability of the Soviet navy must be regarded as threatening.

As platform committee chairman at the 1980 Republican Convention, I had been involved in getting the six-hundred-ship-navy plank included in the document. And during the transition, I urged President-elect Reagan to nominate John F. Lehman, Jr., as secretary of the Navy. Lehman, a former Nixon National Security Council aide, got the post and from the first day was working hard to realize the goal. His tenure as Navy secretary illustrated many of the problems associated with managing the Pentagon. He was a skilled political tactician. By harnessing the Navy's prestige and influence, Lehman was able to generate support for an ambitious ship-, aircraft-, and weapons-acquisition program that was rarely successfully challenged in Congress. Lehman's example, coupled with Reagan's expansive attitude toward the military and Weinberger's dogged insistence on measured increases in the level of defense funding, inspired the other services.

As a result, by 1983 Weinberger had a difficult management situation on his hands: the individual military services began networking with their respective advocates on Capitol Hill and sometimes operating with impunity outside the budgetary and policy parameters set by the secretary of defense. The Army, Air Force, Navy, and Marine Corps were in competition with each other for defense resources.

It was my intention as defense secretary to put a stop to this laissez-faire approach. I told the Senate Armed Services Committee and President Bush that the members of my Pentagon management team would wear "purple suits" rather than the traditional colors of the Army, Navy, Air Force, and Marines. Only by basing resource allocation squarely on a foundation of roles and mission priorities can we hope to manage the Pentagon in a rational manner.

President Reagan and Weinberger took steps early in the first term to resurrect the B-1 bomber, which had been unwisely canceled by Jimmy Carter in the middle of the SALT II negotiations without exacting a quid pro quo from the Soviets. I was in Geneva soon after that decision was made, as a Senate monitor of the SALT II negotiations. In a meeting with members of the Soviet delegation, I asked their scientific adviser, Alexander Shukin, what the Kremlin was prepared to offer Carter in return for canceling the B-1. He replied emphatically, "Senator, I am neither a pacifist nor a philanthropist."

*   *   *

In the 1980 campaign, Ronald Reagan had embraced the national security plank of the Republican platform adopted by the party's national convention in Detroit that summer. I served as overall chairman of the platform committee with then-congressman (now senator) Trent Lott from Mississippi as vice chairman. The plank was crafted by Rhett Dawson and Robert "Bud" McFarlane, at the time minority staff members of the Senate Armed Services Committee. It was based largely on positions taken by the Republican members of that committee and a comprehensive national security position paper prepared under my supervision by the Republican Policy Committee of the Senate. It had been adopted by the Republican Conference (a caucus of all Republican senators) during the latter months of the Carter administration. It provided the philosophic and empirical foundation for the Reagan defense buildup and modernization programs.

On one critical matter, my advice to President Reagan was rejected, precipitating my only major break with the administration on defense policy. I argued strenuously against the decision to scrap entirely the basing mode for the MX that had been inherited from the Carter administration. The MX missile itself had broad support in the defense community and in Congress, although it was opposed by a vocal and energetic minority. The missile was, and at this writing still is, the most capable ICBM in anybody's inventory. It is highly accurate and carries ten multiple independently targetable reentry vehicles. The basing mode, however, had been a matter of considerable controversy, and many alternatives had been researched and evaluated. Some were air and seaborne systems that would have made Rube Goldberg seem unimaginative. The ultimate goal of the exercise was to assure the greatest possible survivability of the system in any likely Soviet preemptive, or first-strike, scenario.

It was generally agreed in the defense community that the preferred means of deployment would be a land-based multiple protective shelter mode, a method for moving the missiles around from shelter to shelter and thus complicating the Soviets' strategic targeting by denying them a sitting duck. This was eventually refined into a modified "shell game," a grid system with underground launching silos placed at intervals. The plan orginally envisioned 4,600 of these silos, housing 200 MX missiles. The missiles would be moved from silo to silo by transporters that could either place the missile in the silo or simulate placement without observable confirmation of which holes were loaded. The Soviets would thus be forced to launch 9,200 warheads to achieve reasonable certainty of destroying 90 to 95 percent of our MX force. That would leave them a severely depleted number of land-based warheads to launch against our Minuteman IIs and IIIs and other strategic targets. The program was authorized with bipartisan support in Congress.

Yes, the shell game system could be overwhelmed, but at the price of an unfavorable force-exchange ratio. That is to say, the surviving U.S. strategic missile force, in all of its triad (land, sea, and airborne) elements, would be greater than the remaining Soviet force. This would be an unacceptable risk for any Soviet planners contemplating a first strike. That is the essence of strategic deterrence.

President Reagan and his advisers had an almost visceral contempt for Carter's position on defense issues, and I think it was easy to play to that bias, even though reopening the MX debate meant stirring up needless controversy and endangering the weapons system.

During the campaign Reagan had ridiculed the "racetrack" version of the MX basing mode considered by the Carter administration. Following his confirmation as defense secretary, Weinberger was ordered by the White House to look at alternative methods of deploying the MX. The whole question of MX basing was put on hold while Weinberger went through the repetitious process of reexamining all the options discarded by the Carter administration, some of which had never been taken seriously by the Department of Defense. I remember one in particular, called Big Bird, essentially an airborne missile silo. The concept was to feature a huge, lumbering plane with a 360-foot wingspan, powered by six diesel engines, flying at an altitude of five thousand feet at 100 knots, with a radar signature that looked like Buckingham Palace.

As this exercise went on it became increasingly apparent that the authorized basing mode was being excluded from consideration entirely while the Pentagon groped for an alternative acceptable to the administration. Support for the MX in an impatient Congress was beginning to falter, and senior military officers were privately expressing their alarm to me. After discussions with some of my congressional colleagues and trusted staff, I decided to intervene directly with the president. I contacted Congressman Bill Dickinson of Alabama, the ranking Republican on the House Armed Services Committee, whose experience and insights I esteemed, and he agreed to join me in the endeavor. Ron Lehman, who was my professional staffer on strategic matters, was assigned the task of preparing for a meeting with President Reagan. Lehman was, and is, one of the best strategic thinkers in the country.

During a congressional recess one morning in late August 1981, Ron and I flew to Offutt Air Force Base, in Omaha, for a briefing with General Davy Jones, chairman of the Joint Chiefs of Staff, and General Bennie Davis, commander in chief of the Strategic Air Command. That afternoon we flew to Los Angeles and checked in at the Century Plaza Hotel, where the president was vacationing. Dickinson joined us that evening, and we spent the balance of the day and the next morning reviewing the presentation Dickinson and I were to make to the president at lunch.

At lunchtime we entered the president's suite and he greeted us warmly, as is his custom. The only White House staff member present was Ed Meese, who, in the White House triumvirate of Jim Baker, Meese, and Michael Deaver, supervised national security affairs. The National Security Council adviser, Richard Allen, who answered to Meese, was not present. I knew that persuasion would be difficult, not only because of the president's bias, but also because Meese had scant comprehension of the arcane theories and theology of nuclear deterrence. Nor did Meese, being new to Washington, have any experience with Congress or sensitivity to the difficulties encountered in securing congressional authorization in the first place. Having discussed MX with him earlier and finding him unreceptive, I felt he did not appreciate the jeopardy posed to the future of the system by delay in deployment.

Dickinson and I spent more than two hours with the president. Using appropriate graphic aids, we made our case. Occasionally during the presentation Meese would interject, "It's not survivable, it's not survivable," ignoring force-exchange ratios and the fact that as important as ICBM survivability is the necessity to hold the Soviet ICBM force at risk by deploying in sufficient numbers in any mode.

We warned the president that if he got MX off track he risked losing the whole system. He listened while I explained that a phased-in approach, working with 100 missiles moving among 1,000 shelters, would get the program started while the planners pursued whatever options might emerge from evolving technology to enhance the survivability of the system. Delay had already permitted opposition to the basing mode to spring up in Nevada and

Utah, where the deployment was to be sited. Senators and congressmen from those two states, including the president's good friend Senator Paul Laxalt, were reflecting constituent pressure and were in active opposition. I therefore suggested the trans-Pecos region of Texas for consideration as an alternative location. I also suggested that he look at an even smaller deployment — 100 missiles in a system of 100 silos — which could be expanded.

I felt at the time that the president had given us a fair hearing. We said as much to the White House press corps, which was congregated in the corridor leading to the president's suite, staking out the meeting. In October, however, the administration announced its final decision to cancel the shell game basing mode. In frustration and anger (never hold a news conference when you are angry), I went to the Senate press gallery and blasted the administration for the decision. Cancellation was a politically fatal mistake, one that was likely to jeopardize the entire ICBM modernization program. I felt strongly that if we surrendered on MX we would be undermining our own negotiating position with the Soviets, perhaps to the point that setting an agenda for arms control talks would be impossible. For years thereafter, Senator Nunn and other Democrats would tweak the president by pointedly (usually in my presence) quoting my words on MX. And that, I have to admit, is fair game.

After several months of intensive searching for a "survivable" mode, the Department of Defense came up with a concept called Dense Pack. It was introduced to me by Major General Guy Hecker, head of Air Force congressional liaison, and Lieutenant General Kelly Burke, head of research and development for the Air Force. They came to my Capitol office one afternoon, closed the door, smiled, unbuttoned their tunics, and said, "Boy, have we got a deal for you!"

The concept, as they presented it, was based on the assumption that incoming missiles, massed together, would commit fratricide on detonation. Hecker and Burke took pains to explain the details very carefully, perhaps cognizant that they were dealing with someone who barely passed his minimum requirement in physics as a college undergraduate. The MX silos would be spaced closely together in clusters, thus forcing the Soviets to concentrate a large force of attacking warheads on a small area. The result would be that the exploding warheads would destroy each other.

I agreed to try to sell the proposal to my colleagues. I got shot down early. A skeptical Congress wasn't buying that one. Attempts at straight-faced presentations to congressional committees were met with derision. Dense Pack became Six Pack. I couldn't even persuade my own committee to take it seriously. The outcome was that to salvage the program a reluctant Congress agreed to deploy fifty MXs in vulnerable Minuteman III silos.

So much for survivability.

TWELVE

START

MILITARY SPENDING during the Reagan administration amounted to about $2.4 trillion. While the figure can be pared down by various accounting methods that adjust for the effects of inflation on the dollar's buying power, the total is still awesome. It has been described as the greatest peacetime military buildup in history. The money was well spent. We purchased security for the 1980s and beyond. With any luck, the Cold War is over, thanks to our determination to resist Soviet aggression.

The Pentagon was on a roll in the first two years of Reagan's initial term, but by 1983 it was obvious that the political tide was shifting — obvious, that is, to me and other senior congressional leaders, but not to the White House and Cap Weinberger. As secretary of defense, Weinberger had made the most of the president's immense popularity. After the honeymoon was over, though, Weinberger's style began to grate on members of Congress who expected him to engage in the normal process of political give-and-take. Cap looked on his budget requests as untouchable. I ended up being caught in the middle, trying to persuade Weinberger to make a few compromises and, on the other hand, spending hours dissuading my congressional colleagues from taking out their frustration on the Pentagon with a meat ax.

This mediation broke down in the spring of 1983. By ignoring

the advice from those of us in the Senate who were in a position
to assess the growing restlessness over the impact of the federal
budget deficit on politically popular domestic-spending programs,
and by insisting on a 10 percent increase in the Pentagon's budget,
the administration ended up with less than 4 percent.

In early 1983, I had begun to resolve my reservations about running
for a fifth term in favor of taking the preliminary steps to get
organized and raise money in preparation for the 1984 reelection
campaign. But by July, those reservations had resurfaced, and they
were stronger than ever.

At about this time, Herblock, the *Washington Post* cartoonist,
decided that whenever he drew Defense Secretary Caspar Weinberger he would hang a toilet seat around Cap's neck. Of course,
it was a snide way to remind readers about the six-hundred-dollar
toilet seats the military had purchased, but Weinberger was the
wrong target for Herblock's ridicule. It was Cap who originally
identified many of the procurement problems and put a stop to
them. Congressionally mandated waste is far in excess of anything
that has occurred through Pentagon mismanagement. To please
their constituents and campaign contributors, members of the
House and Senate are quick to rally around redundant facilities,
programs that have outlived their usefulness, and trivia like an
Army band unit at Fort Devens, in Massachusetts, that Edward
Kennedy pleaded with the Senate to fund several years ago despite
the Defense Department's decision that the band and the money
were needed elsewhere. (Kennedy prevailed after beseeching his
colleagues, "Ah c'mon, guys, let me keep my band.")

Waste, fraud, and abuse wouldn't have amounted to even a billion dollars — and that's out of $2.4 trillion in total defense outlays
over eight years, less than .05 percent overall. Although a relatively
small sum in terms of Pentagon funding, it is still worth recovering
if possible. I intervened to resolve a problem with United Technologies at one point when I was chairman of the Armed Services
Committee. The company had overcharged for fan blades in jet
engines that it was supplying to the Air Force. I called the head of
United Technologies, Harry Gray, and said, "Look, Harry, I think
you ought to give this back to the Air Force." Gray's immediate
reaction was "We're not legally bound to do it." In the ensuing
discussion, I suggested that, legal obligations aside, it would be in
the long-term best interest of United Technologies to make resti-

tution. In the end, Gray said he would consider it. When the accountants went back to audit the program they found that United Technologies had undercharged on some parts, overcharged on others. The company finally made a refund to the Air Force of nearly $500,000.

The United Technologies overcharge was one of the media's favorite horror stories, seized on as an example that Pentagon spending had gone too far, too fast. Yet for every horror story about toilet seats and screwdrivers, and while the band played on at Fort Devens, there were a dozen success stories.

During the confirmation battle I was accused of being an opponent of procurement and management reform because I had blocked some efforts to go after the problem in a piecemeal fashion. In fact, in mid-1983, with the concurrence of Senator Henry Jackson, I had ordered a staff study of the entire range of internal problems in the Pentagon with an eye to achieving the most sweeping institutional reform of the Department of Defense (acquisition, management, command structure, et cetera) since the creation of the unified department by the National Security Act of 1947. I assigned Jim Locher of the committee staff to direct the effort. The study, accompanied by recommendations for reform, was completed by the end of the year. It was my original intention that this study would provide the basis for a legislative initiative for comprehensive reform at the Pentagon and would embrace a number of proposals, including one on the reorganization of the Joint Chiefs of Staff drafted by Congressman Bill Nichols, a Democrat from Alabama. I had opposed some of these reform measures, not because they were without merit — many were thoughtful and constructive — but because I felt such proposals should be considered in the broader context of overall reform and that the result should be the product of an orderly process in which all aspects were considered, deliberated upon, and vetted by all interested parties. I wanted to ensure that each component would be considered in its relationship to the whole, conflicting provisions deleted and micromanagement minimized.

Sensing that Congress was getting bogged down with the authorization and appropriations measures, and that there might not be the time and the inclination to tackle a major reform package, I took a copy of our study to Bud McFarlane, the White House National Security Council adviser. I strongly urged the administration to launch an initiative on Pentagon reform or else risk being overtaken by congressional action at some point in the future. McFarlane told me that Cap Weinberger was not sympathetic to the idea and would oppose it. Eventually, however, internal resistance buckled, and the Packard Commission was formed.

The study also provided the foundation for the landmark Goldwater-Nichols Bill, which, among other things, instituted procurement and acquisition reform. When the bill was passed, Barry Goldwater and Sam Nunn very generously gave me credit for my earlier, albeit unfulfilled, initiatives.

At about the time the Locher effort was getting under way, I recognized that our subcommittee structure was not geared to focus on procurement problems. Revelations of so-called waste, fraud, and abuse demanded committee attention. A bright, energetic junior member of the committee, Dan Quayle, had already taken an active and consuming interest in the subject. Dan came to me with some constructive ideas, with the result that I formed an ad hoc subcommittee on procurement, made Quayle the chairman, and assigned him staff assistance.

Clearly, despite these efforts, the congressional process was not functioning as it should have, and there was little immediate prospect of comprehensive reform. Discipline and self-restraint were largely absent. Every year, the Senate seemed to become a less congenial place. The professionalism and dedication to public service that had once been characteristic of the institution were ebbing away.

Furthermore, random congressional incursions into the president's area of initiative and leadership in the national security and foreign policy process were increasing in frequency and creating potential for mischief. These usually took the form of amendments to bills pending before the Senate that were offered from the floor, with some popular appeal at the moment, but detrimental to the orderly and rational pursuit of national objectives. Republican cohesion in the Senate in support of the president on defense and external affairs was fragmenting.

Finally, I was at the point of becoming cynical, frustrated, and burned out. Perhaps twenty-four years was enough. Perhaps it was time to bring in someone else, with a fresher outlook. And, too, in that my intellectual interests had narrowed to military and diplomatic affairs, should some opportunity present itself for further public service confined to those areas, I would want to feel free to pursue it.

With less than sixteen months to go until my 1984 reelection, I knew it was time to make a decision. The chances for another six-year term looked excellent. Reagan's popularity in Texas was strong, my polls looked good, the campaign fund-raising effort was already under way, and the resources promised to be more than adequate. If I made up my mind to retire, I had to give a potential Republican successor enough time to line up the support and re-sources necessary for a successful campaign. Letting it go until the last minute would have put my party at a severe disadvantage.

By midsummer, I made the irrevocable decision to retire from the Senate.

On August 12, 1983, I flew to El Paso, where the president was addressing the American GI Forum. In his suite at the Marriott Hotel, I told him and Jim Baker of my decision. The president asked me to reconsider, and I thanked him for his confidence in me but declined. I did, however, volunteer to chair and manage his reelection campaign in Texas the following year.

From that point, I tried over the next few days to carry on business as usual. The next day I accepted an award from the GI Forum, a pair of bronze cowboy boots on a wooden base with the inscription: "American GI Forum of the United States Responsive Award presented to John Tower, United States Senator, Texas, for his continuing policy to 'kick doors open' on behalf of the American GI Forum and the Hispanic Community as men of small minds and cancerous bureaucracies oppressed our people."

The following week I flew back to Washington, busied myself with routine Senate matters, and informed Will Ball, my administrative assistant, and Mattie McKee, my executive secretary, of my decision. On August 19, I flew from Washington to Dallas with Fred McClure, my staff legislative director. A few minutes into the flight I told him that the purpose of the trip was to announce that I would not be seeking reelection to the Senate. Fred was caught by surprise, and I think he didn't know whether to offer congratulations or try to dissuade me. We talked about the reasons behind my decision; it was good that he was along on the flight. Bright and energetic, McClure had returned to the staff after taking a leave of absence to obtain a law degree and has gone on, most recently, to become chief of President Bush's Legislative Affairs Office.

If I had been looking to trace the high points of my career, I wouldn't have needed to look beyond the person who was sitting at my side on the plane. I don't want to be overly sentimental or claim credit for the accomplishments of my former staff, but as I contemplated retirement, it was satisfying to know that those men and women, about four hundred strong, would continue to make significant contributions to our society well into the future.

Fred flew on to Austin, where I planned to make my announcement the following week, and by the time he got there he had a hard time overcoming the emotional urge to tell his wife about the decision that I had made to bring my Senate career to a close.

On Saturday morning, August 20, I flew to Houston and boarded a helicopter to view the damage wrought by Hurricane Alicia, which had blown through the Galveston-Houston area two nights before. I have been through four or five hurricanes and a typhoon at sea, and yet it is always heart-wrenching to see how terribly destructive these phenomena can be. That afternoon, I held a news conference in Houston with Jerry Stephens, the director of the Federal Emergency Management Agency, to discuss the federal government's response to the disaster. I returned to Dallas that night and spent the next two days with Lilla in a room at the Adolphus Hotel, phoning a few friends and political leaders to give them a heads-up signal on the public announcement that I planned for the following Tuesday. Among those I called was Phil Gramm, whom I thought of as my most likely successor.

Tuesday morning, August 23, I flew in a private plane to Austin with Lilla, my longtime friend Paul Eggers, and my very able Texas press secretary, Dottie de la Garza, who had set up a news conference at the state capitol. I met the capitol press corps at 2:00 P.M. in the chamber of the Texas House of Representatives, among them a few who had covered my political career from the outset. I read a brief statement:

I have come to the State Capitol today to announce to the people of Texas that I will not be a candidate for reelection to the United States Senate in 1984. Representing Texas in the Senate has been the highest privilege and the most rewarding experience of my life. But I have recently made a personal decision that after 24 years of elective office and at the peak of my productivity I should step aside and pursue other avenues of endeavor. Upon completion of my term, I intend to come home to Texas, which I deeply love and regard as the best place on earth. For the next 16 months, I will vigorously represent the interests and aspirations of my fellow Texans, as I have in the past.

I owe an enormous debt of gratitude to the people of Texas, who have four times elected me their Senator. To those who have given me their encouragement, support, dedication and friendship, I will never be able to adequately express my profound appreciation. I also wish to thank my colleagues who have entrusted me with positions of leadership in the Senate. These responsibilities I have attempted to meet to the best of my ability. The confidence and trust they have placed in me have been a source of strength and satisfaction that few who enter public service come to know.

I have informed President Reagan of my decision and have volunteered to serve in an appropriate position in his reelection campaign.

As I strode from the capitol that afternoon my emotions ran the gamut of recollection, nostalgia, some sadness, and great relief. I didn't exactly ride off into the sunset — perhaps I should have.

The sixteen months that remained of my Senate tenure were busy ones. I managed the Reagan-Bush reelection campaign in Texas, and from that vantage point I was able to lend a hand to the entire slate of Republican candidates, including Phil Gramm, whom the party had nominated to succeed me in the Senate.

It was a most gratifying last hurrah. The Reagan-Bush ticket won the state by almost 64 percent of the vote. Gramm was elected to the Senate by 59 percent. We put four more Republicans into the Texas congressional delegation, picked up an additional place in the state senate and fifteen in the Texas House.

Although President Reagan soundly defeated Walter Mondale nationwide, his coattails were not nearly as long as they had been in 1980; the Republican party, as a result, lost two seats in the Senate, thus setting the stage for the Democrats to make a comeback in 1986.

For the two years until then, Republicans would continue in the majority. Barry Goldwater approached me for advice as to whether I thought that he could handle the responsibilities of chairman of the Armed Services Committee. Barry's seniority put him in line for the post (so long as Strom Thurmond chose to remain as chairman of Judiciary). I assured him he had the experience, the knowledge, and the respect of his colleagues to do a good job.

The two years that Barry Goldwater served as chairman, before he too retired, gave Sam Nunn the opportunity to position himself as the dominant spokesman on defense matters on Capitol Hill. Goldwater had long had a deep interest in the internal reform of the Pentagon. He turned to the staff work on the subject that had been done during my chairmanship, removed it from the back burner, and made it his top priority. Taken as a whole, the sequence of events described earlier in this chapter — Jim Locher's study, my discussions at the White House, the Packard Commission — eventually paid off by giving the reform effort significant new momentum. Barry saw that the timing was right, and he was determined to move forward on this long-overdue endeavor. He became preoccupied with the Goldwater-Nichols Bill, which prescribed major changes in the organization and processes of the Department of Defense. Meanwhile, Sam Nunn was free to assert himself in other matters within the purview of the committee, exploiting the widening chasm between an immovable defense secretary and an assertive Congress. He held himself out as the real power behind the chairmanship, treating Barry with great deference in public and condescension in private. It would appear that Nunn egged Goldwater on until he got into an open confrontation with President Reagan and Cap Weinberger over reorganizing the Joint Chiefs of Staff, and then stood back and watched the fur fly.

In the last few days before Congress finishes its remaining business and adjourns sine die, there are tributes to those members who are about to retire. My colleagues on the Armed Services Committee presented me with a shadow box displaying my chairman's gavel, a few other mementos, and a series of brass plaques engraved with kind words from friends and associates. Nunn made the presentation, and his remarks were printed in the *Congressional Record:*

> Since 1981, John Tower has served as Chairman of the Armed Services Committee. All of us in this room can attest to his skill, his leadership, and his successes in guiding a strong defense program through Congress.
>
> Senator Tower's success on national security issues can, in part, be attributed to his remarkable understanding of foreign

policy. He came to the Senate with a strong background on foreign relations based upon his education at the London School of Economics and his early career as a college political science professor.

But since coming to the Senate, he has devoted a considerable amount of time to the study of world events. In particular, Senator Tower has taken tremendous amounts of time to meet with foreign officials — Heads of State, Foreign Ministers, Defense Ministers, parliamentarians, and military leaders — during their visits to Washington, as well as in his official travels on behalf of our Committee.

So not only does he know the issues, he also knows well the foreign officials who influence them. This combination has been a tremendous asset to the work of this Committee and the Senate as a whole.

Nunn went on to take note of the changes that had occurred since my first days as a U.S. senator. In fact, the Senate had just lived through one of the most glaring examples of the altered situation. We had struggled mightily to win approval for the upcoming fiscal year's Pentagon budget, whereas in the mid-1960s the same process had been relatively cut and dried. The Senate floor debate and the conference committee on the 1985 defense authorization bill were a grueling valedictory and entirely reflective of the breakdown in the congressional legislative process. The four-hundred-page-long bill, as I note earlier, had 107 amendments made to it and took ten days to pass.

The burden of dealing with the nation's security is heavy enough in its own right, but in addition there is an attitude on the part of many of our legislators that poisons and paralyzes the effective functioning of the system. I remember being badgered by various senators on constituent defense matters and threatened with loss of support on floor votes if I didn't logroll with them. I declined to pay that kind of price. And, at about the same time, Senator Charles Grassley angered me to such an extent that my aides were afraid I was about to explode. Grassley got me going by delivering a lecture on the lessons of Pearl Harbor: to wit, that it was our industrial infrastructure, not military preparedness, that was important. Grassley chalked up the devastating defeat to "poor military planning." Under the circumstances my response was extremely temperate. I said, "They bombed us because they were

militarily superior at the time, I say to the senator." It didn't faze
Grassley. He was playing to his favorite audience — the news
media — and he went on to indignantly note that for all the money
the United States was spending on the military, only two tanks a
day were being produced, as though military preparedness in the
nuclear era depended on a tank a minute rolling off the assembly
lines like Model-T Fords. Only two tanks a day! Grassley was looking for a headline.

The time had come for me to leave the United States Senate.

I became a private citizen again at high noon on January 3, 1985,
when the new Congress convened. Fifteen days later, I was named
by President Reagan to be the chief negotiator at the Strategic
Arms Reduction Talks in Geneva.

Ample speculation about my future plans had followed the announcement that I was retiring from the Senate. There was again
talk that I would become secretary of defense, in Ronald Reagan's
second term, should Cap Weinberger step down. An ambassadorial
appointment figured in some of the crystal ball gazing, with the
embassy in Bonn cited as the most likely posting. A few friends
asked if I was interested in running for governor of Texas. I told
them I'd have to think about that one for about twenty years.

With my work for the Reagan-Bush reelection campaign and the
task of packing up and clearing out of my Senate office, there
wasn't much time left over for considering business opportunities.
I was in the process of moving into a small office a few blocks off
Pennsylvania Avenue, approximately midway between the White
House and the Capitol Building, when I got a telephone call from
Secretary of State George Shultz, who asked me to meet with him
the next morning. My immediate reaction was that Shultz wanted
to discuss the post of ambassador to West Germany, which had
indeed been offered to me by President Reagan a month earlier in
my farewell briefing with him. I suspected that the secretary of
state was going to prod me to accept, or at least make a decision
one way or the other on the offer.

Shultz and Soviet foreign minister Andrei Gromyko had spoken
in Geneva two days earlier and agreed to resume arms reduction
negotiations, which had broken down in December 1983 when the
Soviets walked out of the talks and refused to return to the bargaining table. When the secretary and I met as arranged, he asked

me to take the position of strategic offensive arms negotiator and
summoned Paul Nitze, his principal arms control adviser, to sit in
on the meeting. In his memoirs, Nitze describes what happened
this way: "He listened carefully to what the secretary had to say —
he was visibly moved. The offer was a complete surprise, but John
agreed immediately with no reservations."

I told my secretary Kim Garven to stop unpacking and to get
ready to move again — this time to Geneva.

President Reagan wanted a new team of senior arms control negotiators. It was an opportune time to make a fresh start. The
Soviet public diplomacy campaign had failed to break the NATO
allies' resolve to deploy intermediate-range nuclear weapons on European soil — and that deployment had begun. By introducing
SDI, the Strategic Defense Initiative, in March 1983, Ronald Reagan had changed the arms control equation. There was a clear
opportunity to make a breakthrough. A new senior negotiating
team would both serve as a symbol of the administration's commitment to seizing the chance and provide the political and diplomatic substance to realize the objective.

The president chose Max Kampelman to be overall head of the
delegation and the negotiator on space and defensive systems.
Maynard Glitman was named the chief negotiator for medium-
range weapons. My assignment was to oversee the talks on long-
range nuclear weapons. The selection of Kampelman, a Democrat
formerly allied with Hubert Humphrey, silenced Democrats who
might have fussed about the changes. Glitman was Paul Nitze's
deputy; his elevation was a signal that although Nitze was being
replaced — at his own request — there would be continuity and
no backing away from the progress he had made the previous year.
As for my contribution, I'll quote an editorial from the *Dallas
Times-Herald*:

> His nomination will send a clear signal to the Soviet Union
> that the U.S., while willing to negotiate genuine reductions
> in arms, will not veer from a tough bargaining stance and has
> no intention of granting any concessions that might jeopar-
> dize this nation's security. . . .
>
> The former senator also could prove very helpful to the
> Reagan administration if and when the U.S. and Soviet

negotiators reached an agreement. His contacts on Capitol Hill and his reputation as a "hard-liner" on military matters undoubtedly would enhance the likelihood of ratification of any pact presented to Congress.

I had not planned to resume my career in public service quite so soon. I had already accepted two corporate board memberships and had decided to decline the Bonn post. My intention was to build a firm financial foundation that would support me in my retirement years. As Senator William Cohen noted during the confirmation hearings, I had left the Senate with "more modesty than means." Over the years, when the news media did rundowns on the net worth of members of the Senate, I always ended up around the bottom of the list. As the son and grandson of Methodist clergymen, I inherited no material wealth. My assets were limited to the homes we owned in Washington and Wichita Falls. My only foray into the world of investments was a small stake in a piece of offshore-oil-rig equipment, a blowout preventer, which I leased out for a modest return. Otherwise, I lived off my Senate salary and some honoraria, out of which I also educated my three daughters at Hockaday, a private school in Dallas, and sent them to Southern Methodist University.

By accepting the START negotiating appointment, I postponed my plans to begin achieving a measure of financial security. It was an open-ended assignment and for all I knew could have kept me shuttling between Geneva and Washington for the four years that remained of Ronald Reagan's presidency. Effectively, I would be working during that time for half pay, since under government rules my Senate pension was applied to my State Department salary (to prevent double-dipping), bringing the additional compensation, beyond the retirement income, to about $39,000. To be sure, I wasn't in it for the money; I was serving my country. But such an exaggerated emphasis was placed on the fees that I earned as a consultant during the Senate confirmation fight that I thought it would be helpful to put these financial matters into proper perspective. Given the earning power I demonstrated after leaving Geneva and returning to private life, in 1986, I had clearly made a significant financial sacrifice to serve as the START negotiator. I did not hesitate to make that sacrifice, I do not regret having done so, and I was prepared to make the sacrifice again in 1989, when President-elect Bush called on me to serve in his cabinet.

*   *   *

Viktor Karpov, the chief of the Soviet START delegation, was a skilled negotiator. He only rarely engaged in polemical displays, and on the first occasion when he did I settled back in my chair at the long conference table and listened until he had said his piece. The Marxist monologue lasted about thirty minutes. I felt no useful purpose could be served by an equally lengthy rejoinder and replied, "I don't agree with your assumptions, your premises, or your interpretation of history. Now let's talk about what we came here to discuss." It was the most effective way of dealing with the Russian fondness for dialectical exchanges, which were, at best, tangential to the negotiations. Every now and then, though, Karpov would tempt me into responding to his more sweeping pronouncements. The Soviets frequently remind American officials that it was the United States, not the Soviet Union, that used nuclear weapons in wartime. Karpov chided me for this once. I replied that since I had been assigned to the U.S. invasion force against Japan in World War II, Truman's decision to drop the atomic bombs on Hiroshima and Nagasaki probably saved my life, and undoubtedly the lives of tens of thousands of others. Karpov informed me that the Red Army had by then subdued the Japanese by taking Manchuria and seizing the northern islands, and therefore the action was solely designed to intimidate the Soviet Union. I took a moment to ponder the awesome certitude of Soviet historical revisionism and changed the subject.

Despite the predictable divergence of views, Karpov and I fashioned an effective working relationship. Our first few meetings were crucial in this regard. My instructions were to inform the Soviets that the U.S. negotiating position that had been tabled during the previous negotiations, broken off in December 1983, remained valid and on the table. In addition, we were prepared to be flexible and to move out from our starting point, which included a build-down proposal to allow the superpowers to reduce their arsenals of older weapons systems while modernizing their strategic forces in ways that would not escalate the threat of nuclear war. Our message was unambiguous: let's pick up where we left off.

However, Karpov responded by saying that the NATO deployment of Cruise and Pershing II missiles in Western Europe and President Reagan's continued commitment to SDI had altered the strategic situation. Until we stopped SDI and withdrew the INF missiles, he said, there was no purpose to be served by putting forward a specific Soviet proposal. In effect, Karpov was reiterating the position that had led to the suspension of the talks sixteen months earlier.

The plenary sessions, as these face-to-face encounters between the two delegations were referred to, alternated locations. A session in our ninth-floor conference room in the Botanic Building, near the United Nations complex, would be followed a week later by one at the Soviet mission. The plenaries opened with an exchange of formal statements from each side, after which we adjourned into subgroups in informal sessions known as post-plenaries, which permitted unstructured discussion and argument by the specialists of the respective negotiating teams. These talks were exploratory in nature; neither side was bound by anything that was said in them. They were a far more productive and useful negotiating vehicle than the plenary sessions.

Karpov's statement required a forceful response. Rather than launching into a definitive rationale for the Cruise and Pershing II deployments, or fencing with Karpov about SDI, I focused on the implications of the Russian non-position. I told him that since he would not put a proposal on the table, then perhaps I should inform my government that it would be best if I returned home until the Soviet Union was prepared to make its position known.

Karpov came back with (and I am paraphrasing him) "No, no . . . if you agree to our position, we'll go a lot further than we've ever gone before." It would have served little purpose to remind Karpov that he no longer had a position, and so I did some fishing. "How much further?" I asked.

"A lot further. It's a good deal," Karpov replied. Again, please remember that I am paraphrasing him. Each week at the post-plenaries I pursued this line with logical follow-up questions, not suggesting that there was the slightest chance that SDI or INF deployments would be compromised. "Suppose I agree to your position, what would we get in return?" I inquired. Karpov told me there would be deep reductions in strategic weapons. "How deep?"

"Deeper than we've ever gone before."

A negotiating round lasted from six to eight weeks, after which the two delegations would return to their respective capitals for consultations. We came to the end of the first round, and Karpov was still vague on the Soviet position. Round two, which began in May 1985, repeated the pattern. Karpov assured me that the Soviets were prepared to offer deep reductions in strategic systems if only we would agree to ban "space attack weapons" — in short, scrap our SDI program. "How deep is that?" I asked, noting that the previous Soviet position had proposed a reduction in strategic nuclear delivery vehicles to a total of eighteeen hundred. "That's twenty percent. Is it greater than twenty percent?"

I remember that Karpov said, "Yes, much greater."

"Thirty percent?" I asked. "Forty percent?"

He said, "Yes, or more."

This line was pursued by other members of the team in their encounters with their Soviet counterparts. Our persistence finally paid off. One of the advisers on Max Kampelman's negotiating team had been shocked and offended that I would even entertain the hypothetical notion of "accepting" the Soviet proposal. To him SDI was sacred, and it was to me too. But by refusing to let Karpov off the hook and by prodding for specifics, we had maneuvered the Soviets to the brink of a 50 percent reduction in strategic delivery vehicles.

I told Karpov that we were talking only about delivery vehicles but that the United States was just as interested in reducing nuclear warheads. This was a sensitive area with the Soviets. It took me at least two post-plenaries to get a direct answer. I had to ask point-blank: "Are you talking about weapons, too?" By then, Karpov was locked in to the theme of deep reductions and unable to pull back from the proposition. He acknowledged that the deep reductions would also apply to warheads.

Subsequently, Karpov and his delegation came up with a cunningly devised formula for applying these deep reductions to portions of the strategic triad in a way that would affect our nuclear capability to a greater extent than it would affect theirs. The Soviets are adept at playing the numbers game. Some strategic weapons systems are more destabilizing than others. And I should here make important distinctions between types of delivery systems. Missiles are fast flyers; bombers are slow flyers. It takes an ICBM about twenty-five minutes to reach its target from launch; a bomber takes ten to twelve hours to make the same journey. The warning time of an ICBM attack is, therefore, very short indeed. Submarine-launched ballistic missiles are fast fliers, but real-time communication with subs is difficult without compromising a submarine's greatest asset — concealment. Further, only a fraction of our bomber force is in the air at all times, and no more than half of our submarine force is at sea at one time. An ICBM force can be fully manned and ready at all times. Thus, the ICBM is the principal element and the leading edge of a nuclear first strike. Subs and bombers are essentially retaliatory systems. The Soviet strategic force is heavily oriented toward land-based missiles. At this writing there are approximately 6,500 warheads in the Soviet ICBM force and approximately 2,500 in ours — roughly a three-to-one ratio. In that we do not have an offensive mentality or policy, our strategic triad is more balanced, and more oriented toward retaliation. Our objective in working toward a treaty agreement that enhanced the security of the United States and its allies was clear. It was incumbent upon us to achieve reductions that were both deep and equitable — to remove the threat posed to our safety by the enormous arsenal of Soviet ICBMs.

When Karpov introduced his formula for deep reductions, he explained that it was designed to enhance stability by ensuring that no more than x percent of the permitted number of warheads could be deployed in any one leg of the strategic land-based, submarine-launched, or long-range bomber force, the so-called triad. Therefore, on the surface, it appeared to be responsive to our concerns. The hitch was that Karpov refused to set a value on his x. We didn't know what the number was or how it would affect the overall equation.

After Karpov and I had several exchanges over the Soviet proposal, he continued to resist my efforts to pin him down on a number. Finally I said, "Viktor, I cannot negotiate on the basis of an unknown percentage of an unknown number."

From then on, we were fully engaged in the process of filling in the numbers and the percentages. We had found the concept — deep reductions, on the order of 50 percent — and in fits and starts, the Soviets developed a proposal that accepted this principle, one that had been criticized as unrealistic and unattainable when it was first outlined by President Reagan in 1981. By the time Mikhail Gorbachev and Ronald Reagan met for the Geneva summit in November 1985, they were able to agree on "the principle of 50 percent reductions in nuclear arms of the U.S. and the U.S.S.R. appropriately applied."

*   *   *

One of the keys to negotiating successfully with Viktor Karpov was my determination to avoid allowing the talks to degenerate into a harangue, with each side laying down unproductive salvos of rhetoric. Most of the real work of the START talks was done in the post-plenaries, once the formal opening statements had been delivered. I do not mean to minimize the importance of the plenaries. The statements, seven- or eight-page papers, were an effective way to ensure that a message went straight from Geneva to Moscow, or from Geneva to Washington. To make sure that nothing got lost in translation, the paper, after being read, was handed to the other side so that it could be transmitted verbatim back to the State Department or the Kremlin.

There was an early-nineteenth-century Congress of Vienna quality to the proceedings that made them cumbersome at times. On the other hand, the post-plenaries and other private meetings gave me an opportunity to get involved in a give-and-take with Karpov. When he would start running on about some alleged U.S. outrage, I'd cut him off. One time I just said, "Bull——." The interpreters couldn't believe their ears; they practically dropped their pencils in amazement. Karpov stopped and broke into a smile. "Okay, okay," he said in English. "We will talk turkey."

Occasionally, we would invite the Russian delegation to social events, which were more relaxed, and they would reciprocate. Gorbachev's policy of restricting the flow of vodka at the Soviet mission tended to make our invitations the more prized.

These social contacts with the Soviets might have raised a few eyebrows among those who believe that the atmosphere around negotiations must be tense and combative. The Soviets are perceived by some to have an inferiority complex. They are very sensitive to slights and what they interpret as contemptuous treatment. By dealing with them as equals, I sought to create a spirit of cooperation rather than confrontation.

Karpov's fifty-seventh birthday happened to coincide with a plenary session that was being held in our building. After both sides had finished delivering their statements, I adjourned the meeting and announced that there would be a small celebration. We had champagne, presented Karpov with a cowboy hat, and sang "Happy Birthday." He didn't know what to make of the hat, which turned out to be a bit too large for him; it came down over his ears. We had asked one of the Soviet delegation's military ad-

visers to get his chief's hat size, and Karpov shook his head mourn-
fully at this intelligence lapse. I have no reason to believe it was
part of the Soviet misinformation campaign, but one never knows.

There were congenial moments; however, I never lost sight of
the fact that Viktor Karpov was a formidable adversary. He was
well read, shrewd, and sophisticated. Occasionally, he'd try to pull
something over on us, and I would cluck my tongue and say, "Viktor, I can't believe a man of your erudition would make such a
statement!"

Karpov couldn't resist the temptation to engage in a little media
manipulation, and from time to time he would tell reporters that
the U.S. side was not cooperating, dragging its feet or whatever.
I rebuked him once after reading a headline in the *International
Herald Tribune* that read: "SOVIET ACCUSES U.S. OF FAILING TO
RESPOND POSITIVELY ON ARMS." Seeing that the Soviets were still
in the process of outlining their proposal to us, there had not yet
been an opportunity to respond. When I pointed that out, Karpov
said he had been misquoted, which indeed proved to be the case.
Thus, the press can sometimes make mischief in a delicate negotiating process.

Karpov also had a penchant for "linkage" that we had to keep
in check. The Soviets wanted to conduct the arms control talks by
way of one grand negotiating forum broken into three subgroups.
The U.S. position was that there should be three separate and
distinct negotiating teams loosely gathered under one umbrella organization. By way of a compromise, Max Kampelman served as
first among equals, should the need arise for an overall approach
involving the three teams. Karpov, who was chief of the Soviet
arms control delegation as well as START negotiator, regularly
insisted on meetings that would result in linking the teams together. His objective was to merge the three major categories of
issues together to achieve maximum negotiating leverage.

Diplomatic negotiations are carefully orchestrated to mesh with
strategic and political objectives. The balance can easily be upset.
Karpov's attempts to fuse the tripartite talks into an agglomerate
could have paralyzed any movement toward an agreement on strategic weapons by injecting the SDI controversy into the proceedings. The genius of Ronald Reagan's Strategic Defense Initiative
rested squarely on its ability to convince the Soviets that they were
faced with the choice of negotiating seriously or watching the

United States embark on a program that could change the strategic balance in its favor.

SDI was not so much a bargaining chip as a live option that, given its considerable cost and technological complexity, the Soviets could not hope to achieve in the near term. Yet the United States, with its superior resources and technical skills, could dream the impossible dream, and if we realized a significant portion of its potential benefits, the Soviets would be put at a marked disadvantage. The notion of erecting a perfect umbrella to shield the entire U.S. population from nuclear attack is not attainable, and most responsible strategic analysts knew it from the beginning. Ronald Reagan's vision of SDI was inspired by his buoyant optimism. Essentially, this vision held the promise of shifting the emphasis from reliance on the threat of nuclear destruction as a deterrent to reliance on a nuclear defense that would discourage attack. It was a signal to the Soviets that they could not continue to modernize their strategic nuclear forces without risking the possibility that America would proceed with research, development, and deployment of a defensive system that would render those forces obsolete.

Throughout my time as chief START negotiator, Soviet respect for U.S. technology and concern about SDI were manifest. The Soviets seemed to be more certain than many of our own scientists that a workable and cost-effective system would emerge from President Reagan's initiative. This attitude gave the United States a diplomatic advantage. I was naturally disturbed when I was told by Ambassador Glitman that a member of a delegation of congressional observers had taken Karpov aside at a reception in Geneva and told him not to worry about SDI. Glitman had heard this senator and, I should add, Democratic presidential aspirant say, "Congress is going to take care of" the program. I could only imagine how much comfort that might give the Soviets, and I was appalled by the lack of judgment and discretion. No matter what this senator's opinion about SDI, he was undercutting his own country's negotiating posture.

The U.S. START team made a significant contribution to arms control while I served as the chief negotiator, and it pained me to see our accomplishments cast in an unfavorable light during the fight over my confirmation. The men and women who worked with me were dedicated professionals. They served well and under

difficult conditions. The two-month stint in Geneva for each round
of negotiations, followed by an interval back in Washington,
tended to disrupt everyone's private life. Unlike someone with a
normal diplomatic assignment, which permits an individual to settle in one place, fall into a routine, and make friends among the
local residents, our personnel were unable to settle in. Except for
the senior principals in the delegation, they lived in cramped little
flats or hotel rooms.

Delegation members were thrown together for ten- and twelve-
hour (and sometimes longer) workdays. There was very little contact with anyone who wasn't a co-worker. Groups of hikers or
skiers or sightseers would get together on the weekends, but there
was scarcely any time for socializing. On a couple of occasions,
low-stakes poker nights were arranged in the conference room to
give everyone a little fun and relaxation. They were pretty tame
events and certainly not wild parties by any stretch of the imagination.

Unfortunately, during the course of my confirmation battle,
Congressman John Dingell of Michigan, chairman of the Subcommittee on Oversight and Investigations of the House Committee
on Energy and Commerce and a chronic publicity hound, was
holding hearings on an unrelated matter. The committee was probing a report drawn up by the General Accounting Office to the
effect that a contractor for the Department of Energy had violated
regulations in a government-funded lobbying campaign. Retired
Air Force lieutenant colonel Robert Moser, whom I identify earlier
in the book as Ambassador Kampelman's executive secretary in
Geneva, was supposedly employed by the contractor to assist in
the lobbying effort against a congressional ban on nuclear testing.
In a 1986 investigation, the Air Force Office of Special Investigations reportedly identified some security violations by Moser but
apparently did not make a finding that the violations resulted in a
compromise of sensitive information. Although the initial investigation was focused on Moser, the fact that I was a part of the
Geneva team triggered what appeared to be a separate investigation
of me. Such was not the case.

In a February 6, 1989, letter to Senator Nunn, Dingell said he
possessed "boxes of documents related to questionable activities"
in Geneva and that the subcommittee had "extensive information
that may be of use to you." According to the letter, the documents

included files from various investigative agencies. The letter was leaked to the *Detroit News*.

To his credit, Sam Nunn attempted to warn off reporters who inquired about the significance of the events in Geneva vis-à-vis my fitness for the post of secretary of defense. According to various press reports, Nunn cautioned journalists to be very careful in dealing with the Dingell information. He said nothing had been found to corroborate allegations of security violations in Geneva by me or my staff. His admonition fell on deaf ears. Reporters would not be deterred from a juicy story, regardless of the unreliability of the sources. CBS even ran a piece that featured a woman, described as a former secretary in the arms control delegation, her face concealed by shadows, who said she had personally seen me chasing a secretary around my desk. It was an absurd lie. I would have had to be a high hurdler to chase anybody around the desk, since it was L-shaped and linked to a wall credenza. Besides, I have always treated my secretaries with professional respect, and they would have told CBS that — on camera, without benefit of dramatic shadows — if the network had bothered to ask.

The Dingell investigation, however, is what muddied the waters. It generated an atmosphere of intrigue and mistrust and gave a State Department security officer by the name of Berne Indahl the ammunition he needed to attempt to show that the Arms Control and Disarmament Agency was guilty of violating security procedures. Proving this would allow Indahl to one-up Kenneth Adelman, the ACDA director during the Reagan years, with whom he had been feuding.

To defend himself against charges that included sexual harassment, Moser apparently informed the investigators that he knew of fourteen other members of the ACDA delegations in Geneva who were involved in extramarital relationships. He later told the FBI that I was *not* one of those fourteen. But by then Indahl's report had been leaked to the press, and it contained the false allegations about my secretaries.

The smallest administrative infractions by members of the START team were exaggerated by the press into major lapses. As part of the routine in Geneva, Marine guards, in accordance with the regulations, used to make the rounds at night through the delegation offices, looking for any classified material that had not been locked away or for windows that had been left unlocked. The

Marines took their job very seriously, and when they found any-thing even marginally confidential they wrote up a pink slip re-porting a violation. Once, early in my tenure, I was written up for leaving on my desk a list of staff phone numbers marked "For Office Use Only." The numbers wouldn't have been very useful to the Soviets — they probably had them already. To my knowledge, no member of my negotiating team was ever cited for a major security violation. Yet the press reports conveyed the impression that the office was lax and vulnerable to Soviet espionage.

As Dingell's hearings were under way, the *Baltimore Sun* was leaked a six-page report based on an interview that Office of Per-sonnel Management investigators conducted with Berne Indahl. These are the last five paragraphs of the story:

> Mr. Indahl told the OPM investigators that he had "inde-pendent corroboration" of Mr. Tower's relationships with the unnamed and unspecified number of secretaries.
>
> "John Grassle, the Geneva security officer, told Indahl that Ambassador Tower's wife threw him out in February 1986 because of his involvement with secretaries and Grassle helped Ambassador Tower find an apartment in a hotel in Geneva after Tower's wife had ejected him from their home," the report said.
>
> Mr. Grassle, in an interview last night after Mr. Billmire alerted him to the contentions of the report, denied ever tell-ing Mr. Indahl any such thing.
>
> "If Berne was here right now, I'd ask him where the heck he got that information because he didn't get it from John Grassle," Mr. Grassle said. "Berne and I were good friends," he added, saying that he hasn't seen Mr. Indahl in recent years.
>
> Mr. Indahl, now stationed with the State Department in Africa, could not be reached for comment.

I can only describe the Indahl report, the starting point and key premise of this story, as an astounding lie; of all the things that were said during the confirmation, it was the one that made me the angriest. Innocent people were being vilified in order to dam-age me. It was despicable.

By late 1985, married life with Lilla had grown too difficult to continue. My daughters were becoming estranged from me, and staff morale was sagging. Lilla was a perfectionist who was extremely demanding of my staff. She heaped verbal abuse on them when they failed to meet her standards of performance. Before dinners and other social engagements, she would order a complete guest list and biographies of all those attending. Lilla wanted to be able to say things like "I understand you graduated from Vassar in 1961 . . ." If the staff didn't hop to it, she'd call them "incompetent slugs" and worse. It was not unusual for me to see a secretary dissolve into tears after one of Lilla's tongue-lashings. I felt very sorry for Lilla, but in November, after the final round of talks for 1985, I informed her that I had decided on a permanent separation. We were in Washington at the time and agreed that I would return to Geneva without her. I left the house in Washington on November 11, 1985.

The START talks were to resume in January. My daughter Marian accompanied me back to Geneva. She speaks French, and I asked her to come along so that we could spend some time together. The idea was to have Marian help me run the official residence and discharge the social obligations that were mine as ambassador.

It made for a pleasant but brief interlude. Lilla broke our agreement that she would come to Geneva only at the end of the round of talks to obtain the personal belongings she had left behind. Without warning, on the morning of February 5, a Wednesday, Lilla appeared at the residence. She may have been hoping for a reconciliation. I do not know for sure. However, I do know that was an impossibility. Marian and I immediately moved out to temporary quarters. In a visit planned weeks earlier, my eldest daughter, Penny, joined us the following Saturday. A few days later, I arranged to borrow the apartment of Ron Lehman, who had been detained in Washington on National Security Council business.

Lilla did not throw me out of the house; in fact, she asked me to stay. In any case, the house was not hers to begin with, since it was *my* official residence. But rather than insisting that she be the one to depart, I elected to leave. With Marian already in Geneva, and Penny soon to arrive, other arrangements would have been necessary anyway, given the animus between Lilla and my daughters.

The press, which seemed to have such an interest in my divorce papers, failed to note that I had at that point been separated from

Lilla for three months — since November 11 of the previous year, as clearly stated in the divorce petition Lilla herself filed.

My much-maligned secretaries, Brenda Hudson and Kim Garven, were highly competent and trusted aides. Brenda had been on my Senate staff after a stint with the Air Force. She had been stationed in Tehran during the fall of the shah and threatened by an Iranian mob. Kim, an Army officer's daughter, had also served on my Senate staff. In Geneva, I rarely saw them after working hours or on weekends, except at occasional social functions. They lived in a dormitory hotel along with a dozen or more other delegation staff. At this writing, Brenda is Ron Lehman's executive secretary, and Kim runs my Washington office — and does it well. It is significant to note that neither of their names appeared in Lilla's interrogatories during our divorce settlement process.

When the START talks reopened in January 1986, the Soviet delegation went into a holding pattern that seemed to reflect disappointment on its part with the Geneva summit conference between Reagan and Gorbachev the previous November. The atmosphere was friendly (they said *nyet* with a smile instead of a frown), but the Soviets would not offer substantive responses to our proposals or elaborate on theirs. Apparently, Karpov was waiting for instructions from Moscow, and Moscow was taking its own sweet time.

On March 12, I released the text of this letter to the news media:

> I would like to confirm that I have submitted to the President my resignation as U.S. Chief Negotiator for the Strategic Arms Talks. My resignation will be effective in April, although I will remain available to the President for a longer period should I be needed.
>
> I wish to note that reports which represent my resignation as due to frustration with the substantive progress of the negotiations are incorrect. The negotiation of an arms control agreement is, by nature, a complex, lengthy, and difficult process which requires a great deal of patience. I have always recognized this and have been at the forefront of those counseling patience as well as perseverance in the negotiating process. I have found my work challenging, engrossing, and gratifying. I have been privileged to be associated with the best professional team in the arms control business. The reason for my resignation, rather, is a desire to return to teaching

at Southern Methodist University as well as to explore various business opportunities.

I feel honored to have served the President and the Nation in such an important endeavor as that in which we are engaged in Geneva. I am in complete accord with the President's arms control policy. I believe that the negotiations are fundamental to the U.S. national interest and that the objective of securing deep reductions in strategic offensive nuclear weapons at equitable, stabilizing, and verifiable levels is in the mutual interest of both the United States and the Soviet Union. I believe an agreement based on these criteria will ultimately be possible and can be achieved.

In mid-February I had sent a back-channel message to the president submitting my resignation as ambassador and chief START negotiator. I had been considering the move for several weeks and mentioned the possibility to Ron Lehman so that I wouldn't catch him by surprise. He urged me to wait and think it over. I knew Ron was trying to buy time to mobilize senior administration officials to persuade me to stay on. I outflanked him by going immediately to the president to submit my resignation and recommend that Lehman be named as my replacement. When he went to the White House several days later to alert National Security Adviser John Poindexter to the "problem," it was too late. Poindexter said, "There's a bigger problem than you think. Tower has resigned and urged the president to appoint you in his place. You're it."

Ron Lehman was the right man for the job. A former Senate staffer of mine, he had agreed to become the deputy START negotiator even though it meant passing up the opportunity to achieve full ambassadorial rank and run his own show at the Mutual Balanced Force Reduction Talks in Vienna. The progress we had made in Geneva since March 1985 was a team effort, and I knew he would build on that foundation. Ron was later named assistant secretary of defense for national security policy in the Reagan administration, and President Bush appointed him to head the Arms Control and Disarmament Agency.

I left the START talks in good hands.

THIRTEEN

THE PRESIDENT'S SPECIAL REVIEW BOARD

ON MY REENTRY into private life, I hung out my shingle as a consultant, primarily in the defense field, with offices in Washington and Dallas. British Aerospace was my first client. My initial impression was that their primary interest in me would be focused on military sales, but as it turned out I functioned in the area of civil aircraft sales and related matters. Rockwell and LTV soon joined my client list as well.

I served on the board of directors of three corporations — British Aerospace, Astrotech International, and Brassey's International Defense Publishers — and took on speaking engagements on college campuses and before civic, trade, and professional groups. One of the more rewarding aspects of returning to private life was the opportunity to resume my teaching career, as a Distinguished Lecturer in political science at Southern Methodist University, a post that had been offered to me as I was retiring from the Senate.

Any new enterprise or life-style takes six or seven months to shake down and settle into a productive routine. Just over seven months after I had given up my START negotiator's portfolio, I was called on by President Reagan to once again return to government service.

On Tuesday, November 25, 1986, President Reagan accepted the resignation of National Security Adviser John Poindexter, fired

Lieutenant Colonel Oliver North from the National Security Council, and summoned Attorney General Edwin Meese to the White House. Meese announced to the press that without the president's knowledge, $30 million received from the secret sale of U.S. arms to Iran had been transferred to the contra rebels in Nicaragua.

Meese attempted to insulate the president from the damage: "The president knew nothing about it until I reported it to him" on Monday. Meese told a news conference that Poindexter and North also hadn't informed the secretary of defense, the secretary of state, or the CIA director of the arrangement. He went on to point out that his investigation had not been completed and would continue.

But congressional critics were quick to suggest that the removal of the two White House aides and Meese's comments had not cleared the air. "There is something wrong when the president doesn't know what's going on in the basement of the White House," charged Senate Democratic leader Robert Byrd. Democratic congressman Stephen Solarz of New York declared, "This has profound political and possibly even criminal implications," adding, "I don't think Congress will accept this explanation from Meese and I don't think the country will."

The Democrats were being predictably partisan, but Republicans were not exactly rushing to the support of the president either. "That's an NSC run amok," charged House GOP leader Robert Michel. "This is a major problem facing the administration," said Congressman William Broomfield of Michigan, the ranking Republican on the House Foreign Affairs Committee. "I think there is more to come in this investigation. There are probably others involved."

The next day, with the Iran-contra situation at a full boil, the White House released a written presidential statement announcing the establishment of a "special review board" to examine the operations of the NSC. I was named to serve as the board's chairman. The press immediately began clamoring for a statement from me. I met with them in the lobby of the building in which my Dallas office is located. I kept it short and to the point: "I have accepted the Chairmanship of the Special Review Board to study the role and procedures of the NSC staff. I am delighted to be associated with two such distinguished Americans as Ed Muskie and Brent Scowcroft. I intend to pursue this task with diligence and objectivity. We will meet with the President Monday to receive our mandate, and I feel that no other comment from me would be appropriate until after that meeting."

The decision to establish the Special Review Board did not immediately pull the administration back from the brink of crisis. However, there was a sea change in attitude, as reflected in this *Washington Post* editorial:

President Reagan was quick off the mark to name the members of the commission that is to survey the workings of the National Security Council staff, "in particular" its "operational activities, especially extremely sensitive diplomatic, military and intelligence missions." His choices — former senator and arms control negotiator John Tower, former Democratic senator and secretary of state Edmund Muskie and former [Ford] national security adviser and retired Air Force lieutenant general Brent Scowcroft — have among them the experience in government and the reputation for straight shooting that should ensure a penetrating inquiry and a respectful official and public audience for its findings. In handling his Iran challenge, Mr. Reagan has done well here.

What should the Tower commission look into? Offices reporting to the president, as the NSC staff does, are free of the congressional oversight — including Senate confirmation of the person in charge — that is exercised upon the executive departments. Almost everyone grants that a president should have this flexible tool of a personal staff. The devices of secrecy available to a personal staff that operates in the national security area, however, create special difficulties. President Reagan himself now declares that he was "not fully informed" of at least one activity — the fund diversion — in the arms shipments to Iran. The information reaching the secretary of state was incomplete and episodic. The information reaching Congress was practically nil.

The task of the new commission is to recalibrate the balance between the responsiveness and the responsibility of the NSC staff. It must serve the president, but it must serve him well in the broadest sense, and it cannot be a law unto itself.

President Reagan is not the first chief executive to have trouble assembling, keeping and managing his national security team . . . there is no sure model or formula on hand to guide him. A president has to decide what he wants. No outsider can dictate to him. But in the Tower commission President Reagan has available an expert and sympathetic panel. If, by turning to outside advice, he is serious about regrouping for his last two years in office, he has the right men.

By the time Muskie, Scowcroft, and I had our first meeting with President Reagan, his popularity, as measured by a *New York Times* / CBS news poll, had plunged twenty-one points to 46 percent, the sharpest one-month decline since public opinion surveys of presidential job performance began in 1936. He told us that he wanted "all the facts to come out." White House reporters were ushered into the Cabinet Room to witness the official establishment of the commission. Reagan was somber as he read his statement to the cameras:

> You will have the full cooperation of all agencies of the executive branch and the White House staff in carrying out your assignment. And I want to assure you and the American people that I want all the facts to come out — about learning of a possible transfer of funds from the sale of arms to Iran, to those fighting the Sandinista Government — we acted to learn the facts. And we'll continue to share the actions we take and the information we obtain with the American people and the Congress. . . .
>
> If we're to maintain confidence in our Government's foreign policy apparatus, there must be a full and complete airing of all the facts. And I am determined to get all of the facts out and take whatever action is necessary. The work of this board and the Department of Justice investigation will do just that. Just as soon as your findings and recommendations are complete, they will be shared with the American people and the Congress. So with that, I say, go to it.

As soon as the president finished reading his statement, the reporters in the pool began to shout questions. Helen Thomas of UPI made herself heard above the din. "Mr. President, when the attorney general said that you were not fully informed, did that mean that you never knew anything about contra funding with Iran sales money?" she asked. Reagan was used to sparring with the White House press, but clearly he did not relish the prospect of a full-blown news conference on Iran-contra. He said, "Helen, I've answered that question. I'm not going to take — we have a meeting now to go into, but I answered that question a couple of times."

Thomas shot back, "Well, does that mean that you had no knowledge at all?"

"That's what I said."

The president's order establishing the review board gave us just sixty days to complete our work. Unlike a congressional committee or a special prosecutor, we did not have subpoena power, nor did we have the power to take sworn testimony, which meant that witnesses could only be "invited" to testify, and should they speak untruthfully, the board was powerless to apply legal sanctions for perjury.

Nonetheless, Muskie, Scowcroft, and I were confident that we could fulfill our mandate. Although I had been named chairman, the board members were absolute equals. We consulted closely on the selection of staff. I recommended Rhett Dawson to serve as executive director, and Muskie proposed a former Democratic Senate staffer, Clark McFadden, for the position of general counsel. From that starting point, we went on to choose a small cadre of experienced Washington hands to give the Special Review Board its investigative and analytical muscle. There were twenty-six of us in all, counting clerical, security, and public relations personnel. From day one, this team worked with uncommon energy and dedication.

The board was given office space in the New Executive Office Building, on Seventeenth Street, just around the corner from the White House. It was not an ideal arrangement by any means. Muskie, Scowcroft, and I shared a small suite of offices on the fifth floor and borrowed a conference room from the Office of Science and Technology. Most of the rest of the staff was crammed into a single room on the floor below. It was togetherness in the extreme, but it did allow for close interaction and coordination, which proved to be invaluable as the investigation progressed.

I had already announced to the press that the board's objective was not to ascertain guilt or innocence. Yet the Special Review Board still needed a more precise definition of its role and a determination of the direction it would take. Had the three members decided to read the president's instructions in a narrow and literal manner, we could have chosen to conduct a largely academic examination of the NSC's history and functions. That, however,

would have been totally inadequate. Neither Muskie, Scowcroft,
nor I would have been content with such an approach.

We gathered the staff together — such as it was, since our mea-
ger ranks were still being filled out — for what was arguably our
most important meeting. Although I moderated the discussion, the
instructions issued that chilly December morning were a product
of the collective sentiments of all three board members. The objective of the board's inquiry, as enunciated at the session, came
down to this: the board, to the best of its ability, was to find out
what had happened and why. Muskie, Scowcroft, and I told the
staff to dig as deeply as it could into the transfer of arms to Iran
and the financial arrangements associated with the transactions.
Moreover, the ultimate disposition of the funds — i.e., did the
money go to the contras, and if it did, under whose authority? —
was to be fully explored. The board was to lay out *all* the facts.

The task at hand was to pull together the pertinent documents,
in effect, to locate the paper trail that could lead us to our objective.
In the initial stages of the investigation, Michele Markoff and Ken
Krieg ended up wheeling shopping carts full of NSC documents
between the White House and our offices. Markoff, the executive
secretary of the Strategic Arms Control Talks, and Krieg, on the
staff of the secretary of defense, had the requisite security clearances
to receive and process the classified material; hence they ended up
functioning as both common stevedores and skilled analysts. Still
juggling her START duties with one hand, with the other Markoff
went to work to develop a day-to-day chronology of decisions and
events based on the documents. Normally, it can take up to three
months to obtain security clearances — thirty days beyond the life
of the board — but by begging, borrowing, and stealing individuals with active clearances, we were able to jump start the investigation.

Documents alone would not have been sufficient. The board
members knew that an extensive series of interviews with the principal and secondary figures involved in the Iran-contra affair had
to be conducted. Simultaneously, it would be necessary to talk with
the living former presidents, their advisers, and others who had
direct knowledge of NSC procedures. We did not have time for a
slow and leisurely examination that would begin at the beginning
of the NSC's origins. It was essential to pick up the end of the
thread that was the closest to hand.

Our first interview, on December 11, was with Robert

McFarlane, President Reagan's former NSC adviser. Unlike John Poindexter and Oliver North, McFarlane cooperated fully with the board. Letters sent out to Poindexter and North by our general counsel, requesting that they appear before the board on December 17, drew responses from two of Washington's premier law firms. Brendan V. Sullivan, Jr., of Williams & Connolly, who represented North, wrote, "As you know, Lt. Col. North has asserted his constitutional right not to answer questions with respect to the subject matter of your . . . letter. We regret that we cannot be of assistance to you at this time. Lt. Col. North looks forward to the opportunity of answering all your questions at the appropriate time." Attorney Richard W. Beckler, of Fulbright and Jaworski, similarly notified us that "at the present time, Admiral Poindexter must respectfully decline to appear before the Board." Like Sullivan, Beckler left the door open to future cooperation by adding, "He [Poindexter] has asked us, however, to assure you that he would be pleased, at the appropriate time, to discuss and respond to the Board's questions."

North and Poindexter were facing the possibility of criminal indictment (as was McFarlane at the time) and were well within their constitutional rights to refuse to testify. The board, however, pursued the possibility of compelling North and Poindexter to answer our questions by sending a letter to President Reagan that requested him to use his authority as commander in chief to order the two men to cooperate fully. As active-duty military officers, North and Poindexter could not refuse a lawful order, but there was serious debate over whether such an order from the president would, in fact, be lawful. We were duly informed by the White House counsel that in his opinion, should the president agree to the board's request, the order would violate not only the Constitution's protection against self-incrimination but also the Uniform Code of Military Justice. H. Lawrence Garrett, the general counsel of the Department of Defense, concurred. He sent the board a memorandum that maintained that a grant of immunity from prosecution would be necessary if the president ordered North and Poindexter to testify, and that probably would have meant that the pair would escape subsequent criminal proceedings entirely. The matter was dropped, and wisely so, since the board could have been — and no doubt would have been — accused of deliberately short-circuiting the legal process and subverting justice.

No presidential order or offer of immunity was necessary to

induce Bud McFarlane to appear before the board. His voluntary appearance was typical of the man. Duty to his country came before self-interest. McFarlane, a retired Marine colonel, had been on the minority staff of the Armed Services Committee. He had once served a stint at the White House on President Ford's NSC staff. We worked closely together while I was Armed Services Committee chairman after he moved to the State Department on a route that eventually led him back to the White House as Ronald Reagan's NSC adviser. McFarlane held that post until December 1985, when he crossed swords with the new White House chief of staff, Donald Regan, and was replaced by Poindexter.

The board interviewed McFarlane three times. On the second and third occasions, we went to see him at Bethesda Naval Hospital, where he was being treated for swallowing an overdose of Valium. I believe the overdose reflected the severe stress he had been under in the months since the Iran-contra affair surfaced in the press. Of the three interviews, it was the first that helped us begin to assemble the narrative of events.

Bud McFarlane said that David Kimche, the director general of the Israeli Foreign Ministry, had approached him in July 1985 to ascertain the position of the U.S. government "toward engaging in a political discourse with Iranian officials." According to McFarlane, Kimche thought that the Iranians would ultimately need something, namely arms, to show for the discussions. McFarlane, our first witness, gave us the first face-to-face testimony that implicitly linked the idea of supplying arms to Iran with the release of the U.S. hostages in Lebanon. He quoted Kimche as saying,

> They [the Iranians in contact with the Israelis] understood that they needed to demonstrate their own bona fides, and that they believed that they could influence the Hizballah in Lebanon to release the hostages, and in fact went as far as to convey through him [Kimche] on July 3rd that they had three approaches, just in terms of formats, of where they might deliver the seven hostages, and sought our comment on which of these was preferable.

What we obtained from McFarlane in that interview was invaluable. He pointed the board in the right direction, and we were able to focus on the documents and other witnesses to flesh out the Israeli connection, which appeared to be the starting point of the initiative. By backtracking, we could go from Kimche to

Michael Ledeen, the NSC consultant who made the first officially sanctioned inquiries, which yielded the contacts with Israeli government officials in 1985, including a meeting with then–prime minister Shimon Peres. We asked Ledeen to submit to an interview, and he agreed to appear in early January.

The Israeli government, however, was not so cooperative. Our requests for interviews with David Kimche and other officials were simply ignored. This attitude created a major obstacle for the investigation, but in the end we succeeded in spite of the Israeli effort to obscure its role in the Iran-contra affair.

McFarlane's interview of December 11 was also important in that it brought President Reagan into the picture early on, as noted in this excerpt from the Special Review Board's final report:

> McFarlane told the Board he then reported this conversation [with Kimche] to the President before he entered the hospital for his cancer operation in the second week of July. He informed the Secretaries of State and Defense and the Director of Central Intelligence in separate conversations. He also said he visited with the President in hospital, and the Secretary of State "to discuss it in brief." . . . According to McFarlane, the President considered the question in a broad context, including Kimche's suggestion that eventually arms transfers would become an issue.

Based on McFarlane's statement, it appeared that providing arms to Iran was discussed, but not in terms that would have made it a quid pro quo exchange. Later, President Reagan told the board he could not recall this meeting with McFarlane and had no notes to confirm that it had occurred.

The board interviewed Vice President George Bush on December 18. We knew from our research that Bush had met with one of the key Israeli figures in the arms-for-hostage transaction three days after Father Lawrence Jenco was released by his captors in Beirut, on July 26, 1986. By then, the United States had sold Iran 508 TOW missiles (after which the Reverend Benjamin Weir had been freed) and eighteen HAWK missiles and spare parts. Following Jenco's release, the Iranians who were in contact with North and Poindexter were pushing for another shipment of HAWK spare parts. In a memorandum written the day of the vice president's meeting in Jerusalem, Oliver North warned John Poindexter that a hostage "will probably be killed to demonstrate displeasure" if the United States didn't supply the parts. Bush told the board that he had been uneasy about meeting the Amiram Nir, Prime Minister Peres's adviser on counterterrorism, and had attempted to contact Poindexter to discuss the situation. However, Poindexter wasn't available, and the vice president said he talked with Oliver North, who indicated that the prime minister of Israel thought it was important for Bush to meet with Nir.

This excerpt from the report of the President's Special Review Board summarized Vice President Bush's version of the meeting:

> The Vice President expressed concern to the Board about what he perceived as the extent to which the interests of the United States were in the grip of the Israelis. Now, according to the Vice President, the Israelis themselves may be in some sense seeking cover. Vice President Bush related that his discussion with Mr. Nir was generally about counter-terrorism. There was no discussion of specifics relating to arms going to the Iranians; e.g., the price of TOW missiles was never raised.

A memorandum written by the vice president's chief of staff, Craig Fuller, was also included in our report. The memo's first paragraph reported that Nir "described the details of the efforts from last year through the current period to gain the release of the U.S. hostages." It continued:

> He reviewed what had been learned which was essentially that the radical group was the group that could deliver. He reviewed the issues to be considered — namely that there needed to be [a] decision as to whether the items requested would be delivered in separate shipments or whether we would continue to press for the release of the hostages prior to delivering the items in an amount agreed to previously.

On July 30, 1986, the day after George Bush's meeting with Amiram Nir, President Reagan approved the shipment of twelve pallets of HAWK missile spare parts to Iran.

This sequence of events alerted the board to the possibility that the vice president's involvement with the arms-for-hostage phase of Iran-contra might have been deeper and more intimate than originally thought. The staff was instructed to search diligently for additional evidence linking George Bush to the matters that we were investigating. Backstopped by Clark McFadden, who had been involved in the Bush interview, the board investigators and analysts looked for the vice president's fingerprints. George Bush said he was "out of the loop," but we knew that he had not been a passive vice president. He had been actively involved in policy formulation and implementation in the Reagan administration. The attorneys and analysts on our staff did not have to be told that their efforts would be scrutinized for the slightest indication that the board had gone easy on the man who could well succeed Ronald Reagan in the presidency. As a result, the working assumption was — and indeed had to be if we were going to conduct an honest, credible inquiry — that George Bush was directly involved. That assumption was *never* borne out by our investigation.

By mid-January, the board's staff had stuffed six filing cabinet safes, each with four drawers, full of documents. It was nearly an overwhelming volume of material to sort and analyze. We were at an important crossroads. Decisions had to be made on how the board would proceed, otherwise there was a risk that our final product could end up being so unfocused and broad as to be useless. At that point, Ed Muskie, Brent Scowcroft, and I stepped back from the task. Without going through a lengthy and agonizing appraisal — between us we had a total of about a hundred years of hands-on government experience, and certain things don't need to be discussed very much — we concluded that, taken as one massive problem, process, and puzzle, Iran-contra would overpower us. To succeed, the board had to break that prodigious complexity into its component parts; each of us needed to assume responsibility for the area of inquiry that best fit his individual strength and experience.

Accordingly, Ed Muskie took on the job of doing the rigorous legal analysis and evaluation. Trained as a lawyer and seasoned as a legislator, he immersed himself in the thick layer of legal ambiguities that threatened to smother us. The board had to know which laws had been broken, by whom, and in what way.

As a retired senior military officer, scholar, and presidential national security adviser, Brent Scowcroft was a natural for the job of examining the NSC mechanism. Having a sense for how it was supposed to function, he set out to discover the flaws and what needed to be done to fix them.

Meanwhile, I homed in on the political dynamics of the Iran-contra affair: the ideas that motivated the participants and the cause-and-effect relationships that had to be identified if we were to satisfactorily explain exactly what had happened and why.

By blocking out the Special Review Board's work in the form of a triangle — legal, administrative, and political — we found an effective strategy for dealing with the Iran-contra investigation. In addition, we decided to divide the board's report into two major parts. The first half would be the introduction, overview, conclusions, and recommendations. Stephen Hadley, a partner in the law firm of Shea and Garner, was assigned to write it. The second half would be a narrative, event-by-event account of the affair. Nick Rostow, special assistant to the State Department legal adviser, drew that job, and both men spent weeks chained to word processors.

The board interviewed fifty-three individuals, including the three living former presidents and the surviving ex-secretaries of state and defense. Most of the interviews were conducted in Washington, although we did travel to Plains, Georgia, to meet with Jimmy Carter, and to Paris for sessions with Manucher Ghorbanifar and Adnan Khashoggi. The interviews with Ghorbanifar and Khashoggi became in-house jokes among the board members and staff. Ghorbanifar proved to be so verbally adroit and persuasive that we came away from the interview convinced he had provided us with missing pieces of the Iran-contra puzzle. Back in Washington, after reviewing the transcripts closely, it became obvious that Ghorbanifar's statements were glib, but not nearly as useful as we had first imagined. In every sense of the phrase, he was definitely not a man from whom you would buy a used car. Effusive, articulate, the complete con man, he handed us a line about how he was acting as a go-between with Iran to promote peace between our two countries. In reality, he was just trying to make a buck . . . millions of bucks. Khashoggi, for his part, after we were ushered into his lavish Paris apartment just a block away from the Plaza Athénée, where we were staying, wasted the board's time with complaints about all the money he had lost by acting as a middleman and financier for the arms transfers. As I looked around at the sumptuous furnishings in the apartment, I couldn't muster much sympathy for the man's tale of woe.

President Reagan met with the board on two occasions. The first time, January 26, 1987, he told us that he had approved the shipment of U.S. arms by Israel to Iran in August 1985. He was, he said, uncertain of the precise date. And it was during this interview that he also maintained that he could not remember being briefed in the hospital by Bud McFarlane on the efforts that were being made to free the hostages and the possible link to arms sales.

The interview was conducted in the Oval Office of the White House. I asked most of the questions, at the suggestion of Muskie and Scowcroft, who figured that the president would feel more at ease with me, given our long-standing relationship. I had ample experience with the president's tendency to ramble on and tell stories, and I tried to gently guide him back to the main point. I could see that he was working off notes prepared by his staff and that portions of testimony given to the Senate Foreign Relations Committee by McFarlane were specifically highlighted in yellow on one of the pages. The crux of the McFarlane testimony, delivered in January 1986, took the same position as the one we had just heard from the president — to wit, Reagan had approved the arms shipments sometime in August 1985.

The board had its second interview with Ronald Reagan on February 11. The logistics of that session were not nearly as complicated as those for our first interview, which had coincided with a four-inch snowfall, an amount that was more than enough to bring Washington to a standstill and that forced Rhett Dawson to do some quick improvising. To get us to the White House on time, Rhett had arranged for a convoy of four-wheel-drive vehicles.

The Special Review Board's report detailed the substance of what happened that morning in the Oval Office:

> In his meeting with the Board . . . the President said that he and Regan had gone over the matter repeatedly and that Regan had a firm recollection that the President had not authorized the August shipment in advance. In response to a question from the Board, the President said he did not authorize the August shipment. He noted that very possibly, the transfer was brought to him as already completed. He said that subsequently there were arms shipments he authorized that may have had to do with replenishment, and that these could have taken place in September. A memorandum from Peter Wallison, White House Counsel, on which the President heavily relied, stated that the President had been "surprised" that the Israelis had shipped arms to Iran in September, and that this fact caused the President to conclude that he had not approved the transfer in advance.

For meetings in the Oval Office the president usually took a seat in an upholstered wing chair placed to the right of the fireplace across from his desk. There are a matching wing chair and a pair of sofas for visitors. It was in that comfortable setting that we conducted the interview. A log fire burned cheerily in the grate under the carved marble mantel. The characteristic luminosity of the Oval Office — a burnished, almost pewterlike quality of light — was intensified by the snow that still covered the South Lawn.

I sat opposite the president in the other armchair. I was concentrating, listening hard to Reagan's rather convoluted statement, and I could not observe the reaction from Muskie or Scowcroft. But I, for one, was shocked at what I was hearing. The president was recanting his previous testimony — testimony fully consistent with documentary evidence that we had obtained and with the statements of McFarlane and other individuals.

I asked the president a few clarifying questions. While starting to repeat his previous answer, he stood up and went over to his desk. He picked up a sheet of paper and, as I remember his words, said to the board, "This is what I am supposed to say," and proceeded to read us an answer prepared by Peter Wallison, the White House counsel.

It was obvious that the president had been prepped by Wallison and words were being put into his mouth.

If there was ever a day when one could honestly say there was good news and there was bad news, February 11 was it. I don't think any of the board's members said more than a few words as we left the White House and returned to our offices. Rhett Dawson and Clark McFadden, who had sat in on the interview, were equally pensive. I believe I broke the silence when we got back to the New Executive Office Building. I said to Rhett, "What the hell are we going to do now?"

At that point, we had already begun to write our report, a key element of which was to be the president's January 26 statement that he had approved the shipment of U.S. arms to Iran in August 1985. There was no way the board was going to expunge it from the record, but we were left with a major contradiction to deal with, which bore all the earmarks of a deliberate effort to conceal White House Chief of Staff Donald Regan's involvement in the Iran-contra affair. By convincing the president that he, the president, had not authorized the arms shipment, Regan was

buttressing his own contention that he had been completely un-
aware of the transaction despite a reputation for tightly controlling
the chain of command within the White House staff. It appeared
that Regan was putting his own interests ahead of those of the
president, who had promised the American people a "full and complete airing of all the facts." Given the Wallison memo, this seemed
to us to be the only logical explanation for the altered testimony.
Perhaps by making that seemingly innocent comment before reading from it, the president was deliberately tipping us off that Donald Regan was up to something fishy. Who knew?

Muskie, Scowcroft, and I were sitting on the couch in my office
somberly pondering the dilemma when Ken Krieg walked in and
delivered the good news. His enthusiasm was easily the mirror
image of our bleakness. He told us he had just discovered a backup
system for the White House computer that preserved copies of the
files Oliver North and John Poindexter had apparently attempted
to destroy as the Iran-contra affair started to come to light. According to Krieg, unbeknownst to Poindexter and North (or other
White House officials, for that matter), messages that went
through the so-called PROF system (professional office system),
an electronic mailbox run by an IBM mainframe computer that
handled everything from top-secret policy exchanges to notes
about lunch dates, were copied onto backup disks from the main
memory of the central White House computer. Those who used
PROF were given a code word to access the system, and they were
under the mistaken impression that any messages they deleted were
gone forever.

As they examined NSC documents, Krieg and other members
of the staff had spotted occasional messages between North and
Poindexter that had been generated by PROF. The flavor and substance of these messages were tantalizing, but huge gaps in the
sequence of the dates indicated that the record was incomplete. In
going back to check on PROF, Krieg found that North was a pack
rat. Unlike Poindexter, who periodically deleted his accumulated
PROF messages, North kept them in a special file. When the White
House computer operators made backup disks to protect the system from a catastrophic failure, this material was also transferred,
since it was stored and active in the system. And the disks, normally
preserved for only a few weeks, were held for safekeeping after the
attorney general issued instructions to the White House staff to

maintain all records associated with the Iran-contra affair. Thus, when North apparently purged his PROF files after being removed from the NSC staff, the copies were already beyond his reach.

Thanks to this feature of the White House computer, the board was able to obtain printouts of hundreds of messages between North and Poindexter. Ken Krieg read through a four-foot-high stack of documents, turning up about seventy messages that gave us unique insight into what was going on in Ollie North's head at critical moments of the process. He dashed off some of the messages the way another person might pick up a phone to make a spontaneous observation or request. And what came back from Poindexter was equally revealing.

Although there were no earthshaking revelations, the notes provided us with enough corroborative detail and texture to solidify our investigation and give the final report enormous credibility. We went from groping around in a dark room, bumping into the furniture, to switching on a bright overhead light.

The PROF notes came to our attention about two weeks before the board's mandate was due to expire. I had already asked for and received a two-week extension, and we now needed even more extra time to digest this material. My request for another two-week extension on the deadline was granted.

Hammering out our recommendations and drafting the report was a seven-day-a-week job, and many of those days were eighteen- and twenty-hour marathons. We borrowed space in the Old Executive Office Building to get Nick Rostow out of the cramped communal "bullpen" — where he had been trying to write the narrative — and into a less hectic environment. On many nights, Steve Hadley would take an hour off from his writing chores to go home for dinner with his wife and newborn child, and then return to work through the night, catching a few hours' sleep on an office couch. Domino's pizza, McDonald's, and Chinese carryout kept the team going.

The board scrubbed every sentence of the report, discussing, so it seemed, each adjective and adverb. Any lingering partisanship would have exploded at that point, but there were no blowups and no major substantive disagreements. We worked in harmony toward the common goal of getting at the truth.

On February 20, the board received a letter from President

Reagan informing us that in trying to recall the events of 1985 and 1986, "I let myself be influenced by others' recollections, not my own." The president went on to state:

I have no personal notes or records to help my recollection on this matter. The only honest answer is to state that try as I might, I cannot recall anything whatsoever about whether I approved an Israeli sale in advance or whether I approved replenishment of Israeli stocks around August of 1985. My answer therefore and the simple truth is, "I don't remember — period."

Six days later we released the board's final report. The president's last-minute recantation of his recantation did not affect our conclusions. The report noted that the president was "deeply committed to securing the release of the hostages."

In his obvious commitment, the President appears to have proceeded with a concept of the initiative that was not accurately reflected in the reality of the operation. The President did not seem to be aware of the way in which the operation was implemented and the full consequences of U.S. participation.

The President's expressed concern for the safety of both the hostages and the Iranians who could have been at risk may have been conveyed in a manner so as to inhibit the full functioning of the system.

The President's management style is to put the principal responsibility for policy review and implementation on the shoulders of his advisors. Nevertheless, with such a complex, high-risk operation and so much at stake, the President should have ensured that the NSC system did not fail him. He did not force his policy to undergo the most critical review of which the NSC participants and the process were capable. At no time did he insist upon accountability and performance review. Had the President chosen to drive the NSC system, the outcome could well have been different.

The board went on to criticize the actions of several others, including White House Chief of Staff Donald Regan, Secretary of State George Shultz, Secretary of Defense Caspar Weinberger, and the late director of Central Intelligence, William Casey. Regan, who was known to have "asserted personal control over the White

House staff and sought to extend this control to the National Security Advisor," was faulted for failing to ensure an "orderly process" throughout the Iran initiative. He did not see to it that plans were made for handling public disclosure and "must bear primary responsibility for the chaos that descended upon the White House when such disclosure did occur," the report said.

Shultz and Weinberger were taken to task for having "distanced themselves from the march of events." Casey, the board found, among other lapses, "encouraged North's direct operational control" and should have "pressed for operational responsibility to be transferred to the CIA." And it is my personal opinion that William Casey's role in the affair was highly significant; his illness and death deprived the board of fully exploring that involvement.

The board met with President Reagan on Thursday, February 26, 1987, in the White House Cabinet Room at ten o'clock in the morning, an hour before a news conference was scheduled to begin in the fourth-floor auditorium of the Old Executive Office Building. As we took our places at the table, the board's staff was beginning to distribute copies of the report to the news media, embargoed for release until the end of the question-and-answer session. Ronald Reagan was getting his first glimpse of the report at the same time as the rest of the American people. There had been no pressure — at least none that was felt by the board — to give the White House a sneak preview.

In his memoirs, *For the Record,* Donald Regan says he believes the arrangement "was unfair and demeaning for the President in addition to being unheard of." Regan by that point was apparently convinced that he was being set up as the scapegoat for the Iran-contra mess and was lashing out at those he perceived to be his enemies. Although we were asked by Frank Carlucci, the new NSC adviser, for general guidance in advance on the direction of the reforms that would be recommended, anything else would have been criticized as collusion between the board and the White House. It was only prudent to stay at arm's length.

As the meeting began, I told the president that the board had found no evidence that he had participated in a cover-up or had authorized one. "There is no need for the slashing of wrists" is what Donald Regan in his memoirs recalls that I said, although I don't remember using the phrase.

At the news conference, the president made a brief opening statement, and when he was done, I literally rushed him off the stage at the request of White House aides who were afraid he would be tempted to answer the questions that were immediately hurled at him from the audience. Muskie, Scowcroft, and I spent about an hour on the firing line. The three of us stood behind every word in that report. I told reporters that in my view Iran-contra was an "aberration." Overall, the report was favorably received. "THE BUCK STOPS THERE" was the headline in the *Los Angeles Times* the next morning over the lead editorial, which commented, "The Tower Commission report is a bleak but vital examination of how a government went astray because its President failed to meet his responsibility to be in charge."

Although the meaning of the Special Review Board's report was clear to the editorial writers, the man who had appointed us to investigate the Iran-contra affair was still having trouble coming to terms with what had happened and why. With my official duties at an end, I was asked to meet with the president and Mrs. Reagan in the early evening of Friday, February 27, in the family quarters of the White House. Before I accepted the invitation, I checked with Ed Muskie and Brent Scowcroft to see whether they thought it would be appropriate. Neither of them thought there was any reason to decline, seeing that the report had been issued and that the president was the one who had created the board in the first place.

Stuart Spencer, the president's old friend and political adviser, was there when I arrived, as was a White House speechwriter. Reagan was preparing for a nationwide television and radio address on the Iran-contra affair, and Spencer asked me to summarize the report again for the president. I said that the board had concluded that arms had been traded for hostages. The president interrupted to say that that was not his intention or policy. He started to explain that the arms were a way to establish the bona fides of the Iranian contacts. I think he genuinely believed that. I heard him out and said, "Mr. President, that just won't wash." I said the arms shipment had been perceived as a ransom payment for the release of the hostages, no matter what his real intentions had been. I told him that I felt it was in his best interest to recognize it as an error in judgment. Stu Spencer spoke up to support and amplify my comments. I looked over at Nancy Reagan, well aware of her fierce protectiveness of her husband. She seemed not at all perturbed by the conversation; occasionally, as I made additional points, she nodded her head in agreement. The First Lady,

I believe, felt strongly that her husband's associates had failed him and that it was best to get all this out on the table — say it was a mistake and get it over with.

Ronald Reagan is a very humane man who is sometimes naive. I had seen that side of him before, and it was both a frustrating and endearing trait. When I sensed that my message was getting through to him, I stood up to go. Nancy took my arm and led me toward the elevator. I wondered if I was going to be scolded for bearing down too hard on the man she loved. In the hallway, we stopped and she hugged me. "I know how difficult this has been for you," she said. "But you did a good job."

FOURTEEN

GUNNED DOWN

M R. PRESIDENT, the FBI's final — or presumably final —
report on Senator Tower is now in. You are reported to have read
some of it. The Senate committee has it." George Bush stood at
the podium in the White House briefing room waiting for the
reporter to complete the preamble to his question. The president
was preparing to leave for Tokyo the next day to attend the funeral
of Japanese emperor Hirohito, and the news conference was a way
to clean off his desk before the trip. He had opened the session by
introducing Congressman Bill Grant, from the Second District of
Florida, who was metamorphosing from a Democrat into a Republican. The president described the decision as "good news for
our party not only in Florida, not only in the South, but nationally."

When the President called for questions, he mentioned his impending trip to Japan as a way of suggesting to the reporters that
it was a subject he would like to discuss. In response, he was asked
about Iran's death threats against novelist Salman Rushdie and
what another correspondent characterized as "a widespread perception that you don't have a foreign policy." The third set of
questions also ignored the president's preference, but George Bush
did not show any irritation as the correspondent arrived at the nub
of the issue:

Q. — I would like to know what you got from it [the FBI report], and also whether you have any reason to believe that the Senate will go forward — any reason from private conversations with members of the Armed Services Committee — will go forward with a favorable vote on this nomination?

PRESIDENT BUSH — What I got from it, and I reviewed some of the more — the parts that related to the allegations against Tower — what I got from it is that there has been a very unfair treatment of this man by rumor and innuendo, over and over again rumors surfacing. With no facts to back them up.

And I saw this as an affirmation of what I felt all along, and that is that John Tower is qualified to be Secretary of Defense. He will be a good Secretary of Defense, although the report didn't answer that. But the allegations against him that have been hanging over this simply have been gunned down in terms of fact. And so that's positive. . . .

And I hope that the Senate will move forthrightly on this nomination. So — and I don't know, Britt, where it stands. I talked to — I had some of the leaders down this morning but the only one I got to talk to on this was Bob Dole. And I'd like to see it go forward, obviously. I never wavered in my support for John Tower.

The ten-day Senate recess had ended the day before, on Monday, February 20, 1989. The break had been a welcome respite. I devoted my attention to the backlog of work at the Pentagon without having to face what seemed like a crisis a day over my confirmation. The recess also gave my friends and political allies an opportunity to mobilize and present our side of the story for a change. Richard A. Viguerie, chairman of the United Conservatives of America, who had helped in my first Senate campaign, told the *New York Times* that he had "never personally encountered anything" that "would cast aspersions on Tower's reputation." Viguerie said, "I have never seen Tower drink in excess." Those comments were similar to those offered to the news media by Richard Perle, an assistant secretary of defense in the Reagan administration: "In the 19 years I have known him — and I saw a lot of him over the years in late night sessions and when I traveled with him to international conferences — I have never seen John Tower drunk."

It is important to recall again that throughout December, January, and early February, White House policy forbade me, as well as other cabinet nominees, from making any public comment, and I was also under the constraints of traditional congressional protocol as to what I could say and do on behalf of my nomination.

The recess, however, did have negative consequences. As I had feared, with Congress out of Washington, which reduced the daily flow of news, the press simply recycled and rehashed many of the allegations that in any normal course of events would have been long forgotten. The *Baltimore Sun* ran the Knight-Ridder News Service story about the alleged mistresses in Geneva during this period, and a wholly misleading account surfaced about alleged discrepancies in my testimony to the Senate Armed Services Committee on the subject of my business relationship with British Aerospace. The story wrongly suggested that, contrary to my statements to the committee that I advised the British firm on nondefense matters, I was actually involved in helping it attempt to sell military systems to the Pentagon. It pulled fragments out of a partial deposition, given during a property-settlement dispute with Lilla, which was not completed or reviewed for accuracy and was never signed. The document was not in the public domain, and I had given it to the FBI myself.

I concluded, therefore, that the Senate Armed Services Committee staff was involved in planting the British Aerospace story. I had provided the committee with extensive, detailed records on my consulting activities, and bits and pieces of that material were scattered through the articles that appeared in the press. A reporter for a major national publication called one of my associates at about that time and said, "Why is Arnold Punaro doing this?" It suggested to me that Sam Nunn's chief committee staffer wasn't as innocent of leaking as he professed to be.

Having material from the divorce reemerge was also troubling. My press adviser, Dan Howard, was so fed up with Lilla's machinations against the nomination, he urged me to consider sending her a message through my lawyers to the effect that if she persisted, I would exercise my right under the terms of the divorce agreement to have the settlement overturned on the grounds that she was engaged in harassment. I told Howard that I felt sorry for Lilla and just couldn't bring myself to do that, even though it did seem to be a clear case of harassment, which was specifically forbidden in the settlement.

Fortunately, not all of the news coverage was adverse to my cause. William Safire, the *New York Times* columnist, weighed in with a characteristically blunt assessment of the situation:

> The ordeal of John Tower is the shame of the United States Senate. The man permitting the prolonged besmearing of the next Secretary of Defense is his successor as Chairman of the Senate Armed Services Committee, Sam Nunn. . . .
>
> The committee should have demanded weeks ago that the F.B.I. answer a set of questions about the nominee against a reasonable deadline. Instead, we have an open-ended hunt for anybody who has seen the former Senator drunk, for a sexual liaison that may have been a security risk, or for an aide on the take.
>
> Senator Tower now stands accused of being a drunk, a womanizer (a new noun for which no female equivalent has been coined) and a revolving-door sleaze; in fairness, it should be recorded that he has not been charged with pederasty, insider trading, the smoking of cornsilk, or moppery — at least not yet.

Safire's column went on to note that only eight cabinet nominees had been turned down by the Senate. The most recent, Admiral Lewis Strauss, was refused confirmation to be Eisenhower's secretary of commerce in a bitter fight with undertones of anti-Semitism led by Senator Clinton Anderson, who reportedly loathed the nominee. Safire correctly pointed out that the separation of power presumes that the president has the right to choose his own team, just as the selection of a senator's staff should not be dependent on the executive branch. I also agree with his contention that the advice-and-consent function as applied to cabinet nominees "has nothing to do with jointly selecting judges, in which the two branches join together to people the third." The precedent that Sam Nunn was attempting to establish with my nomination was one that flies in the face of American history and our governing traditions. He sought to extend the Senate's legitimate prerogatives (although they are often stretched beyond the breaking point) vis-à-vis judicial nominees (one fourth of whom have been rejected by the Senate) to the president's cabinet and the executive branch as a whole. "But what about drinking? Isn't it dangerous to appoint a man charged in hearings with inebriation to be boss of the Pentagon?" Safire asked, and then answered:

The responsibility for choosing a Secretary of Defense with cool nerves and a steady hand rests squarely on the President. We cannot all go sniffing breaths at the Cabinet table; we elect Presidents for their judgment on this.

Fully aware of the talk, George Bush vouches for John Tower, who has sworn he has no drinking problem. It is not necessary that Sam Nunn assume that heavy Presidential responsibility — unless, in the Senator's long association with the nominee in the Senate, he can testify to the contrary.

This is an endurance-building ordeal for Mr. Tower, a restraint-measuring test for the Senate, and a character trial for the President.

The other night, a former aide to Jimmy Carter advised that Mr. Bush distance himself from the nominee rather than risk his prestige so soon. That was precisely the craven action taken by Mr. Carter when his choice for C.I.A. came under fire, causing the abandoned nominee to withdraw — and signaling Washington and the world that the new President was a wimp.

Mr. Bush should continue to support forthrightly the man he chose. Mr. Tower should stand fast. The Senate Armed Services Committee should stop making a spectacle of itself and confirm.

The political crosscurrents were working both for and against my nomination. Obviously, a vote before the recess would have been preferable. If Nunn had been pressured into scheduling it, I might have won. As it was, he had two weeks to dig in for the final showdown. Even so, I could argue that I was gaining strength during that period — or at least holding my own. The Bush administration did not give Sam Nunn the slightest indication that the nomination would be withdrawn. If he was determined to block it, he would have to engage in hand-to-hand political combat, and in the past Nunn had shown little enthusiasm for such bloody and bruising work. Safire's slashing column gave him a taste of what it would be like.

The president's statement at his Tuesday news conference was calculated to propel my nomination over the last obstacles and bring it to a vote in the committee. By declaring that the FBI report "gunned down" the allegations, George Bush was offering a powerful interpretation of the report that would be difficult to refute without suggesting that this newly elected and popular national leader was a liar. The phrases he used defined the issue in terms of fairness versus unfairness. The president's interpretation gave every senator — even those who had spoken against the nomination — a way to climb down from the confrontation without losing face. In so many words, Bush was saying to the Senate, "Read my lips: the FBI report guns down the allegations; repeat those words and we can all walk away from this with dignity." An even closer reading of the presidential lips also indicated that a vote against John Tower would be a vote *for* rumor and innuendo.

The FBI report that the White House delivered to the Senate Armed Services Committee on February 20 was the product of a field investigation that had begun the previous December 1. Eighty-two days — more than eleven weeks — had gone into examining my private life and personal conduct. And even though the report went far beyond the scope of any background check ever conducted on a cabinet nominee, with more than four hundred interviews, there wasn't one scrap of substantiation to support any disqualifying allegations made against me. Under pressure to come up with something, the FBI had widened its investigatory perimeter to an unprecedented degree. The questions asked, the techniques employed, the territory covered, would have been appropriate to a homicide investigation, not an inquiry into my fitness to hold high government office. The report, for example, included more than three years' worth of photocopied receipts from my neighborhood delicatessen and liquor store in Dallas; ten pages of receipts for bottles of mineral water, beer, wine, pâté, hors d'oeuvres, and gift items. I have a charge account at the store, and I can tell at a glance when Marian, who is the family gourmet, went in to make purchases, or when parties were being planned and gifts purchased. Over the course of three years, the total bill came to about $3,000. Broken out, that is an expenditure of $19.23 a week.

There is no point in overdoing this aspect of the FBI file, but I am placing emphasis on the deli receipts because they are illustrative of the extent to which the investigators pursued their work without coming up with evidence of improper conduct. In fact, if the purpose of the investigation was to prove that I had acted soberly, the receipts could have been cited as substantiation. However, through no fault of the FBI's, the purpose of the investigation became one of demonstrating the validity of the proposition "Where there's smoke, there's fire."

There was no fire — much to the consternation of Sam Nunn, who kept sending the FBI back to find it — and the smoke was generated by the sources I identified early in the book: scandal-mongers in the news media, which by that point had turned into a lynch mob; political opponents; my ex-wife Lilla; and an assortment of cranks.

The Russian-ballerina allegation is another example. An individual contacted the FBI to inform them that in 1987 he had been present at a private party in a home near the River Oaks Country Club, in Houston. He said that I was also a guest. There was drinking and dancing. As the evening advanced, this person claimed, I told him the hostess of the party was a Russian émigré ballerina whom I kept in lavish style as a mistress. The FBI was informed that when the other guests left, the man, who said he was a pianist, was asked to stay and play the piano while the Russian ballerina and I danced. He said that he excused himself when the woman and I, now atop the piano, began to disrobe.

Naturally, the FBI was galvanized into action by such a salacious story. Agents fanned out all over the River Oaks area searching for a Russian émigré, a Russian ballerina, a Russian female, a Russian of any description. They drew a blank. The best the FBI could do was to interview Natasha Rawson, a woman of upstanding character and some maturity, an old friend of mine and of many prominent Houstonians; I had not seen her in ten years. Natasha told the agents that if there had been such a person as the Russian ballerina, she, as a benefactor of the Houston Ballet, a member of its board of directors, and a person of Russian heritage who speaks the language fluently, would have known of her — and there was no such person.

The FBI went back to its source, who by then had decided he was being harassed and refused to answer further questions. One of his neighbors told the agents — who noted it in the FBI file — that the man was a recluse and used several different aliases, was "a pathological liar" and "weird, weird, weird." Leslie Stahl of CBS was told by a member of the Senate Armed Services Committee that the story had no substance. She ran with it anyway.

Once they completed their interviews in the field, the FBI agents came back to me for what they referred to as an exit interview. The purpose was to determine whether my statements on a particular subject would contradict or corroborate what had been learned from an informant. Whenever possible, the agents were not supposed to reveal the nature of the allegations. I had to guess what they were driving at. But with the Russian-ballerina absurdity, they were forced to ask me direct questions, like "Do you know a Russian émigré ballerina?" Thinking that she might have been trained in the ballet as a young girl, I mentioned Natasha Rawson. "Have you ever danced on the furniture?" they asked. "I have a hard enough time dancing on the floor," I said. The agent was plainly embarrassed, but persisted: "Have you ever danced on a piano and taken off your clothing?" Later, when I repeated the question to my daughters, the three of them reacted the same way, and Penny put it best: "Daddy take his clothes off? Hell, you can't even get him out of his suit jacket in public!" It's true, and I told the agents that I didn't even like to wear short-sleeved shirts.

It was a ludicrous and chilling sequence of questions. Maybe somebody else would have thrown in the towel at that point, but it made me all the more determined to fight. If I had quit, all that crap would have been left out in the public domain unanswered.

The FBI report that went to the Senate for the members of the Armed Services Committee to review was filled with such stuff. The president accurately described the contents as rumor and innuendo, and when he said the allegations had been gunned down, he was referring to the logical conclusions that flowed out of the investigations of things like the Russian ballerina. My records showed one party at the River Oaks Country Club, in 1987, a testimonial dinner in honor of A. Frank Smith, the chairman of the board of directors of Southwestern University. I spent the entire evening with Southwestern's president, Roy Shilling, and Dr. Shilling confirmed that fact to the FBI. On other allegations that had made the rounds, senators who bothered to look could see that the flight attendant who accused me of drinking to excess on an international flight flunked a lie detector test; the woman accused by a member of the Senate Armed Services Committee staff of having an affair with me during a committee staff management and policy retreat at Fort A.P. Hill, in Virginia, flatly denied it, and her description of the evening was corroborated by others who were there; and the anonymous tipster who called the FBI to accuse me of taking bribes from the "Independent Oil Producers," a Texas association that he said was based in Wichita Falls, was talking about a nonexistent group. And Larry Combest clarified his damaging statement to Nunn and Warner, telling the FBI that I had never been "a captive" of alcohol in the 1970s.

Indeed, if my former Senate colleagues had read as far as the exit interview I gave to the FBI on February 7, when I was asked if I had ever chased my secretary around the desk in Geneva, they would have seen a definitive statement from me that could have been applied to every last one of the allegations — "Hell, no."

With the president in the air en route to Tokyo, Sam Nunn hit back at him. The February 23, 1989, *New York Times* reported it this way:

> Sam Nunn, the Senator everyone is watching to determine the fate of John G. Tower's nomination to be Secretary of Defense, said [on February 22] that the inquiry by the Federal Bureau of Investigation did not resolve whether Mr. Tower still has a drinking problem.
>
> Addressing President Bush's contention that all allegations against the nominee had been "gunned down," Mr. Nunn . . . said: "That's the President's opinion. I'm sure that he has thought about that carefully. That is not my opinion."
>
> The ranking Republican on the committee, Senator John W. Warner of Virginia, said that he had reviewed the F.B.I. report and that "reasonable men and women can have credible differences of opinion" based on the evidence presented. Both Mr. Warner and Mr. Nunn said they had not decided how they would vote.
>
> But Senator J. James Exon of Nebraska, the second-ranking Democrat on Armed Services, said he would vote against Mr. Tower's nomination. He predicted a close vote in both the committee and on the floor of the Senate.

With Exon pointing the way for the other Democrats on the committee to follow, Sam Nunn announced that he hoped to bring the nomination to a vote on Thursday, February 23.

I believe that Nunn was beginning to feel the heat and figured that he'd better move quickly to maximize what shock value he could derive from the sheer mass of allegations collected in the FBI report. Those who were inclined to assume the worst or vote against me for ideological reasons might be stampeded by the report. Well aware that some of his colleagues might be looking for an easy way out, Senator Robert Dole noted that "if you want to vote against him, you'll find ten reasons in that report." And, subsequently, Dole went on to cite at least a hundred good reasons to vote for me.

Misgivings about the report weren't restricted to Republicans. Patrick Leahy, the Democratic senator from Vermont, acknowledged that the FBI report was being used as camouflage to conceal ideological motives: "I think there are some who are more interested in fobbing it off on the FBI report." Leahy, a former prosecutor, added, "Others are genuinely concerned about the vague nature of the FBI report. I have been frustrated in the past by the very vague and sometimes worthless nature of the FBI reports, because they sometimes quote people without any indication of accuracy."

Sam Nunn could not afford to give his colleagues time for second thoughts or reflection, otherwise they would begin to see that the allegations did not hold water. A quick, ill-considered vote is an old tactic. Even those who are being manipulated know that they can explain away actions that were taken in the heat of the moment. In addition, Nunn had committed the Democrats to a direct confrontation with the White House. Any Democratic member of the committee who might have been inclined to vote for my nomination on its merits could see that the issue had evolved into a purely partisan battle. Since Nunn had made my defeat a personal crusade, those who defected would be accused of inflicting a serious wound on one of their own party's senior leaders. Still bleeding from the drubbing they took in the November presidential elections, the Democrats viewed the prospect of allowing the chairman of the Senate Armed Services Committee to be humiliated — even though the humiliation would have been largely self-inflicted — as not at all palatable.

There were eleven Democrats and nine Republicans on the Senate Armed Services Committee. With one exception my Republican ranks were holding firm. John Warner's vote was in doubt, but I was certain that he would, in the end, be persuaded to do the right thing. My hopes rested on three Democrats: Edward Kennedy, John Glenn, and Richard Shelby. The Senate recess had undermined Shelby's once-firm support for confirmation. By his own account to the press, he went home to Alabama to attend town meetings in twenty Alabama counties to find that I was becoming "more and more controversial" among his Bible Belt constituents. "I could feel the heat building in my own state," he said. Shelby returned from the recess and sent word to us that he was nervous and needed "company" if he was going to vote for me. What Shelby meant was that he could not be counted on to cast a vote for confirmation unless he knew that other Democrats would cross over to join him — an understandable, although not a particularly laudable, position. I am also afraid that Shelby saw an opportunity to score some political points with religious fundamentalists in Alabama.

If I had set out to identify one Democratic senator on the committee who would be immune to a purely partisan argument when it came to a national security matter, it would have been John Glenn. Glenn had an unblemished record as a Marine aviator, astronaut, and legislator for being above politics on defense policy. In addition, I considered Glenn to be a friend, and it was a friendship forged out of our occasional collaboration on plans, programs, and policies in the 1970s and 1980s. John Glenn had been one of the senators who told me not to even bother paying them a courtesy call before the opening of the hearings; he said he knew I would make a fine secretary of defense. A few weeks earlier, at a defense symposium in Munich, I had incorporated his suggestions in the paper I presented. Glenn, who also attended the symposium, had suggested that I mention force projection and the need to protect choke points like the Strait of Malacca. I thought it was a good way to get the Western Europeans to focus on issues outside of NATO. As I was summarizing the paper to the conference, I dropped in Glenn's ideas, and as I did so I gave him the okay sign, making a circle with my thumb and index finger. He gave it back to me from across the room. One of the West Germans saw it and said, "What does that mean?"

But then, inside of a month, Glenn was not just making pro forma statements of opposition in the interest of Democratic unity, he was going after me with a vengeance. Glenn's not the brightest guy in Washington, but it disturbed me more to get blindsided by him than to be attacked by Sam Nunn, who I knew harbored personal animosity. To add insult to injury, after the recess, once Nunn's position was obvious, Glenn refused to even return my telephone calls.

John Glenn's sudden abandonment of principle and friendship is still baffling, and his subsequent behavior on the Senate floor still shocks me; it was as though he had become a totally different person.

Edward Kennedy, the third Democrat whose vote I was hoping for, had made a supportive statement before my testimony to the committee. Kennedy's seniority and prestige put him beyond the reach of Nunn's arm-twisting. He was too powerful to be threatened. Kennedy's life-style also made him vulnerable to the sort of personal attacks to which I had been unfairly subjected. Still, Edward Kennedy is a loyal Democrat, and Nunn recognized that he could be held in line if a rationale was presented other than drinking and womanizing — two issues that, if cited by Kennedy as the reason for voting against me, would subject him to ridicule and the justifiable charge of hypocrisy.

Accordingly, on the afternoon of February 22, the day before the committee was scheduled to vote, Sam Nunn convened a meeting of the committee's Democrats to discuss my nomination. "As Nunn recalls the session," the *Washington Post* reported, "he outlined the pros and cons that he had made in making his own decision. On the one hand, he said, there was the President's prerogative and the importance of a top cabinet post in a new administration. On the other hand was 'the signal we were sending to the people who work in defense . . . what kind of advice and consent role do we have left for everyone else.' " In addition to his concerns about drinking, Nunn also said he was troubled by my role as a former consultant to defense contractors. I am told that he referred to my testimony on the issue and claimed that he was struck by my "almost total insensitivity" to the appearance of a conflict of interest, an insensitivity he believed would make it virtually impossible to establish high standards at the Pentagon.

An incongruous statement from a man who, during the hearings, said to me, "I am not one of those who believe we can afford to be so strict in our rules on conflict that we send nothing but inexperienced people who have no knowledge of defense to run the toughest department in the world."

Nunn seemed to have been afflicted with amnesia. "Well, I know you, so the problem for me is not one of fearing that you are going to do something improper on behalf of a client. I don't worry about that. I know you, and I know you to be an honest person" — another statement Nunn had made at the hearings that was lost from his memory bank.

And this exchange was forgotten as well: "Would you feel compelled to bend over backwards [to demonstrate impartiality] for clients that you formerly represented [so] that those clients themselves would be treated unfairly?" Nunn had asked me, and I answered, "I think the likelihood is that, if anything, I would bend over backward." Nunn took a sip from his water glass for dramatic effect, folded his arms across his chest, and with a faint smile said, "So the people who ought to be worried are the former clients?" The audience laughed. "Well, that may be true," I answered.

As he spoke to his Democratic colleagues, Sam Nunn was engaged in rewriting the record. Every one of them had to know what was happening. By telling them that I had shown insensitivity, he was asking them to join in a conspiracy to fictionalize the clear and demonstrable facts of the confirmation process and to disregard their own personal experience from the years of working with me in the Senate. Those men had sat in the hearing room and heard me recall my service as chairman of the President's Special Review Board, of having to investigate the actions of a president to whom I was deeply loyal. "It was not a pleasant experience," I told the committee,

> and I dealt with that as objectively as I could because, as I said in response to a question when I was appointed to the Board,* my loyalty to my country transcends any other loyalties, and I would repeat that today. I think that in the past, my public life has been characterized by integrity. I don't believe that I have ever violated the trust of my stewardship of the people's power, and so I would have to stand primarily on my reputation as an honest public servant.

Sam Nunn and his Democratic colleagues knew that when it came to my country and my integrity, I was the last person they could fairly accuse of "almost total insensitivity." Nevertheless, Nunn needed to give Edward Kennedy and a few of the others who had qualms a fig leaf with which to hide their moral nakedness.

Nunn has refused to this day to own up to his pivotal role in defeating my nomination. The attitude, I believe, reflects a desire to cling to his apolitical image while operating in a ruthless and purely partisan manner. He has assured Washington journalists that he did not pressure his colleagues to vote against me. Nunn has even gone as far as describing his caucus with the committee Democrats as reaching "a joint kind of decision." As he described

---

*"How can you be objective because of your loyalty to Ronald Reagan and your association with [Robert McFarlane]?"

it, "We came to the decision collectively . . . the committee members helped shape my thinking." However, Democratic leader George Mitchell brushed aside that specious contention by telling the *Washington Post:* "It's fair to conclude that, had Sen. Nunn supported the nomination, Sen. Tower would have been confirmed."

Nunn was so determined to avoid being accused of partisanship that he continued to attempt to seduce John Warner to his cause. When the Armed Services Committee's Republican members met before the vote, Warner said to his colleagues, "Tell me why I should vote for this man." For a moment the other Republicans, I understand, were speechless. John McCain, still incredulous at what he had just heard, said, "Tell me why you *shouldn't* vote for this man!" From then on it was a free-for-all. Warner was tongue-lashed by Strom Thurmond and some of the others. Strom closed in on Warner, jabbing his index finger into the Virginian's chest like a bayonet. He's a guy who isn't about to buy a on-the-one-hand-and-on-the-other-hand argument. One observer said my friends were so angry at what they considered Warner's dereliction of duty as the ranking Republican that in a figurative sense they threw him at the wall, picked him up, and threw him back at the wall again. They apparently explained to him that if he did not begin to actively support my nomination, in all likelihood he would lose his position as ranking member. It was not a moment of comity and collegiality. I've been told, in fact, that there was a lot of yelling.

Finally, John Warner saw the light. He went off to a noon meeting with Sam Nunn and informed him that he was parting company with the chairman.

The committee was called to order at 6:35 P.M. At the outset, Sam Nunn announced he would vote against my nomination, and he summarized the reasons. As I expected, Nunn built his case around the FBI report. He pointed to what he called "a clear pattern of excessive drinking and of alcohol abuse by the nominee in the 1970's." Nunn grudgingly noted my service as Senate Armed Services Committee chairman, START negotiator, and chairman of the President's Special Review Board, all of which had occurred in the intervening years — I say "grudgingly" because it amounted to only one brief sentence.

By attempting to be forthright with the committee, I had acknowledged that while alcohol had never affected the performance of my duty, I did drink too much in the early 1970s, had recognized that fact, and put a stop to it. However, that wasn't good enough for Sam Nunn. Plus, it gave him a weapon to use against me. "I have searched in vain for several weeks," he said, "for a point in time when the nominee himself acknowledged this problem and dealt with it decisively. The nominee made it clear that he has never sought medical assistance for his drinking problem. There are a number of inconsistencies in Senator Tower's own comments to the FBI and to the committee in terms of his use of alcohol."

After posturing on the question of booze, Nunn turned to — women. He was forced to concede that there was no finding of impropriety involving "female foreign nationals" (i.e., spies). Nor was there anything to the allegations of sexual harassment of my female employees. Yet Nunn couldn't resist saying: "There are, however, some examples of conduct which I find indiscreet and which call into question both judgment and example. These are not decisive, in my judgment, but they add to a cumulative body of concern that I have about this nomination."

With that comment, I saw illuminated the underlying Democrat strategy: bury John Tower under a "cumulative body" of "garbage" — the word James Exon had used to describe the allegations.

As he neared the end of his statement, Nunn came to a theme he would use repeatedly to justify his actions:

> There is much in Senator Tower's record which is highly commendable. I believe that John Tower is a loyal, patriotic American, who has a solid record of public service. I also believe he is dedicated to our Nation's security.
>
> For me, however, this is not enough.
>
> I am skeptical as to the nominee's ability to restore public trust in Pentagon management.
>
> I am concerned as to his ability to command the respect of his subordinates and to set the moral standards for the men and women in uniform.
>
> Finally, I cannot in good conscience vote to put an individual at the top of the chain of command when his history of excessive drinking is such that he would not be selected to command a missile wing, a SAC bomber squadron or a Trident missile submarine.
>
> Leadership must be established from the top down.

After thirty-seven years in politics, I did not consider myself particularly naive. But as I sat watching the proceedings on television, I was struck by the blatant misrepresentation that was occurring. Sam Nunn had the votes to defeat me. I knew it and he knew it. Yet the chairman of one of the Senate's most powerful committees found it necessary to go to such extreme lengths to destroy my reputation that he wouldn't even stop at engaging in a form of Orwellian double-talk that was intended to turn reality inside out and upside down.

I don't like to refer to myself in these terms because it may sound immodest — and as an opponent of mine once said, "John Tower has got a great deal to be modest about" — but I probably had more personal contact with the enlisted men and women of the U.S. military than any other member of the Senate Armed Services Committee. And I don't mean sitting comfortably in a reviewing stand. If Nunn had turned to his immediate left, he could have asked John Warner about the helicopter ride he and I took at terrain-following level, skimming low and fast to avoid antiaircraft fire, at times dropping below the rooftops of Beirut's scarred streetscape, literally whipping the drying laundry off the clotheslines as we headed for the beleaguered U.S. Marine position on the seafront; they were dug in down there after the tragic truck bombing of their barracks. It was a trip I made because I knew that, as chairman of the Senate Armed Services Committee, I had to see firsthand the conditions faced by our troops. At the time, the State Department wanted to keep those Marines there. They were a symbol of America's commitment. They were, in fact, bunkered down in a defensive position, immobile and frustrated, serving no positive purpose. It wasn't long before they were brought home.

Sam Nunn could sit comfortably behind his desk and talk all he wanted about leadership. I stand by my record of leadership.

"Leadership must be established from the top down" is a bad joke when it comes from a man who equates leadership and commanding "the respect of his subordinates" with being aloof and authoritarian with his Senate staff, and a bad joke when it comes from a man whose subordinates have rarely distinguished themselves beyond the small, confining world of a congressional office.

Nunn's contention that my "history of excessive drinking [was] such that [I] would not be selected" to command a SAC bomber squadron or a Trident submarine was based on extremely

questionable assumptions. A formal, factually substantiated, medically corroborated finding of alcohol abuse is necessary to remove a military officer from his or her post. The military does not rely on hearsay, innuendo, and rumor to determine an individual's fitness for command. Nunn's own fitness to command would be questioned in today's military if he proposed to base personnel decisions on the same standards he used to judge my nomination to be secretary of defense.

It was, I have to say, absolutely searing to have to listen to that statement, a political death sentence mitigated only by the kind words of my friends. John Warner, recalling our extensive international travels together:

> Never once did I ever see that man ever indulge in any way in terms of his personal habits that would reflect anything but credit and honor upon the institution of the U.S. Senate and a country that he loves so dearly and has served so long.
>
> Now that is my observation, but I have talked with every single Senator who has served with him in this institution and who is here today, and many of those who have gone on to retirement and other ventures. Not one single U.S. Senator, not one, who has served with John Tower, can ever recall a single instance where any of his personal habits interfered with his duty.

Strom Thurmond:

> I want to say, first, that I have known John Tower since 1961 when he came to the Senate to succeed Lyndon Johnson.
>
> I have known him all these years, and I do not think anyone questions his integrity, his courage, his dedication or his ability. I do not think anyone questions his military expertise. He is probably one of the best informed men in this Nation on military matters. He knows the military establishment. He knows the Pentagon. He knows what needs to be done.

I could go on and quote from the statement of every Republican member of the committee, but I will add just one more, that of William Cohen, who asked his colleagues to square their own personal experiences with the hearsay, the rumor, and the innuendo:

> And so, I have to ask the question — is the committee to give greater probative value to the unsworn statements by largely

unidentified people, than to our own experience, than to that of a General Scowcroft, to a Howard Baker, to a Max Kampelman, or, indeed, to President Bush himself?

To that I must conclude an overwhelming no. This is an extraordinary action that is being taken tonight, and it should not go without notice that President Bush is in Japan tonight.

And I believe we do a great disservice to him and to John Tower himself. And a final point, on appearances. Certainly all of us should be concerned about appearances, but if appearance is to govern, rather than actuality, then I would respectfully submit that most of the Members of Congress would have to disqualify themselves from passing judgment upon legislative matters that come before the Congress.

Each of us solicits, we receive contributions, substantial in total, from a variety of sources — agriculture, telecommunications, business, defense — and yet, we are able to pass judgment upon the merits or demerits of those respective interests.

I think that we have a double standard in saying that John Tower, because of his past associations, is unable to look at the merits of a case and pass judgment on those merits. . . .

So, Mr. Chairman, I said I was not going to take long and I am taking long. But I think when you weigh the totality of the evidence, and measure that against the standard as to whether or not we can find by clear and convincing evidence that President Bush is not as concerned about the chain of command as we are, then I believe that we have been found wanting in that regard. I believe the President deserves to have John Tower and that John Tower deserves the position.

To use T. S. Eliot's phrase, the proceedings ended not with a bang but with a whimper. It was snowing and some of the senators wanted to get it over with and leave for home before the roads became slippery, but Sam Nunn had to stall for time, waiting for Robert Byrd, who was off attending a cocktail party in the Capitol to promote a book he had just authored (ironically, a collection of his speeches on great moments in U.S. Senate history). Byrd finally appeared to inform the committee members that they had missed "a very nice reception." He announced that they could pick up autographed copies of his book the next day and then, because time was short, asked to have his written statement opposing my nomination inserted in the record. Nunn agreed to the request and moved on:

> CHAIRMAN NUNN — I think we are ready for a motion, and I recognize Senator Warner for the purpose of making the motion.
>
> SENATOR WARNER — Mr. Chairman, on behalf of all of us on this side of the aisle, we are privileged to move to report the nomination of John Goodwin Tower to be Secretary of Defense to the Senate with the recommendation that the Senate act favorably thereon and give its advice and consent to this nomination submitted by the President of the United States.
>
> CHAIRMAN NUNN — There is a motion, is there a second?
>
> SENATOR COHEN — Mr. Chairman, I second the motion.
>
> CHAIRMAN NUNN — Senator Cohen seconded the motion. The Clerk will call the roll.

The motion was rejected, and a moment later a second motion — to report the nomination unfavorably to the full Senate with the recommendation that it not be confirmed — was carried by a mirror-image vote, also along party lines: eleven Democrats voting aye, nine Republicans voting nay.

FIFTEEN

TAKING THE PLEDGE

THE COMMITTEE'S REJECTION of the nomination was
a heavy blow, but there was consolation in it. At last, after more
than three months of being required to undergo a relentless daily
pounding in the press and on Capitol Hill without fighting back,
I could answer my critics and attempt, as best I could, to salvage
my personal reputation.

I realized at once that I could not wait for President Bush to
return from Asia to begin the counterattack. He was not due back
until the following Monday night, and nearly four days would be
lost. Besides, I had been deferring to the White House since December, when I was informed by a member of the transition operation that I was not to talk to the press or actively promote the
nomination. Effectively, I had been bound and gagged since then,
almost totally dependent on others for my defense.

With the president out of the country, I suppose, I felt less
constrained to consult with the White House on every move. This
freedom of action also worked to George Bush's advantage, in that
the news media were describing the committee's vote as a personal
defeat for the president, and I felt that any further damage should
fall on me and not him. But Bush wasn't about to run from the
fight. Unable to sleep, he called White House congressional liaison
Fred McClure in the middle of the night, Tokyo time, to find out

what he could do. McClure told the president that he would need
him to lead the lobbying effort with phone calls to and meetings
with Senate members as soon as he arrived back in Washington.
President Bush gave McClure the authority to clear his schedule
and reprogram it as necessary. And in the meantime, as he traveled
to Beijing and Seoul, he used the communications facilities on
board *Air Force One* to get a head start on contacting key members
of the Senate.

Dan Howard had been urging me for several days to consider a
more aggressive approach toward the press. The day after the committee voted, I agreed to give it a try. Howard presented a plan
that featured interviews with representatives of the major media
and appearances on the weekend network TV talk shows. I decided
that ABC's *This Week with David Brinkley* would be the best forum.
But I knew it wouldn't be enough to simply show up and field
questions from Brinkley and his colleagues. There had to be something dramatic to breathe life into the nomination.

After conferring with Rhett Dawson, I was leaning in favor of
the idea of announcing that I would forgo the consumption of any
alcoholic beverages while I held the post of secretary of defense. It
seemed to be the kind of thing that would be bold enough to make
headlines and to knock down the contention that my "problem
with alcohol" — I should say Sam Nunn's problem with alcohol,
for it did appear to be something of an obsession with him —
made me unfit for a place in the military chain of command.

As my doctors had observed during my convalescence from
colon surgery, I had no difficulty abstaining from alcohol. My consumption of wine was already limited to such an extent that to give
it up entirely was hardly a significant sacrifice. If Sam Nunn was
honestly concerned about my use of alcohol, total abstention
seemed like the best way to satisfy him; after all, Nunn had said
that he had looked in vain for a point in time when I had "acknowledged this problem and dealt with it decisively." Besides, as
secretary of defense I would be living in a goldfish bowl; any back-
sliding from the promise would be immediately observed and, no
doubt, turned into headline news that would have the effect of
forcing my resignation.

Taking the pledge, as it came to be called, also was an effort to
generate public support in parts of the country where the allegations about my personal conduct seemed to be having the most
impact — the South and the Midwest. Wherever the doctrine of

Christian redemption was accepted as an article of faith, there was a predisposition to forgiveness in response to those who mend their errant ways. I do not regard the consumption of alcohol as a sin or an act of immorality. However, I am enough of a realist to accept that there are great numbers of people who see it in exactly those terms, and many of those who don't might genuinely consider it an impediment to reliable performance.

At the same time, to demonstrate that my pledge was not interpreted as a backdoor confirmation of alcoholism, I decided to release a letter from Warren Lichliter, one of the physicians who had treated me in the postoperative phase of my colon surgery. Dr. Lichliter made these observations:

> The normal preoperative assessment for a patient with possible colon cancer includes evaluation of the liver in order to determine the presence or absence of metastatic disease. The liver function tests were entirely within normal limits. This indicated that there was no evidence of involvement with liver metastasis nor, incidentally, of any acute or chronic liver dysfunction which one would expect to see in the presence of chronic alcoholism.
>
> Senator Tower underwent abdominal surgery on 5 January 1989. Findings at the time of surgery showed a normal-appearing liver without any evidence of metastasis or acute or chronic liver disease. Again, such findings are not compatible with chronic alcoholism.
>
> Most importantly, Senator Tower's post-operative course went very well. He exhibited no evidence of alcoholic withdrawal or anxiety during his entire post-operative course and, in fact, was on the telephone almost continuously throughout his hospital confinement with Defense Department and White House transition personnel coordinating strategy for the incoming Administration. The medical personnel involved with his post-operative care were amazed by his ability to return to such a demanding work schedule so soon after major abdominal surgery. This was definitely not the typical post-operative course of a patient with any degree of alcohol dependency.

The physician said, in conclusion, "Based on these facts, it can be stated with relative certainty that Senator Tower shows no evidence at all of alcoholic impairment or alcoholism. It is my professional view that there is little basis for statements made concerning the possible impairment by alcohol of his ability to perform his duties as Secretary of Defense."

I read parts of the letter on the Brinkley show before announcing that I would not consume alcohol of any kind — wine, beer, or spirits — while serving as secretary of defense. "Now what I want to do is to try to remove the obstacles to my confirmation. I've already gone a step further than I'm required to do on recusals, more than the law requires me to do," I said.

> And I'd like to take another step, which I hope will remove what appears to be the principal obstacle and the principal concern expressed by Senator Nunn and other senators, and I would like to read this pledge, if you want to call it that:
>
> Noting the principal concern of Senator Nunn and other members of the Senate, relative to my confirmation as Secretary of Defense, namely the extent to which I may engage in excessive use of beverage alcohol, let me state that I have never been an alcoholic nor dependent on alcohol.
>
> However, to allay any fears or doubts on this matter, I hereby swear and undertake that if confirmed, during the course of my tenure as Secretary of Defense, I will not consume beverage alcohol of any type or form, including wine, beer, or spirits of any kind.

The night before, I had signed the pledge in the presence of Dr. William Narva, the attending physician of Congress, and Transportation Secretary Samuel K. Skinner, both residents of the Jefferson Hotel, whom I asked to sign as witnesses.

I did not expect that the gesture would earn me a free ride on the issue, and I had been warned by my advisers that it might be construed as an admission of alcoholism. Knowing ABC's Sam Donaldson, the substitute anchor of the Brinkley show, as I do, I was fully prepared for his response: "Senator, I want to go back to your pledge. By making that pledge today, it seems to me you're admitting you have a drinking problem."

"No, I said in the statement that I am not an alcoholic nor have I ever been dependent on alcohol."

"Then why would you make a pledge when you say there's no reason to?" Donaldson asked.

"Why not? . . . It's a small thing to do to allay doubts and fears."

Donaldson kept on: "Now when allegations are raised that you're a womanizer, should you take a pledge not to go out with women?"

"I'm a single man," I said. "I do date women."

"Well, exactly. I'm asking you . . ."

"I've been a single man for three and a half years."

Donaldson was determined to change the focus: "When you start down this road . . ."

But if he was going to change it, I was going to shape the discussion: "What's your definition of womanizing, Sam? . . ."

"I don't know. I simply —"

"Well, all right," I said.

In the meantime, Sam Nunn was appearing on NBC's *Meet the Press,* threatening to reopen the Senate Armed Services Committee hearings, subpoena witnesses, and "have a full public airing" of the allegations. Nunn said that reconvening the committee would be "unfortunate," which prompted George Will to ask in his syndicated newspaper column:

> Oh? For whom? Not Tower, who can hardly be more injured. It might be unfortunate for the patrons of the Monocle Restaurant because all the employees would be testifying. (One claims to have seen Tower drunk, a dozen say they never did.) And it would be interesting to hear from the man who says he saw Tower drunk in Washington on [days] when Tower was in Pakistan, Texas and Seattle.
>
> If it is fair to judge Tower by "appearances," it is fair to note that Nunn "appears" to be taking this personally.

When I reviewed the videotape of *Meet the Press,* I could see a flicker of fear in Nunn's eyes as he told Andrea Mitchell that he was in "a hopeless situation" and that the White House was "grossly unfair" to leak portions of the FBI report that exonerated me from charges of misconduct. George Will heaped scorn on this bizarre appeal for sympathy. He wrote that Nunn was "simply smarmy" and issuing "simpering disclaimers" rather than offering clear reasons for his opposition to my nomination.

Nunn wanted to play rough, but the idea that his opponents would actually hit back appeared to offend and frighten him. From the beginning, he had attempted to impose a double standard on the White House. George Bush was supposed to be nonpartisan, while Sam Nunn and the Democrats took full partisan advantage of their opportunities.

The reporters that I talked to didn't even try to hide the fact that Nunn's staff had been distributing material since the confirmation process got under way that they thought would damage my chances. I did not have the FBI report, so I could not do any leaking, but I imagine that White House officials, in a legitimate attempt to defend the president's nominee from attack, did give journalists guidance about what the FBI had found in the course of its investigation. On the Sunday after the Armed Services Committee had voted against my nomination, the *New York Times* reported that a summary containing descriptions of twelve of the allegations was being drafted at the White House, and the newspaper published seven brief accounts of incidents that had not been substantiated by the FBI:

- Mr. Tower was alleged to have seduced a woman at a party. But the woman who was the ostensible object of his affections told the F.B.I. that he helped her to the bathroom when she was ill, the official said.
- Mr. Tower had an affair with a Russian ballerina in Houston. The White House official said the F.B.I. found "no substance" to the allegation.
- An Arizona businessman told the F.B.I. that he saw Mr. Tower drunk on three occasions at the Jefferson Hotel in Washington. The F.B.I. found that on the dates cited, Mr. Tower was in Pakistan, Texas and Seattle.
- A businessman said he saw Mr. Tower drunk at a party in West Germany and named five other American businessmen who attended. Two of the businessmen named said they did not see Mr. Tower drunk. The three others said they did not attend the party, with one saying he never met Mr. Tower, the White House official said.
- A male flight attendant claimed that on a trip to Paris, Mr. Tower consumed so much vodka that he had difficulty getting off the plane. But a female flight attendant in the first-class cabin, where Mr. Tower sat, said she did not see Mr. Tower drunk, the White House official said.
- Mr. Tower was alleged to be drunk at the Monocle Restaurant, a popular dining spot near the Capitol. But waiters at

the restaurant said they did not see him drunk there, the official said.

• Mr. Tower was seen drunk at his neighborhood in Dallas, where he owns a condominium. But a detailed F.B.I. check of the neighborhood, including interviews with neighbors, maids and liquor store owners, found nothing to corroborate the allegation, the official said.

This summary was probably what Nunn was referring to, but the proposition is untenable that the president was somehow required to sit passively and silently by while an individual that he had selected for his cabinet was smeared. Under Sam Nunn's definition of fair play, not only was his staff permitted to hand out portions of the FBI report to the press, but he could sit in an open meeting of the committee and make sweeping statements about my alleged abuse of alcohol, indiscretions, and lack of judgment — all without substantiation. Then he could appear on television and complain that if the White House didn't behave itself, he was going to reopen the hearings, which, I am convinced, amounted to an empty threat, since the allegations, if fully aired with subpoenaed and sworn witnesses, could be shown to be false. Sam Nunn didn't want that to happen.

The reporters on *Meet the Press* were friendly and nonconfrontational. However, the tape shows Nunn fairly twitching with hostility. In the most polite terms, he was being asked to justify his actions, and for a man who had created a pristine image of probity, substance, and wisdom, that was hard to take. Steve Daley, writing in the *Chicago Tribune,* noted the impact the confirmation battle was having on Nunn's image and on his carefully nurtured presidential ambitions:

Whatever happens to Tower . . . the world according to Sam Nunn looks different these days.

Everybody's political darling has been bloodied. Nunn has been savaged by conservative editorial writers and columnists, leaked on by the White House and grouped with those much despised congressional "micromanagers" we heard about during the Iran-contra hearings and the doomed nomination of Robert Bork to the Supreme Court. . . .

He does not appear to be enjoying himself in the midst of the whirlwind, a whirlwind that would surely come with any national campaign. As a politician, Sam Nunn has never been this far from shore.

Indeed, Nunn was far from shore, and he was afraid. I could see that from the videotape, and I knew that I was up against a very dangerous opponent. For Sam Nunn, it wasn't just politics or business, where you fight hard and shake hands when it's over — it was personal. Nunn was out to win, and he was determined to do whatever was necessary to accomplish his objective.

Immediately after the Brinkley show, most of my friends and advisers felt that the pledge had served its purpose well. Former senator Howard Baker called to congratulate me on my performance. But while it was probably a major factor in persuading Senator Howell Heflin to vote for my nomination on the Senate floor, the pledge could have hurt as much as it helped. The press played it as an admission that I had a problem with alcohol, and in Washington, among those who were the most politically savvy, it was read — and read accurately — as a measure of my desperation. I was looking for a button to push or a lever to pull that would begin to hoist the nomination out of the pit it had tumbled into, and nothing seemed to work.

I was caught in a classic damned-if-you-do / damned-if-you-don't situation. If I had gone on the attack against Sam Nunn, which I was itching to do, any chance of persuading Democratic senators to cross over and vote for me out of principle would probably have been lost. The Democrats would have circled the wagons. I knew that the president wanted to avoid an overtly partisan battle. On Saturday, February 25, he told the press pool on *Air Force One* that it would be pointless to "start hurling charges." The president said, "I don't see any point in making this personal. I have enough respect for Senator Nunn to know that he is not pursuing a frivolous course in this matter at all. I know everyone would like to see a great confrontation and love to hold my coat, and maybe hold his, as we get into a big brawl. But there's no need for that."

From the president's standpoint it was a wise course of action. No matter what happened to me, he had to go on working with Sam Nunn and the Democratic congressional leadership. In late February 1989, George Bush had not yet consolidated his political position and popularity. Unlike Ronald Reagan, who favored all-out assaults on Congress when it seemed to be attempting to thwart him, President Bush was inclined toward a more conciliatory approach. The danger, however, was that by being reasonable, the president was likely to lose both his defense secretary designate and a measure of his political clout. When he returned to Washington Monday night and was able to personally assess the situation, George Bush saw that danger for what it was. He is an intensely competitive man, and that aspect of his character had not been fully appreciated at that time; Manuel Noriega had yet to be dragged back to the United States in manacles. But those who knew him well could have testified that George Bush is stubborn and gutsy. I was aware of that side of his character, but I did not want to inflict damage on his presidency. I suggested that he might consider withdrawing my nomination.

I made the offer at the outset of a strategy session held in the president's private study in the family living quarters of the White House on Tuesday evening, February 28. The president had just come back in from a jog. He was still wearing his sweat suit; there wasn't a trace of any jet lag after the long trip from the Far East. On the contrary, he seemed to be energized by the prospect of his first tough battle on Capitol Hill and raring to go. "Mr. President, I am prepared to withdraw," I said. "I don't want to be an embarrassment to you."

George Bush flatly and immediately rejected the idea. I thought he would. It was his call, though. Withdrawing the nomination would have ended the agony, but it would have left all the lies unanswered. I wasn't looking for revenge on the Democrats. I wanted a week or ten days to tell my side of the story. George Bush didn't bother with a pep talk or a speech to rally the troops. As I recall, it was as plain and simple as could be: "The hell with it. Let's fight this one out."

The president's support was reassuring. I can't say that I felt optimistic about the chances — but he gave me a second wind. I knew I could get through to the end.

His preliminary contacts with senators while he traveled in the Far East had not succeeded in changing any votes, but the president was receiving a fair hearing, and that morning he had begun a round of face-to-face meetings with Democrats whom Fred McClure and the other White House congressional liaison people

had identified as the most likely possibilities. As the next step, using
Senator Robert Dole as the flamethrower, he was about to turn
up the heat on Sam Nunn.

After the strategy meeting, Dole and John Warner went downstairs to the White House briefing room to talk with reporters. I
accompanied them as far as the door to the press area and continued on through the West Lobby to my car. The Republican leader
was about to demonstrate to the Democrats that their free and
highly partisan ride was over.

Bob Dole spent about thirty minutes doing the job that John
Warner should have been handling all along. He said I was the
victim of a "hatchet job" and had been "shabbily treated." Even
though he voted in committee for my confirmation, Warner was
clearly uncomfortable at being associated with comments that
might be interpreted as criticism of Sam Nunn. I suspect that Dole
knew Warner would have preferred to be just about anywhere
other than that briefing room and took great pleasure in making
his colleague squirm. And I say that by way of underscoring one
of Bob Dole's greatest attributes. He enjoys the rough-and-tumble
of politics, but it is not just an adrenaline high that comes from a
battle. Dole taps into deep convictions that give him boundless
courage, enthusiasm, and wit. He's got a sharp tongue and a sharp
mind and isn't afraid to use them on behalf of his beliefs.

All in all, it was a bad day for Nunn, who had already been
stung by a *Wall Street Journal* article that morning reminding the
newspaper's readers that the Georgia Democrat had been involved
in an alcohol-related hit-and-run traffic accident in 1964. The *Journal* reprinted a December 4, 1972, story from the *Atlanta Journal:*

> Perry, Ga. — Newly elected U.S. Senator Sam Nunn's ac-
> count of an auto wreck he was involved in differs substantially
> from the official accident report, The Atlanta Journal has
> learned in an extensive investigation.
>
> The probe was undertaken after sources in Nunn's home
> town of Perry took issue with his version of the accident that
> occurred there Oct. 31, 1964.
>
> Nunn's detailed explanation was published by The Journal
> Nov. 9, two days after he had defeated Republican Fletcher
> Thompson in Georgia's U.S. Senate race.
>
> (Following the election — "to show how honest a cam-
> paign Fletcher ran" — a Thompson aide furnished The Jour-

nal with a copy of the summons growing out of the incident. According to the aide, Thompson had vetoed the idea of making the accident a campaign issue.)

Nunn said on Nov. 9 that the accident "took place around 12 o'clock midnight."

The accident report on file at the police department here lists the time as 2:45 a.m.

Nunn said, "I hit a parked car — kind of half in the yard and half on the road — there was nobody in it."

According to the official report, Boyd Hathaway Jr.'s unoccupied 1964 Mercury Comet was entirely off the pavement, parked in front of his home, when Nunn's vehicle struck it, damaging the right front and side of the Hathaway car — an estimated $300.

"I sort of sideswiped it. I went on down the road and ran in a ditch," Nunn said.

From the Hathaway home at 1424 Elizabeth Ave., the report shows, Nunn continued on Elizabeth Avenue until its intersection with Forrest Avenue. He turned left onto Forrest, then drove another two blocks to the intersection of Forrest and U.S. 341 (Main Street) there. Nunn crashed down an embankment while attempting to negotiate a right-hand turn onto U.S. 341, the police report adds.

Investigating officers Pat Padgett and Charles Lewis, neither of whom is a Perry policeman today, said in their report that Nunn traveled three-tenths of a mile after hitting the parked car.

Nunn was going in the direction of his family's farm on U.S. 341 when he plunged down the embankment. Patrolmen Padgett and Lewis estimated damage to the "complete front" of Nunn's 1963 Pontiac at $600. In the report, they described the vehicle as "not driveable."

Nunn said on Nov. 9 that when his car went into the ditch, his head hit the steering wheel, resulting in a bloody nose. "Some people came along, picked me up and took me home," he said. "I told them to call the police, and they went back and told the man whose car it was."

The report says police reached the scene 10 minutes after the accident happened. Nunn was not there, and Padgett and Lewis charged him with hit and run, and with leaving the scene of the accident.

Authorities did find a friend of Nunn's, George B. Wells Jr., trying to tow the heavily damaged car out of the ditch.

In an interview here, Wells admitted it, but denied any wrongdoing on his part. If Nunn had run into a parked car that night, he said, "It's news to me."

Charles Rodgers, whose wrecker service was called to the scene, said he was instructed to haul the car to the farm owned by Nunn's prominent father, a wealthy lawyer-land-owner and one-time state legislator. Rodgers said he complied.

Nunn said in his Nov. 9 statement that the day after his accident, he went to Perry Police court and paid a $100 fine, pleading either guilty or nolo contendere (no contest).

"I was guilty of leaving the scene, but I was not guilty of hit and run. If I had known it (the summons) said hit and run, I would not have pled guilty. Hit and run, I emphatically deny," said Nunn, who in 1964 was 26 years old, practicing law, and the President of the Perry Chamber of Commerce. He was first elected to the Georgia General Assembly in 1968.

Although both the accident report and the summons specified the charges as "hit and run, also leaving the scene of accident," the docket for Perry Recorders Court shows that on Nov. 21, 1964, Nunn forfeited bond of $115.50 on a single charge — leaving the scene. The docket makes no reference to the hit-and-run charge.

The Journal learned that the accident happened moments after Nunn left a party at 1433 Baker St., just behind the Hathaway home, which at the time was the residence of Jack Ragland.

The Journal established that among those at the party were Ragland, Wells and Dr. William R. Jeries.

Questioned about Nunn's condition when he left the party that morning, Ragland, the comptroller for Macon Junior College, replied, "I don't remember"; Wells, the owner of the Heart of Perry Motel, responded, "I don't know"; and Dr. Jeries, a Perry dentist, said, "No comment."

Nunn's driving record at the Department of Public Safety in Atlanta contains no reference to the court action stemming from his 1964 accident. Police chief Bernard Dennard said the Perry Police Department did not begin filing copies of traffic violation convictions with the state until several years ago.

His record at the Department of Public Safety does include four moving violations, though. It shows that Nunn violated an unspecified Macon traffic ordinance in 1955, ran a stop sign in Macon in 1958 and was detected speeding (70 in a 60 mile per hour zone) in Butts County in 1960. Fines for these offenses were $4, $5, and $25, respectively. The fourth violation occurred two months after his wreck.

According to the record, at 1:30 a.m. on New Year's Day, 1965, Nunn passed a Georgia State Patrol car on a curve, despite a solid yellow line on Georgia 247, three miles south of Warner Robins.

He entered a nolo contendere in the Court of the Ordinary in his native Houston County on Jan. 6, 1965. The record indicates that he was fined $25 and that the fine was suspended.

The story was picked up by the Associated Press, stripped of all but the most rudimentary detail, including the portion that highlighted Nunn's inconsistent statements and nocturnal vehicular encounter with the police two months after the original incident, and circulated nationally. Immediately, there were howls of outrage and indignation from the Democrats. To distract attention from the substance of the story and the obvious implication that this skeleton in their leader's closet might explain his obsession with drinking, they fussed about how Tower partisans had "planted" the story.

The AP's stripped-down, six-paragraph version of the story ran on page D27 of the *New York Times*, which put it behind the classified ads and obituaries, near the stock market quotations. I have no way of determining whether it was sanitized by the editors at the wire service or at the *New York Times*. In either event, the effect was that only readers of the *Wall Street Journal* saw the full account, along with an accompanying editorial:

By the standards of a more civilized era, an incident 24 years ago wouldn't be relevant. Indeed, in 1972 Mr. Nunn's opponent chose not to use the driving episode against Mr. Nunn in the campaign. The race was close, and Fletcher Thompson might be a Georgia Senator today if he had followed the standards Sam Nunn has now introduced into American politics.

The Nunn standard has been put on the table by an 11–9 vote of the Armed Services Committee. The winning margin was provided by Senator Edward Kennedy, who charmingly failed to note that the vote had something to do with drink and women. Despite a lot of graveyard-whistling about the chain of command, Senators themselves will not long be exempted. . . .

That would be far less distressing than what is actually happening — the development of a new gutter standard in Washington: not to fight on the merits at all if possible, but to cripple on grounds of personal behavior and innuendo. This reached a watershed in the campaign against Robert Bork, with demagoguery about the eminent jurist as a racist and sterilizer.

The editorial went on to refer to an issue that, at the time of the confirmation battle, I was willing to address only obliquely — honoraria, PAC (political action committee) money, and junkets paid for by special interest groups. It was and is a raw nerve. Every member of the Senate has been tainted in the eyes of many people by accepting money from sources that seek to influence Congress. Perhaps I should have made more of it — but I wasn't seeking a confrontation — to convince the Democrats that by damning me for the appearance of a conflict of interest involving conduct that occurred after I left the Senate, conduct that was never shown to be illegal, unethical, or a breach of government regulations, they were damning themselves for conduct that occurs every week in the U.S. Senate.

In 1987, the members of the Senate Armed Services Committee accepted a total of $500,000 in political honoraria. Sam Nunn benefited the most from this largesse, by collecting $50,500. To comply with the Senate rules, he gave $16,000 to charity and pocketed the rest, a large portion of which came directly from defense contractors or groups that front for them.

Nunn and his wife spent ten days in Honolulu that same year, with round-trip airfare and two nights' lodging paid for by Sea-Land Corporation, which had federal contracts for carrying supplies to U.S. forces to Europe. Alan Dixon, who joined in the conflict-of-interest chorus, spent three days along with his wife in February 1987 in Palm Beach, Florida, at the expense of Pratt and Whitney, another defense contractor. A month later he was in Phoenix, courtesy of McDonnell Douglas.

More recent figures for 1989, on file with the Federal Elections

Commission, show that Nunn received a total of $472,400 in contributions from special-interest PACs, including those sponsored by Rockwell International, United Technologies, and General Electric, three of the nation's largest defense contractors. United Technologies was the most generous of all; it gave the chairman of the Senate Armed Services Committee $5,000, and individuals employed by some twenty other major defense contractors ponied up a total of $58,800, their generosity toward Sam Nunn underwritten by paychecks from the likes of Boeing, General Dynamics, Martin Marietta, Grumman, and Hughes Aircraft. And Senator Nunn's Senate salary was augmented by honoraria in 1989 of more than $35,000, with another $11,000 of these speaking fees going to charity, as required by Senate rules.

I point this out now, not to play the infantile game of "Well, you do it too!" but to show how the debate degenerated into unfairness and hypocrisy. There was an almost irrational, self-destructive quality to it that I could never adequately counter. One of the first rules of negotiating is that your adversary will never knowingly inflict damage on his own cause. Yet the Democrats were doing just that. Why? I can only theorize: anger and frustration at going from a twenty-point lead in the polls in July 1988 to defeat four months later in the presidential elections; fear that they were being permanently locked out of the White House; panic over the way the public lashed out at the attempt to raise congressional salaries; consternation that George Bush had grabbed the high ground on the ethics issue; paranoia about the success of negative campaigning. There is no simple, neat answer. The explanation is obviously a composite of many different factors, some of which I mention earlier, including Nunn's presidential ambitions and the desire on the part of some to conceal their own human failings by vilifying me. I do know that it is inadequate to say that what happened was "just politics" or, as one of my associates said at the time, "You walked into Sam Nunn's gunsights, and he pulled the trigger." Anybody with a fraction of Nunn's experience as a politician should have known the consequences of pulling the trigger, consequences that would fall on Democrats as well as Republicans, the U.S. Senate, the political process, and the country as a whole.

In announcing his intention to vote against me, Sam Nunn spoke of providing an example, restoring public confidence, and setting moral standards. What kind of example is it when the chairman of the Armed Services Committee descends into the gutter and takes every Democratic member of the Senate along with him?

By Wednesday, March 1, we had shaped our strategy for waging the confirmation fight on the Senate floor and had begun to implement it. At a series of meetings at the White House and on Capitol Hill, John Sununu, Fred McClure, and other White House staffers, along with Senator Bob Dole and his assistants, compiled a list of about a dozen Democratic senators who seemed to be the most likely candidates for taking an independent line. My staff and I participated in this process, as did such former legislative liaison people as Powell Moore, Tom Korologos, and Pam Turner. The president dedicated every moment he possibly could to the effort through phone calls and personal meetings with individual senators. The effort rivaled or surpassed any I'd ever been a party to in my lengthy Senate career.

I made some phone calls to senators with whom I felt I had enjoyed a collegial relationship. I was turned down flat by some. As I've mentioned, David Boren was one who said he had to side with his friend Sam Nunn. Claiborne Pell, the chairman of the Foreign Relations Committee, told me he was distressed at what was happening but quickly added that I should not read that as an indication that he would vote for my confirmation. In the latter days of the lobbying effort, I phoned three others I didn't really know. One I remember in particular was a call to freshman Democrat Joseph Lieberman of Connecticut. Lieberman had defeated my friend Lowell Weicker, a liberal Republican, with the help of conservatives in his home state. He told me that he would like to support me, but that he had been in the Senate only eight weeks and was getting enormous pressure from his party leadership to cast a negative vote. He feared the consequences if he broke ranks.

The president, on the other hand, was trying to appeal to reason. He knew me well, could vouch for my fitness as well as my qualifications, and wanted and needed me on his team. His persuasiveness seemed to give some members pause.

Howell Heflin of Alabama told reporters after meeting with the president that he was open-minded, adding, "I want to be fair." Heflin went on: "The issue is what is his drinking problem today. Another is if his pledge [to stop drinking] is sincere and does he have a temptation or propensity to return to drink." And the former judge fell back on personal experience, which is precisely what

I hoped my former colleagues would do, by saying, "I never saw him when I thought he was under the influence of any alcoholic beverage, but I wasn't with him 24 hours a day."

The pledge was apparently having an impact on Heflin, as was the experience of reading the FBI file, which had been placed in S-407 — a secure room in the Capitol — for members of the Senate to review. Heflin spent three hours perusing it.

Lieberman had also gone to S-407 and had characterized the material as "ultimately inconclusive." He said of it, "You certainly don't feel there's enough, at the extreme, to indict somebody."

It was a high-risk proposition to make the file available to the entire Senate plus selected staff members. This opened the door to the possibility that raw summaries of the FBI investigation of my affairs could have virtually unrestricted circulation. Even so, without providing the FBI file to Howell Heflin, it could be argued, he would not have decided to vote for my confirmation. Again, there was no clear-cut answer as to the best course of action.

Senator Bob Dole and White House Chief of Staff John Sununu were in favor of providing the news media with a version of the file identical to the one in S-407, with the exception that it would not include the names of those who gave information to the federal agents in the belief that their identities would be withheld. The president, in the end, however, decided that since not even the most careful editing could fully protect the confidentiality of the witnesses, we could not release an abridged version of the file. He said we would just have to make the best of a bad situation.

Thus, I was left without decisive means to counter the leaks from S-407, which were turning into a torrent of negative stories. To compound the problem, the Democratic staff of the Armed Services Committee had prepared its own summary of the FBI file for senators who couldn't spare the time to read the original. When Senator John McCain read what purported to be an unbiased presentation, he hit the roof. The Democratic staffers had "summarized" by eliminating the material that was favorable to my cause. McCain and the other Republicans insisted that they be given the right to develop an alternative summary, which would also be available in S-407. Nunn's staff agreed but seemed puzzled that the Republicans would object to their stacking the deck. And they were probably relieved and amused that we had not caught on to another surprise that they had slipped into their summary — but I will get to that in due time.

*   *   *

A word about John McCain before I move on. He was badly injured when his A-4 crashed near Hanoi during the Vietnam War
and severely mistreated as a prisoner of war. A man of considerable
physical courage and stamina, he bears the lasting effects of his
injuries with fortitude. He is prematurely white-haired, quiet-
mannered, courteous, sometimes impetuous. He never minces
words. I have deep admiration for McCain, and when he retired
from the Navy, I broke an old political rule of mine and actively
supported him in his quest for the Republican nomination for
Congress in a hotly contested Arizona primary.

As a Navy captain, McCain was my escort officer when I visited
Sultan Qabus of Oman out in the desert of his kingdom. We sat
cross-legged on a brightly hued Persian rug in a large tent. One
must be careful how one sits during such an audience, since it is
an insult to show the soles of one's feet to the sultan. McCain was
having some difficulty with his gimpy leg, and his shoe sole
pointed directly at the sultan. There were a few awkward moments
as the sultan's bodyguards glared at us. I quietly explained Mc-
Cain's war wound to His Majesty, who graciously dismissed the
incident by reminding me that he was a graduate of Sandhurst and
a former captain in the British Army of the Rhine.

John McCain worked hard for my nomination. Senator Richard
Shelby was overheard on an elevator telling a colleague that he was
being lobbied intensely by Sam Nunn. "They're twisting my arm
so hard to vote against Tower, I think it's broken. But if I do,
McCain will break the other one," Shelby said.

Just before the full Senate made its decision, McCain had a final
comment that I will always treasure. It was simply this: "God bless
you, John Tower. You're a damned fine sailor."

On March 1, Bob Dole had also let his counterpart, Democratic
leader George Mitchell, know that the Republican side intended
to fully debate my nomination before it was brought to a vote.
Mitchell understood Dole's meaning: there would be at least a
week of debate once the nomination was formally taken up on the
Senate floor, and the debate was not going to be genteel.

The easy way out for Bob Dole would have been a perfunctory
debate and a quick vote. But to his credit, he wanted to fight — if
for no other reason than to exact a price from the Democrats. They
were not going to be allowed to savage me and wound the presi-

dent without doing some public bleeding of their own. Furthermore, the debate was the only opportunity to publicly answer the allegations that had been leveled against me. The press, for the most part, was doggedly illuminating the allegations, regardless of how outlandish they were, and making scant effort to inform the public when substantial evidence was available to disprove them.

I took the opportunity to speak out whenever I could find an appropriate forum. I availed myself of an invitation from the National Press Club to respond to a flurry of reports that the Pentagon had been drifting, rudderless, because of my contentious confirmation battle. I explained in substantial detail that I had spent much of the previous month working on two important initiatives:

First, a comprehensive review of America's national defense strategy; and second, the development of a plan for implementing sorely needed reforms of Defense Department management and procurement practices. Our review of the strategic options open to President Bush has gone virtually unnoticed in the general clamor surrounding my nomination. It has been in the works for many weeks, and it is a serious undertaking.

I then ticked off three elements of the review:

The review will analyze how current trends and uncertainties affect the appropriateness and effectiveness of our national defense strategy for the 1990's. It will identify those elements that should continue to guide our strategy and those elements that should be reexamined.

The review will address specific force posture issues in light of the reexamined national defense strategy and current budget constraints. The goal will be a military force that provides the most effective deterrent while offering the greatest competitive leverage for our defense investment.

The review will examine how arms control can be used to enhance our national security objectives. It will examine the basic premises underlying our approach to current and prospective negotiations and insure that they are consistent with our defense strategy and force posture.

As for procurement reform, I was emphatic:

I want it said: "Tower never flinched." Major and expensive systems will not survive the defense strategy review. I cannot give you a "cut list" of weapons, because such cuts should follow, not precede, our strategy review. But in making those cuts, I will not succumb to the temptation of stretch outs and postponing the tough decisions. Nor will I assume that any weapon, or any force structure, is sacrosanct.

I particularly wanted to include those two excerpts from my National Press Club speech here because they were not reported anywhere else. The news media — which so often clamor for substance, sneer at the twenty-second sound bite, and solemnly forswear sensationalism — totally ignored a serious presentation on a most serious subject.

Actually, I was deliberately testing the news media. I suspected that my speech would go unreported, and I was correct. The questions that followed, with three or four exceptions, were about the confirmation. I was prepared for that eventuality, and when I was asked what angered me the most about the way the nomination was being considered, this was my reply:

I suppose one thing that I think engenders some resentment is the fact that there was no clearly defined standard against which I should be judged. The standard seemed to be developed and seemed to evolve to fit the situation. Now, several senators have said that the Secretary of Defense must adhere to a higher standard than members of the United States Senate. I accept that. I accept that the Secretary of Defense must adhere to a higher standard than members of the United States Senate. But my question is, how much lower an acceptable standard is there for members of the Senate? Is it an acceptable standard for senators late in the evening who've had a few drinks in the hideaways and offices of the Capitol, a few steps away from the Senate chamber, to come onto the floor late in the evening and vote on vital issues of nuclear deterrence? Is it an acceptable standard for senators to accept honoraria, PAC contributions, and paid vacations from special interests who have a vested interest in the legislative process? I think, in the course of formulating a standard for the Secretary of Defense or indeed for any other Cabinet officer, that it is time that the Congress articulated what its own standards are.

The statement managed to get the press's attention. The headline, however, the snappy twenty-second sound bite, came when I was asked about my pledge to abstain from consuming beverage alcohol: "You said Sunday you've never broken a pledge in your life. Does this include wedding vows?" A few members of the audience groaned when they heard the question. The moderator stepped back from the podium to allow me to answer. I instantly decided that the only way to handle the question was to hit it head-on. "As a matter of fact, I have broken wedding vows. I think I'm probably not alone in that connection."

The answer could have been refined somewhat. "Unto death do us part" is a wedding vow. Having been divorced twice, I broke that vow, as have millions of other men and women. There was a connotation of infidelity that was not intended in the answer I gave, and of course the news media made the most of it.

At that point, though, it hardly mattered if the networks and newspapers squeezed another drop of titillation out of the story at my expense. From the beginning, the news media, by and large, had eschewed higher journalistic standards in favor of those practiced by the gossipmongering supermarket tabloids. I don't think Andrea Mitchell of NBC has ever heard the term "second source." She appeared to be ready to run with anything that she was told — without bothering to double-check it — particularly if it was whispered to her by Senate sources. Among my staff, Andrea picked up the well-deserved nickname High Priestess of the Lynch Mob, and in spite of it all we actually got a few laughs out of her single-minded determination to rake up the muck. She is the most viciously partisan reporter I've ever seen. Andrea's daily phone calls — especially those inquiring about the Russian ballerina in Houston, which featured subtle questions like "Well, he did buy her an apartment, didn't he?" — furnished a bit of comic relief. Richard Billmire, who got stuck handling most of these questions, demonstrated the patience of a saint by pointing out that the River Oaks section of Houston has some of the most expensive real estate in the country and that a brief analysis of my personal net worth would reveal that I did not have the financial means to maintain a mistress in the style that Andrea Mitchell and her colleagues had fantasized.

While Dan Rather of CBS was generally fair and objective, his colleague Bob Schieffer, the network's chief Washington correspondent and a golfing buddy of Sam Nunn's at the exclusive

Burning Tree Country Club, gave a convincing performance as surrogate prosecutor for Nunn when I appeared on *Face the Nation*. He couldn't resist making snide interjections as I attempted to answer his questions: "So that's false?" . . . "All right, all right" . . . "So what information did you give 'em?" And when he had run the drinking allegations into the ground, Schieffer archly announced, "Senator, let's switch from whiskey to money." He suggested that I had provided inside information on the START talks to my consulting clients, a favorite Sam Nunn line of attack, but when I started to answer he kept interrupting until I finally said, "Wait a minute!" Schieffer grimaced at me, threw his weight back into the swivel chair, and folded his arms petulantly. As I explained that the premise of his question was incorrect — that a decision had not yet been made on when to switch from the MX missile to Midgetman and therefore I could not possibly have advised my clients on the issue — he snapped at me, "Senator, I am aware of that!"

CBS also had a tendency to use lurid graphic effects on the screen — like the words "Fondling Women" — while the substance of the anchor's or reporter's news copy contradicted the allegation, which left viewers confused or, if they weren't paying careful attention, gave them the wrong impression. The *Face the Nation* program I mention was a good example. The segment that I appeared on ended with a little clip of tape showing Barry Goldwater making a classic Barry Goldwater comment: "If they chased every man or woman out of this town who had shacked up with somebody else or gotten drunk, there'd be no government."

Cute. Entertaining. It left the impression that Goldwater was providing the viewer with the bottom line on John Tower. "A nice kicker," as they say in broadcast journalism. The only problem is that broadcast journalism has turned into nothing but nice kickers, and journalism has gone by the board.

I've been told that television news people have the attitude that if it didn't happen in front of a camera, it didn't happen, unless of course it was some damaging allegation — even an anonymous charge. The attitude of David Martin, CBS's Pentagon correspondent, seemed to bear that out. In an effort to refute the false allegations concerning my conduct in Geneva, Richard Billmire located the chief administrator of the U.S. arms control operation in Geneva, John Grassle, who had been cited as the source for the report that I had been thrown out of the residence in Switzerland by my wife. Grassle denied everything, and he was quoted in the *Baltimore Sun* and other newspapers. But when he declined to appear on camera, Martin refused to report his statement.

Some of the usual media suspects, however, acquitted themselves well. The *Washington Post* coverage was generally straightforward, with the exception of its "Style" section, which, I was told by a senior *Post* writer, hews to a lower journalistic standard, to the extent that accuracy, balance, and fairness must give way to the entertainment value of the material. Unfortunately, however, other newspapers pick up these stories and treat them as hard news.

The *Los Angeles Times* offered readers reasonably thorough and balanced stories. However, its correspondent John Broder was suckered into running a story that is older than he is. Broder reported that in 1973 I boarded an elevator in the Capitol dressed in Western garb in the company of several other people from Texas. Senator Edmund Muskie was also on the elevator, and when the operator passed the floor I had requested without stopping, Broder wrote, I said, "Son, I told you I wanted three and you went right past my floor." To which the young summer intern was reported to have replied, "Hold your horses, cowboy, we take care of the senators first." The elevator operator was fired that afternoon, Broder informed his readers, at my insistence. The story was offered as an example of "vindictiveness and arrogance by Tower." The only problem was that the yarn goes all the way back, in various permutations, to Teddy Roosevelt. More recently, it was told about my immediate Senate predecessor, Bill Blakley, who held the seat with an interim appointment after LBJ resigned to be vice president. And although it is apocryphal, the tale fits Blakley better than me, since he favored Western-style attire, which I have never worn in the Capitol. In another version of the story, the other senator on the elevator was Ken Keating of New York, Bobby Kennedy's predecessor. Broder assured his readers in the article that the 1973 incident was "a widely circulated story affirmed by several sources." Les Carpenter, a Washington correspondent for several Texas newspapers in the 1960s, once ran the story, later found it to be untrue, and apologized in print. Ken Towery, my former Senate press secretary and administrative assistant, remembers the story cropping up on another occasion, in the *Washington Post,* and receiving a letter of apology from the publisher after we pointed out that it was, to use a charitable term, a tall tale.

The elevator story is best summed up by a comment made by Harry Truman to writer Merle Miller in the book *Plain Speaking:* "Newspapermen, and they're all a bunch of lazy cusses, once one of them writes something, the others rewrite it and rewrite it, and they keep right on doing it without ever stopping to find out if the first fellow was telling the truth or not." I think this one incident amply illustrates just how anxious the news media were to print or broadcast whatever damaging material fell into their hands without making a serious effort to check its authenticity. John Broder promised his readers that the elevator story had been "affirmed by several sources." He obviously neglected to ascertain whether they were *reliable* sources.

Indeed, Broder and all Washington reporters are extremely dependent on their news sources. Our government is like the tip of an iceberg, and without reliable sources, much of what goes on cannot be accurately conveyed to the American people. News sources have an obligation to take responsibility for the accuracy of the information they dispense to the press, which was exactly why George Bush told the members of his new cabinet to go on the record with the press whenever possible. Those who hide their identity while purporting to offer factual information may also be hiding their motives, their self-interest, and, in some cases, their duplicity.

Be that as it may, I think the press ultimately gets the kind of sources it deserves. Sloppy, shallow, sensation-seeking, and irresponsible journalists are prime candidates for running afoul of those who fancy themselves media manipulators. The Washington press corps allows itself to be manipulated because it's easier than digging out stories the hard way; also, it's rewarding. Reporters with a modicum of seniority command salaries that are equivalent to those of members of Congress. The lecture fees are also hefty, and some of them are paid by the same special interest groups that the news media condemn for corrupting members of the House and Senate with PAC money and honoraria.

The double standard that is engendered, in consequence, is equally corrupting. It lowers the news media to the level of the duplicitous and the deceitful. I think many honest reporters know this and struggle to guard against it. On occasion, I suspect, the *Los Angeles Times* tested the legitimacy of its sources by running a dubious story first in its sister publication, the *Baltimore Sun,* which seemed willing to publish just about anything. Such testing, however, left something to be desired from the standpoint of a resident of Baltimore or of the story's principal subject.

Reporters from two major publications, one of which was the *New York Times,* told a colleague of mine that they were under orders from their editors to come up with a new John Tower story every day, no matter what. The result of that kind of pressure — as any reputable editor will attest — creates a posse of journalists riding hard in pursuit of even the most worthless item, which is duly blown out of proportion, invested with bogus significance, and presented to millions of people, who assume that the journalists involved are using common sense and adhering to the highest standards of their profession.

I don't think I will ever forget the mob scene in front of the Jefferson Hotel at the height of the confirmation battle. Every morning I had to run the gauntlet out the front door to my car. The moment I hit the sidewalk, I would be surrounded by reporters yelling questions at me, sound technicians, their microphones attached to long poles, jabbing and shoving, photographers scrambling backward, colliding with each other, cursing and grunting. If anyone had stumbled, he would have been trampled.

We had a view of the entrance from our rooms; my daughters would look down, and Penny or Marian would say, "Daddy, don't they ever leave?" The sidewalk was a pigsty of fast food wrappers and coffee cups. We could hear them down below, laughing and horsing around at all hours. They could have cared less about disturbing the hotel guests or pedestrians trying to pass by.

The stakeout moved around as well. It followed me to the Pentagon each morning. Or if I went to the White House, there would be a car or van following me. Bill Johnson, my driver, would routinely ask me if I wanted him to lose them. Usually I told him not to bother, but on a couple of occasions I let him do it. Superbly trained in evasive driving techniques, he'd look in the rearview mirror, slow down for a light to change to yellow, and zoom through the intersection, leaving the news media caught in the traffic behind the light. Frustrated by this, the networks hired a motorcyclist to trail after me.

It was an obscene manifestation of lynch mob mentality. I don't think I would have been all that surprised to come down one morning and find the ladies and gentlemen of the press wearing the red caps of the French Revolution, waiting beside a rickety wooden tumbrel to take me off to the guillotine.

The phenomenon that I experienced has been described in terms of a shark feeding frenzy. But that implies an insensate pattern of behavior, and I prefer the characterization offered to me by Mike Wallace, of *60 Minutes,* when we crossed paths in New York a few weeks after the confirmation fight was over. Unlike the tumbrel and guillotine scene, there was something uniquely all-American about it. "Tower," Wallace said, "you were lynched."

Senate debate began on March 2. As a curtain raiser, the *Washington Post* splashed this story across its front page, under the byline of Bob Woodward:

FBI CITES 2 INCIDENTS AT BASE
Nominee Allegedly Drunk, Fondled Women

One section of the material on former Senator John G. Tower that has attracted attention from senators considering his nomination as defense secretary concerns two visits Tower made to Bergstrom Air Force Base in Austin, Tex., in 1976–78, when he allegedly appeared to be drunk and fondled two women, according to informed sources.

Retired Air Force sergeant Bob Jackson first told the Senate Armed Services Committee and later the Federal Bureau of Investigation of the two incidents at Bergstrom when Tower toured the base. Jackson, who was the noncommissioned officer-in-charge of base public relations and VIP tours, said he observed both incidents.

During the two tours of the base Tower "had liquor on his breath and he had trouble talking and was staggering out of the car and up the steps," according to Jackson's account.

In one incident, Jackson told the FBI, while Tower was touring the office of the base chief of maintenance, "a secretary started to get up and Tower put his hand on her shoulder as she started to rise. His hand slid off her shoulder and onto her breast. She drew back and nothing was said. There was no great caressing or fondling. It was just untoward and unseemly."

In the second incident, "an enlisted female crew chief on an F4 aircraft was standing at attention or parade rest and Tower was told her name and put his hand on her shoulder and it traveled down, resting on her rump for a short period of time," according to Jackson's account.

The story went on to report that Jackson retired from the military in 1978, and quoted him directly as saying, "Had she been my daughter, well, he is too little to hit — that would have put me down to his level. But if I did what I wanted at the time, you'd be talking to me now from Leavenworth." Fort Leavenworth, Kansas, is the site of a military prison.

When I got to the Pentagon that morning, Dan Howard was already at work dissecting the story, pulling out the names, dates, and places so that we could hunt for eyewitnesses or other evidence in rebuttal. Like any professional public relations person, Dan started by asking me flat out if the story had any substance. I assured him that it was a complete lie.

It is a nightmarish task to shoot down a story that is alleged to have happened years before. Just coming up with my appointment diaries for the period wasn't easy. The bulk of my Senate files had been shipped to a federal repository in Austin, where they were being sorted and catalogued before going to the archive I established at Southwestern University. Fortunately, Senator John McCain got a telephone call that same morning from a retired Air Force officer who had read the Jackson story in the *Arizona Republic*. The man said he had been assigned to Bergstrom during the period mentioned and would have been involved in any visit to the base by a member of the Armed Services Committee, and he didn't recall the visit at all. McCain asked him to come up with a list of other senior officers with whom he had served at Bergstrom. The caller had a good memory, and the names were called in to the Pentagon for current telephone numbers and addresses.

In the meantime, the *Post*'s Jackson story rang a few bells with the Republican staff on the Senate Armed Services Committee. A similar allegation had been sent to the committee. In the screening process that took place during the confirmation, Democratic and Republican staff members reviewed each allegation to decide if there was sufficient merit to warrant further action. Nothing was thrown out, but the wildest accusations were put in an *X* file, which was designated to hold material that would not be used by the committee. The allegations included in the Jackson story, by mutual agreement of the majority and minority staffs, had been relegated to the *X* file.

The surprise in the Democratic summary of the FBI report that I refer to earlier in the chapter was this: the Jackson material was surreptitiously removed from the *X* file and included in the

Democratic summary. From there, it found its way to the *Wash-ington Post*. Relations between the Republican and Democratic committee staffs, already badly strained, degenerated even more. The Republicans, justifiably so, felt that they had been set up and sandbagged by Arnold Punaro. And all the talk of cooperation between the two sides that Sam Nunn offered to the Senate as the debate began, shortly after 1:00 P.M., was belied by that incident of double-dealing.

Nunn escalated his attack on me in his opening statement. The pitch of his voice rose as he declared, "I believe personally that Senator Tower has had a serious drinking problem in the 1970's and 1980's, including in recent years." To buttress his contention that "we are talking about someone that is next to the President, at the very top of the nuclear chain of command," Nunn went on to read a Department of Defense directive that he said defined alcohol abuse as "any irresponsible use of an alcoholic beverage causing misconduct or unacceptable social behavior, or impairing work performance, physical or mental health, financial responsibility or personal relationships." It didn't seem to occur to Sam Nunn that by the very standard he was citing, I would not have been disqualified from holding a military assignment involving nuclear weapons. There had been no substantiation to demonstrate misconduct, unacceptable social behavior, or impaired work performance, physical or mental health, financial responsibility, or personal relationships. On the contrary, I had provided evidence, as had my associates, neighbors, family, colleagues, and the FBI, that satisfied each criterion.

But Nunn had an issue that he thought would transcend the dubious methods and assumptions in his approach. He even went so far as to suggest that my confirmation as secretary of defense would increase the risk of a nuclear holocaust:

> Senator Warner and I spent 3 years or 4 years working on what we call "risk reduction," the risk of nuclear war. We have even succeeded partially in getting a risk reduction center set up between the United States and the Soviet Union. Every step we can take to reduce the risk of nuclear war, to reduce the mistake, must be taken, and I think all senators need to consider the importance of this chain of command as well as the importance the military themselves give this chain of command, and the example we set here in this nomination is

going to work its way down in the military forces of our nation one way or the other — one way or the other.

The picture he painted was as astounding as it was lurid. A drunken defense secretary was going to push the nuclear button if the Senate didn't intervene. Short of that, this inebriated member of the president's cabinet was going to seduce the men and women of the military into a life of alcoholism, which could lead them to accidentally start a nuclear war. The overwrought and simplistic nature of Sam Nunn's presentation did much to discredit the chairman of the Armed Services Committee in the eyes of many of his former admirers. Until Nunn launched his crusade against my nomination, he was considered a serious student of national security issues. But by asking the Senate to believe such simpleminded notions, Nunn badly undermined his own credibility as a defense expert. Political exaggeration, even invective, is understandable in some circumstances, but not the comic-book quality of an argument that relies on the so-called bolt-out-of-the-blue theory, which postulates a Soviet attack without warning of any kind and a prelaunch sequence that goes totally undetected, catching the United States by surprise, with the president unable to act and the secretary of defense — dead drunk — at the top of the chain of command. I am even willing to concede that perhaps Sam Nunn genuinely thought I had an alcohol problem and was concerned about the ramifications such a problem would have at the Defense Department. But nuclear war? Demoralization of the entire military structure? Arguments such as those made me wonder if Nunn hadn't permitted his hostility to overtake his intellectual composure. Aside from this lack of composure, his reasoning can be explained only by all-consuming ambition or — and here I may be getting as close to an explanation as we will ever come — political inexperience. Nunn went directly from the Georgia legislature to the U.S. Senate, rose to the position of ranking member of the Armed Services Committee in just eleven years, and along the way was studiously apolitical, never cultivating the arts of compromise, persuasion, and tactical retreat. Propelled into battle with the president of the United States, for whatever objective, his inexperience led him to make a series of damaging blunders.

SIXTEEN

A HIGH PRICE TO PAY
FOR PUBLIC SERVICE

THE DEMOCRATS played a destructive game of follow the leader for the next week. John Glenn demonstrated his disequilibrium by reading words and phrases from the FBI report into the Senate record, touching off an angry dispute about his flagrant breach of the rules. Glenn was in such a hurry to say words like "crocked" and "obviously drunk" in front of C-SPAN's cameras that he violated the rule, established at the outset, that the FBI report could not be directly quoted. Glenn's remarks were finally expunged from the record, but not from reporters' notebooks or TV screens. It was so venomous, so unexpected from John Glenn.

The Democrats were obviously feeling the heat from the Republican position that the FBI investigation had not substantiated the allegations. The impulse was to point to the gossip and innuendo contained in the report and cite them as fact. At one point, a thoroughly seething Senator Ernest Hollings proclaimed: "The report contains facts. And I know facts. I have practiced law for 40 years." A subsequent remark by Hollings also indicated that I had gotten under his skin with my National Press Club comments about Senate standards. He said, "The American people ought not to be led to believe that Senators are off in their hideaways having a party and drinking together." Hollings is a tall man. His silver hair, square-cut jaw, and thick Southern accent give him an imposing air. He is the Senate bully, quick to attack with harsh and personal invective. Once he commences an onslaught, Hollings gives no quarter. He is a true demagogue whose wild statements are intended to intimidate and to silence. He is a study in arrogance and pomposity, and as the confirmation fight was drawing to a close, I was to feel the full force of those traits.

To say the least, the timing of the *Post*'s Jackson story couldn't have been worse. Senator Phil Gramm said his stomach hurt when he read the references to the allegations in the FBI report in S-407. Mine was a little queasy, too, but I had passed the point of registering much pain or anger by then. John Warner, whose responsibility it was to open the Republican side of the debate, was left without a rebuttal when he took the floor. We were still tracking down Air Force officers and information that could be used in my defense. Warner is a good speaker, however, and his presentation was effective and well balanced. Prudently, he stepped around the Jackson story:

This morning's newspaper carries a story. The chairman referred to it. I guess we will hear more about it. I sincerely hope that it can be disproved. Some facts relative to that are in S-407. But before this Senator attaches any credibility, a great deal of corroboration will be necessary.

But I thought I would bring out today, not a secret document, but another, I think, credible source of evidence. I ask unanimous consent that it be printed in the Record in its entirety.

The document, a letter, was addressed to Sam Nunn:

Dear Mr. Chairman:

We have known Senator John Tower professionally and personally for a number of years. We are aware of his 26-year record of outstanding public service to this country.

He served the people of Texas in the United States Senate for 24 years. They endorsed his performance in office by re-electing him three times, in each instance over a well-financed and strong opponent.

After retiring from the Senate where he held important policy and leadership positions, Senator Tower was asked by the President to handle some of the toughest and most delicate problems facing our country. He received public acclaim for his work as Chief Negotiator for the U.S. Strategic Arms Talks in Geneva, and for his fairness and candor as Chairman of the President's Special Review Board which studied National Security Council operations in light of the Iran-Contra matter.

We all know the Senator well. Many of us worked as volunteers in his campaigns or as members of his staff. Many of us counseled with him on domestic policy or on sensitive matters of national security and defense. Others of us are simply his friend. But we are all convinced that President Bush has made an excellent choice in nominating Senator Tower as Secretary of Defense.

We urge you to bring his nomination to a prompt vote in the Senate Armed Services Committee and to recommend his confirmation as Secretary of Defense.

> Sincerely,
> *Honey Alexander, Member, Corporation for Public Broadcasting, Nashville, TN; Carol E. Dinkins, Former U.S. Deputy Attorney General, Houston, TX; Anne Armstrong, Former Ambassador to Great Britain, Armstrong, TX; Elizabeth H. Dole, Secretary of Labor, Washington, DC; Patricia Hill, Member, Texas House of Representatives, Dallas, TX; Kay Bailey Hutchison, Former Chairman, National Transportation Safety Board, Dallas, TX; Cyndi T. Krier, Member, Texas State Senate, San Antonio, TX; Beryl B. Milburn, Former Chairman, Higher Education Coordinating Board, Austin, TX; Cynthia Root Moran, Former Assistant Secretary for Legislation (Acting), Department of Health and Human Services, Washington, DC; Jocelyn L. Straus, Member, National Council on the Arts, San Antonio, TX; Carla A. Hills, U.S. Trade Representative, Washington, DC; Jeane J. Kirkpatrick, Leavy Professor of Government, Georgetown University, Washington, DC; Sally F. McKenzie, Vice Chairman, Texas Women's Commission, Dallas, TX; Catherine Clark Mosbacher, Attorney, Houston, TX; Anna Mowery, Member, Texas House of Representatives, Fort Worth, TX; Irene Wischer, President and CEO,*

Panhandle Producing Co., San Antonio, TX; Greer Garson Fogelson, Dallas, TX; Jessica Catto, Builder, Woody Creek, CO; Nancy Kissinger, New York, NY

As far as I know, Sam Nunn never bothered to respond to the letter. The news media, totally swept away by the Jackson story and the rancorous Senate debate, took no notice of the views of nineteen prominent women who were willing to speak out on my behalf. The statements of a "retired" Air Force sergeant were far more credible than those of someone like Anne Armstrong, who had known me for nearly thirty years. More credible, that is, until Senator John McCain strode back into the Senate chamber late Thursday afternoon, March 2.

McCain interrupted a dispute that was raging over John Glenn's attempt to read portions of the FBI report into the record. Democratic leader George Mitchell was trying to repair the damage Glenn had done by breaching the Senate rules when the Arizona Republican asked to be recognized:

Mr. President, I have some information I think would be very interesting to Members of this body and others concerning the allegation that was printed on the front page of the Washington Post this morning concerning an allegation made by a retired Technical Sergeant Jackson concerning some alleged behavior on the part of Senator John Tower during some period between 1976 and 1978.

I remind my colleagues it was on the front page of the Washington Post. We have now received information that this individual's last duty was when he reported to Bergstrom Air Force Base on February 21, 1976. His last duty day was March 16, 1977. He was referred to the Wilford Hall Medical Center for psychological evaluation and was later retired for psychiatric disability, and the details of that can be made available. He was permanently retired April 19, 1978, for a psychiatric condition.

I also point out that the 12th Air Force commander from June 1975 through June 1978 recalls John Tower to be in Bergstrom only once during the period, the first Saturday of August 1975 for an air show. That memory has been confirmed by the wing commander and vice wing commander and master chief of the Air Force.

Mr. President, the reason I am bringing this very important

information to the attention of this body is that the allegation was obviously given great credibility by the media by being printed on the front page of the Washington Post. I think it clearly indicates there is no validity to that and very little we can do to repair the damage that is done by this allegation which I understand was going to be carried on national media tonight.

CBS, I was informed, was ready to put Jackson on the evening news, but one of my aides relayed McCain's information to a network producer at the last minute and Jackson, the source of the allegation — a source who had not been at Bergstrom when I visited in 1975 — was dropped from the lineup. It was, to be sure, a close-run thing. Dan Howard and Rhett Dawson had been working the phones all day at the Pentagon, attempting to track down officers who had served at Bergstrom. Rhett requested a routine check of Jackson's military records to verify his assignment to the base, and that's how the information about his psychiatric condition came to light. Rhett then placed a call to Pat Tucker, the Republican counsel to the Senate Armed Services committee, who was in the cloakroom just off the Senate floor. Tucker, suspicious about Jackson's rank, given his years of service, had also made inquiries and was anxiously waiting for a response. He scribbled a few notes, grabbed McCain, and gave him a quick briefing. There was an unfunny comedy of errors getting the material faxed from the Pentagon to the Senate — somebody had the wrong numbers — but eventually, with much running back and forth and urgent calls, it got there.

When McCain yielded the floor, John Glenn picked up right where he had left off as though nothing of significance had occurred. Glenn even worked a reference into his speech about "fraternization." He said the issue had received "much press attention" and used the term "manhandling." With that, William Cohen rose to his feet. "Will the Senator yield?" he asked. Glenn pushed on, ignoring Cohen's request: "The perception is there. The perception is in the press. I cannot verify them but it is a perception that is out."

Cohen persisted. "Is the Senator suggesting there is evidence that Senator Tower manhandled a woman in the military?"

"No, I did not say that. I did not say that at all," Glenn replied.

"That is what you are implying."

Glenn beat a hasty retreat: "I did not use Senator Tower's name. What I said with regard to manhandling was that I do not like the term 'womanizing.' That is the point I was making . . . I was not referring to Senator Tower at all. I think the Record will show that."

Having made his point, Cohen said, "I thank the Senator," and sat down.

When Cohen and McCain left the Senate floor, they went to the press galleries to talk about the Jackson story. They got a quick taste of the news media's attitude. One reporter demanded to know if McCain "didn't feel bad about what he had done to Sergeant Jackson." Needless to say, McCain and Cohen were flabbergasted by the question.

To its credit, and Bob Woodward's, the *Washington Post* all but issued a retraction of the story. The news media are loath to admit fallibility. Mistakes are usually dealt with in one- or two-sentence corrections that are run in the back pages. The *Post,* however, fashioned its correction into a full-fledged news story reporting Jackson's background and the fact that I had not been at Bergstrom at the time the incidents were alleged to have taken place. It was an effort to right the wrong that had been done, but the *New York Times,* no doubt with its competitive instincts aroused by being scooped on the original — albeit false — story, sprang to Jackson's defense. I was interviewed by *Times* reporter Andrew Rosenthal on Friday afternoon, one of only a handful of encounters with the press in the last days of the confirmation battle. It was a straightforward, businesslike session, which was apparently not what Rosenthal's editors were seeking. The interview was killed, and in its place the next day, March 4, one of the newspaper's headlines read "TOWER ACCUSER WAS ATTACKED IN SELECTIVE WAY." The *Times* quoted an expert in privacy law who was of the opinion that the sergeant's right to privacy had been violated.

The refutation of the Jackson story provided a vivid example of the kind of allegations that were being used against me by the Democrats. Some of them complained that they had been set up by the White House on the Jackson story, the implication being that we planted the false allegations for our opponents to discover and leak. The logic was twisted and ludicrous — akin to blaming the murder victim for his own death.

*   *   *

I was headed to the White House at about the time John McCain and Bill Cohen were shooting down the Jackson story. Dorothy, my daughter Penny, and I had been invited to a small dinner and movie party. Barbara Bush had called previously to make sure that Penny, who had arrived in Washington earlier in the week, knew that she was also included in the evening. Barbara had apparently seen or heard about Penny's appearance on CNN's *Sonya Live* call-in program. As my eldest child, she had taken it upon herself to become the Tower family's primary public spokesperson on my behalf. And I think that her efforts were one reason the phone calls and letters received at the White House in the preceding week to ten days had started to shift in my favor. I was not aware before-hand that the CNN program was a call-in, and my heart sank when I realized what she could be subjected to, if worse came to worst. However, Penny handled the challenge with consummate skill. She made several excellent points, among them the observations that my drinking in the 1960s and 1970s reflected the era and that as the times changed, so had I. "His generation drank cocktails at five," she said. "It was a life-style, not a dependence. He changed that life-style. Just as he doesn't eat a lot of red meat anymore, he doesn't drink scotch anymore." It was pure common sense, and I am sure many TV viewers could relate to it in terms of their own changing life-styles. I was very proud of Penny.

At the White House party, Penny ended up sitting beside Senator Bennett Johnston of Louisiana. It was very informal. Dinner plates were propped on coffee tables and knees. I've been asked if Penny lobbied Johnston for his vote, but Washington and the Senate do not really work that way. I knew he was going to be on the guest list, and although it was extremely tempting, I decided it would be inappropriate to use the occasion to advance my nomination. Johnston was open and friendly throughout. After the buffet dinner we went down to the theater ("theater" is rather a grand term for a room with a large screen and armchairs, but that's how it is described), which is on the lower level of the White House, near the library where FDR broadcast his famous fireside chats, to see the film titled — appropriately enough — *Chances Are*.

Jeanne Tower Cox, Penny's youngest sister, remained in Dallas; but she too was effectively aiding my cause. Jeanne sent out Mailgrams to key senators, including this one to Sam Nunn:

For several weeks my sisters and I have endured tremendous pain watching the confirmation process of our father to become secretary of defense. I can't tell you the heartache in reading and watching inaccurate and untrue portrayals of our father. Endless unfavorable leaks appeared in the news media for weeks, and I don't recall anyone complaining about those. I have the highest respect for you, Senator Nunn, and I know this has been difficult for you also. I simply wanted you to know that my father is the most decent, honorable, patriotic and Christian man I know. If I did not truly believe that, my husband and I would not have named our nine-week-old son John Goodwin Tower Cox. My sisters, Penny Tower Cook and Marian Tower, join me in this letter to you.

Naturally, a letter from a man's daughter can be dismissed as nothing more than an expression of family loyalty. But is this next letter also without merit?

Last Wednesday, 19 retired Generals and Admirals from the Army, Navy, Air Force and Marine Corps, all of whom have known the honorable John Tower for many years, forwarded a telegram to the Commander-in-Chief of the Armed Forces, strongly supporting the nomination for Secretary of Defense of this exceptional American. I believe that this act is unprecedented in the history of our Country, and have attached a copy of the text for your examination.

I have known Senator Tower professionally, socially, and personally for over a decade, and one of my sincerest regrets is that I retired before having an opportunity to serve under him while he is our Secretary of Defense. It is my strong conviction that history will identify him as one of the greatest patriots and statesmen of our generation.

I urge you to judge Senator Tower on his unique professional qualifications to lead our defense establishment. The young men and women who today are serving in the uniform of their country deserve to have John Tower at the helm. I am sending this letter to all members of the United States Senate.

With warmest best wishes, I am,
Most respectfully,

P. X. Kelley

General Kelley, the former commandant of the Marine Corps, sent his letter first to Senator Ted Stevens, who put it into the *Congressional Record* along with a copy of the telegram:

We have served as General and Flag officers in the Armed Forces of the United States.

We commanded the military forces upon whose successful performance the security of the American people depends.

We know John Tower well, and have known him for many years.

In our relationship with Senator Tower, we have found him superbly qualified in every respect, both professionally and personally, to serve the nation as Secretary of Defense and in the chain-of-command. We would be honored to serve under him, and the uniformed men and women of our country would unquestionably benefit from his leadership.

We strongly support your nomination of this exceptional American.

I won't list all the names of those who signed the telegram, but there was a cross section of the senior military leadership stretching back for more than a quarter of a century, including General Bennie L. Davis, former commander in chief of the Strategic Air Command; General Charles A. Gabriel, the former chief of staff of the Air Force; and three former chiefs of naval operations, Thomas B. Haywood, James L. Holloway, and Elmo R. Zumwalt. At one time, all were key links in the military chain of command who were routinely asked to pass judgment on the fitness of those serving in our strategic nuclear forces. I don't think there could be a more effective rebuttal to Sam Nunn's claim that I would be found unfit to serve as the commander of a SAC wing or a guided missile sub than the above telegram signed by a Bennie Davis or a Thomas Haywood.

After the Jackson travesty and the first two days of Senate debate, the misgivings felt by all but one of the wavering Republicans gave way to solid support. Larry Pressler of South Dakota, who had been talking about possibly voting against my nomination, fell in line. He said he was concerned about the unfair treatment I had been receiving. Ken Krieg, who had served on the staff of the Special Review Board and had joined the defense secretary's staff at the Pentagon, prepared a comprehensive study that answered the doubts Pressler had expressed as to my commitment to Pentagon management and procurement reform.

And, yes, we did do some arm-twisting. When a party leader like Bob Dole says, "I need your vote on this one," the request usually carries great weight. Nancy Kassebaum told Dole that if her vote was needed to tip the balance, she would support me. Kassebaum fancies herself an independent thinker and makes a fetish of independence. I called her, and she was obviously being swayed by the Democrats' arguments that I would not set a good example and would be unfair to women in the military. I pointed to my record of advancing the careers of women who had worked for me, my cosponsorship of the original Equal Rights Amendment, and the testimonials that I had received from women like Elizabeth Dole and Jeane Kirkpatrick. Even though she was giving the Democrats bipartisan cover, Kassebaum had her mind made up already.

I did hope, though, that an op-ed piece that appeared in the *Wall Street Journal* on Tuesday, March 7, would have some impact. Written by Karen Elliott House, former Washington correspondent, foreign editor, and a top executive at Dow Jones, the newspaper's parent corporation, the article directly addressed the womanizing allegations and the way the FBI investigation had been conducted:

> I was a source for the Federal Bureau of Investigation's probe of Sen. John Tower. And, if my experience is in any way typical of the 500 or more interviews conducted by FBI agents in compiling the secret dossier on Sen. Tower's career and character, the U.S. Senate is pursuing its debate on the basis of rumor, gossip and innuendo that any American citizen clearly would consider character assassination.
>
> Since not one of the 100 Senators, many of whom have served, worked and traveled with John Tower for decades, has testified to any firsthand knowledge of his alleged drinking and skirt-chasing, it is the FBI report that is being wielded as the murder weapon to destroy not only his nomination but his name. Thus, it seems instructive to senators and citizens to recount one FBI interview, how it originated, what it produced and most important, how easy it would have been

to pile additional innuendo on the bonfire around which the Senate is gleefully dancing. . . .

My interview began with a call one afternoon a few weeks ago from a polite FBI agent, requesting a meeting. I guessed the topic was John Tower. Two days earlier I had received a call from the Los Angeles Times correspondent in Houston requesting a copy of a newspaper article that he had been told contained an account of John Tower propositioning me 17 years ago when I was a young Washington correspondent for The Dallas Morning News. I had indeed written a lengthy profile of Sen. Tower during his re-election campaign in 1972 in which I queried him on rumors of his frequent appearances with women other than his wife and on several auto accidents in which he was involved. It might have been a better story if Sen. Tower had propositioned me, but he didn't.

The only offer I ever had from Sen. Tower was a polite and public invitation to me and by inference a table of Dallas Morning News colleagues to join him for "jazz and scrambled eggs" after a White House correspondents' dinner 17 years ago — an invitation I declined and which seems as innocuous in retrospect as it did at the time. But the rumor mill was obviously grinding away.

Within hours of the FBI phone call, two polite but persistent young agents, one male, one female, showed up at my New York office for what turned out to be a half-hour interview. They quickly explained they had received an anonymous letter saying that if they wanted "derogatory information on John Tower," to contact me or my then-roommate, Sally Shelton, at the time a legislative assistant to Sen. Lloyd Bentsen (D., Texas).

Having passed on the anonymous charge, the FBI agents then graciously offered me anonymity to confirm and expand on it or on any other information I might have about misconduct by Sen. Tower. I declined the offer of anonymity. I also explained that not only did I have no firsthand experience with any misconduct by Sen. Tower, in my reporting efforts 17 years ago to track down similar rumors, I'd been unable to substantiate gossip about Sen. Tower's "womanizing."

So, we now had the odd situation of a reporter who had been unable to confirm rumors about John Tower and other women at that time now being asked by the FBI to anonymously confirm rumors about John Tower propositioning her. With this trail clearly leading nowhere, the agents politely pressed for any other information I might have — or any rumors I might have heard. All I could do was acknowledge that rumors of Sen. Tower's interest in women have abounded in Washington for many years.

House went on to relate that she suggested the FBI contact her ex-roommate, who had gone on to serve as a U.S. ambassador. The FBI did so, and according to House, Sally Shelton was asked about rumors of sexual harassment against my female employees. House continued:

> Ms. Shelton is as perplexed as I am by the rumor process that has led us to be even peripherally involved in the Tower investigation. The experience also leads to some other reflections. For one thing, a process of rumors begetting rumors offers anyone with the slightest shred of gossip to pass it on through official channels, to instigate additional FBI inquiries and to widen further the web of innuendo in which the senator is snared. Had either Ms. Shelton or I sought to play a mischievous role in the nomination process, we had ample opportunity — indeed an FBI invitation — to do so.

By Tuesday morning, when Karen Elliott House's article appeared, I had won my first convert. The day before, Howell Heflin of Alabama announced that he had come to a decision:

> Because of my personal observations, his background, qualifications, and intelligence, the uncertain state of the evidence, his pledge and the safeguards, I am willing to rely on his pledge and give him a chance to prove himself. Giving one a chance to prove himself or herself is one of the great redeeming values of the American way of life. I will vote for confirmation.

I was deeply appreciative of Senator Heflin's decision. However, I had not made the progress I had hoped to in persuading other Democrats to come to the same conclusion. One by one, the senators on my list of the most likely candidates to support me were succumbing to Nunn's pressure.

Nunn was working hard to convince Joseph Lieberman and

Charles Robb. I am told that he based his argument on purely personal grounds. He needed the senators' support, and without it, as chairman of the Armed Services Committee, he would suffer serious political damage. It was remarkable that Lieberman was still undecided, seeing that Nunn's arm-twisting had gotten to such stalwarts as Claiborne Pell, who told me over the phone, clearly in anguish, that he was deeply disturbed by what was happening, but be that as it may, I could not count on him for support. Although Heflin's defection was welcome, some of my more pessimistic advisers read it as an indication that Nunn and George Mitchell had locked up the necessary votes to defeat me and had released Heflin to vote his conscience.

Mitchell had gone from playing a bit part in the drama to a central role. The confirmation battle was his first major Senate showdown as majority leader. Mitchell is intensely partisan, and he had to know that the press would judge him harshly if the Democrats lost the fight. Furthermore, Nunn was beginning to show signs of battle fatigue. Since the first day, the debate had been extraordinarily bitter. I don't think the Senate had seen such sustained vitriol since the days before the Civil War. By the Monday that preceded the final vote, Mitchell had taken to throwing himself in front of the guns to shield Nunn from the pounding that Republican senators were giving him. The majority leader, himself under strain and growing testy, got into a verbal slugging match with Senator Warren Rudman of New Hampshire. Rudman, a former attorney general of his home state, delivered a devastating legal critique of the Armed Services Committee's report on my nomination. He told the Senate he had tried hundreds of cases and had never seen anyone "trashed on such flimsy evidence in my entire life":

> In many cases the witnesses are anonymous; in others, they are clearly mentally deranged or, from my reading of the evidence, personally vindictive. They were not subject to any kind of cross-examination. Nor in the great majority of cases were polygraphs used. And yet it is on that kind of uncorroborated, unsworn, unchallenged, uncross-examined junk in most cases that John Tower will probably see his nomination go down to defeat.

Both Rudman and Senator Arlen Specter, another skilled trial lawyer, were punching huge holes in the Democrats' case. Earlier,

to blunt Specter's attacks, Senator Dennis DeConcini declared that
he had seen me under the influence of alcohol on the Senate floor.
He quickly amended this falsehood by adding, "Was he inebriated
to the point that he could not operate? The answer is no." De-
Concini sat on the other side of the Senate chamber and was
never in a position to observe me closely on the floor, and yet he
was the only one of my former colleagues to make such an assertion.

Mitchell wasn't as rash as DeConcini. He sat through Rudman's
presentation without interrupting, and he must have been acutely
uncomfortable as Rudman ridiculed the portion of the committee
report that was based on the tone of the Democrats' favorite issue:
the appearance of a conflict of interest after I resigned as chief
START negotiator. Senator Rudman read an excerpt that quoted
State Department regulations about the disclosure of classified inside information, and then said:

> I thought of that hook in the report, and I thought to myself:
> "The fellow who wrote that is really clever, because there is
> not one iota of evidence that any such thing occurred." In
> fact, there is no evidence to the contrary. The only evidence
> is John Tower's statement that he never divulged any classified
> information of any kind to any client.
>
> Then the committee in this very artful report which, with
> all due respect to all in the Chamber, is worthy of the kind
> of indictment one would find in a people's court in the Soviet
> Union goes on to say: "The committee has no evidence that
> Senator Tower provided his clients with classified informa-
> tion. In the committee's judgment, however, this situation
> created the appearance of using public office for private gain
> and casts doubt on his ability to command public confidence
> in the integrity of the system."

Rudman followed the committee's logic to its obvious conclusion:

> This report says he did not violate one law, one rule, one
> code. But Senators say, "Oh, well, we are Talmudic scholars.
> We are going to apply our own standard." So beware, nom-
> inees: If you ever served in government, do not just look at
> the ethics codes and the statutes. Get into the heads of every-
> body on the committee and everybody in the Senate, because

it is their personal judgment that will determine whether you rise or fall. If that is fairness, I do not understand the word.

George Mitchell bided his time and later in the day rose to observe that Rudman had only been expressing his personal opinion about the committee report. Mitchell said, "I very strongly disagree with that description of what is in that report. You are perfectly entitled to your opinion . . . but it cannot be permitted to stand as though that were an undisputed fact."

> SENATOR RUDMAN — The Majority Leader is entitled to his opinion. I would make an offer to any Senator on this floor to join me now, this minute, to go up to room S-407. I will go through the report line by line with any Senator from either side of the aisle, trained lawyer, judge, investigator, whatever, read every line of that report and, Mr. Majority Leader, my dear friend from Maine, I stand on that statement because it is correct. Because one thing I learned in 24 years of practicing law is I know how to read evidence, and I know how to state it and I know how not to misstate it.
>
> SENATOR MITCHELL — I think I know how to do that just as well as you do.
>
> SENATOR RUDMAN — I am sure.

With Mitchell losing his composure, and Bob Dole and Ernest Hollings tearing into each other, the Senate was in turmoil. An excerpt from the Dole-Hollings exchange captures the venomous atmosphere:

> SENATOR DOLE — You served with the Senator from Texas for a long time. You observed him. You were in an exchange the other day with the Senator from Wyoming and you said, "Drunk is enough for me."
>
> And I have been on the floor when the Senator from South Carolina has attacked other Senators by name.
>
> SENATOR HOLLINGS — Oh, now we have attacked other senators. Let us stick to Mr. Tower.
>
> SENATOR DOLE — Let us recall each attack, one at a time.
>
> SENATOR HOLLINGS — One at a time; namely Tower.
>
> SENATOR DOLE — I recall a comment made about the Senator from Ohio, Senator Metzenbaum; and a comment about the Senator from Texas, "the Senator from Texaco."

These are the words I recall the Senator from South Carolina saying.

When you stand on this floor and talk about Mr. Alcohol Abuser you are talking about John Tower. And there is no evidence in that record that he is an alcohol abuser.

SENATOR HOLLINGS — There absolutely is, Mr. President, and he knows it.

SENATOR DOLE — You would not speak to anybody else that way.

SENATOR BYRD — Mr. President, I asked for the regular order, that Senators not address other Senators in the second person and that they make their questions through the Chair.

Bob Dole was too polite to use the words Hollings had actually directed at Senator Howard Metzenbaum a few years back; Hollings called him the senator from B'nai B'rith. The remark caused such a stir that it was expunged from the record. Hollings's other target of abuse, Lloyd Bentsen — the senator from Texaco — chose to ignore the slur.

By Tuesday afternoon, March 7, the fourth day of the debate, the mood of the Senate was ugly and growing uglier by the hour. I think at about that point there was growing sentiment on both sides that things had already gone too far. The Democrats were starting to lose their momentum, and I had picked up my second defector, Senator Christopher Dodd. The vote I had cast against the censure of his father, Dodd said, "heightened the personal dimensions" of his decision, but he added, "I owe John Tower fairness . . . I do not owe John Tower my vote" — a clear suggestion that his Democratic colleagues were not adhering to a standard of fairness.

Public opinion was shifting my way for the first time since the confirmation battle had escalated. The phone calls and mail to Bob Dole's office had gone from two- or three-to-one against me to two- or three-to-one in my favor. A significant percentage of these messages expressed the opinion that President Bush should be allowed to choose his own secretary of defense. This nascent change in sentiment coincided with Sam Nunn's unprecedented decision to send investigators from his Permanent Investigations Subcommittee to Dallas in search of the elusive smoking gun to finish off

my nomination. (One Democrat, Tim Wirth of Colorado, suggested that since no smoking gun had been found, the Senate
should make do with "smoking cartridges.") When Bob Dole took
Nunn to task for this outrageous maneuver, he lamely contended
that new allegations had been received the previous weekend about
my behavior at the American Airlines Admirals Club in Dallas, and
since the FBI had concluded its investigation, there was "no other
choice" but to send a former district attorney and two other investigators on the staff of the subcommittee down to Texas to
pursue the charges. On the floor of the Senate, Dole demanded to
know how long Nunn planned to keep at it. "I guess we can make
the case we are going to investigate until the last vote is cast," Dole
said. "Maybe somebody will run in right before somebody votes
aye or no, and say hold it, I just got something, I got it over the
transom. We will go out and investigate that."

Again, George Mitchell was forced to intervene to shield Senator
Nunn from the consequences of his actions. Mitchell tried to side-
track Senator Specter, who rose to point out that, under the rules,
when a matter has been reported to the full Senate, even the reporting committee loses jurisdiction and cannot take up the issue
again unless there is a motion to recommit. My nomination had
been voted on by the Armed Services Committee and sent to the
full Senate for final disposition. Nunn rashly responded to Senator
Specter by asserting that his subcommittee — a subcommittee that
is not even connected to the Armed Services Committee — had
the right and the authority to proceed with an investigation "over
almost any activity of government" despite all the rules and prec-
edents. It was a preposterous and arrogant notion, and I suspect
that Mitchell knew it; at the earliest opportunity he got Nunn and
the Democrats off the hook by arranging to have the investigation
quietly terminated.

But, of course, the charge involving the Admirals Club was
leaked by Senator Nunn's staff. No one else could have done it.
Nunn was in sole possession of the allegation, the Republican
members and the White House having been shut out of the
process. The Permanent Investigations Subcommittee staff was ad-
mittedly being used for partisan purposes. Andrea Mitchell breath-
lessly reported on NBC the previous evening — Monday, March
6 — that I had been seen drunk in the Admirals Club at the Dallas–
Fort Worth airport. The answer never caught up with the charge.
I rarely spend more than twenty minutes in the club when I check

in for flights. Every member of the club staff interviewed by Nunn's gumshoes denied the charge was true and attested to my consistently gentlemanly conduct.

The White House lobbyists were still trying to find the right combination to convince Lieberman and Robb. The best and last hope was to give them cover by persuading Bennett Johnston to vote for me. Johnston is fond of letting it be known that he is one of George Bush's tennis partners — an arrangement that dates back at least to the Bush vice presidency. And the Louisiana Democrat had lost the majority leader's race to George Mitchell, which we also thought might give us an opening.

Some former Democratic senators weighed in on my behalf, including Russell Long, Gary Hart, and Gene McCarthy. Years earlier, McCarthy and I participated in forums that pitted liberals against conservatives. Gene once said, "Tower and I are like old carnival wrestlers; we know each other's holds." He wrote an editorial on my behalf in *Roll Call,* a Capitol Hill newspaper. And Gary Hart has told me that despite our differences, I always gave him a fair hearing in the Armed Services Committee. Hart called Tim Wirth and leaned pretty hard on him, I understand, but to no avail. Russ Long made phone calls on my behalf. They all apparently were appalled at the way the Senate was doing in one of its own.

Although Johnston held out almost to the end, he wasn't willing to buck the Democratic leadership. Soon thereafter, Lieberman announced that he would vote against confirmation. And Robb capitulated to Nunn. He was overheard saying to the chairman of the Senate Armed Services Committee, "Okay, Sam, I'll do it. I don't want to do it, and don't ask for anything else."

Lloyd Bentsen, as I knew he would, stood by me. "I found myself comparing the John Tower in the FBI reports to the John Tower I have known for years and worked with on Texas projects in the Senate. They were not the same man," Bentsen said, and he noted the personal aspects of the ordeal that I had been through:

In the passion of debate, pundits writing editorials in the isolation of their offices . . . sometimes have a tendency to forget that public officials have personal feelings also. We have seen witnesses have their sanity, their integrity impugned as they try to reach back to try to remember facts in the record of things that happened years ago. And we have seen every

imperfection in an essentially good man dragged into the piti-
less glare of television while his lovely daughters sat there and
were subjected to it. It has been a high price to pay for public
service.

George Mitchell had promised to inform Bob Dole and the White
House when he had obtained the votes necessary to defeat the
nomination. We were so notified on Wednesday, March 8, and
Dole agreed to allow the vote to be scheduled for the next day. I
would have preferred a few more days of debate to make the most
of the public support that seemed to be moving my way. But Dole
had to use his best judgment of the situation.

At 10:30 Thursday morning, the assistant legislative clerk of the
Senate read the document nominating me to be secretary of defense. Bob Dole was recognized by the presiding officer. Dole
noted that his request that I be allowed to address the Senate in
person had been objected to by George Mitchell. I had broached
the idea a week earlier, in the hope that I would be given that basic
courtesy by my former colleagues. After all, I had spent twenty-
four years in that body. My reputation had been destroyed in large
measure by the actions of Sam Nunn and the Democratic majority,
and the least they could have done was to allow me to stand on
the Senate floor and speak for a few moments on my own behalf,
answer whatever questions the senators cared to put to me, and
then submit to their judgment. In the end, I think, Mitchell and
the rest of the Democrats couldn't risk it. The embarrassment of
having to look me in the eye and confront me directly would have
been too much to bear.

Dole continued his statement:

I then proposed what some have referred to as sort of a six
month trial period [for me to serve as defense secretary] after
talking with Senator Tower, after at least advising the President, and advising the chief of staff, John Sununu, at the
White House.

It was our hope that that good faith effort might convince
some that this man is certainly deserving of that chance, and
that it would be another indication of good faith on the part
of the nominee and on the part of the President — that coupled with Senator Tower's pledge on national television, sobriety pledge. . . . The Majority Leader was kind enough to

say that he would consider it. The Chairman of the Armed Services Committee said he would sleep on it. I have now had the opportunity to visit with the Majority Leader, and also briefly with the Chairman of the Armed Services Committee.

The bottom line in this place is how many votes do you have? How many votes can you change? Can you change any?

I think it is fairly clear, notwithstanding what was a good faith shot, it is not going to change any votes.

George Mitchell rose to offer a unanimous-consent request setting a final vote for 4:00 that afternoon. In reply, Bob Dole simply said, "We are ready."

The debate continued until the appointed hour. Vice President Dan Quayle moved into the presiding officer's chair and declared: "Under the previous order, the hour of 4 o'clock having lapsed, the question is: Will the Senate advise and consent to the nomination of John G. Tower of Texas to be Secretary of the Department of Defense? On this question, the yeas and nays have been ordered. The clerk will call the roll."

A period of fifteen minutes is allotted for each roll call.

"Are there other Senators in the chamber who desire to vote, or change their vote?" the vice president asked. There was silence in the chamber. "Yeas 47, nays 53 . . . the nomination is not confirmed."

The transition staff had been told to remain in the office once the vote was complete. I did not want a large entourage trooping downstairs with me to the secretary of defense's private dining room, where a press pool was gathered. Dan Howard was standing in the doorway, waiting. I slid off the arm of the chair I had been perched on and followed him down the corridor to the escalator. There was one more thing to do. I focused all my energy and concentration on it. Once more unto the breach. The news media wanted a last shot at me, but this time it would be on my terms. We were accompanied by a single security agent and my secretary Kim Garven. We walked briskly and in silence.

I had written out a statement in longhand that morning, and one of the clerks typed it onto a single sheet of paper:

It is time for the bitterness, rancor and anger to fade and for those elements of government who have been involved in the confirmation process to unite and be about the people's business. I will be recorded as the first cabinet nominee in the history of the Republic to be rejected in the first 90 days of a Presidency and perhaps be harshly judged. But I depart from this place at peace with myself knowing that I have given a full measure of devotion to my country. No public figure in my memory has been subjected to such a far-reaching and thorough investigation nor had his human foibles bared to such intensive and demeaning public scrutiny. And yet there is no finding that I have ever breached established ethical standards nor been derelict in my duty.

I am deeply grateful to our great President for his continuing confidence in me and his unflagging support in the most difficult of circumstances. I am obliged to my old colleagues in the Senate who rallied to me with fervor, zeal, and eloquence in the face of staggering political odds. I shall always be in their debt. I am thankful to the thousands of Americans who have inundated me with messages of encouragement and support.

It is my intention to return to private life in my beloved Texas. But I shall speak out from time to time on national issues when my knowledge, experience and insights may contribute to public debate.

I hope that my successor will be speedily and expeditiously confirmed, and I wish him Godspeed.

I stood before the cameras, read the statement, and departed the Pentagon.

EPILOGUE

I DON'T so much resent my rejection by the Senate as the way it was done.

My life as a full-time public servant has ended. I can live with that fact, although I must confess a certain frustration at not being able to put my acquired experience, knowledge, judgment, and sense of history to good use. I am much better off economically than I would have been otherwise, free to pursue various outside interests, and free to spend more time with my loved ones. Certainly, I am not happy with being held out as a bad example and being remembered by many only in the context of the publicity surrounding my confirmation struggle. Lost is the fact that I was once regarded as a competent leader, worthy of trust and capable of bearing the heavy responsibilities of sensitive and demanding assignments.

If, indeed, any significant new evidence regarding my personal life or my business associations had surfaced after the confirmation hearings, raising additional questions about my fitness for office, I should have been recalled to answer them before the Armed Services Committee. I do not believe there was any credible evidence that I acted unethically, illegally, or, more important, in a manner incompatible with the national interest in my consulting work. To the contrary, I advised defense contractors to closely examine costs for possible economies and to sharpen their pencils in responding to requests for proposals. I always made it clear to my staff and clients that I would never support any programs for which there was not a valid requirement.

Absent another hearing, given the unprecedented nature of what was taking place, there is another step Senator Nunn could have taken. At the time he arrived at the conclusions that the president's nomination was ill advised and that it was his duty to oppose confirmation, rather than resorting to hints, leaks to the news media, and stalking-horses, he could have personally informed me of his views. At the very least, I would have had a chance to see and hear for myself that Nunn's decision was irreversible.

Finally, it seems that by any standard of courtesy or fair play, I should have been permitted the opportunity to address the Senate and respond to any questions regarding my behavior — particularly in light of the fact that some senators were quoting from raw FBI files, contrary to the Senate's own rules. Any argument against such an appearance on the grounds of precedent or rules is an excuse, not a reason. It could have been accomplished by unanimous consent. What were they afraid of? By availing myself of the courtesy afforded former senators, which permits them to come on the Senate floor (but not to address the Senate), I could have done a little personal lobbying in the chamber. I elected not to do that, however, believing it would be inappropriate and tasteless.

Of lasting concern to many is the cavalier treatment given to the confidentiality of FBI files compiled from background checks. Much of this material, as noted earlier, is unevaluated and uncorroborated. I received many letters from thoughtful people, including some prominent liberals, expressing dismay. The *Washington Post,* in its lead editorial the day after the Senate vote, referred with discomfort to "the dependence of the Senators on untested raw data from an FBI file":

> The Democrats, taking offense when this is brought up, reply that it was the president's power alone to release the file to the public. But surely they cannot have thought that such release was a good idea or that it was what those of us who were troubled by the importance of this file in the proceedings thought would be a good solution. It would, if anything, have been worse than the use to which the file was already being put, to dump it into the public domain. It was the untested

character of the material that we found disturbing, along with the anonymity of so many of the accusers; and this sentiment is in no way assuaged by the assurance being lavishly offered by the Democrats yesterday afternoon that the confirmation proceeding is, after all, not a criminal trial, and thus carries no requirement for the kinds of safeguards we and others thought were lacking. The same defense was made when loyalty boards and congressional investigating committees and other instrumentalities made use of this kind of material over the years, and it is no more reassuring now than it was then.

Former secretary of defense Don Rumsfeld sent an open letter to the FBI director on March 27, 1989, which said in part:

For more than twenty-five years, I have cooperated with the FBI by meeting with agents concerning the backgrounds of literally dozens of individuals under consideration for senior positions in the federal government. Indeed it has never crossed my mind to not cooperate — until very recently.

However, this letter is to advise you that I have come to the end of the road. In the future, I do not intend to cooperate with FBI agents on background checks, until significant changes are made in the way the information is handled.

I followed carefully the confirmation consideration with respect to former Senator John Tower. While I have no criticism of the FBI in this regard, I strongly disapprove of the way the process was handled. Unverified information received in the course of the FBI background checks apparently was made available to the members of the United States Senate by the executive branch of the government. Such information was leaked to the press either by individuals in the executive or legislative branches, or both, to the detriment of the government, to say nothing of the disservice to John Tower. I do not care to be a part of or contribute to a process that works in that manner.

I recognize that background checks are necessary. I also recognize that the legislative branch needs access to some of the information gathered during such checks. My concern is that, prior to making such information available outside of the investigative process, there appears to be no test as to whether or not information is valid, no test as to whether information is relevant to a candidate's qualification for the office involved, no judgment made as to the number of people given access to FBI information, and insufficient attention given to the ability of the individuals involved in the process, in both branches of the government, to handle confidential information.

In an op-ed piece in the *Washington Post* of April 18, 1990, Lloyd Cutler, a prominent Washington lawyer and former counsel to President Carter, made some cogent observations on this flawed process:

> It is a violation of the Senate's rules to make anything public contained in the confidential FBI summary of its investigation of the nominee, and most of the time these rules are observed. But when an appointment is controversial for other reasons . . . opponents are sorely tempted to throw in additional juicy tidbits from the FBI report that could swing the balance in their favor. With so many senators now allowed to read these reports and to share the contents with their staffs, one or two may find the temptation too hard to resist.
>   This is what happened in the confirmation battle over John Tower's nomination to be secretary of defense.

The Senate should live up to its own rules and preserve the confidentiality of the personal information contained in the FBI reports. It is fair to say that if the Senate does not become more circumspect in its treatment of the FBI product, many highly competent people, with some embarrassing but not disqualifying blemishes in their background, may be deterred from accepting appointments to positions requiring Senate confirmation. There is the added risk that some thoughtful and responsible people, like Don Rumsfeld, will be reluctant to cooperate with background investigators.

In a sense, the Senate demeaned itself in the manner in which it rejected a man four times elected to that body and elevated to positions of leadership within it. My performance as a senator and as a committee chairman was not widely questioned by my former colleagues except on philosophical grounds. In fact, many who voted against my confirmation, including Senator Nunn, gave me high marks. I was being rejected on the grounds of some illusive and ill-defined standard of personal conduct that senators are not expected to observe. The *Washington Post* noted, "The rhetoric put to this purpose frequently reached awesome new levels of inconsistency and hypocrisy." During the course of my appearance at the National Press Club, I said, "I accept that the Secretary of Defense must adhere to a higher standard than members of the United States Senate." On reflection, I now recant that statement.

Is the public prepared to endorse a lower standard for senators and House members than for cabinet officers? Legislators are powerful people — the ultimate source of statutory law. They now claim an equal right of participation in the national security policy process to that of the executive branch. If, indeed, there is a valid fear of the possibility of the secretary of defense's being under the influence of alcohol during a highly unlikely, million-to-one, bolt-out-of-the-blue nuclear attack on the United States without any strategic warning (Senator Nunn likes to say "at two in the morning" — although I think that evening rush hour is more likely), then there is another matter that should be of concern: those dispassionate, clear-headed judgments on strategic deterrence and defense that reduce the likelihood of attack, judgments the Congress is frequently called on to make. In this and all other sensitive matters, the Senate should insist on a high standard of sobriety.

There is no question that liquor is kept and consumed in various Capitol hideaways and Senate and House offices. Liquor is served at receptions in the Capitol Building and in the Senate and House office buildings. Furthermore, as of this writing, wine is sold in the Senate restaurant, beer and wine in the House restaurants. It would be a simple matter for the Congress to set an example and enhance public confidence in the institution by prohibiting any alcoholic beverages from being kept or served or consumed in any of the Capitol environs, including the office buildings. Although this would not guarantee sober deliberation (members frequently leave the Capitol to attend cocktail parties and dinners elsewhere, returning for late-evening votes), it would reduce the likelihood of less than sober conduct.

On the matter of conflict of interest, there are already rigid standards set for members of the executive branch — far higher than exist for the legislative branch. At this writing, there are so many well-publicized cases pending before the Senate Ethics Committee that it seems almost superfluous to discuss them here. In my confirmation process, much was made of appearance of conflict of interest by senators who apparently maintain the outrageous pretense that there is nothing in their own public actions that gives rise to such appearances. While there is occasional press comment on PAC contributions, honoraria from interest groups, and other favors, the news media seemed to be more interested in the propriety of what I did after I left the Senate (ignoring the obvious fact that my business activities were entirely consistent with those conducted by many highly respected former senators and representatives after leaving public life). The attention should be focused on the current practices of those who are still active legislators.

I do not support campaign-financing-reform proposals that feature public funding. These, in my view, would diminish the role of political parties in the process and deny participation to those unable to do volunteer work in a campaign — not to mention compelling taxpayers to foot the bill. PAC contributions, however, should be narrowly limited, honoraria abolished (at the same time, salaries for legislators should be increased, a point I will come back to later), and limits on individual contributions should be raised to more realistic levels.

Without impugning the integrity, character, or fitness of Richard Cheney (I applaud his selection), I will close these comments on standards by asking a rhetorical question: What standards were applied to his nomination? Rushed through the Senate to confirmation in less than a week, the FBI barely had enough time for even the most cursory of background checks. A thorough, thoughtful examination by the Senate of the nominee's views and qualifications was impossible. Sam Nunn and the rest of the Democratic majority were so eager to get out of the bind they had created for themselves that all the fine sentiments about standards and process were tossed aside and forgotten. Awesome new levels of inconsistency and hypocrisy indeed.

There is no institution in Washington in more urgent need of reform than the Congress of the United States, and yet no institution is more inherently resistant to reform. I recognized this when I was still in the Senate and offered recommendations in committee testimony. My views track fairly closely with proposals contained in legislation introduced by Senators Nancy Kassebaum and Daniel Inouye in the 100th Congress. Having expounded on reform in considerable detail in Chapter Eleven and elsewhere, I will simply summarize:

- The authorizing and appropriating process should be merged into the authorizing committees.
- The Budget Committee should be abolished and its functions taken over by the Appropriations Committee, which could also appropriate monies for those purposes not dealt with in the authorizing committees.
- Biennial budgeting and appropriating should be instituted to permit better planning by the spending agencies, better economies of scale, and more legislative time to consider substantive issues and exercise oversight.
- The committee system should be overhauled to avoid overlapping jurisdiction and replication of effort.

Given its present structure, practices, and diffusion of power and responsibility, the Congress is unable to do its work with due deliberation in a reasonable time. Congress has become a bloated bureaucracy that makes the Pentagon look like a model of efficiency and economy by comparison. It succumbs to the temptation to statutorily micromanage some elements of the executive branch. A better alternative is to hold administrators strictly accountable for their performance, making clear what is expected of them and authorizing the management tools necessary. Congress should not mandate inflexible procedures that inhibit clear lines of control and authority running downward through the system or commensurately clear lines of responsibility and accountability running upward.

Unfortunately, no spur is given to congressional reform by the mass media. They are too preoccupied with their perceived responsibility to maintain an adversarial relationship with the executive branch. Sam Donaldson once said, "It is the function of the press to hold the President's heels to the fire." In playing out this role, the press too often abjures balance and rarely questions the motives or enlightenment of the president's critics. Congress becomes a conscious or fortuitous ally in the process that has the net effect of not just holding the president's heels to the fire but undermining the institution of the presidency. The press, in encouraging congressional encroachment in areas traditionally considered within the purview of presidential authority and responsibility, is intolerant of flawed performance by the chief executive and indifferent to that of Congress; it does not insist on congressional cohesion, consistency, orderly process, or the acceptance of responsibility for the consequences of its actions.

To be sure, the news media do bear down on individual members of the legislative branch for junketing, professional misconduct, or personal misbehavior. But a highly focused chorus of
institutional disapproval seems to be heard only when Congress
considers raising its own pay — absolutely the wrong issue. Despite what I have said about institutional shortcomings and individual foibles, it is only fair to note that members of Congress
generally work hard and long at their job, usually at the cost of a
normal family life. With dedication, they shoulder heavy and multifarious responsibilities that are unique to their profession. The
private sector pays much more for much less demanding work.
Many promising legislators feel compelled to retire from Congress
when it comes time to pay for educating their children.

Congressional pay should be raised to levels more nearly commensurate with the responsibilities of the members, and honoraria,
presently used to augment salaries, eliminated. The cost to the
taxpayer would be more than recovered by cutting congressional
staff to manageable levels.

In the current struggle between Congress and the president on
national security matters and the climate of mutual distrust that
characterizes it, I believe it is timely to draw attention to a passage
from the report issued by the President's Special Review Board,
which I chaired:

> There is a natural tension between the desire for secrecy and
> the need to consult Congress on covert operations. Presidents
> seem to become increasingly concerned about leaks of classi
> fied information as their administrations progress. They
> blame Congress disproportionately. Various cabinet officials
> from prior administrations indicated to the Board that they
> believe Congress bears no more blame than the Executive
> Branch.
>
> However, the number of members and staff involved in
> reviewing covert activities is large; it provides cause for con
> cern and a convenient excuse for presidents to avoid Congres
> sional consultation.
>
> We recommend that Congress consider replacing the exist
> ing Intelligence committees of the respective Houses with a

new joint committee with a restricted staff to oversee the intelligence community, patterned after the Joint Committee on Atomic Energy that existed until the mid-1970's.

I would expand on that recommendation by suggesting that the committee be composed of the majority and minority leaders of the respective houses, plus the chairman and ranking minority members of the Senate and House Armed Services Committees, the Senate Foreign Relations Committee, and the House Committee on Foreign Affairs. This would impose additional burden and responsibility on already busy people, but this is a matter of such critical importance to the national security interest of the country that the most mature and experienced judgment should be brought to bear on the sensitive work of the committee. The staff should be small, highly professional, and experienced in handling classified information.

I would go a step further. Senators and representatives who have access to material classified above top secret should be submitted to the same background checks required of those in the executive branch. An individual's ability to be elected by a regional constituency does not automatically make that individual risk-free. If the voters of a district want to elect a man who consorts with male prostitutes, that's their business; but it is the nation's business to have assurances that this person is not a security risk. Such checks are required for all former members, regardless of stature and reputation, who accept intelligence-sensitive positions in the executive branch. Why not present members? Reports from the investigations could be evaluated, at least initially, by the Joint Committee on Intelligence (or by the intelligence committees of the respective chambers, absent the formation of a joint committee). In the alternative, the reports could be acted upon by the respective ethics committees.

The executive branch has a tradition of forming temporary boards and commissions made up of distinguished people to advise and make recommendations on matters of current, critical, and sometimes time-urgent importance. The Grace, Scowcroft, Kissinger, and Packard commissions, and the President's Special Review Board, are recent examples. Reform-minded legislators might want to consider, as an alternative to comprehensive efforts at internal reform that start from scratch, the establishment of an outside commission on legislative reform. Such a commission could be made

up, in large part, of former members of the legislative branch, who
could bring both experience and objectivity to the task of recommending constructive measures for change. It could spark public
debate and focus press and popular attention on the responsiveness
of Congress to the needs and aspirations of a complex society in a
fast-changing world.

Finally, in offering these recommendations, I must also acknowledge that there are limits beyond which we are unable to go in
enacting reforms. The news media are afflicted with serious shortcomings. It was the intent of the framers of the Bill of Rights to
guarantee freedom of the press in order to protect the free flow of
information to the citizenry — so necessary to the viability of a
democratic society — not simply to protect those who gather and
disseminate information. Too many journalists today vigorously
assert their privileges and immunities under the First Amendment
but ignore the concomitant responsibilities. The most serious con-
straint on free access to information these days comes not from
government censorship but from news management by many of
the major news organizations. This is a problem that is beyond
remedy, however. It would entail dangerous tinkering with the
First Amendment, and my purpose in raising the issue here is to
enhance public awareness, not to suggest there are any corrective
measures that could or should ever be undertaken.

I put forward these observations and ideas without rancor. Many
occurred to me before I departed the Senate. I revere and cherish
the Congress as an institution. It is the ultimate repository of the
people's power, which is why I want so much to see it perfect itself
to fulfill its promise. The genius of American democracy has been
its capacity for self-analysis, self-criticism, self-refinement, and accommodation to change. We must never lose it.

SOURCES

Books

Davis, John H. *Mafia Kingfish*. New York: McGraw-Hill, 1989.

Kearns, Doris. *Lyndon Johnson and the American Dream*. New York: Harper and Row, 1976.

Knaggs, John R. *Two-Party Texas*. Austin, Tex.: Eakin Press, 1986.

Lehman, John F., Jr. *Command of the Seas*. New York: Charles Scribner's Sons, 1988.

Miller, Merle. *Plain Speaking: Conversations with Harry S. Truman*. London: Victor Gollancz, 1974.

Nitze, Paul. *From Hiroshima to Glasnost*. New York: Grove Weidenfeld, 1989.

Nixon, Richard M. *The Memoirs of Richard Nixon*. New York: Grosset and Dunlap, 1978.

Regan, Donald T. *For the Record*. New York: St. Martin's Press, 1989.

Smith, Hedrick. *The Power Game: How Washington Works*. New York: Ballantine Books, 1989.

Sorenson, Theodore C. *Kennedy*. New York: Harper and Row, 1965.

Tower, Beryl Goodwin. *Poesy and Mirth*. Austin, Tex.: Clearstream Press, 1983.

Truman, Harry S. *Years of Trial and Hope*. Vol. 2 of *Memoirs*. Garden City, N.Y.: Doubleday, 1956.

White, Theodore H. *The Making of the President 1960*. New York: Atheneum, 1961.

Newspaper and Magazine Articles

Almond, Peter. "Even After Closed Hearing, Tower's Approval Seen Sure." *Washington Times,* February 1, 1989.

"Arms Negotiator Tower" (editorial). *Dallas Times-Herald,* January 23, 1985.

Associated Press. "Nunn Admitted Guilt in '64 Traffic Accident." *New York Times,* March 1, 1989.

Atkinson, Rick. "The Once and Future Kennedy." *Washington Post Magazine,* April 29, 1990.

Barta, Carolyn. "Viewpoints" (column). *Dallas Morning News,* March 13, 1989.

Broder, John M. "Tower's Ordeal Illustrates Capital Power Games." *Los Angeles Times,* December 7, 1988.

Broder, John M., and Melissa Healy. "Rumors Hurt Tower's Bid to Be Secretary of Defense." *Los Angeles Times,* November 19, 1988.

————. "New Ethics, Democrats Pose Hurdle for Tower." *Los Angeles Times,* February 9, 1989.

"The Buck Stops There" (editorial). *Los Angeles Times,* February 27, 1987.

"A Case of Nunn Hit-and-Run" (column). *Wall Street Journal,* February 28, 1989.

Conconi, Chuck. "Style" (column). *Washington Post,* February 2, 1989.

Cutler, Lloyd. "Let's Not Get Personal." *Washington Post,* April 18, 1990.

Daley, Steve. "Politics Comes Crashing in on Nunn." *Chicago Tribune,* February 26, 1989.

Devroy, Ann. "Delays Are Weakening Tower, Lawmakers Say." *Washington Post,* December 9, 1988.

Dewar, Helen. "Committee Vote Due Today." *Washington Post,* February 2, 1989.

Dewar, Helen, and Dan Balz. "Tracing the Steps in Tower's Downfall." *Washington Post,* March 29, 1989.

Elvin, John. "Weyrich Attack on Tower Draws Conservative Fire." *Washington Times,* January 2, 1989.

Furgurson, Ernest. "The Surprising Mr. Tower." *Baltimore Sun,* December 21, 1988.

"GOP Brass Plans VIP Reception." *Houston Post,* May 28, 1961.

Greenberger, Robert S., and Jane Mayer. "Deepening Crisis. Reagan Effort to Clear Air About Arms to Iran Raises More Questions." *Wall Street Journal,* November 26, 1986.

"Grumbling Continues Within Tower Camp." *Houston Post,* August 6, 1978.

Hoffman, David. "Bush Expected to Name Tower Defense Chief." *Washington Post,* November 22, 1988.

House, Karen Elliott. "Really, FBI: I Have No Dirt on Tower." *Wall Street Journal,* March 7, 1989.

Kaplan, Fred, and Walter Robinson. "Confirmation of Tower Said to Be in Danger." *Boston Globe,* February 9, 1989.

Lee, Jessica. "New Items Put Tower Vote on Hold." *USA Today,* February 3, 1989.

McGrory, Mary. "Sweet Babble of Tower." *Washington Post,* January 29, 1989.

Noah, Timothy. "Born to Be Mild." *Washington Monthly,* December 1989.

"Nunn's Tower Play" (editorial). *Wall Street Journal,* February 9, 1989.

Oreskes, Michael. "Nunn Asserts Issue of Tower Drinking Is Still Unresolved." *New York Times,* February 23, 1989.

Ostrow, Ronald J. "He Sees 'More of a Conflict' Than Personal Life." *Los Angeles Times,* February 6, 1989.

Pincus, Walter. "Bush Team, Tower Negotiate on Filling Key Pentagon Slots." *Washington Post,* November 23, 1988.

Pincus, Walter, and David Hoffman. "Bush Plans Review of Defense." *Washington Post,* November 26, 1988.

Rosenthal, Andrew. "Tower Nomination." *New York Times,* February 8, 1989.

Safire, William. "Towering Inferno." *New York Times,* February 13, 1989.

Shram, Martin. "Towering Inferno." *Washingtonian,* May 1989.

Stewart, Jim. "Tower: Too Hot for Bush to Handle?" *Atlanta Constitution,* November 13, 1988.

Thompson, Mark. "Tower Backed Arms-Talks Aide Found to Be a Security Risk." *Philadelphia Inquirer,* February 5, 1989.

———. "Tower Kept Mistresses in Geneva, Report Alleges." *Baltimore Sun,* February 16, 1989.

"Tower Capital Welcome: Tower Capitol Acclaim Exceeds All Precedent." *Houston Chronicle,* May 31, 1961.

"The Tower Commission" (editorial). *Washington Post,* November 27, 1986.

"The Tower Vote" (editorial). *Washington Post,* March 10, 1989.

Weinraub, Bernard. "White House Outlines Drive to Save Tower Nomination." *New York Times,* February 26, 1989.

West, Paul. "Top Tower Aide Resigns." *Dallas Times-Herald,* August 22, 1978.

Wilson, George C. "Advisers Press Bush to Reform the Pentagon." *Washington Post,* November 12, 1988.

Woodward, Bob. "FBI Cites Two Incidents at Base." *Washington Post,* March 2, 1989.

Woodward, Bob, and Charles Babcock. "FBI Undertakes Exhaustive Check on Tower." *Washington Post,* December 11, 1988.

Government Publications and Documents

Congressional Record: 98th Cong., 2nd sess., 1984, vol. 130, no. 131; 101st Cong., 1st sess., 1989, vol. 135, nos. 21, 22, 23, 24, 25, 26. Washington, D.C.: Government Printing Office.

Report of the President's Special Review Board, February 26, 1987. John G. Tower, chairman.

U.S. Congress. Senate. *Alleged Assassination Plots Involving Foreign Leader. Interim Report on the Select Committee to Study Government Operations with Respect to Intelligence Activities.* 94th Cong., 2nd sess., November 20, 1974. S. Doc. 94-465.

U.S. Congress. Senate. *Hearings Before the Committee on Armed Services on Nomination of John G. Tower to Be Secretary of Defense.* 101st Cong., 1st sess., Jan.

25, 26, 31; Feb. 1, 2, 3, 1989. Washington, D.C.: Government Printing Office, 1989.

Unpublished Materials

Rumsfeld, Donald. Open letter to William Sessions, director of the Federal Bureau of Investigation, March 27, 1989.

INDEX

Dodd, Christopher, 5–6, 353
Dodd, Thomas, 6, 353
Dole, Elizabeth H., 340, 347
Dole, Robert, 193–194, 217, 291, 318,
324, 325; and "Dole mole," 93; at
hearings, 96–97, 106; and roll call
vote, 298–299, 326, 347, 354, 356–
357; in Senate debate, 352–353, 354
Donaldson, Sam, 312–313, 365
Douglas, Stephen, 61
Dow Jones, 347
Draft Goldwater Committee, 165
drinking: by congressmen, 56–59, 363
drinking allegations, 129, 293, 297;
Nunn and, 6, 77, 159, 195, 200–
201, 212–214, 298, 303–315 *passim*,
336–337, 354–355, (raises subject at
hearings) 125–126, 157; news
media and, 42, 48, 50, 126, 155,
180, 204, 205, 216, 291, 298, 312,
314–315, 330; anonymous, 46, 160;
unsubstantiated, 83, 121, 123, 124,
140, 313, 334; refuted, 181–182, 291,
311–312, 314–315, 344, 355; abstention promised, 200, 201, 310–312,
316, 325, 329, 356; in Senate debate, 351, 353
Dukakis, Michael, 9, 10–11, 216;
Nunn-Warner letter to, 70–71,
101, 102, 114
Dukakis, Mrs. Michael (Kitty), 11

Eagleton Amendment (1973), 147
Eastland, James, 57
Eaton, Charles A., 151
Ecevit, Bülent, 150
Eggers, Paul, 206, 250
Ehrlichman, John, 208
Eisenhower, Dwight, 17, 19, 60–61,
64, 86, 146, 178, 293; JT manages
1956 Texas campaign of, 33
El Paso Herald-Post, 233
Elson, Edward, 29
Energy, U.S. Department of, 227, 264
Equal Rights Amendment, 347
Ervin, Sam J., Jr., and Ervin Commit-
tee, 133
Estrich, Susan, 11
Ethics Committee (Senate). *See* Senate
committees
ethics issue, 43, 187, 323
Exon, J. James, 107, 195, 201; and roll
call vote, 6, 108, 202, 203, 298; al-

legations as "garbage," 123, 304;
Nunn and, 213–214, 216
Export Administration Act, 227
extremism, 119, 167, 168

Face the Nation (TV program), 330
Fahd, king of Saudi Arabia, 144–
145
Farenthold, Sissy, 217
FBI (Federal Bureau of Investigation),
132, 136, 137; and Ill Wind scandal,
43; reports to Reagan administration, 69, 70; and Watergate,
74
FBI investigation, 98, 159–160, 187,
204, 354; begins, 39–40; need for,
40–41; unsubstantiated information, 41, 77, 120, 140, 141, 158, 192,
199, 295–298, 338, (refuted) 181,
314–315, 347–349, (anonymous)
199, (Jackson story) 334–335; lack
of deadline in, 41, 99, 293;
Nunn's use/misuse of, 41, 44, 69,
70, 100, 192–193, 200–201, 303,
(information leaked) 90, 313–314,
315; exhaustiveness of, 44, 45, 46,
51, 100, 199, 295–297; Bush
briefed, comments on, 46, 49–50,
291, 294–295, 325; news media
and, 49–51, 160, 192–193, 194, 313–
314; JT supplies information, 69,
292, 304; continuation of, 69, 72,
140, 158, 195, 196, 201, 202, 203,
296; availability of file, 70, 192,
325, 339, 360; Combest interviewed, 181–182, 297–298; Warner's statement on, 192–193;
"exit" interview, 296–298; as
"camouflage," 299; "summarized," 325, 335–336; Glenn quotes
material from, 338, 341
Federal Communications Commission, 69
Federal Elections Commission (FEC),
32, 322–323
Federal Emergency Management
Agency, 250
filibuster, 56, 167–168
Finance Committee (Senate). *See* Senate committees
Fitzwater, Marlin, 198, 200, 204
Flannigan, J. W., 67
Fogelson, Greer Garson, 341

COPYRIGHT ACKNOWLEDGMENTS